Greening the Academy

Ecopedagogy Through the Liberal Arts

Edited by
Samuel Day Fassbinder
DeVry University, Chicago, USA

Anthony J. Nocella II
Hamline University, Saint Paul, Minnesota, USA

and

Richard Kahn
Antioch University Los Angeles, USA

SENSE PUBLISHERS
ROTTERDAM/BOSTON/TAIPEI

A C.I.P. record for this book is available from the Library of Congress.

ISBN: 978-94-6209-099-6 (paperback)
ISBN: 978-94-6209-100-9 (hardback)
ISBN: 978-94-6209-101-6 (e-book)

Published by: Sense Publishers,
P.O. Box 21858,
3001 AW Rotterdam,
The Netherlands
https://www.sensepublishers.com/

Printed on acid-free paper

Greening the Academy

WHAT PEOPLE ARE SAYING ABOUT
GREENING THE ACADEMY

The necessity of linking together single issue social justice pursuits cannot be overstated, nor can the crucial role higher education must play in helping to solve international social justice dilemmas. *Greening the Academy* provides a much-needed analysis focusing on the importance of these issues as a means to progress global peace and justice issues. A must read for anyone seriously interested in making a difference in the world.

- Craig Rosebraugh,
Author of *Burning Rage of a Dying Planet*

Many of the most important forces for social change in human history have taken root in our universities, and today the academy is a crucial site where scholars are working to integrate ecological sustainability and social justice. *Greening the Academy* is a clarion call for deep green approaches to thinking, teaching, research, and action that can make a dramatic and positive difference for the future of all species.

- Dr. David Naguib Pellow,
Author of *Garbage Wars: The Struggle for Environmental Justice in Chicago*

Critical, crucial, and challenging, this book initiates a dialogue essential to the survival of our planet and all the species on it, including our own. Ignored for far too long by leaders of the major social institutions around the world, this book poses the question of whether the academy will belatedly tackle the urgent policies and actions necessary to ameliorate the ecological destruction wrought by predatory capitalism. University Centers for Teaching and Learning should use this book to generate meaningful discussions of curriculum transformation wherever possible.

- Dr. Julie Andrzejewski,
Co-Director, Social Responsibility Masters Program,
St. Cloud State University

Greening the Academy breaks through barriers that continue to enervate higher education's contribution to environmental education and ecological justice. By connecting radical "cognitive praxis" and authentic Indigenous perspectives to a variety of relevant topics, it offers educators motivation and maps for helping us all regain our lost balance before it is too late.

- Four Arrows,
Editor of *Unlearning the Language of Conquest:
Scholars Expose Anti-Indianism in America*

This is an important and urgent book that represents a landmark for higher education. It is a book that must be heeded, and, more importantly acted upon.

- Dr. Peter McLaren,
Author of *Che Guevara, Paulo Freire, and the Pedagogy of Revolution*

Higher education plays an increasingly important role globally in determining responses to human-induced environmental change. *Greening the Academy* shows us that it is crucial that educational policy, curriculum, institutional practice, and scholarly research go beyond greenwashing business as usual and instead engage critically with environmental issues. The book highlights how environmental concerns are not only the purview of the sciences but are centrally a result of cultural and economic practices and priorities, and thus must be engaged interdisciplinarily and in relation to community and place. To change the path we have set for the planet, it will take collaboration and persistence; this book offers hope in moving forward.

- Dr. Marcia McKenzie,
Editor of *Fields of Green: Restorying Culture, Environment, and Education*

TABLE OF CONTENTS

FOREWORD

BILL MCKIBBEN

I've had the privilege, for more than a decade now, of being associated with Middlebury College's Environmental Studies Department. It's the oldest such beast in the country, dating back to the early 1960s, and it produces an astonishing number of graduates who go on to leadership roles in advocacy groups, state and federal agencies, and green business. The entire original leadership of 350.org, which in 18 months grew to be the largest grassroots climate campaign in the planet's history, was made up of kids who'd graduated Middlebury six months before they began.

My theory for why Middlebury was punching above its weight involved more than simply the superb instruction my colleagues were offering. It was also, I think, the design of the program—in particular, the fact that the humanities have always been a central part of the program, as important as science and policy. In most places, environmental studies have been focused on the natural sciences, or captured over time by them. And this makes a certain kind of sense: they're the easiest part of the equation to systematize, and the hardest to screw up. There's little danger of fuzzy thinking; for deans worried that programs will be partisan or ideological, there's comfort in biology and chemistry being at the core.

But the great insight of ecology—the greatest scientific insight of the 20th century, far more important in the long run than cracking the atom—was that everything was hooked together. And that's as true, in a way, in our political and economic ecosystem as it is in any vernal pool or alpine meadow. When we deal with a problem like global warming, the physics and chemistry are, at this point, the least of the issue. We understand them well enough to know *how* to act; that we *don't* act has something to do with other parts of our brain and heart. We need to understand the economic forces that constrain us, and also the cultural patterns, psychological intuitions, and visceral fears that keep us from doing what we must. And so—among other things— we need voices from people like Wendell Berry, Terry Tempest Williams, Leslie Marmon Silko, Ed Abbey, Henry Thoreau, Gary Snyder, Richard Cizik.

More, we need the kind of interdisciplinary insight that only a college or university can offer. The ag school needs to be in touch with the theology school, and the psych department needs to be talking to the chemists. If there was ever an argument for escaping the deep silos of academe, the environmental crisis is it. It's not a "subject" as much as a lens through which to view the world. These papers begin to postulate how different disciplines—right down to criminology—might deal with the environmental dilemma. That's exciting to read, but it's even more exciting to see them all gathered in the same place, speaking to each other. It's a rich conversation, and one we need to have urgently, because there's nothing timeless about the trouble we face. We're in an emergency, and in an emergency you call on all hands.

ACKNOWLEDGEMENTS

We would like to thank the planet Earth, all of the elements, and the creatures of the world for the possibility of life. Also, we thank Peter de Liefde and Sense Publishers for believing in this project and for being so passionate about its completion during the editing stage. It goes without saying that *Greening the Academy* could not have been put together without the fine contributions of its many preeminent authors: Bill McKibben, Piers Beirne, Nigel South, Kishi Animashaun, Timothy Luke, Steven Best, Miriam Kennet, Michelle Gale de Oliveira, Donna Houston, Eva Swidler, Brian McKenna, Tema Milstein, Corey Lewis, Greta Gaard, and David Greenwood. We would also like to thank Craig Rosebraugh, David Naguib Pellow, Four Arrows, Peter McLaren, Julie Andrzejewski, and Marcia McKenzie for their support of this book. Finally, we thank our universities, colleagues, many friends, and our families for granting us the time and strength to see this project through to its eventual completion.

DEDICATION

This book is dedicated to those who struggle against the antidemocratic privatization and militarization of the academy. We side with and salute all those who work to oppose an academic industrial complex that vivisects animals, engineers dangerous genetic modifications of life, and pollutes the commons (including the minds of a potentially just community). Happily, there is resistance in higher education still and, with it, hope. Occupy the curriculum. Occupy the disciplines. Occupy the campuses. Occupy everywhere.

INTRODUCTION

RICHARD KAHN, ANTHONY J. NOCELLA II
AND SAMUEL DAY FASSBINDER

Who will prepare the scientists, technicians, engineers, entrepreneurs and global humanitarians that can convert urgency into opportunity, replace fossil fuel dependence with clean energy innovation, and rebuild our economy and society on a new and greener foundation? Who will educate citizens ready to master these new realities and ensure exemplary stewardship of our planet for now and for future generations? The answer is right here in this room. America's educators, in fact, our nation's entire education system must rise to this challenge, and our higher education leaders and communities, in particular, must lead the way. Secretary Duncan—who will speak with you tomorrow—often says that we must educate our way to a better economy. To expand on his remarks, we must educate our way to a green economy and a better environment!

—U.S. Under Secretary of Education, Martha Kanter, (2010)
Remarks at the Department of Education's "Sustainability Education
Summit: Citizenship and Pathways for a Green Economy"[1]

The university…has become a service for sale, ever more ready to hire itself out to governments or multinationals. It makes itself important through communal navel-gazing. Pedagogues and astronomers, gene researchers and sociologists, all work to process data and present them for verification to a management committee of peers, that is, likeminded data producers. What goes on in the lab has lost all but a tenuous tie to sense and meaning, let alone truth. Why is it…that so few of those who share our conviction are willing to come out and confess this?

—Ivan Illich (1991)

So long as there is a dysfunction in a system, a departure from known laws governing its operation, there is always the prospect of transcending the problem. But when a system rides roughshod over its own basic assumptions, supersedes its own ends…then we are contemplating not crisis but catastrophe.

—Jean Baudrillard (2009)

One cosmogonic story we can tell about education for sustainability concerns the birth of academe. To speak of academia today is to signify a collection of institutions of "higher" learning, research and instruction. These may be located on traditional campuses with ivy-covered buildings surrounding grand central lawns, or in a series of urban buildings amidst bustling city downtowns, or even in suburban corporate office parks. Increasingly, such institutions also virtually inhabit the Internet as either a primary or significant auxiliary domain.

Initially, however, long ago in the centuries prior to the Common Era, the Ancient Greek *Akademia* was a large grove of sacred olive trees dedicated to Athena, the Goddess of Wisdom. Surrounded by a wall containing various statues of the great individuals of Athens, and dotted here and there with ceremonial temples, the place functioned as a regional parkland for citizens' recreation and ritual. Within this civic wooded area, a smaller garden plot belonging to Plato was additionally established. It was here in this verdant space that Plato began his famous philosophical school—with its students becoming known as the "academics."

The Platonic academic corpus contributed significantly to the educational heights of Athenian *paideia*, which in turn became the paradigmatic example of civilized life through its cultural reproduction as the Roman tradition of *humanitas*—the foundation for what we have come to designate in modern times as the humanities curriculum (Kahn, 2010). Ironically, and somewhat tellingly, the Romans paid their debt to the Academy by invading and devastating it, while felling its lauded trees in support of the Roman military machine's imperial conquest of the Aegean that was then taking place during the Hellenistic era. The recent movie *Avatar* perhaps lends a useful set of images to help us envision what the siege of the *Akademia* must have looked and felt like to those Greeks who had consecrated it as the presumed navel of universal learning. Thus, to speak of "greening the academy" suggests that there is something much deeper (and even archetypal) at stake than the "green campus movement" (Orr, 2010; Beringer & Adombent, 2008; Koester, 2006) now in vogue—that reforms, however welcome, like STARS,[2] the gathering of college and university Presidents as signatories for a campus climate agreement, or schools investing in the creation of LEED certified architecture,[3] are woefully insufficient ends that must themselves be reformed. Indeed, the history of academia (per this origin story) correspondingly functions as a secular mythopoetic narrative to the Biblical—and other similarly religious—tales that chronicle the devastating spiritual loss of an Edenic habitat, even as it likewise suggests a conclusion in which the "garden" is hopefully restored through a process of continual renovation in accordance with the spirit of moral progress: *universitas semper reformanda.*

Unfortunately, we need only look at the state of higher education today to see, despite its undoubtedly remaining a contested terrain (this book being one such contestation), that the 21st century finds academia moving steadily from a position characterized by continual crisis towards one of epochal catastrophe. In a world in which global industrial systems have clearly emerged as major powers, thereby generating unprecedented historical outcomes of planetary genocide, ecocide, zoöcide—and likewise, epistemicide (see McLaren, 2012)—the idea of "sustainability" must thus strive to take rigorously oppositional and tactically concrete forms both on and off campus, if it is to transcend greenwashing by the public relations industry as purchased by the "power complex" (Best et al., 2011) of said systems. Sustainability cannot simply be handed over to STEM (science, technology, engineering and mathematics) programs to coordinate as a field of endeavor without being falsified. Neither is it sufficient merely to offer interdisciplinary environmental studies programs (themselves often tilted toward and disciplinarily controlled by the environmental sciences) as a reasonable reform in sustainability's name. What is required is not a curricular addendum within the campus that passes under the happy buzzword of furthering "sustainable development," but rather a sustained critical intervention by visionary educational leaders, critical faculty, agitated students, and emancipatory movements belonging to the communities in which academic institutions are based, all organized together in order to morally transfigure the relationship between the school and the society as part of a collective aspiration for the total liberation of the potential peace, justice, joy, and the vital well-being of our emerging planetary community.

By contrast, as Henry Giroux (2007) has aptly put it, the academic contribution to the project of human freedom—denoted clearly since antiquity by the moniker "liberal arts" (artes liberales), the literacy curriculum requisite for a vibrant and democratic public citizenry—must now be understood to be in chains. The last few decades especially have found universities and other post-secondary education institutions in the grips of an American-styled marketization paradigm (Slaughter & Rhoades, 2009), in which their traditional role as a resourceful public sphere is being creatively destroyed in order to fashion academe as a global network of corporate-statist bureaucracies (Pusser et al., 2011) focused upon obtaining short-term, quantifiably measurable goals of increased knowledge productivity, maximized economic efficiency, and the manufacture of a biopolitical social totality (Pierce, 2013). Such might be termed the Age of the Neoliberal Arts.

For these reasons, this introduction asserts that education for sustainability must now take the insurgent standpoints[4] of "militant research" (Shukaitis et al., 2007) that are demanded by ecopedagogy as an affiliated movement-of-movements.[5] It does so to refuse the systemic greening of the academy, where "greening" is but a hegemonic code for the transmutation of the diverse array of human values produced and conserved within the academy into the singular value of the greenback standard as a commodity in service to regimes of imperialist finance. When Greening the Academy herein interrogates the liberal arts disciplines, then, it does so pedagogically to explicate the qualitative differences between capitalist (and related oppressive forms of) disciplinary "greenspeak," on the one hand, and the disruptive, democratic types of ecological disciplinarity (Fassbinder, 2008) that move beyond mere speech and to which we must now transition by any means necessary, on the other.

Ecopedagogy as Environmental Justice and Green Critical Criminology

It has been nearly a decade since Julian Agyeman and Craig Crouch (in Corcoran & Wals, 2004) offered their own powerful critique of what passes for sustainability education in colleges and universities. It is worth repeating at length:

> The current, predominant orientation of sustainability discourses in higher education is one of *environmental sustainability*. At the university level, themes associated with sustainability are therefore taught in departments of environmental science and environmental studies, emphasizing ecology, resource management, and environmental economics.
>
> This pedagogical approach means that aspects of sustainability having to do with justice and equity are, if at all, dealt with in departments outside the environmental studies...The domination of '*sustainability as science*', together with its polarization against '*sustainability as justice and equity*', is not only an inaccurate representation of the reality of sustainability issues, but also imparts a distorted picture to students. As a result, it is possible to graduate from university programs with credentials implying expertise in sustainability issues with a full understanding of the science of sustainability, but not the fundamental justice and equity issues that are inseparable from holistic considerations of sustainability (pg. 113).

We have yet to see much, if any, progress in re-orienting the dominant academic tendency—in the name of "sustainability"—of un-tethering issues of environmental literacy from prevailing ethical concerns such as being "summoned politically to work in pursuit of cultural and linguistic democracy, Indigenous sovereignty, and human rights" (Darder, 2011, pg. 329). As justice-seeking activists and critical pedagogues well know, the inability to find meaningful institutional reform in the face of clearly stipulated requests generally speaks less to the failure of those requests being understood and more to the reality that such demands are understood to be generally unwelcome.

The ways in which power works in education in this way, at both the macro and micro levels, to at once block and advance the liberation movement(s) for sustainability is the curricular purview of ecopedagogy. Such involves an ongoing interrogation of the campus through "a critical pedagogy of place" (Greenwood, 2010; 2008; Gruenewald, 2003), in which "place" is achieved through a justice-seeking lens. In this regard, Dave Hill and Simon Boxley helpfully summarize that "Recent developments in critical ecopedagogy emphasize an education within a 'dialectics of justice' (McLaren & Houston, 2005, p. 169), the two sides of this dialectic being *environmental justice*—the question of the unequal distribution of harmful environments between people—and *ecological justice*—the justice of the relationship between humans and the rest of the world."

Ecopedagogues tackling the problems of sustainability will find that the dialectics of justice cast the academy in a pretty unsavory light. Campuses, for example, are well known as major polluters and the pollution they produce goes far beyond any anthropogenic greenhouse gas contributions that they may provide. Consider a 2001 audit by an office of the U.S. Environmental Protection Agency that listed a representative sample of 175 academic institutions as commonly violating, by turn: the Clean Air Act, the Clean Water Act, the Emergency Planning and Community Right-to-Know Act, the Resource Conservation Recovery Act, the Toxic Substance Control Act, the Federal Insecticide, Fungicide, and Rodenticide Act, various state measures, as well as these colleges and universities having committed failures to properly institute spill prevention controls and countermeasures or to ensure the safe working of their underground storage tanks.[6] As gross industrial pollution is both a major social and biological harm that disproportionately affects the poor and people of color,[7] as well as being a primary contributor to the ruination of the land and destruction of species diversity, ecopedagogical research concerned with "greening the academy" suggests the topic of pollution should serve as a thematic focal point around which to organize change.[8]

For sure, when campuses pollute, all associated must bear some of the yoke of the responsibility for it. Yet, Weyerhaeuser paper contracts and air-conditioned offices aside, it seems conservatively plausible to suggest that those in the social sciences and humanities do not contribute anything resembling as much pollution as do those scientists, engineers and other campus lab workers whose careers revolve around projects granted by the military, corporations, and other governmental agencies interested in manufacturing research. If this is true, it suggests that charges of academic crimes against environmental and ecological justice should be properly brought to bear first and foremost upon the STEM initiatives that have come to pervade colleges and universities, and that the liberal arts' biggest offense may be in not helping these allegations to be effectively made both near and far.

In speaking of charges against the academy, and to suggest that universities must be brought to bear responsibility for the socio-ecological crimes wrought by their disciplinary technics, here the movements for ecopedagogy and environmental justice enter into an active partnership with the emerging movement for critical criminology (see Nocella II, 2011). Though beyond the scope of *Greening the Academy* to treat at any length, it bears mentioning here that it is the opinion of this book's editors that it is highly unlikely that curricular and disciplinary formations in higher education will change in order to better accord with demands for environmental and ecological justice without an organized sustainability movement also concerned with:

1. Teaching and learning the differences between retributive, restorative/ reparative, and transformative justice approaches across the curriculum;
2. Actively working with those who have been unjustly harmed inside and outside of the academy in order to bring these criminological approaches to bear on both singular and systematic matters of environmental and ecological justice, with offending parties and their institutional representatives being held accountable and made available for healing encounters; and

3. Committing campuses widely to the peacebuilding processes that are inherent in transformative justice approaches, such that an educational culture of nonviolence, empowerment, and flourishing social/cultural/ environmental diversity can replace unsustainable academic systems characterized by technocratic social control, authoritarian repression, and the complex stigmitization of forms of pedagogical dissent.

It is our hope that this text serves as a foundation stone in this regard. Our readers are thus advised that, if such a movement cannot materialize (and soon!) throughout academia, those truly interested in sustainability and the pursuit of knowledge should pursue ways to begin "escaping education" (Prakash & Esteva, 2008) rather than enduring it.

An Overview of the Chapters

In the essays that follow one will find a good deal of analysis of the history of academic research within a range of the social sciences and humanities, as deemed (by each author) to be relevant to the dream of achieving a more insurgent formation of sustainability studies characterized by "supradisciplinary" (Horkheimer, 1989: 31–32; Kellner, 1989: 7, 44) praxis. Importantly, though not surprisingly, many of the essays in this edited volume reveal that disciplinary constraints upon the diverse types of academic speech required to serve moral progress work to reproduce forms of academic voice that are out of step with our catastrophic scholarly conditions (see similarly Orr, 2009). Still, though the hope for the organizational transformation required for critically "greening the academy" poses a number of dire and dystopic problems to those who would undertake such a project, it must not be forgotten that university life (and the society to which it is dialectically tethered) maintains "objective ambiguity" (Marcuse, 1964). Despite the omnipresence of academic repression[9] for those who would seek to challenge its technical partnership with the "matrix of domination" (Collins, 2000), contemporary higher educational reality should be broadly seen as complex and contested by a variety of forces, rich with alternatives that are immediately present and yet ideologically, normatively, or otherwise blocked from achieving its full realization in service to society (Marcuse, 1972: 13).

Greening the Academy thus takes up the challenge to radicalize our social practices and higher educational institutions through the application of new diagnostic critical theories and alternative pedagogies such that unsustainable cultural and political features of academic life are negated, even as progressive tendencies within liberal arts scholarship are articulated and reaffirmed. Notably, this process has been conceptualized as "reconstruction" by progressive educators like John Dewey (1897) and revolutionaries like Antonio Gramsci, who importantly noted that "every crisis is also a moment of reconstruction" in which "the normal functioning of the old economic, social, cultural order, provides the opportunity to reorganize it in new ways" (Hall, 1987). Thus, in the chapters that follow herein, the book's varied authors were asked to reflect upon possible academic openings for ideological reconstruction in their disciplines in which holistic, affiliated, and practical approaches to systemic socio-ecological problems might be addressed in the context of the present-day university.

Samuel Day Fassbinder begins the anthology with a look at environmental education titled "Greening Education," suggesting that educational efforts could productively focus on the thematic direction provided by three texts: Curry Stephenson Malott's *A Call To Action* (2008), about the redemption of Native American Traditional Ecological Knowledge; John Vandermeer's *The Ecology of Agroecosystems* (2009), an interdisciplinary text bridging sustainable agriculture and political economy, and Margaret Atwood's *Oryx and Crake* (2004) and *The Year of the Flood* (2010), fictional works of speculation into a future of environmental catastrophe.

Piers Beirne and Nigel South then investigate how criminology might productively take up issues of environmental justice as issues of harm toward nature and animals, pitching for a turn in the field that accords with the social, cultural and juridical demands that hail from a radical ecological/animal rights perspective.

In the third chapter, Kishi Animashaun critically examines environmental sociology from a rigorous historical perspective, beginning with Dunlap and Catton's (1979) piece "Environmental Sociology," through its productive grappling with issues of political economy and the social construction of environmental problems. Specifically, Animashaun highlights Shellenberger and Nordhaus's infamous essay "The Death of Environmentalism" and the controversy surrounding it as a measurement of where environmental sociology is today.

With "Greening Political Science," Timothy Luke theorizes the need for an intriguing typology of discourses in political ecology: from environmental justice to critical climatology, ecomodernization to green statism, and natural capitalism to resource managerialism. The difference between a discipline based in critical social theory and one committed to a banal ecologism emerges.

Steven Best's contribution fuses a historical reading of revolutionary environmentalism with a philosophy of liberationist activism to anticipate a movement that promotes "ecological democracy" as opposed to the pervasive barbarism which he believes is likely to be the outcome of corporate domination in this era.

"Greening Economics" has Miriam Kennet and Michelle Gale de Oliveira probe recent developments in mainstream and alternative economies for a descriptive engagement with the analysts of existing economic structures to see how far they will go in advocating for humanitarian change.

An historical critique of the field of geography frames the seventh chapter, in which Donna Houston argues "Environmental determinism—though discredited—created conditions for the 'jettisoning' of nature from geography." She then pushes for geographical research to work compellingly to re-integrate the analysis of nature into its workings, a task she finds as already tentatively underway in the disciplinary discourse.

Eva Swidler's own "Greening History" meanwhile suggests that historians have generally been obtuse to theoretical problems, and that until historians wake up to the critical problems of historical theory, we are not likely to see important progress in environmental history. As an alternative, her essay specifies a "way through" by which history could redeem itself from its insensitivities.

Next, Brian McKenna's brilliant essay contextualizes the history of environmental anthropology in light of the various divisions of the academic discipline of anthropology. On the one hand, he sees these as relating to the ongoing history of primitive accumulation and, on the other, to various attempts to preserve the commons as a social and environmental construct.

In the tenth chapter, "Greening Communication," Tema Milstein surveys a broader history of the concept of "the environment" in communication studies, research which culminates with a recognition of an emergent investigative paradigm: "ecological theory: nature as co-communicant."

Taking up the study of literature, Corey Lewis's poetic piece argues that literature—especially American writing of the 18th, 19th, and early 20th centuries— was instrumental in forming changing attitudes toward the land and environment. The relationship between literature and the broader social and cultural trajectory that has unfolded within the development of modern industrial capitalism and political liberalism is raised for the reader's consideration.

"Greening Dis-Ability," a definitive contribution by book editor, Anthony J. Nocella II, boldly argues for a new paradigm of "ecoability" as a critical-theoretic contribution to sustainability that (at the same time) respects the differently-abled among us.

Finally, with the concluding essay, Greta Gaard's "Greening Feminism" offers a cross-disciplinary, comprehensive history of the contribution of women to the history of environmentalism.

A Concluding Statement of the Book's Limits and Possibilities

In closing, it remains for us to make a brief accounting of the possibly avoided and hidden curricula of *Greening the Academy* itself. Careful readers will undoubtedly wonder: If it is important to "green" feminist scholarship (or to "green" scholarship by feministing it), and if it is a similarly notable sustainability issue that we challenge the "normalization" of academic life through ecoability frameworks, etc., then is it not equally crucial to specifically highlight in a book such as this the contribution to sustainability education that every type of single-issue identity politics could advance against the myriad of disciplinary antagonisms they face? In short, we agree—while also asserting that sustainability education demands learning to move beyond identity politics as part of a broad-based dialogical alliance for academic reconstruction and social change.

To this end, the authors comprising this book were solicited or chosen with a careful understanding of their ideological locations and approaches, and it is the hope of the editorial team that the book thus blends anti-capitalist, antiracist, feminist, Queer, and other insurgent standpoints with a plurality of progressive political viewpoints, including those that can be classified as anarchist, socialist, or radically democratic. We did not—after considerable discussion—include a chapter on Native American (or American Indian) Studies, or on the need to indigenize the academy.[10] Arguably, this can be read as a significant limitation. On the other hand, projects such as bringing TribCrit (tribal critical race theory) to bear upon the entire academy, while additionally challenging the compartmentalization or denigration of tribal knowledge on campuses, seemed a particularly immense a task for any one author to handle fairly in the limited space that a book chapter could provide. Additionally, we asked the question: Whose purpose would such a chapter serve— the non-idealized struggle of specific Indigenous scholars and peoples or the radical pedagogical dream articulated by the three white editors of this collection? Moreover, considering the long-standing contribution made by universities to furthering the histories of colonization and settler colonization of Indigenous places, we as editors wondered if it was at all just to subsume the topic of academic indigeneity as merely one among many other academic contestations? Would doing so, in other words, be more representative of the "Colonial Model of Education" or a properly "critical interstitial methodology" (on the difference, see Calderón, 2011)?

The cognitive praxis of such deliberations suggests that situations exist, especially when whites are formally situated within positions of leadership, in which some struggles (both academic and non-) within the movement-of-movements must be heard internally on different terms, in different registers, or at different magnitudes in order to properly achieve a collective political ecology based in solidarity. Without hereby calling for a problematic return to the "ranking of oppressions," then, for this specific project the editors decided that the sovereignty of Indigenous knowledge traditions could best be respected in the manner set before you now. We recognize that this decision may amount to a "strategic essentialism" (Spivak, 1987), and that such essentializing—even if strategic—still runs the risk of silencing, marginalizing, or even further erasing the Indigenous scholars that we would seek here to symbolically stand with. Yet, we cannot emphasize enough that if we are to seriously "green the academy" it means that non-Indigenous scholars must demonstrate a disciplined sensitivity to the dangers for Indigenous peoples that their academic work can help further as historical settler agents, even when such non-Indigenous scholars are themselves self-consciously oppositional as they attempt to negotiate "the teaching machine" (Spivak, 2008) of which they are a part.

Besides questions about the array of cultural and political locations emphasized (or not) within *Greening the Academy*, still other readers will inevitably wonder about why our treatment of the "liberal arts" takes the form of this particular set of disciplines enclosed herein. Why is American literature treated and not Chinese? What about American or Cultural Studies? Where are the natural, physical, and mathematical sciences—aren't these traditionally conceived of as part of the liberal arts tradition? In fact, the history of the liberal arts reveals that it has never been a merely static curriculum. Rather, the liberal arts have been transformed again and again during varying periods by a range of educational institutions depending upon perceived institutional and social needs, as well as the understanding of human nature current at the time. Therefore, based on contemporary conditions of unfolding global technocapitalist biopolitics, which would reduce education and ethics to mere investment and security instruments for the unsustainable growth of new economic sectors, we seek to argue here for a renewed critical deliberation on what form the liberal arts can best take today in support of humane futures.

Certainly, the collection of subjects examined within *Greening the Academy* is ultimately tentative, partial, and arbitrary. Still, in our opinion, the freedom not to worry overly much about providing a more definitive list is provided by the emergence of an affiliated literature that also takes up questions concerning the form and goals of a reconstructed academic sustainability curriculum (See, e.g., Wals & Corcoran, 2012; McKenzie et al., 2009; Bartlett & Chase, 2004; Corcoran & Wals, 2004; Jones et al., 2010; Bowers, 2011; McDonald, 2011; Orr, 2010; McGonigle & Starke, 2006; Martin & Samels, 2012; Johnston, 2012; Andrzejewski, 2009; Myers, 2012; and Blewitt & Callingford, 2004). Taken together these texts offer a plethora of methods and educational models for how we might begin to undo harmful disciplinary standards, allow transdisciplinary and complex conversations to emerge from the disciplinary margins, tether academic work to place-based and bioregional cultural work, seriously engage national and international policy related to education for sustainable development, support widespread campus greening, and stimulate proactive types of critical educational leadership within academic administrations.[11] No two books (including our own) provide a congruent disciplinary or curricular template, and readers will find that many of these texts concerned with "greening the academy" include treatments of, or otherwise pitch, for interdisciplinary types of environmental science.

Readers of this volume should understand that in no way is it, its contributors, or its editors, advancing a pedagogical or political position that can be typified as anti-science. We recognize the value of the environmental sciences (broadly conceived) and believe that if we ever are to realize a "green academy" then our colleagues in the sciences must play an important role toward that endeavor by re-integrating with a critical *humanitas* (Marcuse, in Kellner, 2001: 74–76). On the other hand, the dialogical performance of this integration does not happen in the abstract, but rather in the objectively ambiguous conditions of academic domination as this Introduction has set out. Thus, while our purpose in *Greening the Academy* is to critique the liberal arts, we do so in order for them to speak more powerfully back to the environmental sciences such that the liberal arts might provide the moral authority on campuses for institutional reconstruction on behalf of a "new science of the multitude" (Kahn, 2010). In the absence of such, during this Age of the Neoliberal Arts and the Dehumanities, we find the social and humanistic fields are riddled with "science envy" (Agger, 2007)—an affective disorder that is only primed to grow worse the more such fields are marginalized on campus or altogether cut back. Again, what is at stake here is much more than just the self-esteem of the liberal arts. *Greening the Academy* intends the unshackling of the liberal arts once and for all from the oppressively economistic scientism (Margison & Naseem, 2010; Baez & Boyles, 2009) that seeks to define what counts as legitimate academic knowledge and, in this way, culturally reproduces the unsustainable dominant ideology of the global industrial complex.

In summary, then, this book strives to support researchers, students, administrators, and community activists interested in sustainability education work of this order by contributing to the disciplinary archaeology and deconstruction of the social and humanistic sciences from a total liberation standpoint, while also providing a type of critical intervention into the green campus movement that we see as overly concerned with achieving the positive piecemeal reforms of grabbing "low-hanging fruit." By contrast, at this time, education for sustainability requires a sweeping moral indictment of academic institutions as primary (and knowing) contributors to numerous historical crimes against humanity and the rest of the planetary community. If there is an apple that we must bite, then it is this.

NOTES

[1] According to her biography, in her role as Under Secretary, "Kanter reports to Secretary of Education Arne Duncan and oversees policies, programs, and activities related to postsecondary education, adult and career-technical education, federal student aid, and five White House Initiatives on Asian Americans and Pacific Islanders, Educational Excellence for Hispanics, Historically Black Colleges and Universities, Tribal Colleges and Universities, and Faith-Based and Neighborhood Partnerships." See: http://www2.ed.gov/news/staff/bios/kanter.html.

[2] The Sustainability Tracking, Assessment & Rating System created by the Association for the Advancement for Sustainability in Higher Education (see https://stars.aashe.org/).

[3] This is the agenda proffered by the leading sustainability education non-profit, Second Nature, founded by Sen. John Kerry, Teresa Heinz, and Dr. Anthony Cortese in 1993. See http://planetforward.org/idea/introducing-second-nature-transforming-higher-education-for-a-sustainable-society/. For our purposes here, the organization's name is a precious conceit that connotes the ideal work of *humanitas*—the use of education to improve both naturally given matter and manner.

[4] While the notion of "a standpoint" did not originate in feminist scholarship, we use the language here very much in line with its treatment in *The Feminist Standpoint Theory Reader* (Harding, 2003).

[5] For a compelling example of how militant research into the problem of sustainability might be conducted outside of academic disciplines, see Best & Nocella, 2006.

[6] See http://www.epa.gov/region1/assistance/univ/vio.html.

[7] Some additionally argue that this list includes women, children, the elderly, and other groups still.

[8] However, pollution is not the *only* thematic point for productive organization. For a treatment organizing the dialectics of justice in education around the plethora of issues related to human exceptionalism, see Lewis & Kahn (2010).

[9] On the ubiquitous academic repression of critical scholars and activists, see the startling collection of accounts in Best et al. (2010).

[10] However, this is a key concern for and pillar of ecopedagogy. See, for instance, Fassbinder (Ch. 1) and Kahn (2010).

[11] It goes beyond the work of this text to critically and comparatively evaluate these books in order to highlight contradictions, limitations, and possible alliances in approach. It goes without saying that this is an important *next step* for work in this area. *Greening the Academy*'s contribution, besides offering curricular data, is to singularly challenge the approach to sustainability in academia that stops short of a supradisciplinary movement and which delimits "sustainability" overly much as related to issues of facilities management, scientific and technological literacy, and business innovation, while failing to understand it first and foremost as a humanization concern requiring justice, liberty, and the interrogation of the many ways in which academe furthers the domination of nature.

REFERENCES

Agger, B. (2007). *Public Sociology.* Lanham MD: Rowman and Littlefield. 2nd ed.

Andrzejewski, J., Baltadano, M. P., & Symcox, L. (2009). *Social Justice, Peace, and Environmental Education: Transformative Standards.* New York: Routledge.

Baez, B., & Boyles, D. (2009). *The Politics of Inquiry: Education Research and the Politics of Science.* Albany, NY: SUNY Press.

Bartlett, P., & Chase, G. (2004). *Sustainability on Campus: Stories and Strategies for Change.* Cambridge, MA: MIT Press.

Baudrillard, J. (2009). *The Transparency of Evil: Essays on Extreme Phenomena.* New York: Verso Books.

Beringer, A., & Adombent, M. (2008). Sustainability in Higher Education Research. *Environmental Education Research, 14*(6), pp. 607–623.

Best, S., Kahn, R., Nocella II, A. J., & McLaren, P. (2011). *The Global Industrial Complex: Systems of Domination.* Lanham, MD: Lexington Books.

Best, S., & Nocella II, A. J. (2006). *Igniting a Revolution: Voices in Defense of the Earth.* Oakland, CA: AK Press.

Best, S., Nocella II, A. J., & McLaren, P. (2010). *Academic Repression: Reflections from the Academic Industrial Complex.* Oakland, CA: AK Press.

Blewitt, J., & Callingford, C. (2004). *The Sustainability Curriculum: The Challenge for Higher Education.* New York: Routledge.

Bowers, C. A. (2011). *University Reforms in an Era of Global Warming.* Eugene, OR: Eco-Justice Press.

Calderón, D. (2011). Locating the Foundations of Epsitemologies of Ignorance in Education Theory and Practice (pp. 105–128). In E. Malewski & N. Jaramillo (Eds.), *Epistemologies of Ignorance in Education.* Charlotte, NC: Information Age Publishing.

Collins, P. H. (2000). *Black Feminist Thought: Knowledge, Consciousness, and the Politics of Empowerment.* New York: Routledge.

Corcoran, P. A., & Wals, A. E. J. (2004). *Higher Education and the Challenge of Sustainability: Problematics, Promise and Practice.* Netherlands: Kluwer Academic.

Darder, A. (2011). *A Dissident Voice: Essays on Culture, Pedagogy and Power.* New York: Peter Lang.

Dewey, J. (1897). My Pedagogic Creed. *The School Journal, 54.*

Fassbinder, S. D. (2008). Capitalist Discipline and Ecological Discipline. *Green Theory & Praxis, 4*(2).

Giroux, H. (2007). *The University in Chains: Confronting the Military-Industrial-Academic Complex.* Boulder, CO: Paradigm Publishers.

Greenwood, D. A. (2010). Education in a Culture of Violence: A Critical Pedagogy of Place in Wartime. *Cultural Studies of Science Education,* 5, pp. 351–359.

———. (2008). A Critical Pedagogy of Place: From Gridlock to Parallax. *Environmental Education Research, 14*(3), pp. 336–348.

Gruenewald, D. A. (2003). The Best of Both Worlds: A Critical Pedagogy of Place. *Educational Researcher, 32*(4), pp. 3–12.

Hall, S. (1987). Gramsci and Us. *Marxism Today,* (June), 19.

Harding, S. (2003). *The Feminist Standpoint Theory Reader: Intellectual and Political Controversies.* New York: Routledge.

Hill, D., & Boxley, S. (2007). Critical Teacher Education for Economic, Environmental and Social Justice: An Ecosocialist Manifesto. *Journal for Critical Education Policy Studies,* 5 (2). Retrieved from http://www.jceps.com/index.php?pageID=article&articleID=96.

Horkheimer, M. (1989). *Traditional and Critical Theory in Critical Theory: Selected essays.* New York: Continuum.

Illich, I. (1991). Text and University: On the Idea and History of a Unique Institution. A translation by Lee Hoinacki of the keynote address delivered at the Bremen Rathaus, September 23, 1991. Retrieved from http://www.davidtinapple.com/illich/1991_text_and_university.PDF.

Johnston, L. F. (2012). *Higher Education for Sustainability: Cases, Challenges, and Opportunities from Across the Curriculum.* New York: Routledge.

Jones, P., Selby, D., & Sterling, S. (2010). *Sustainability Education: Perspectives and Practice Across Higher Education*. London: Earthscan.

Kahn, R. (2010). *Critical Pedagogy, Ecoliteracy, and Planetary Crisis: The Ecopedagogy Movement*. New York: Peter Lang.

Kellner, D. (2001). *Herbert Marcuse: Towards a Critical Theory of Society. Collected Papers of Herbert Marcuse, Volume Two*. New York: Routledge.

———. (1989). *Critical Theory, Marxism and Modernity*. Oxford: Polity Press.

Koester, R. E. (2006). Beyond Disciplines: Integrating Academia, Operations, and Community for Campuswide Education for Sustainability. In R. &. Forrant (Ed.), *Inside and Out*, pp. 41–61. Amityville, NY: Baywood Publishing Company.

Lewis, T., & Kahn, R. (2010). *Education out of Bounds: Reimagining Cultural Studies for a Posthuman Age*. New York: Palgrave Macmillan.

Marcuse, H. (1972). *An Essay on Liberation*. Harmondsworth, PA: Penguin.

———. (1964). *One-dimensional Man*. Boston, MA: Beacon Press.

Margison, E. H., & Naseem, A. (2010). *Scientism and Education: Empirical Research as Neo-liberal Ideology*. New York: Springer Publishing Co.

Martin, J., & Samels, J. (2012). *The Sustainable University: Green Goals and New Challenges for Higher Education Leaders*. Baltimore: Johns Hopkins University Press.

McDonald, T. (2011). *Social Responsibility and Sustainability: Multidisciplinary Perspectives Through Service Learning*. Sterling, VA: Stylus Publishing.

McLaren, P., & Houston, D. (2005). Revolutionary Ecologies: Ecosocialism and Critical Pedagogy. In P. McLaren, *Capitalists & Conquerors: A Critical Pedagogy Against Empire*. Lanham, MD: Rowman & Littlefield.

M'Gonigle, M., & Starke, J. (2006). *Planet U: Sustaining the World, Reinventing the University*. Gabriola Island, BC: New Society Publishers.

McKenzie, M., Hart, P., Bai, H., & Jickling, B. (2009). *Fields of Green: Restorying Culture, Environment and Education*. New York: Hampton Press.

McLaren, P. (2012). Objection Sustained: Revolutionary Pedagogical Praxis as an Occupying Force. *Policy Futures in Education, 10*(4), pp. 487–494.

Myers, W. A. (2012). *Sustainability in Higher Education: Best Practices, Trends and Obstacles Impacting Champions of Sustainability on College Campuses*. Unpublished Dissertation. Prescott, AZ: Prescott College.

Nocella II, A. J. (2011). *A Dis-Ability Perspective on the Stigmatization of Dissent: Critical Pedagogy, Critical Criminology, and Critical Animal Studies*. Unpublished Dissertation. Syracuse, NY: Syracuse University.

Orr, D. (2010). *Hope is an Imperative: The Essential David Orr*. Washington, DC: Island Press.

———. (2009). *Down to the Wire: Confronting Climate Collapse*. Oxford: Oxford University Press.

Pierce, C. (2013). *Education in the Biocapitalist Era: Optimizing Students for a Flat World*. New York: Palgrave Macmillan.

Prakash, M., & Esteva, G. (2008). *Escaping Education: Living and Learning Within Grassroots Cultures*. 2nd ed. New York: Peter Lang.

Pusser, B., Kempner, K., Marginson, S., & Ordorika, I. (2011). *Universities and the Public Sphere: Knowledge Creation and State Building in the Era of Globalization*. New York: Routledge.

Shukaitis, S., Graeber, D., & Biddle, E. (2007). *Constituent Imagination: Militant Investigations, Collective Theorization*. Oakland, CA: AK Press.

Slaughter, S., & Rhoades, G. (2009). *Academic Capitalism and the New Economy: Markets, State, and Higher Education*. Baltimore: Johns Hopkins University Press.

Spivak, G. C. (2008). *Outside in the Teaching Machine*. New York: Routledge.

———. (1987). *In Other Worlds: Essays in Cultural Politics*. New York: Taylor and Francis.

Wals, A. E. J., & Corcoran, P. (2012). *Learning for Sustainability in Times of Accelerating Change*. Wageningen, The Netherlands: Wageningen Academic Publishers.

GREENING EDUCATION

SAMUEL DAY FASSBINDER

INTRODUCTION

Environmental education in all eras has taught about the natural world: the passing on of knowledge about nature is what has counted as education over most of the human race's 200,000-year existence. "Environmental education" is, however, a term now connected to the relatively recent birth of environmentalism, and of the perception of environmental problems: Joy A. Palmer's *Environmental Education in the 21st Century* suggests that environmental education began on a global level with the 1968 UNESCO Biosphere Conference, in Paris, which "called for the development of curriculum materials relating to studying the environment for all levels of education, the promotion of technical training, and the stimulation of global awareness of environmental problems." (p. 5) Environmental education's modern being coincides, then, with environmentalism's modern being: Ramachandra Guha (*Environmentalism: A Global History*) tells us that "the environmental movement is a child of the sixties" (p. 1). Much of this "birth" is typically traced to the explosive appearance of Rachel Carson's *Silent Spring* in 1962 and of the first Earth Day and of the beginning of the Environmental Protection Agency in 1970, each of which, as events, increased the popular perception that there were such things as environmental problems.

The term "environmental education" is in fact a broad, general term that could encompass practically any learning process. "The environment" is where we live: it encompasses the whole world, and not just the outdoors; "education" encompasses practically any process of teaching and learning, and we are learning all the time. This modern definition of "environmental education," however, comes into being with a recent increase in the scale of what are called "environmental problems."

Our present-day desperation as regards environmental problems demands a form of environmental education which would prompt solutions, both in terms of dealing with the physical manifestations of pollution, depletion, climate change and so on, and in terms of the social structures which underlie environmental problems. Toward this end, the idea of "cognitive praxis," a term suggested by Richard Kahn in his book *Critical Pedagogy, Ecoliteracy, and Planetary Crisis*, deserves examination. The term "praxis," as used in this context, suggests Karl Marx's concept of "practical-critical activity," or the educator Paulo Freire's idea of "reflection and action upon the world in order to transform it" (p. 36). "Cognitive praxis" is a form of teaching and learning which contributes to praxis, to practical (essentially problem-solving)

S. D. Fassbinder, A. J. Nocella II and R. Kahn (Eds.), Greening the Academy:
Ecopedagogy Through the Liberal Arts, 1–22.

activity that embodies a critique of society. Kahn develops "cognitive praxis" in tandem with "ecopedagogy," a movement combining the philosophies of teaching of the critical pedagogy movement (specifically of Paulo Freire but engaging other educators as well) with the urgency of an environmental education dedicated to the current environmental crisis.

In his book, Kahn suggests that a "cognitive praxis" is an attempt to teach society about the environment, to inspire both thought and action ("praxis") such that environmental problems can be solved. "Cognitive praxis," then, is an expansion of the realm of knowledge and action, to put humanity as a whole in service of the goals of environmentalism. Kahn defines it as follows:

> Environmental movements engage pedagogically with society, with their own membership, and with other movements. They thereby generate theories, new strategic possibilities, and emergent forms of identity that can be accepted, rejected, or otherwise co-opted by dominant institutional power. This, then, is what can be called the collective cognitive praxis of disparate environmental movements... (p. 27)

Kahn holds out "cognitive praxis," then, as a tool for social change in light of the present-day ecological crisis:

> Part of the development of cognitive praxis is to wage transformative campaigns on behalf of (innovative) thoughts and practices, and to attempt to march through all manner of social institutions with them, especially those overtly concerned with the function of education. (p. 27).

Given such a definition and such a motivation, then, we can expect that, as anxiety over environmental crises (perhaps specifically abrupt climate change) increases, a wide variety of attempts at "cognitive praxis" will be tried toward environmental solutions. Clearly, a multitude of changes in social practice, resulting in an overall transformation of world-society, will be needed to overcome the ecological crisis. This essay will suggest possibilities for "cognitive praxis," specifically in college-level education, in reflections upon environmental education in the past and the present, and in anticipation of what it might be in the future.

In Kahn's discussion of "cognitive praxis" there is a prominently-placed suggestion of the "long march through the institutions," a reference to Marcuse (*Counterrevolution and Revolt*, page 55). The suggestion is that an open engagement with social institutions will be necessary in order to transform the logic of the system as a whole, and thus to solve environmental problems. In this light, colleges and universities are importantly positioned as places of academic freedom and of the preparation of young adults for existence within present-day social structures. There is also a tradition of collegiate activism to which the expected audience for this essay, professors, students, and other participants in college life, might hope to contribute.

Vital to the pursuit of effective cognitive praxis is an engagement with society's existing institutional structures. Put more straightforwardly: the overall organization of society needs to be examined if overall environmental problems are to be solved. This can be conceptualized in an academic sense in terms of political economy. Two principles guide a political economy analysis of environmental problems: 1) from Saul Alinsky's *Rules for Radicals*: "The basic requirement for the understanding of the politics of change is to recognize the world as it is" (p. 12) and 2) Kees van der Pijl's definition, "(Global) Political Economy refers to those approaches to analysing world society which seek to overcome the disciplinary divisions of social science" (p. 1). The van der Pijl definition may seem fairly abstract, but will become important in light of the problems encountered by cognitive praxis in the context of academic life. One's right to participate in a university or college is often constrained by one's affiliation with a "discipline" or "field," in the sense of having a major, or by the name of the department granting one's graduate degrees or tenure-track position – but it's important that disciplinary divisions not interfere with cognitive praxis.

In summary, if environmental education is to adopt any form of cognitive praxis it needs to remain as education while at the same time opening doors to new manifestations of activist participation in the "world as it is." Toward this end, an effective cognitive praxis at the college/university level must offer an open discussion of our relation to existing structures of political economy. As Peter McLaren (2005) argues, "humans are conditioned by structures and social relations just as they create and transform those structures and relations" and so the language of political economy is useful in discussing structures and social relations as such. Or, as McLaren asks more polemically, "do we know whose hands ground the capitalist lenses through which we comprehend the world and do we know from whence came the bloodstains on the lens grinder's workbench?" (p. 9)

The ultimate aim of classroom discussion about the political economy of the "real world" is going to be diverse – Kahn makes that clear with his emphasis (above) upon the "generat(ion of) theories, new strategic possibilities, and emergent forms of identity" (p. 27). Ultimately, however, an educational cognitive praxis would pry open for examination what Cornelius Castoriadis called the "social imaginary." The social imaginary is the set of symbolic ingredients for our construction of social existence. Cognitive praxis uses the social imaginary, as such, as a terrain for activist struggle, through its manifold and diverse representation of alternatives to the current way of life.

Environmental education authors Charles Saylan and Daniel T. Blunstein have recognized much of what is stated above, and their recent (2011) book *The Failure of Environmental Education and How We Can Fix It* reflects this. Saylan and Blunstein start from a deep concern about environmental problems, and enthusiastically embrace a discussion of society and social behaviors. The first sentence of Chapter One of their book sets a tone: "Environmental education has failed to bring about the changes in attitude and behavior necessary to stave off the detrimental effects of climate change, biodiversity loss, and environmental degradation that our planet is experiencing at an alarmingly accelerated rate." (p. 1) So the human race must change its behaviors, and environmental education can be assigned the task of teaching the wisdom to know how. The question prompted by this pronouncement is one of "how can educators do this?" Later in the book, the authors advocate a specifically activist pedagogy to fix environmental education:

> We think environmental education should develop an informed and thereby active citizenry, but we realize that this will not be accomplished solely by incorporating environmental education curricula into national teaching standards. Instead, the tenets of individual responsibility, development of community, social engagement, and appreciation of nature will have to permeate educational systems at all levels. (p. 174)

Advocates of cognitive praxis would welcome Saylan and Blunstein's proposal as a positive development. The questions they would have about "development of community" and "social engagement," though, would be ones of whether or not environmental education can address the immediate needs of working people, of whether or not it can do more with social engagement than lobby Congress for measures without "political traction," and if it can or can't dislodge the economic and political interests that stand in its way. Saylan and Blumstein's book starts an important (though unfinished) discussion in political economy.

An important starting point for the self-understanding of environmental educators wishing to practice "cognitive praxis" (in the North American context) is reflection upon the past, and specifically upon traditional ecological knowledge as advanced by Native American peoples. In bringing this wisdom to the present moment, however, it must be placed in the context of their conquest and assimilation in the history of the expansion of the United States. Environmental educators can effectively appropriate traditional ecological knowledge, but not on the grounds of continuing imperialism. Also important to the history of environmental education is the "nature study" movement of early 20th century America, the most significant movement of the prehistory of environmental education, and in discussing it I will touch upon practices of "playing Indian" it adopted, out of some felt need to imitate America's possessors of traditional ecological knowledge. An alternative path to "playing Indian" for present-day audiences is suggested by the politically-engaged, "of the land" pedagogy of Curry Stephenson Malott as depicted in his book *A Call To Action*.

Cognitive praxis in environmental education must also look for openings within present-day social structures. In the context of present-day college/ university work, the science of agroecology offers promise in that it combines the human realm of necessity, as addressed in food production through agriculture, with a wholistic scientific understanding of nature, as addressed in ecology. Agroecology education offers the academic study of sustainability beyond the unsustainable structures of political economy that currently rule the land. Moreover, agroecology education offers opportunities to apply traditional ecological knowledge to modern ecological dilemmas while at the same time addressing political economy.

Given the uninhibited trends of industrialization and capital accumulation, future attempts at cognitive praxis will have to contend with an environment significantly more challenging than that of previous eras. Contemplation of the future of the environment, which is to say the future, will require that we open a social imaginary – which for the future means the symbolic register of the dominant trend, the governing concepts of where we are headed as a world-society. Of relevance to acts of questioning the dominant trend as such are Margaret Atwood's novels *Oryx and Crake* and *In The Year Of The Flood*. Atwood's novels speculate about a world in which ecological knowledge has been forgotten and the gossip of consumer life substituted in its place. In Atwood's speculative world, what is left of ecological knowledge has been gathered up as bits and fragments of a "past" by a religious cult. The central event of both of these novels is depicted as an ultimate instrumentalization of the world – an attempt by one person to put an end to the human race and to substitute in its place a "perfected," genetically-engineered, new human species. Atwood asks us to imagine what kind of ecological decisions we would make if we were to have to live in such a world.

In one sense it could be argued that the historical beginnings of environmental education were in the wisdom passed down from elders in traditional societies, for much of that wisdom is what we today call "traditional ecological knowledge." Today, however, traditional ecological knowledge is integrated into frameworks that its preindustrial sponsors would not recognize. While the metabolic rift between society and nature has never been as wide as it is today, the goal of sustainability today can be spelled out more clearly than ever in a vision of a post-capitalist world in harmony with Earth's ecosystems substrate.

BORROWING FROM THE PAST: A PEDAGOGY OF UNITY

The past, present and future are all of course locations in time; but when we deal with them cognitively, as aspects of cognitive praxis, they are part of the social imaginary. Past, present, and future exist in the symbolic realm as ingredients for our construction of social existence, and as such, past, present and future are contested terrains of activist struggle.

Each of these temporal concepts puts a distinctive stamp on life. The real-life past is lost to us forever; we reconstruct it through historical documentation and unearth its clues in archaeological digs, but it remains a contested zone: "what happened back then" is partially forgotten, and partially reshaped, to meet present-day needs. The present moment is the location of our direct experience, our time of living, the site of our struggles. The future is conceived as a speculation, using terms borrowed from the present.

As far as environmental education is concerned, the debate about the past is a debate about traditional "environmental education," which is to say, education before it was called "environmental" and supplemented with industrial/consumer society's concern with environmental problems. As the past is a terrain of appropriation by

5

the present, the question at hand in the North American context is that of whether traditional First Nations practices can be made congruent with "environmental education," and made to solve environmental problems. The discussion about this was dramatized effectively by Shepard Krech III's (1999) book The Ecological Indian, which claimed an assessment from a conservationist perspective upon a number of historic First Nations practices. Krech gives the natives of North America a mixed review: he can find some native practices which count as conservation, and others which don't.

Whatever else the debate about the "ecological Indian" was about (Krech, also Harkin and Lewis), it was really about the relationship between the settler society of the late 19th and early 20th century (Euro-)America, as it eventually developed concepts of "ecology" and "conservation," and the various First Nations societies, whose traditional practices are then later evaluated as "traditional ecological knowledge" long after they have been subjected to conquest and assimilation. Perhaps not all traditional practices of First Nations societies count as "ecological" – but nevertheless traditional ecological knowledge was the beginning of "environmental education." In having to cope with the natural world, earlier peoples had to be educated about their environments, whereas modern consumers in mass industrial society live in architectural and technologized communication complexes that substitute consumer convenience and instrumental relationships (both to society and to nature) for knowledge of the land once regarded as essential to survival. Traditional ecological knowledge is useful as a subject of present-day environmental education because its users had to "live outdoors" in a way in which present-day human beings don't.

In the settler society that subjected Native Americans to conquest and forced assimilation, the first important mainstreaming of environmental education was the "nature study movement," and it was this movement which provided us with many of our current motivations for pursuing environmental education. The "nature study movement," as depicted in Kevin Armitage's brilliant (2009) book *The Nature Study Movement*, was largely an educational movement that attempted to educate young children about nature through simple versions of outdoor study – birdwatching, for instance, or gardening or animal husbandry. It flourished in the Progressive Era of American history, in the first quarter of the 20th century. Its advocates typically recommended outdoor education for young people (typically in elementary schools) as an antidote to the corrupting effects upon character of industrial life. As Liberty Hyde Bailey suggested in his book "The Nature Study Idea," the point of the nature study movement was to "enable every person to live a richer life, whatever his business or profession may be" (p. 4). The nature study movement also borrowed liberally from child-centered, progressive education in the Progressive Era.

Indeed, readers can observe that even before the nature study movement there were the beginnings of a concept of environmentalism concerned with environmental problems. Most famously, George Perkins Marsh's *Man and Nature*, published in 1864, greatly advanced the idea that conservation would be necessary if human beings were not to destroy their environmental substrates. Moreover, as Armitage repeatedly points out, the nature study movement was motivated by conservationist impulses throughout its history.

However, I think that it's meaningful to look at environmentalism as Joan Martinez-Alier (2002) does, as divided into three currents: (1) the cult of wilderness, engaged primarily in the "defence of immaculate nature" (p. 1), (2) the gospel of eco-efficiency, which has translated today into the movements for "sustainable development" and "ecological modernization " (p. 5), and (3) environmental justice and the environmentalism of the poor, concerned largely for the "material interest in the environment as a source and a requirement for livelihood; not so much a concern with the rights of other species and of future generations of humans as a concern for today's poor humans" (p. 11). One can see in the nature study movement the beginnings of the first two currents, whereas what society needs today is participation in the third current – people who are concerned with the environment not because it's wilderness in need of preservation, nor because the capitalist system needs improved management, but rather because they live there, and want to continue to do so. The environmentalism of the poor, then, was the First Nations contribution to the history of environmental education in North America.

Interestingly enough, one part of the nature study movement, insofar as it promoted outdoor education, engaged practices of "playing Indian," and thus from the beginnings of environmental education there was a certain appropriation of the images of the knowers of traditional ecological knowledge. As Armitage points out, a number of educators of the early 20th century thought that, for children, "playing Indian" would be a good antidote to the ills of modern life: they also imagined that "playing Indian" would recapitulate the stages of human development, from savagery to civilization, as depicted by the racialist anthropologies of that time.

The practice of "playing Indian" may have been a sideshow of the nature study movement – but its popularization along with nature study highlights what was missing from nature study; a confrontation with colonialism, with the ways in which the descendants of Europeans colonized North America, conceptualized as an imprint upon the land. The history of "playing Indian" reveals that "Indian," like "nature," was the obverse face of conquest in the colonial imaginary of the American consciousness. The Boy Scouts, for instance "played Indian," and this allowed them to reinforce notions of European superiority: "by emulating Natives, boys reenacted the stages of progress outlined earlier in the century by Morgan and echoed by Turner, thus ironically affirming racialized conceptions of social development and their own superiority." (Huhndorf, p. 74)

One of the most prominent advocates of "nature study" through "playing Indian" was Ernest Thompson Seton, who indeed imagined "playing Indian" as a developmental stage for little boys. Seton, a Canadian and one of the cofounders of the Boy Scouts of America, identified "playing Indian" with what he called "woodcraft," which incorporated a number of different outdoor skills. Seton's

(1903) juvenile novel *Two Little Savages* lays out Seton's plan: in the novel, the boy protagonists make a wigwam, a teepee, a peace pipe, bows, arrows, a war bonnet, and an "Indian drum." The flip side of Seton's romanticization of "playing Indian" was the ethic of Daniel Carter Beard, who (as member of the Boy Scout bureaucracy) promoted outdoor skills through the romanticization of Euro-American pioneers, of Daniel Boone and Davy Crockett.

As full, published books, two important historical commentaries on "playing Indian" are Philip J. Deloria's (1998) *Playing Indian*, and Shari M. Huhndorf's (2001) *Going Native*. Deloria sums up the problem with "playing Indian" as follows: "the ways in which white Americans have used Indianness in creative self-shaping have continued to be pried apart from questions about inequality, the uneven workings of power, and the social settings in which Indians and non-Indians might actually meet" (p. 190). One can see this even more vividly in the practices of New Age hucksters who sell cheap versions of Native American spirituality today. But here we are actually concerned with the integration of "playing Indian" into nature study, as an object lesson about forms of environmental education which don't critique the colonial/capitalist context in which they are embedded.

Nature study in the Progressive Era as a whole was an educational reaction to an era of growing industrialization in which the remaining political threat to white, European-ancestry hegemony posed by the First Nations peoples had been somewhat recently been neutralized, and in which the actual progeny of First Nations people were being deprived of their cultural heritages in BIA schools. It took refuge in innocuous images of nature, and went forth to study the environment. Some of the promoters of nature study used "Indians" as images of an idealized past in order to make child's play of them, to teach the progeny of European ancestry the values of outdoor life. The preponderance of nature study literature is innocuous: a gander through Anna Botsford Comstock's (1911) *Handbook of Nature Study for Teachers and Parents* would find a good deal of simple discussion about animals, plants, minerals, the land and sky. Or for further innocuous reading one could peruse the book Seton published just before *Two Little Savages: Wild Animals I Have Known* (1898) tells (in Seton's juvenile-fiction prose style) the life-stories of a gray wolf, a crow, a cottontail rabbit, a dog, a fox, a jackal, and a partridge, most of whom Seton gave pet names.

The examples of "playing Indian" in Armitage's book on nature study also point to a greater truth about the nature study movement and about environmental education in general. The modern sense of environmental education is a rediscovery, faux or real, of a natural world left behind by industrial society, and in its prehistory in the nature study movement we can see how "environmental education" (in the modern sense) became a byproduct of the colonization and exploitation of the land and of human beings under conditions of capitalist industry. Indeed, traditional ecological knowledge can be validated by its integration into what is today called "natural resource management" (see e.g. Menzies (2006)) for a variety of applications) – historical societies have left behind practices which still prove useful in the maintenance of the heritage of a livable planet Earth under industrial conditions.[1] The educational value of the Native American past in the history of North America, however, extends beyond bits of knowledge (e.g. "woodcraft), to the history of peoples who "lived outdoors" (rather than on technological-industrial landscapes) and who did what they could with the "native science" they gained therein. The real question for environmental educators, however, is one of whether or not in going "back to nature," as the nature-study advocates did, they can (or can't) get past the industrialist/colonial/capitalist visions of environmentalism and position themselves to demand environmental justice.

Chapter 4 of Kahn's book, titled "Organizational Transformation as Ecopedagogy: Traditional Ecological Knowledge as Real and New Science," makes the admirable case that

> ecopedagogy works strategically for (traditional ecological knowledge) to be taught unabashedly as science in order to achieve a redistribution of "the cognitive and social benefits of scientific and technological changes" (Harding, 1998, p. 168) along more equitable and sustainable lines, while also reducing the sociocultural and environmental costs often brought on by the introduction of such changes. In so doing, ecopedagogy supports transformative research into who is excluded from the canons of sustainability scholarship, the methods it undertakes, and the normative sociopolitical frameworks of WMS ("Western modern science") generally. (p. 106–107)

Having established the possibility, then, of an ecopedagogy which could teach what Gregory Cajete (2000) calls "native science," Kahn then proceeds in his narrative to a rather advanced discussion of his chosen example of traditional ecological knowledge, the Peace Camp at the Nevada Test Site. Kahn's narrative brings the reader to a realization of the ultimate political value of projects such as the Peace Camp; here it is important to identify a set of cognitive praxes that can integrate traditional ecological knowledge.

The starting point for Native American cognitive praxis should be the core vision of "native science," in a form which can be adapted to the present, industrialized, situation as a foundation for long-term land stewardship. With an eye toward political economy, in this core we can identify concepts such as communal land use (as opposed to private property), respect for nature (as opposed to "natural resources" philosophy), and local sovereignty (as opposed to "global governance" in the service of empire). The power of this vision derives from a history of conquest and colonization in which Native American concepts of land are seen as having been displaced. From Jace Weaver's essay "Notes from a Miner's Canary":

> When Europeans came to the Western hemisphere, they deposed communal Native notions of land. Though systems varied from tribe to tribe, in general land was considered a common resource, available for all. George Barnaby (Dene) speaks of the rationale for such a system and captures the essence of many Native beliefs about the earth when he says, "Our life is part of the land.

> We live on the land and are satisfied with what we get from it. No one person owns the land, it belongs to all of us. We choose where we want to go and our choice is respected by others whether in the settlement or in the bush. We have no word in our language that means wilderness, as anywhere we go is our home. (19)

Thus Weaver, and Barnaby whom he quotes, spell out a Native American land ethic. Readers can see the power of this sort of vision in light of the stock notion, made into the lyric of a Joni Mitchell song, that "you don't know what you've got 'til it's gone." The core of this knowledge, however, has to be adapted to the the present day, of a world characterized by empire in decline and by the continuing spread of capitalist discipline over planetary society and nature. Curry Stephenson Malott's *A Call To Action* suggests one way of restoring a pedagogy of Native American ecological knowledge, toward cognitive praxis in environmental education.

At first glance Malott's book appears as an unlikely candidate for environmental education. It advertises itself as a text in cultural studies dealing with Native Americans, and might also be suitable for upper-division or graduate education classes. In short, the modern university can easily marginalize it. A large portion of its content is concerned with retelling the history of domination and colonization to which native peoples in North America have been subjected. It is, however, organized around a pedagogy that is "endowed with a land-centered revolutionary consciousness" (p. 90). Malott points to traditional knowledge, for instance, of the native peoples of the Pacific Northwest and of how they were able to manage the salmon population in their areas through "ancient fishing practices that protected the natural balance of the land and its ecosystems" (p. 95) before the invasion of settlers of European origin. He continues the narrative by discussing how legal battles in the current era are informed by the reuse of traditional knowledge as possessed by tribal elders (p. 102).

Malott also endorses revolutionary critical pedagogy, as voiced by Peter McLaren, as a means of recognizing this history and of humanizing oneself against the debilitating effects of the colonization and predation which came before the current era and which continues in different guises to this day. He chooses, as an example of native peoples who are today resisting the system, the Zapatistas of Chiapas, prizing their radical democracy, their cultural diversity, and their anticapitalism as appropriate to struggles against the sort of domination that has (from our perspective) waged war against Indigenous visions of ecological sustainability.

Malott's text offers specifically a pedagogy of unity. Not only does it extend outside of the past of North America's native peoples, but it also engages populations outside of the existing First Nations peoples. The author quotes approvingly of Winona LaDuke:

> I would argue that Americans of "foreign" descent must become Americans. That is not to become a patriot of the United States, a patriot of the flag, but a patriot of the land of this continent... You were born here, you will not

likely go away, or live anywhere else, and there are simply no more frontiers to follow. We must all relearn a way of thinking, a state of mind that is from this common ground... if we are in this together, we must rebuild, redevelop, and reclaim an understanding/ analysis which is uniquely ours. (p. 89)

Thus in attempting to enact what Martinez-Alier calls "the environmentalism of the poor," it becomes an open question of activism, and of pedagogy, of how to create coalitions around what Malott calls "Indigenous resistance" (p. 73). Above all, Malott urges us to think clearly without fear of philosophy, and to see clearly without shrinking from the conditions of the world as it is.

Environmental Education Now: Agroecology as College Ecopedagogy

David W. Orr's (1996) contribution to the ancestor volume to this one (*Greening the College Curriculum*) gives a set of institutional reasons for the failure of today's universities to address the ecological crisis. They are, in brief:

1. The dominant belief in technical progress in universities has meant that university research has often failed to recognize dangerous aspects of technology.
2. An obsession with departmentalization and specialization has dominated curricular organization within universities.
3. Universities have become expensive places to attend, thus creating an increased emphasis upon fundraising and corporate dependence.
4. University administrations have not shown leadership in addressing the ecological crisis. (Orr pp. 9–12)

Orr's critique of university education points to the fact that we might look for cognitive praxis in university education in its margins, in places within the university outside of its dominant institutional frameworks. Curry Stephenson Malott's *A Call To Action*, for instance, will receive its biggest audience in departments of education, as typically marginalized by universities.[2]

In *Critical Pedagogy, Ecoliteracy, and Planetary Crisis*, Richard Kahn criticizes environmental studies, as such, for having been institutionalized as a "hard science" specialization within the modern university:

Even the field's new nationwide professional society, the Association for Environmental Studies and Sciences...emphasizes the centrality of physical and biological science to environmental studies issues. (p. 104)

We can expect environmental education – especially at the university level – to follow suit in many places, as being about the teaching of a hard-science perspective upon "nature" without much reflection upon the diversity of possible changes in the human social arrangement and how these would change our relationship to "nature." Thus an appropriately marginal place for cognitive praxis in university education would be agroecology education. Now ecology is itself an "interdisciplinary discipline," which combines various sciences in regard for the whole of nature, and avoids the instrumental specialization typical of hard-science disciplinary research. Typically, however, the problem with ecology as a "hard science" is that it does not consider human beings as existing within ecosystems, and so the social sciences tend to be overlooked in ecological analysis. Agroecology, as a subset of ecology, can be an exception to this general observation: agroecology combines a practical art, agronomy, with a hard science, ecology, to discover or invent measurable forms of sustainable agriculture. Agroecology, moreover, is qualitatively different from other fields in which the term "sustainability" is used (e.g. "sustainable development") in that it attempts to make of the concept "sustainability" a connection between the distant past and the present rather than using the term "sustainability" to merely advertise the merits of particular programs. Agroecology is thus open to the academic representation of traditional ecological knowledge, with its superior understanding of sustainability in its own contexts.

In discussing agroecology, here, we may wish to include discussion of another field which counts more as a practical art than agroecology: permaculture. Permaculture is interesting to advocates of sustainability because its advocates use rigorous methods to promote sustainable living through an "earthcare ethics" (Mollison p. 3): these involve fundamental reductions in energy use, localization of production, promoting biodiversity, and restoration of land wasted in industrialization. For the purposes outlined in this essay, permaculture suggests that the "science of sustainability" focus currently granted to agroecology education can be made to apply to all of the practical arts, and not just to agronomy and to the growing of crops.

In the area where I live, there is one course at a local college (Pomona College, in Claremont, California) that offers a course in agroecology education: "Food, Land, and the Environment," Environmental Analysis 85, taught Spring Semester each year. Indeed, another nearby college, Cal Poly Pomona, offers more extensive courses in agriculture – but I would like to focus upon one of the texts used in the Pomona College course: John H. Vandermeer's *The Ecology of Agroecosystems*, because I think that this text points to the "way in" for consideration of human social life within ecology, and thus a fuller reckoning with the goal of sustainability than has typically been the case in academic work.

Now it needs to be said here that other college agroecology textbooks have been informed by the sort of traditional ecological knowledge that informs Vandermeer's book, and that also informs the vision of sustainability that is described in the previous section. Vandermeer's book is exceptional in its treatment of social issues nonetheless. Stephen Gliessman's *Agroecology: Ecological Processes in Sustainable Agriculture*, for instance, was a book used by the abovementioned Pomona College class in previous terms. It is full of pictures from the author's studies of native agricultural practices in the state of Tabasco, in Mexico. Gliessman's book, however, sticks pretty closely to discussions of biology, agronomy, and physics. Miguel Altieri's (1987) *Agroecology: The Science of Sustainable Agriculture* contains a chapter by Richard B. Norgaard and Thomas O. Sikor ("The Methodology and

Practice of Agroecology," pp. 21–40) which importantly discusses the socially beneficial aspects of the social employment of agroecology by non-governmental organizations in Latin America. Vandermeer's book is nonetheless exceptional in that it ties the "hard science" and the social science together in a way which is unmatched by other textbooks.[3]

Vandermeer's book starts with a set of vignettes (chapter 1) discussing different agricultural situations (the Irish potato famine, the Sun coffee crisis, and the Cuban experience with organic production), all of which illustrate the effect the capitalist system has had upon agricultural production.

The narrative of this book then shifts to a discussion of the history of agriculture, and the different ways in which agriculture came into being in different parts of the world. Vandermeer's history of agriculture concludes with a discussion of the dramatic changes in agriculture that took place upon the introduction of capitalism, and of crop production for capitalist purposes.

In Chapter 4, Vandermeer shifts to a discussion of the chemistry of soil science and of industrial agriculture with artificial fertilizers, though Chapter 3, which discusses various aspects of agroecology as a mainstream science, prefaces this discussion. But it is the fifth chapter of Vandermeer's book which ties together his "hard science" discussion of agricultural processes with his "social science" discussion of the history of agriculture and of the political economy of agriculture in a way which matters to cognitive praxis in environmental education.

Vandermeer starts by discussing, briefly, the beginnings of the movement for organic agriculture, which was institutionalized around the thesis that the biological life of the soil, and not just its chemical competition, mattered in terms of agricultural production. Vandermeer:

> Although understanding the basics of soil physics and chemistry, as covered in the previous chapter, is certainly a prerequisite for understanding the ecology of agroecosystems, the real key for more ecological forms of agriculture comes with the biology of the soil. From the moles, to the ants and termites, to the earthworms, to the springtails, to the ciliates, the bacteria, the roots of the vascular plants, the algae and fungi, an enormous range of living organisms is involved in the formation, function, and maintenance of the soil. A great many of the physical and chemical changes that occur in soils are a direct consequence of living organisms. And there is general agreement that the extent to which this complex biological community is disrupted the "health" of the agroecosystem may become compromised. (p. 167)

Now, *The Ecology of Agroecosystems* might appear at first glance to be a textbook limited to college courses in soil science, biology, chemistry, or agronomy. But there is some heavy politics-of-science lifting going on here. Vandermeer's claim is that industrial agriculture is in crisis today because it does not adequately take into account the biological makeup of soils, instead choosing to increase agricultural productivity through chemical means (artificial fertilizers, chemical pesticides and herbicides, and so on). He also argues that the crises of industrial agriculture as such are part of the expanding capitalist system as it exists today.

The journey to Vandermeer's thesis, attempting to provide a scientific/academic basis for small-scale, "ecological" agriculture as an optimal way to produce food, proceeds rapidly and logically after this paragraph. This takes place both as a critique of the industrial model of agriculture as well as of the capitalist system. In the end, Vandermeer concludes that "the deep and local knowledge of the farmer, especially the traditional farmer, is essential to the development of the alternative model (of agriculture)." (p. 329) Moreover, Vandermeer suggests that in the process of industrialization of agriculture and of the process of proletarianization of farmers, both conditioned by the expansion of capitalism, this deep and local knowledge is becoming lost (p. 330). This agrees at least in spirit with the critique of capitalism presented in Malott's book.

Richard Kahn's criticism of "sustainability" in university discourse is that "sustainability is uncritically organized on campus such that it fundamentally accords with scientistic types of technicism, instrumentalism, positivism, and naïve empiricism" (p. 104). Vandermeer's book is replete with graphs and equations, doubtless granting him respectability in academic science departments, yet in *The Ecology of Agroecosystems* the number-crunchers are put to work to support the small-scale farmers, using traditional ecological knowledge, to whom the book is dedicated. One of Vandermeer's most prominent moments of cognitive praxis is when he rebuts the most prominent arguments against organic agriculture, and (as with Malott's book) there is a discussion in this book of the Zapatistas as protagonists of agroecological knowledge, and of their relationship to the land.

Ecopedagogy about the future, using two Margaret Atwood novels

The future is itself unknowable. Predictions typically extrapolate – they imagine human beings to be predictable and then follow assumed trends forward. An example can serve to illustrate this point: If the technology of today is more complex than that of yesterday, then futurists are likely to assume that tomorrow's technology will be even more complex than that of today. Futurology, then, mines the world of the present for clues about the future. Typically this mining leans on science; futurology looks at scientific discovery and extrapolates from it.

Science fiction is like futurology in extrapolating from the present. Science fiction differs in that the science fiction text does not just tell us what the future will be like, but instead depicts human situations in an imagined future, narrated as dramas. Science fiction, then, offers imaginary futures in an educationally accessible, embodied form. However, as Samuel Delany (2005) says, "science fiction is not about the future;" it "uses the future as a narrative convention to present significant distortions of the present" (p. 291). Much of what science fiction predicts is not really likely at all to happen, but we would miss out on keen observations about the future as a psychological object if we were to think of "sci-fi" as merely a form of entertainment about an impossible world. Science fiction as used in a literature class, for instance, could be a starting point for reflection upon human beings as versatile beings; any particular text might be read as expanding or shrinking their versatility (through mutations, technological amplifications, new environments, new forms of government, or encounters with extraterrestrial aliens). Science fiction has pedagogic value in suggesting a human world of possibility, of versatility, and of limitation, all of which are of relevance to the search for an effective cognitive praxis in our time and (ultimately) for the solutions to our environmental problems.

Certainly, one aspect of human versatility (or possibility) is what Cornelius Castoriadis (2007) calls "autonomy." Autonomy according to Castoriadis is easy to define but hard to exemplify. "An autonomous person," said Castoriadis, "is someone who gives herself her own laws." (p. 94) The idea of a autonomous person is important in Castoriadis as an idea of an autonomous society, a grouping of people empowered to direct their own fates and decide matters amongst themselves, freely. So for Castoriadis "the institution of the overwhelming majority of known societies has been heteronomous," i.e. not autonomous, as such (p. 97). An autonomous society, then, would be a somewhat utopian construct, a construct of a world far better than ours. It's easy to see how Castoriadis' idea of autonomy incorporates a number of social ideals: freedom, democracy, (libertarian) socialism, social responsibility, and so on. Because autonomy is the ability to change the social imaginary, it is also an important value of cognitive praxis. A critical question for environmental educators is one of how our autonomy (or whatever of our autonomy actually exists) can be employed to solve environmental problems in the future. We can work toward an answer to this question by engaging our premonitions of the future – by engaging with futurology, prognostication, and science fiction.

The positive, "describe what we want to see" solution to the problem of the future is enacted in Ernest Callenbach's two novels, *Ecotopia* (1975) and *Ecotopia Emerging* (1981). *Ecotopia* is famous as a "realistic science fiction" tale, of a possible society in which all social institutions are organized autonomously, and with ecological consciousness involved in their planning. *Ecotopia* is, then, a utopian science fiction text – a story of a world organized according to an ideal (in this case, an ecological ideal) of human behavior. Utopian stories say to the reader: here is the world as it could be; go out there and make it like this. *Ecotopia Emerging* is the story, written afterward, of how *Ecotopia* came to be – with *Ecotopia Emerging*, however, the question arose for some book reviewers as to whether or not the idea of *Ecotopia* is at all realistic. Students might, then, not view the promise of an "ecotopia" as credible, especially if it is used in a course taught in the US context. The critical question is one of whether or not the resistance to "ecotopia" can be overcome. It does not appear that, at present, human beings are versatile enough, or autonomous enough, to bring about an ecotopia-on-Earth in the near future.

Given the current political mood of "realism," and consequent conformism of social thought, it may seem more appropriate to the aims of environmental education at present to discuss environmental dystopia (a vision of a future gone bad), rather than a utopia (a vision of a good future), to dramatize the extensive damage people are doing to their planet and, moreover, to dramatize the barriers to understanding which make solutions to today's environmental problems seem so far away.

As Tom Moylan (2000) suggests, dystopia's foremost truth lies in its ability to reflect upon the causes of social and ecological evil as systemic. Its very textual machinery invites the creation of alternate worlds in which the historical spacetime of the author can be re-presented in a way that foregrounds the articulation of its economic, political, and cultural dimensions. (p. xii)

In this vein, environmental education could proceed through dystopian science fiction by presenting future tales of ecological ruin, while at the same time incorporating important lessons about political economy. Of especial promise in this regard are two of Margaret Atwood's recent novels: *Oryx and Crake* and *The Year of the Flood*, for their reflections upon abrupt climate change, genetic engineering, and the social atmosphere of capitalist, consumerist society.

Now, Atwood herself denies that these books are in the category of "science fiction," though readers are likely to interpret them as such, for they take place in a future in which technology and social structure have been extrapolated.[4] These two novels take place in a single, imagined future burned by global warming, brought to social chaos by capitalism, and altered by the genetic engineering of both flora and fauna. In Atwood's future, capitalism has proceeded so far that there are no governments, only corporations (with a spooky military presence calling itself CorpSeCorps), and there are distinct social classes, the upper class living in the Compounds, connected by bullet trains, with the masses living in ghetto conditions in the Pleeblands.

As a one-time teacher of literature in classroom settings, I can tell you that if you are planning to use either of Atwood's novels for a course it's important to be sure your class understands and accepts the conventions of science fiction – you will probably have an easier time persuading students in advanced courses that science fiction is worthy of their time and energies than you will with remedial writers. The fundamental problem of teaching science fiction can be seen more clearly through the lens of Samuel Delany's interpretation. Again, Delany:

> Science fiction is about the contemporary world; and the possibility of its futuristic distortions gives its side of the dialogue its initial force. (p. 291)

So imagine that you've assigned one of these books for a college-level class. If you want students to engage the dialogue invited by the text, you can encourage a receptiveness to the idea that the text is in fact asking questions about our present-day conditions of existence by showing how such conditions could be exaggerated in the future. This is, in fact, what happens in Atwood's recent novels.

Science fiction, moreover, is disconcerting to habitual readers of "regular" fiction because the setting, rather than the characters or the plot, becomes the main focus of the story itself. Delany again: "The SF writer, however, *creates* a world – which is harmonized with (or contrasted with, or played off against) both the story's characters and the given world in a much freer way" (p. 293). Thus science fiction is often a constant invitation to explore the contours of the writer's new world, and then to use the contrast with our world to ask questions about it which are relevant to our current experience.

The fictional *location in time* of the setting is distinctive in a science fiction narrative, and can either be clear or unclear. Readers can discern that *Oryx and Crake* and *The Year of the Flood* take place in an imagined near future; but how long after the present day is not spelled out by the author. Some science fiction settings are spelled out temporally with presumed accuracy; so, for instance, you have the universe of "Star Trek," which depicts action mostly in the 23rd and 24th centuries according to specific "star dates," or Larry Niven's "Known Space" series, which offers different settings for fictional narratives taking place over more than a billion years. Science fiction narratives which take place in a distinctly spelled-out future setting (the 23rd and 24th centuries, for instance, the settings for the various Star Trek series) are often invitations to imagine things which seem fantastic to our time – so in Star Trek you have matter transporters which can "beam" people from place to place, "warp drive" shortening the travel time between stars, and other difficult-to-imagine technological marvels. Atwood's indistinct near future is different: it contains technological marvels (mostly genetically-engineered animals of bizarre combination, such as the "rakunks" (raccoon-skunks) or the "pigoons" (pigs genetically altered to grow human body replacement parts)) which it is assumed could become possible somewhat soon. The difficulty of reading the setting's location in time may become a focal point for science fiction as taught in a college classroom.

The ecopedagogic use of *Oryx and Crake* and of *The Year of the Flood* makes use of science-fiction time in that, as the ecological deterioration of the Earth is said to have accelerated, so also has the world of capitalism expanded to create wider class differences and new, sensuous, and bizarre conveniences. These novels are of merit to environmental education, I feel, because they have characters who make fundamentally ecological decisions in a future in which, to use the voice of the character Toby in *The Year of the Flood*, "We're using up the Earth. It's almost gone" (p. 239). The main ecological decision characterizing both books, of course, is the decision by the character "Crake" to wipe out the human race and start out anew with a genetically modified human race scrubbed of flaws. Thus "the flood" of *The Year of the Flood*: an enormous, programmed plague wipes out almost the entire human race. This brings up some fundamental questions: if humanity isn't worth saving, what are we to make of Crake's decision to wipe out the human race (nearly; there are a few survivors), and to create a new one? What is "human nature," and what are we to make of Crake's notion that human nature is unredeemably flawed? But there are other ecological decisions going on: there is the nature cult, God's Gardeners, largely described *The Year of the Flood*, which the book's two protagonists join, and there is the main character Jimmy/Snowman of *Oryx and Crake*, who is largely an antihero thrust into the role of caretaker for Crake's new human beings, the Crakers, and whose mother, early in his life, joined a guerrilla group dedicated sabotaging the ecologically destructive machineries of this world and is at some point found dead, having obviously been pushed off of an overpass onto a freeway.

In the setting of these novels, nearly everything is for sale, nearly everyone is on the take, and there really is very little of a social reality outside of greed and cheap thrills. In examining the more shocking passages at the beginning of *Oryx and Crake*, for instance, in which Jimmy/Snowman and Crake watch snuff films on the Internet, we might ask students about the social causes of violence, and of how a more peaceful society could be brought into being. In the world of these novels, there is no longer any government, or rights to speak of; the world is ruled by corporations and dominated in totalitarian fashion by a police force called CorpSeCorps. Here we could ask students or teachers of this novel about the extent to which Atwood's vision is plausible, or the extent to which democratic people-power might succeed in preventing corporate dictatorship. In the novels, there is a rigid class structure of corporate employees living in the Compounds amidst impoverished masses living in the Pleeblands. Autonomy (in Castoriadis' sense) has largely disappeared from Atwood's universe. The laws of human existence seem set in stone. Here we might ask students about the extent to which this has already become the case, and about what can be done.

In the numerous reviews of these novels as given on the "GoodReads" website (http://www.goodreads.com), readers often tell of building upon the experience of having read *Oryx and Crake*, the older novel, by reading *The Year of the Flood*, the newer one. The primary differences between the two novels are in characters and plot – in the first, we follow around unsympathetic male characters (Jimmy/Snowman, and Crake himself), and in the second, we follow around two somewhat sympathetic female characters (Ren, and Toby). *The Year of the Flood* has more in-depth discussion of ecological choices, given that its protagonists both join God's Gardeners for a portion of the novel's action. In the future, Atwood speculates, environmentalists will join a cult, because environmentalism will seem cultish when compared to the *homo homini lupus* behavior common to the world then. God's Gardeners struggle, however mightily, to recreate the feeling of "living off of the land" while recycling old culture in homage of environmentalisms and religions past. They grow food, for instance, on rooftop gardens to keep it safe from the vandals who roam the streets below. In teaching Atwood's passages about God's Gardeners, we might ask our students questions about the extent to which environmental consciousness is culturally embedded in our society – would environmentalism be stronger in our society, for instance, if it had its own church or religious cult?

Part of the mythic background preached by God's Gardeners (in *The Year of the Flood*) is a striking appropriation of the story of Noah in the Bible. The character "Adam One," leader of the God's Gardeners cult, phrases it thusly:

We God's Gardeners are a plural Noah: we too have been called, we too forewarned. We can feel the symptoms of coming disaster as a doctor feels a sick man's pulse. We must be ready for the time when those who have broken trust with the Animals – yes, wiped them from the face of the Earth where God placed them – will be swept away by the Waterless Flood… (p. 91)

Thus in Atwood's portrayal of the environmentalist cult of the future, Biblical myth is appropriated not to predict Armageddon and the Rapture in present-day fundamentalist fashion, but a future on this Earth, a future in which the centuries-long experiment in nature-appropriation has been brought to a screeching halt. It is too late to solve environmental problems in Atwood's future, because nobody really has the power to do anything besides look for cheap thrills while conforming to the established standards for "pursuing a career," as Jimmy/Snowman and Crake do, or to survive against predatory men and abusive labor conditions, which is also what Toby and Ren do.

Environmental problems are viewed in Atwood's future as something post-apocalyptic. The present is hopeless, and only a horrific disaster brings back nature. Above all, Atwood is asking us: what kind of collapse will be required before something fundamentally new is to spread over the Earth? This is probably the most prominent question which would come up in a class dedicated to studying the environmental issues posed by The Year of the Flood.

In one of his last essays ("Imaginary and Imagination at the Crossroads"), the philosopher Cornelius Castoriadis painted a vision of the future in stark terms:

> I think we are at a crossroads in history, in History with a capital H. One path is now clearly marked, at least for its general direction. That path leads to the loss of meaning, the repetition of empty forms, conformism, apathy, irresponsibility, and cynicism, along with the growing takeover of the capitalist imaginary of unlimited expansion of "rational mastery" – pseudo-rational pseudo-mastery – of the unlimited expansion of consumption for consumption's sake, which is to say for nothing, and of technoscience racing ahead on its own, and obviously a party to domination by that capitalist imaginary. (p. 86)

Indeed Atwood carries the depiction of "pseudo-rational pseudo-mastery" as such to its ultimate extremes. Castoriadis continues:

> The other path would have to be opened up; it has not been marked out at all. Only a social and political awakening, a renaissance, a fresh upsurge of the project of individual and collective autonomy – that is, of the will to be free – can cut that path. (p. 86)

The challenge of environmental education, then, is to associate the instructional process with a forthcoming renaissance, in the ways shown above, so as to avoid the sort of future predicted by Atwood (and other dystopians in that vein).

CONCLUSION

So far, this essay has offered examples of "cognitive praxis" as a concept linking education, specifically conceptual education, with the idea of activism to solve environmental problems. If cognitive praxis is to be effective in solving environmental problems in a world in environmental crisis, it must open a discussion of political economy, and have something to say about our systems of politics and economics. The "pedagogy of unity" of Curry Stephenson Malott adapts North American traditional ecological knowledge to present-day circumstances, making the past relevant and prompting questions of how we can work together in light of the history of colonization foisted upon the native populations of this land. Agroecology education suggests an academic "in" for traditional ecological knowledge, and for political economy, in an academy today dedicated largely to research using "hard science" models. Margaret Atwood's recent novels can also serve as pedagogic devices to focus environmental education upon the possibility of dystopia.

Saylan and Blumstein's *The Failure of Environmental Education* (*And How We Can Fix It*) suggested that environmental education had failed because it could not solve today's environmental problems. Going beyond the standard definition of environmental education as exposure to wilderness, it argues: "environmental education must clearly illustrate that there is only one earth, and we're all on it together" (p. 45). Its authors recognize that "creating environmentally aware students in a society that does not recognize the gravity of the environmental problems it faces is not likely to have much of an impact on those problems" (p. 47), so its authors recognize the necessity of broad social change.

This book comes closest to a discussion of political economy in a chapter titled "Accountability and Institutional Mind-Set," in which it laments our society's inaction on important and pending issues such as abrupt climate change:

> The issue at hand is not so much the outcome of any specific meeting or bit of legislation. It is rather what might be described as the rise of the institutional mind-set in our societies, wherein bureaucracies create policy based on self-perpetuation, which does not necessarily reflect the will of the people or enhance the public well-being. (p. 61)

The authors then examine institutional inertia in a wide variety of institutions: legislatures, school districts, and environmental organizations. At the end, the authors concede depressingly that "it may seem naïve and utopian to expect a major overhaul in the existing political and social fabric to occur to help slow or reverse the anthropogenic assault on our environment" (p. 71). This institutional inertia, then, is the authors' closest approximation to an explanation of the system's dysfunction.

As educators, the authors of *The Failure of Environmental Education* recognize that they play bit parts in the drama of social change: Blumstein teaches a field biology class in which his students learn about conservation; Saylan promotes conservation studies in professional science education (p. 106). The "good ideas" they promote to expand the academic range of their professions (pp. 108–115) include a number of worthy activist projects, including communities of different ethnic and class backgrounds.

A cognitive praxis approach would take this approach one step further. Specifically, discussing political economy (in its specifics, which have been touched upon in this essay) in conjunction with "good ideas" in environmental education would expose college-level students to the possibility of changing society's institutional logic.

NOTES

1   There are also, in fact, pedagogies and instructional programs which demonstrate the superior time frame in which traditional ecological knowledge "goes back further" than mainstream science: see e.g. Angayuqaq Oscar Kawagley and Ray Barnhardt's "Education Indigenous to Place: Western Science Meets Native Reality," pp. 117–142 of *Ecological Education in Action* (Albany NY: SUNY P, 1999).
2   An excellent social analysis of the marginal position of education departments in the modern university is given in David F. Labaree's (2004) *The Trouble With Ed Schools* (New Haven CT: Yale University Press).
3   Cox and Atkins' (1979) Agricultural Ecology indeed has a section on "Agriculture and the Future," but this is given at a rather general level.
4   Atwood's characterization of her novels as "speculative fiction" and not "science fiction" is treated here as a category choice – arguably "speculative fiction" is a subset of "science fiction."

REFERENCES

Altieri, M. (1987). *Agroecology: The Science of Sustainable Agriculture.* Boulder CO: Westview Press.

Armitage, K. (2009). *The Nature-Study Movement: The Forgotten Popularizer of America's Conservation Ethic.* Lawrence KS: University Press of Kansas.

Atwood, M. (2005). *Oryx and Crake.* Nor York: Random House, 2005.

Atwood, M. (2010). *The Year of the Flood.* New York: Anchor-Random House, 2010.

Bailey, Liberty H. (1905). *The Nature-Study Idea, being an interpretation of the new school-movement to put the child in sympathy with nature.* New York: Doubleday, 1905.

Cajete, G. (2000). *Native Science: Natural Laws of Independence.* Santa Fe, NM: Clear Light Press.

Callenbach, E. (1975). *Ecotopia.* Berkeley CA: Banyan Tree Books.

Callenbach, E. (1981). *Ecotopia Emerging.* Berkeley CA: Banyan Tree Books.

Castoriadis, C. (2007). *Figures of the Thinkable* (Helen Arnold, Trans.). Stanford CA: Stanford UP, 2007.

Comstock, A.B. (1911). *Handbook of Nature Study for Teachers and Parents.* Ithaca NY: Comstock.

Delany, S. (2005). Some Presumptuous Approaches to Science Fiction. In Gunn, J., & Candelaria, M. (Eds.), *Speculations on Speculation: Theories of Science Fiction.* Lanham MD: Rowman and Littlefield.

Deloria, P. (1998). *Playing Indian.* New Haven CT: Yale University Press.

Freire, P. (1993). *Pedagogy of the Oppressed.* 20th anniversary edition. New York: Continuum, 1993.

Gliessman, S. (1998). *Agroecology: Ecological Processes in Sustainable Agriculture.* Chelsea MI: Ann Arbor Press.

Guha, R. (1999). *Environmentalism: A Global History.* New York: Longman, 1999.

Harkin, M.E., & Lewis, D.R. (Eds.) (2007). *Native Americans and the Environment: Perspectives on the Ecological Indian.* Lincoln NE: University of Nebraska Press.

Huhnsdorf, S. M. (2001). *Going Native: Indians in the American Cultural Imagination.* Ithaca NY: Cornell University Press.

Kahn, R. (2010). *Critical Pedagogy, Ecoliteracy, and Planetary Crisis.* New York: Peter Lang.

Kovel, J. (2007). *The Enemy of Nature.* 2nd ed. London: Zed.

Krech, S. (1999). *The Ecological Indian: Myth and History.* New York: W.W. Norton.

Labaree, D. (2004). *The Trouble With Ed Schools.* New Haven CT: Yale University Press.

Malott, C.S. (2008). *A Call To Action.* New York: Peter Lang.

Marcuse, H. (1972). *Counterrevolution and Revolt.* Boston: Beacon Press.

Martinez-Alier, J. (2002). *The Environmentalism of the Poor.* Cheltenham, UK: Edward Elgar.

Marx, K. (1990). *Capital: A Critique of Political Economy, Volume One.* London: Penguin.

McLaren, P. (2005). *Capitalists and Conquerors: A Critical Pedagogy Against Empire.* Boulder CO: Rowman and Littlefield.

Menzies, Charles R. (Ed.) (2006). *Traditional Ecological Knowledge and Natural Resource Management.* Lincoln NE: University of Nebraska P., 2006.

Mollison, B. (1991). *Introduction to Permaculture.* Sisters Creek, Tasmania, Australia: Tagari.

Moylan, T. (2000). *Scraps of the Untainted Sky: Science Fiction, Utopia, Dystopia.* Boulder CO: Westview Press.

Orr, D.W. (1996). Reinventing Higher Education. In Collett, J., and Karakashian,S. (Eds.), *Greening the College Curriculum: A Guide to Environmental Teaching in the Liberal Arts.* Washington DC: Island.

Palmer, J. (1998). *Environmental Education in the 21st Century: Theory, Practice, Progress, and Promise.* New York: Routledge Press.

Saylan, C., & Blumstein, D. (2011). *The Failure of Environmental Education (and How we Can Fix It).* Berkeley CA: University of California Press.

Smith, G. A., & Williams, D.A. (Eds.) (1999). *Ecological Education In Action: On Weaving Education, Culture, and the Environment.* Albany NY: SUNY Press,.

Thompson, E.S. (1899). *Wild Animals I Have Known.* New York: Scribner's Sons.

Thompson, E. S. (1903/1911). *Two Little Savages.* New York: Grosset & Dunlap.

Vandermeer, J. (2011). *The Ecology of Agroecosystems.* Sudbury, MA: Jones and Bartlett.

Weaver, Jace. (Ed.) (1996). *Defending Mother Earth: Native American Perspectives on Environmental Justice.* Maryknoll NY: Orbis.

GREENING CRIMINOLOGY

PIERS BEIRNE AND NIGEL SOUTH[1]

INTRODUCTION

'Criminology' can be defined in a great variety of ways but at its simplest and in the terms most commonly accepted it is taken to be the study of crime, criminals and criminal justice. Characterised by Downes (1988, and see Carrabine et al., 2009, p. 3) as a 'rendezvous subject' and remarked upon by Garland and Sparks (2000, p. 190) as having no monopoly on the study of crime, criminology is well positioned to expand its contribution to interdisciplinary research on local and global environmental issues. A green perspective for criminology therefore promises to provide not only a different way of examining and making sense of various forms of harm and crime and responses to them but also an explication of much wider connections that are not generally well understood.

GREENING CRIMINOLOGY

What do we mean by the term 'green criminology'? At its most abstract level, green criminology refers to the study of those harms against humanity, against the environment and against animals other than humans (hereinafter, "animals") committed both by powerful institutions (for example, governments, transnational corporations, military apparatuses, scientific laboratories) and also by ordinary people. Like most abstractions, of course, this one invites more questions perhaps than it was designed to answer. For example, it is often analytically difficult to disentangle environmental harms from the abuse of animals. Animals of course live in environments, and their own well-being – physical, emotional, psychological – is absolutely and intimately linked to the health and good standing of their environments. The forms of these 'green harms' are numerous, their financial costs alone are staggeringly large and they range from the everyday to the exceptional.

Green harms include the abuse and exploitation of ecological systems, including animal life; corporate disregard for damage to land, air and water quality; profiteering from trades and practices that destroy lives and which leave a legacy of damage for subsequent generations; military actions in war that adversely affect the environment and animals; new challenges to international treaties and to the emerging field of bio-ethics, such as bio-piracy; illicit markets in nuclear materials; and legal monopolisation of natural resources (e.g. privatisation of water, patenting of natural products, etc.) leading to divisions between the resource rich and the resource

S. D. Fassbinder, A. J. Nocella II and R. Kahn (Eds.), Greening the Academy:
Ecopedagogy Through the Liberal Arts, 23–32.

impoverished and the prospects of new forms of conflict, harm, injury, damage and crime. Green harms include, too, both individual acts of cruelty to animals and also the institutional, socially-acceptable human domination of animals in agribusiness, in slaughterhouses and abattoirs, in so-called scientific experimentation and, in less obviously direct ways, in sports, colleges and schools, zoos, aquaria and circuses.

Although the term conceals numerous general and local problems, we believe that, expressed this simply as a harm-based discourse, green criminology serves as a timely and crucial addition to existing critical, democratic and left-oriented perspectives on crime and social harm. Like these allied criminologies, green criminology begins by problematising the nature of crime: how is it defined, by whom and with what purpose(s)? Which harms are defined as crimes? Which are not? Which harms are defined as both harmful and criminal? Which are defined as neither? To each of these questions, moreover, can be added another: with what consequences and for whom?

GREEN CRIMINOLOGY: CHALLENGES, ACHIEVEMENTS, PROSPECTS

Proposing a green perspective for criminology is about more than simply adding a new perspective within criminology – it is a call to expand the range of green critical inquiry. Brief examples serve the purpose of illustrating how the themes of justice and rights have been explored in green criminological work so far.

Environmental Justice

One concept that unifies a now considerable body of work in this field is the idea of environmental justice (Benton, 1998; White, 2007, 2008; Lynch and Stretesky, 2007). Many studies have drawn attention to the environmental victimisation of communities of the poor and powerless due to the frequency with which their locations are also the sites of polluting industry, for instance, and of waste processing plants or other environmentally hazardous facilities (Bullard, 1994). Environmental injustices also include cases where local, Indigenous populations have been forcibly removed from land to which they are spiritually attached or where their land has been exploited for military, agribusiness or other purposes in circumstances depriving them of any control or say (Samson, 2003; Kuletz, 1998). Usually the consequences are damaging, if not devastating, producing community dislocation, relationship breakdowns, mental health and substance misuse problems and so on. Hence, White (2004:281) usefully suggests that:

> Environmental justice refers to the distribution of environments among peoples ... and the impacts of particular social practices on specific populations. The focus of analysis is therefore on human health and well-being and how these are affected by particular types of production and consumption. Here we can distinguish between environmental issues that affect everyone, and those that disproportionately affect specific individuals and groups.

Crimes Against Animals Other than Humans

A green perspective concerned with harm and rights will attend not just to the situation of humans but also to that of animals. Though not quite yet a major field of study, there is nonetheless a substantial and growing body of work on animal abuse in criminology. In 2010, for example, a gathering of 20 or so criminologists and scholar activists was convened in Cardiff, Wales, in order to encourage the study of animal abuse in criminology, one direct result of which is the publication in 2011 of a special double issue on the topic in the journal *Crime, Law and Social Change*.

As it has so far been understood, within green criminology 'animal abuse' is a term which typically refers to those diverse human actions that contribute to the pain, suffering or death of animals or that otherwise adversely affect their welfare. Animal abuse may be physical, psychological or emotional. It may involve active maltreatment or passive neglect, and may be direct or indirect (Beirne, 2007, 2009; Cazaux, 2007). Sometimes, of course, animals are harmed when their environments are degraded through the sheer chaos wrought by natural disasters such as earthquakes, hurricanes and tsunamis, or through human-induced causes like wars, climate change, oil spills and road construction.

If violations of animals' rights are to be central concepts in green criminology, then we could profitably begin by examining why, just like some harms to the environment, some harms to animals are defined as criminal, others as abusive but not criminal and still others as neither criminal nor abusive. In exploring these questions a narrow concept of crimes against animals would necessarily have to be rejected in favour of a more inclusive concept of harm. Regan's (2007) notion of harms to animals as either 'inflictions' or 'deprivations' springs readily to mind here (though he has been strongly criticized for limiting his umbrella of animal rights to mammals). Without this re-thinking, the sources of animal abuse will be found to lie only in the personal biographies of those humans who abuse animals in one-on-one situations of cruelty and neglect. Certainly those cases demand our attention. But so too do those other and far more numerous institutionalised harms to animals, where abuse is routine, invisible, ubiquitous and often defined as socially acceptable.

In the case of both environmental justice and animal rights discourses there are evidently doorways leading to many other questions and disciplines – philosophy, law, psychology, literature, life sciences and so on. Two questions then arise meriting further discussion. First, what kind of interdisciplinary connections can a green criminology make? Second, where can we find the common ground on which to build the intellectual capital to underpin the legitimacy of a 'green criminology'?

INTERDISCIPLINARY CONNECTIONS FOR A GREEN CRIMINOLOGY

Looking across the wide horizons of the social and natural sciences and the humanities, it would seem that a considerable amount of relevant research and debate, concerns and concepts connect surprisingly well with aspects of criminology as a multifaceted subject. This is even more the case in relation to a green criminology where an interdisciplinary and comparative approach, embracing, for example, understandings of context, culture, law, economics and science, will be of real benefit. As Hauck (2007) observes, "criminology is one discipline – among many – with a role to play in politicising environmental harm and mobilising action that is appropriate to sustain resources and livelihoods".

Science, law and literature

Global biotechnology industries have increasingly sought to identify and exploit natural products with medicinal and healing properties 'discovered' in developing nations. The biodiversity of different environments has yielded products with numerous uses for local populations for centuries. However, accusations of 'bio-piracy' and post-colonial exploitation have arisen where subsequent ownership of genetic materials and pharmacological products has been asserted by Western interests via systems of intellectual property rights and patents that are alien to the Indigenous peoples who have previously used these gifts of nature. Where religion and pseudo-scientific notions of evolutionary hierarchies once provided the justifications for practices such as piracy and colonial exploitation, today science, law and commerce play these parts.

Similar practices, issues and concerns are associated with the global expansion of Western bio-agricultural corporations and contestation around ownership of seeds, plants and knowledge derived from Indigenous farmers. Here science and law are harnessed together by the powerful to support a process of disempowerment and exploitation. In a different context, Kuletz (1998, p. 28) reports a similar process affecting the radiation-related health problems facing the Navajo and other peoples of desert areas of the American West. Here uranium has been mined and nuclear tests carried out but the statements of the victims are "in effect, excluded from consideration and the people who speak them are, by extension, excluded from any decision-making process bearing on their welfare" (ibid.). In both sets of circumstances, "anecdotal knowledge" (based on inter-generational folk wisdom as well as real contemporary experience) is de-legitimated and not weighted as strongly as "scientific evidence" (which is privileged as inherently and evidently neutral and unbiased). This perhaps strengthens the argument made by green criminologists such as Lynch and Stretesky (2001) for the development and use of science to support the cause and plight of those who are victimised but frequently excluded from recourse to redress or protest.

Law can also, of course, be employed in defence of the environment and on behalf of the victims of power. The field of environmental law is now well established and although the laws themselves are by no means secure or implemented consistently (O'Hear, 2004), the practical problems that such law turns upon are offences and forms of regulation that will be increasingly central on the global stage of the 21st century. International treaties depend upon compliance and regulation; conflicts will increasingly be fought over environmental resources. The environment is subject to theft and exploitation, in need of protection and – just as in the fight against other forms of crime and harm – will require specialist policing and enforcement of agreements and rules (South, 2011).

Making criminological connections of a literary nature, Ruggiero's (2002, p. 98) insightful essay on Herman Melville's classic novel *Moby Dick* explores the violence and sense of challenge that mark the way of life of Captain Ahab and his crew in their battle with nature and, in particular, the mighty whale, all reflecting Melville's age of "science, exploration, entrepreneurial daring and ... obsession with dominion over nature". However, as is also evident, Melville's book is about discovery in more than one sense and the need for harmony and peace with nature is a central message. Literature, art and music are enormous repositories of the stories and images of the violence we do to our environment and the animals with whom we share planet Earth. For all the progress made in science, society and civilised life since the 19th century of Ahab and his mercantile peers, we continue to live with "contradictory claims about the legitimacy of accumulation, the exploitation of nature, power and hierarchy" (*ibid*, p. 96) and a criminology enriched by interdisciplinary insights is all the better placed to illuminate and investigate this.

THE INTELLECTUAL CURRENTS AND CONTEXT OF GREEN CRIMINOLOGY: GREEN ENVIRONMENTALISM AND ANIMAL RIGHTS

To some extent, there is a certain obviousness about the need to forge some common ground between the environmentalist-based discourse of green criminology and the animal-centred discourse of animal rights. To begin with, they already have much in common. For example, each has been nurtured within a much larger social movement – respectively, various environmentalism(s) and the animal protection community. These larger movements originated at roughly the same time and under similar circumstances, namely, the turbulence, iconoclasm and leftist political activism of the 1960s. Moreover, in terms of their ethical perspectives and much of their theoretical assumptions, both movements have an underlying concern with relations of power and inequality and with the elimination of their undesirable effects. These latter include harm, exclusion, injury and suffering. Both in their own ways are more or less consciously anti-statist and anti-authoritarian. Each embraces participatory democracy. Adherents of one movement often travel seamlessly to the other, and they often support the causes of both, including buying locally and buying less, reusing and recycling, using public transportation, and practising vegetarianism and veganism.

Clearly, the respective concerns of animal rights and green environmentalism broadly coincide on major aspects of climate change, as does their opposition to its perceived perpetrators. Among these latter are agribusinesses, transnational corporations, profit-seeking and ignorant states and ineffective international enforcement machinery. However, a clear moral position that is unimpeachable in logic, philosophical foundations or legal reasoning may not fare quite so well when confronted by the messy complexities and contradictions of the real world of human interaction and forces of nature. Indeed, the identification of common ground between an environmentally- (or ecologically-) based green criminology and an animal-centred animal rights theory, worthwhile as it might be, is not altogether a straightforward one. This is so not only because most of us are normally in a state of denial about animal rights issues, as some sociologists have pointed out. Several other obstacles confront this task: some of them matters of convenience and definition, still others without clear resolution.

By way of illustration, consider, first, the numerous points of conflict among indigenes, animals, colonists and the environment in the mid-seventeenth-century Massachusetts Bay colony. At that time the colonists allowed their animals to wander unattended in Massachusetts Bay because of the relative scarcity of human labour there. The colonists, assuming that their cattle, pigs, sheep and goats would thereby fatten and multiply, not only condoned but also insisted upon the free roaming of their cattle. The result was a very serious conflict over grazing practices between colonists and the Indigenous, Algonquian-speaking people. The colonists typically solved this rivalry simply by appropriating Indian land, so that their cattle could then graze there even more freely. Moreover, as Anderson (2004, p. 116) points out in her book *Creatures of Empire*, the environmental impact of the colonists' rising number of livestock cattle increased over time: pigs who killed smaller trees by gnawing on their roots, congregating cattle who compacted and crushed the soil, which thus led to erosion…which in turn led the livestock to range further afield and the colonists to appropriate yet more land.

To the indigenes it was not only that the colonists' livestock were a detested symbol of foreign power but also that the animals wandered into their traps and trampled their corn. In retaliation some of these animals would doubtless have been killed or mutilated by the indigenes and some would have found their way into their meals (Beirne, 2009, chapter 2).

One wonders, however, what the response of green criminologists would be to those aspects of human-animal relationships described above in seventeenth-century colonial America. Specifically, how should we see the essential facts of resistance involving victimised animals and which were to be repeated in the nineteenth century against landlords in East Anglia and against the English occupation in colonial Ireland? Is the indigenes' mutilation of the colonists' cattle a justifiable practice of retaliation? Some would perhaps see it as justifiable given the overwhelming power differences between the colonists and the indigenes. But some wouldn't. We suspect that the dividing line between one response and the other would be some version of a radical commitment to animal right theory: *ahimsa* (i.e. to do no harm) in any and all circumstances.

Consider, second, the situation of the 155,000 Arctic Inuit ('Eskimos'), whose Indigenous groups inhabit northernmost Canada, Russia, Greenland and the United States. Since 2004 the Inuit have sued the U.S. government claiming that, because it tolerates heat-trapping smokestacks and automobile emissions, which directly cause the melting of the Arctic icecap and environmental degradation, the U.S. has contributed not only to the deaths of individual Inuit but also to the possible extinction of their culture (Watt-Cloutier, 2005). As their legal suit has developed, the Inuit have alleged that they are the victims of environmental crimes and that this violates their basic human rights.

But will the movements in green environmentalism and animal rights find common cause in their respective attitudes to the effects of climate change on animals' lives and animals' habitats in the Arctic? At this point we should add that, with much scientific evidence to support them, the Inuit have further complained that rising temperatures, disappearing glaciers and icecaps, and wind-borne toxic pollution have adversely affected the health of Arctic seals and of the indigenes who regularly eat them. Their hunting of seals and other marine mammals the Inuit see as an essential part not only of their culture and traditions but also, indeed, of their physical survival. Thus, an Inuit elder has stated that "[t]he seal…provides us with more than just food and clothes. It provides us with our identity. It is through sharing and having a seal communion that we regain our strength, physically and mentally" (quoted in Peter et al., 2002, p. 167) In terms of their everyday items the Inuit have traditionally used seals, narwhals and whales for food and clothes. The fur and skin of seals are used for boots, moccasins, snowshoes, gloves and mittens, purses, gut bags, caps, parkas, capers, frontlets and tunics. Seals are also used in the making of kayaks, foumiaks and sleds. Seals' fat or blubber is turned into oil for lamps, as is that of whales and walruses. In a mark of respect for those about to be killed, harpoons are often decorated with carvings of seals. Harpoon lines are made from bearded seal hide. Animal bones – including those of seals, walruses and narwhals – provide fishhooks, lures and utensils and other tools and weapons, including projectile points and parts of the all-purpose knives known as ulus (see *passim*, Stuckenberger, 2007).

The intersection of climate change, traditional Inuit survival practices and seal hunting is a complicated one which naturally elicits a variety of responses from green criminology. Among green criminologists there is likely unanimous condemnation of the continued exploitation of relatively powerless Indigenous peoples, like the Inuit, and the threat posed by climate change to their very survival – physical, economic and cultural. Some green environmentalists and some animal welfarists will bemoan the human-induced poisoning of seals because spoiled or dead seals are a wasted 'wild' or 'natural' resource and a "fishery" to be "harvested" wisely. One section of the animal rights movement will doubtless condemn the hunting and slaughter of adult and infant seals by all humans under any and all circumstances. Clearly, in this odd scenario one type of right is seen to trump all others, i.e., the survival of seals is of greater importance than the health and viability of those Indigenous peoples who live in extreme or arduous climates. But a principled *ahimsa* for all surely entails lethal harm to some. Indeed, we believe that about the killing of seals there is an important distinction to be made between, on the one hand, slaughter of seals by professional hunters for reasons of haute cuisine or fashion ('furs') or sport and, on the other, the killing of seals by the Inuit, given the normal climatic conditions of their environment and their needs for survival.

COMMON GROUND FOR GREENING THE ACADEMY

Environmentalist and feminist studies have demonstrated that we cannot deny the intimate entanglement between humanity and nature. This has a profound message for the teaching and learning of all academic subjects. Furthermore, as Adam (1998) superbly illustrates, time, space and nature interact in ways that suggest that it has been an unhelpful characteristic of all disciplines, whether within the humanities and arts or the sciences, natural and social, to hold too strongly to a separation of nature and culture. Such a separation is not as neat as often presented. Thus,

> ...humans are tied to the rhythms of night and day ... constituted by a multitude of circa rhythms... from the very fast firing of neurones to the heart-beat, from digestive to activity-and-rest cycles, and from the menstrual cycle to the larger regenerative processes of growth and decay, birth and death. ... (p. 13)

We therefore need to:

> steer a path that avoids the unacceptable choices of traditional social theory and analysis: between biological and social determinisn (where people are understood to be governed by either their biology or society), between realism and relativism (where the external world is thought to be either discovered or constructed by the understanding we bring to it), between meta-narratives and particularism (where analyses are considered to be embedded in the worlds of either overarching, universal theories or particular, unique contexts and events). [We need] to take account of nature without succumbing to biological determinism, ... [and] accept relativism as inescapable without losing the ability to talk about the physical world of 'nature' and technology ... (pp. 6–7)

Nature or what is 'natural' is often experienced simply as a manipulated construction, both physically and discursively used and abused. Within this kind of dominant discourse it is also accepted that the superior human (white-male) is also self-evidently and 'naturally' set above nature and therefore holds dominion over it, whether it be in a form that is categorised as strange, wild, farmed or domesticated (Hallsworth, 2008). Stephenson (2008) addresses this well in her analysis of how modern society organises the disposal of unwanted animals: those that are sorted out and found to be 'too unpredictable, too implicated in nature's unruly ways' and end up consigned to a 'programme of sterilisation, testing and extermination'. Nature – the environment we inhabit and the animals who share this with us – is deemed to be 'different'. Humans are held to be above it: we perceive, sense, see, feel everything to do with nature as something 'external' and generally isolate ourselves from any true sense of connection. Yet as Benton (1994, p. 40) argued some years ago, we should instead:

> ...view humans as a species of living organism, comparable in many important respects with other social species, as bound together with those other species and their bio-physical conditions of existence in immensely complex webs of interdependence, and as united, also, by a common evolutionary ancestry.

TOWARDS A GREEN CRIMINOLOGY

In recent years criminology has been influenced by developments in law, public campaigning and social protest to embrace and take seriously 'rights'-based issues relating to human rights generally and to the rights of victims, women, minorities and animals, in particular. The denial of rights – even where not a criminal offence – has been examined in various areas of criminology, such as victimology, restorative justice, crimes of war and colonialism. But rights to traditional ways of life and protection from exploitation of Indigenous lands, culture and folklore (as foundations of traditional knowledge) have been neglected in criminology as well as ineffectively affirmed in national and international law (Orkin, 2003). Perhaps the Inuit's complaint that climate change violates their human rights will mark a turning point in this crucial respect.

The movement in green criminology aims to provide a new perspective on the unjust exploitation of natural resources, ecosystems, humans and animals, and the consequences of this for the health, welfare, heritage and rights of all affected by such actions. It is a progressive and open perspective and offers a fertile point of connection with other areas of the academy concerned with environmental justice and the protection of rights for all beings.

NOTE

[1] We are grateful to Anthony Nocella, Richard Kahn and Samuel Day Fassbinder for their generous editorial advice on the first draft of this chapter.

REFERENCES

Adam, B. (1998). *Timescapes of Modernity.* London: Routledge.

Anderson, V. D. (2004). *Creatures of Empire.* Oxford: Oxford University Press.

Beirne, P. (2007). Animal rights, animal abuse and green criminology. In P. Beirne and N. South (Eds.), *Issues in Green Criminology* (pp. 55–83).

Beirne, P. (2009). *Law, Criminology, and Animal Abuse.* Lanham, Md.: Rowman & Littlefield.

Beirne, P., & South, N. (Eds.) (2007). *Issues in Green Criminology* Cullompton: Willan.

Benton, T. (1994). Biology and social theory in the environmental debate.' In. M. Redclift & T. Benton (Eds.), *Social Theory and the Global Environment* (pp. 28–50). London: Routledge.

Benton, T. (1998). Rights and Justice on a Shared Planet. *Theoretical Criminology, 2*(2), 149–175.

Carrabine, E., Cox, P. Lee, M, Plummer, K., & South, N. (2009). *Criminology: A sociological introduction.* London: Routledge.

Cazaux, G. (2007). Labelling animals: non-speciesist criminology and techniques to identify other animals. In P. Beirne, & N. South (Eds.), *Issues in Green Criminology.* (pp. 87–113). Cullompton: Willan.

Dickens, P. (2001). Linking the social and natural sciences. *Sociology, 35*(1), 93–110.

Downes, D. (1988). 'The sociology of crime and social control in Britain, 1960–87', *British Journal of Criminology, 28*(2), 175–87.

Garland, D., & Sparks, R. (2000). 'Criminology, social theory and the challenge of our times', *British Journal of Criminology, 40*(2), 189–204.

Hallsworth, S. (2008). 'Imaginary spaces and real relations', In R. Sollund (Ed.), *Global Harms: ecological crime and speciesism,* New York: Nova.

Hauck, M. (2007). Non-compliance in small-scale fisheries: a threat to security? In P. Beirne & N. South (Eds.), *Issues in Green Criminology* (pp. 270–289). Cullompton: Willan.

Jamieson, D. (2002). *Morality's Progress: Essays on humans, other animals, and the rest of nature.* Oxford: Clarendon Press.

Kuletz, V. (1998). *The Tainted Desert: Environmental and social ruin in the American West.* Routledge: London.

Lynch, M. J., & Stretesky, P. (2001). Toxic crimes: examining corporate victimization of the general public employing medical and epidemiological evidence, *Critical Criminology, 10*(3), 153–172.

Lynch, M. J., & Stretesky, P. (2007). Green criminology in the United States. In P. Beirne, & N. South (Eds.), *Issues in Green Criminology.* (pp. 248–269). Cullompton: Willan.

O'Hear, M. (2004). Sentencing the green collar offender: punishment, culpability and environmental crime, *Journal of Criminal Law and Criminology, 95*(1), 133–276.

Orkin, A. (2003). When the law breaks down: Aboriginal peoples in Canada and Governmental defiance of the rule of law, *Osgood Hall Law Journal, 41*(2/3), 445–462.

Peter, A.M. Ishulutak, J. Shaimaiyuk, N. Kisa, B. Kootoo and S. Enuara (2002), The Seal: an Integral Part of Our Culture, *Études/Inuit/Studies, 1*(26), 167–174.

Regan, T. (2007). Vivisection: the case for abolition. In P. Beirne & N. South (Eds.) *Issues in Green Criminology* (pp. 114–139). Cullompton: Willan.

Ruggiero, V. (2002). Moby Dick and the crimes of the economy, *British Journal of Criminology, 42*(1), 96–108.

Samson, C. (2003). *A Way of Life that Does Not Exist: Canada and the extinguishment of the Innu.* London: Verso.

South, N. (2011). Environmental offending, regulation and 'the legislative balancing act.' In J. Gobert & A. Pascal (Eds.), *European Developments in Corporate Criminal Liability.* London: Routledge.

Stephenson, S. (2008). The dog that could not bark. In R. Sollund (Ed.) *Global Harms: ecological crime and speciesism* (pp. 151–165). New York: Nova.

Stuckenberger, N. (2007). *Thin Ice: Inuit Traditions Within a Changing Environment.* Hanover, N.H.: University Press of New England.

Watt-Cloutier, S. (2005). "Petition to the Inter American Commission on Human Rights Seeking Relief from Violations Resulting from Global Warming Caused by Acts and Omissions of the United States." Accessed January 30th, 2009 at: http://www.inuitcircumpolar.com/files/uploads/icc-files/FINALPetitionICC.pdf

White, R. (2004) Criminology, social regulation and environmental harm. In R. White (Ed.), *Controversies in Environmental Sociology* (pp. 275–292). Port Melbourne: Cambridge University Press.

White, R. (2007) Green criminology and the pursuit of social and ecological justice. In P. Beirne & N. South (Eds.), *Issues in Green Criminology* (pp. 32–54). Cullompton: Willan.

White, R. (2008). *Crimes against Nature.* Cullompton: Willan.

GREENING SOCIOLOGY

KISHI ANIMASHAUN DUCRE

To characterize my life before entering academia, I usually quip: "I was a community organizer on environmental justice campaigns for Greenpeace for three years. I burned out so, I decided to go to graduate school". Most academic audiences chuckle at the idea of graduate school as a more *relaxing* existence. However, I would not trade my experience as a community organizer for the Greenpeace Toxics Campaign in the 1990s. Those experiences have defined both my teaching philosophy and research agenda.

I was 21 years old when I joined the staff of Greenpeace. During my tenure, I moved four times, helped defeat a proposed power plant in San Francisco, a proposed uranium enrichment plant in Northern Louisiana, and an immense plastics manufacturing complex in Southeast Louisiana.[1] Most of my work with local community activists focused on providing technical training of the environmental hazards that they faced, helping them secure legal resources, media training, crafting a media strategy, and building constituencies.

In 1996, I found myself in the most intense battle for environmental justice to date. In fact, many have referred to the struggle to stop the construction of Shintech's massive petrochemical complex in the small town of Convent, Louisiana as the precedent-setting case of environmental justice policy in the United States. By the end of that campaign, I decided to pursue graduate study because I wanted to shift my focus from the localized frontlines of environmental justice activism. A decade later, it seems that I have come full circle. In my maturity as both a scholar and an environmental justice activist, I have come to realize that the movement for social justice must operate on all levels of engagement: local, national, and international. In my circuitous route from Greenpeace, to graduate school, to a Ph.D., the connecting element has been my strong belief in justice and community action.

However, I learned that the path from activist to scholar is not an easy transition. More specifically, my goal of being a scholar-activist and a junior faculty member may have been naïve. The merit system at a typical research university does not allow for the prioritization of what many have termed public scholarship. The purpose of this chapter is to provide an overview and critique of environmental sociology and the University merit system and propose some measures that would successfully integrated the principles of activism and publically-engaged scholarship for the ultimate purpose of *greening the academy*.

S. D. Fassbinder, A. J. Nocella II and R. Kahn (Eds.), Greening the Academy:
Ecopedagogy Through the Liberal Arts, 33–46.

THE DISCIPLINE OF ENVIRONMENTAL SOCIOLOGY: A BRIEF OVERVIEW

The discipline of sociology centers around social institutions and their impact on group behavior. Although contested, the founding assumptions behind the sociological perspective are *objectivity* and *positivism*. Founding theorist Emile Durkheim legitimized sociological inquiry, in relation to the natural and physical sciences by suggesting there were *social facts*; characteristics external to the individual which are governed by society. Thus, we are products of the successful transmission of the norms and values of society. Social facts are stable principles that govern individual behavior and sociologists are capable of uncovering those social facts through the sociological method (Farganis, 2000). This notion of social facts are the foundation to *positivism or empiricism;* the strict adherence to objective methods to test observations. The founding principles of sociology as a discipline are positivism and objectivity. In 1918, Max Weber, another early and influential sociological theorist, gave a speech entitled *Science as a Vocation:*

> All scientific work presupposes that the rules of logic and method are valid; these are the general foundations of our orientation in the world...these pre-suppositions are the least problematic aspect of science. Science further presupposes that what is yielded by scientific work is important in the sense that is 'worth being known'.......Finally, let us consider the disciplines close to me: sociology, history, economics, political science, and those type of cultural philosophy that make it their task to interpret these sciences. It is said, and I agree, that politics is out of place in the lecture-room. It does not belong there on the part of the students....Neither does politics, however, belong in the lecture-room on the part of the docents, and when the docent is scientifically concerned with politics, it belongs there least of all. To take a practical political stand is one thing, and to analyze political structure and party positions is another. When speaking in a political meeting about democracy, one does not hide one's personal standpoint; indeed to come out clearly as take a stand is one's damned duty. The words one uses in such a meeting are not means of scientific analysis but means of canvassing votes and winning over others...It would be an outrage, however, to use words in this fashion in a lecture or in a lecture-room....But the true teacher will beware of imposing from the platform any political position upon the student,whether it is expressed or suggested. 'To let the facts speak for themselves' is the most unfair way of putting over a political position to the student. (Weber)

Here, Weber is highly critical of scholars who impart personal values in their work. In fact, the bedrock of sociology then and now claims to be value-free or, at least value-neutral. Adopting this principle was difficult for someone like me, whose path to academia was borne out of political struggles. From the environmental justice movement in my early career, but my personal and professional achievements are the results of hard-fought mobilizations for civil rights and gender equality.

My mere presence, as an African American female Ph.D. in the classroom is political. Thus, I am unwilling and for the most part, unable to articulate a research and teaching agenda that separates academic work from political conflict and justice.

In all fairness, this sociology-objective assumption has been contested largely by Marxian sociologists and feminist scholars who understood that inexorable link between epistemology, power, and privilege. C. Wright Mills (1959) acknowledged the link between biography and history in his influential treatise on the sociological imagination. And despite his Weberian influence, he acknowledged that the personal was political. Harding (1987) differentiates between method, methodology, and epistemology where the latter seeks to uncover the nature of knowledge generation and the justification of knowledge claims. Hill Collins (2008 in Jaggar) compares conventional and empirical knowledge claims process with the alternative epistemology of Black feminism. Black feminist epistemology arises from four dimensions: (1) the lived experience, (2) a dialogic process and connectedness with others, (3) an ethic of caring and empathy, and (4) and ethic of personal accountability. These dimensions challenge dominant scientific principles of objectivity.

In regards to environmental sociology, the formal establishment of the sub-specialty of environmental sociology occurred in 1979 with the seminal publication of the essay "Environmental Sociology" in the American Sociological Review by Dunlap and Catton. The authors pointed out that the central task in environmental sociology is to determine: "a) How do interdependent variations in population, technology, cultural, social systems, and personality systems influence the physical environment? b) How do resultant changes (and other variations) in the physical environment modify [these systems] or any of the interrelations among them?" (Dunlap & Catton, 1979, p. 252) The authors enumerated the research areas within this new sub-specialty: the built (man-made) environment, institutional response to environmental problems, the study of natural hazards & disasters, social impact assessment, resources scarcities (such as fossil fuels) and resource allocation, and carrying capacity. Here, the concept of *New Ecological Paradigm* (NEP) emerged, where society is affected by ecological, as well as social facts. NEP served as a compliment, rather than critique of conventional theories well established in sociology (Woodgate, 2010).

In the decades since Dunlap & Catton's piece, the bulk of the work by environmental sociologists can be categorized under two fundamental articulations: (1) political economy explanation of the environment-society interaction and (2) the social construction of environmental problems (McCarthy & King, 2005).

The dominant political economy explanation of phenomena in environmental sociology relies upon the dialectic between capitalism and the environment or industry and society. This framework is the foundation behind much of Allen Schnaiberg's work and his collaboration with Kenneth Gould and David Pellow in the *Treadmill of Production* (1994). The "treadmill of production" refers to the interaction of two processes: expansion of production and ecological disorganization. Hannigan (1995) explains the tension within treadmill of production: boosting consumer demand for new products thereby placing strains on the ecosystem as it exceeds its physical limitation to growth and capacity. The Marxian influence is also seen in environmental sociology with the work of James O'Connor (1989) and John Bellamy Foster (2000) where environmental degradation is inexorably linked to capitalist accumulation.

I was drawn to the discipline of Environmental Sociology specifically because of my evolution as a campaigner against environmental racism and injustice. I viewed myself as a scholar-activist; one who could successfully use my campaigning experience to formal training in research. In fact, my research agenda was designed to seek answers create out of my most frustrating dilemmas as a campaigner; how can present day environmental injustice problems connect with socio-spatial aspects of American development such as segregation and geographic isolation.

The theme of environmental racism as defined by Robert D. Bullard (1996) is *"any policy, practice, or directive that differentially affects or disadvantages (whether intended or unintended) individuals, groups, or communities based on race or color"* while environmental justice is described as *"the principle that all people and communities are entitled to equal protection of the environmental and public health laws and regulations."* David Schlosberg (2007) takes note of the inclusiveness of Bunyan Bryant's articulation of environmental racism and injustice:

> It refers to those cultural norms and values, rules, regulations, behaviors, policies, and decisions to support sustainable communities, where people can interact with confidence that their environment is safe, nurturing and productive. Environmental justice is served when people can realize their highest potential, without experiencing the 'isms'. Environmental justice is supported by decent paying and safe jobs, quality schools and recreation; decent housing and adequate health care; democratic decision-making and personal empowerment; and communities free from violence, drugs, and poverty. These are communities where both cultural and biological diversity are respected and highly revered and where distributive justice prevails. (Bryant in Schlosberg, 2007, 50–51)

Schlosberg also notes the expansiveness of the rights according under environmental justice activism in the US but notes that "academics, however, have not always been so expansive and pluralistic in their attempts at defining environmental justice." (2007, 51). The problem of environmental racism can be best explained within the political economy explanation adopted by Schnaiberg and Gould in their model of the *treadmill of production*. Kreig notes that within the political economy of place, there is a struggle between economic activities and the preservation of environmental quality. If the distribution of power lies in the hands of industry, environmental quality decreases at the expense of the lower classes and minority groups (Kreig, 1998). The political economy argument suggest that the culprit is capitalism and this treadmill of production results in an imbalance of power that weighs in favor of the wealthy and less for minorities and the poor.

In their essay on environmental justice, Meuser and Szasz describe the history on the relationship between the economy and environment:

the great texts of historical sociology and environmental history would be read again as books about environmental inequality. Analysis of environmental inequality would start with the enclosure of commons lands, the transformation of land and labor into commodities, illness and injury in the factory system, conditions in manufacturing cities in industrializing Europe.....and at a time when people no longer believe that exploitation of labor can be the basis for international solidarity, such a conception may also provide the theoretical grounds for proposing that environmental justice might be the viable alternative, the rallying cry that can unify and invigorate a new international movement for social change" (pp. 117–8, 1997).

Previously, environmental sociologists' research on the relationship between class and the environment was limited to resource mobilization behind toxic waste struggles, rather than causal factors in siting (Finsterbusch and Humphrey in Buttel, 1987; Lo in Buttel, 1987). The intersection of race, income, and environmental degradation is a fairly new body of knowledge for environmental sociologists. While Szasz and Mueser (1997) trace the study of environmental quality back to the 1970s, it was not until the 1990s that there was a rapid proliferation of environmental justice analyses. This transition was in direct reaction the growing social movement for environmental justice in the United States. In fact, the first national study investigating the extent to which the poor and people of color were disproportionately impacted by environmental hazards was published in 1987 by a church-based research group, not a University.[2] In previous work, I calculated that there seven studies exploring environmental racism prior to 1994. Within the next six years, there were approximately twenty-two publications investigating environmental justice. While much of the evidence has supported the notion of disproportionate environmental impacts upon poor neighborhoods and communities of color, a UMASS researcher in his team produced a series of publications that attempted to debunk the notion of environmental justice analysis (Anderton et al., 1994a; 1994b; 1997; Davidson & Anderton, 2000). Anderton raises doubts on previous research use of geographic scale (zip codes versus census tracts) and the controlled comparisons. Immediate reactions of other environmental justice researchers were defensive. Thus begins a whole body of work on environmental justice analysis that debated methodological issues.[3] Here, we see a reflection of founding principles of objectivity and determinism of social facts. Environmental justice had become limited to debates around methodology. Likewise, there has been relatively little theoretical growth.[4]

Social constructions emphasize the ways in which problems are framed through social interaction. In terms of environmental problems, exploring their social construction has generally focuses on the establishment and maintenance of social movements and the characterization of public environmental concern. Thus, many environmental sociologists work focuses on environmental movements and framing, along with differences in environmental attitudes.

In 2005, environmental political consultants Michael Shellenberg and Ted Norhaus published an essay called "The Death of Environmentalism: Global Warming Politics in a Post-Environmental World" (S&N). They suggested that the contemporary environmental movement was dead. Its demise was a result of its establishment as a special interest group and its narrow policies that failed to gain public support. Shellenberger and Norhaus concluded that the future of the environmental movement depended on public-private partnerships. The impact of this essay on environmental sociologists was almost instant; the Environmental, Technology and Society section of the American Sociological Association organized a symposium in August 2005 entitled, *The Death of Environmentalism and the Future of Environmental Sociology* (Cohen, 2006). The reaction was inevitable, given the dedication of many environmental sociologists to the exploration of the environmental movement. When it comes to empirical analyses, a significant amount of the work in environmental sociology has come in the form of investigations on differences in environmental attitudes as well as disproportionate impacts of environmental hazards. However, a perusal of the top three journals for Sociology has paid little interest in environmental sociology.[5] The bulk of environmental sociology work during this period was published in interdisciplinary journals focuses on broad environmental issues like *Organization and Environment*, *Environmental Planning*, and *Natural Resources and the Environment*.

Rudy & Konefal: (2007) recognized environmental racism and the movement for environmental justice as a major influence on the intellectual discourse in environmental sociology. In a review of course syllabi, they acknowledge that while the subject of environmental justice is covered in many environmental courses, that coverage is limited. The intersections between race, class, gender, and the environment are depicted within these courses solely on the basis of the extent of disproportionately, rather than an articulation of the historically embedded processes of racism, sexism, and classism that produce environmental inequalities. Thus, Rudy and Konefal advocate for a "historicizing" of environmental sociology pedagogy: integrating the history of nature along with the historical development of society and emphasizing the role of science, technology, private property, capital, and political power within these developments that lead to stratification.

To suggest that the academy must be *greener* refers to the notion that the academic pursuits must also account for social justice. But environmental sociology has neglected to fully explore notions that theorize justice, whether it is environmental justice or climate justice. The sociological precept of objectivity and the preponderance of positivism and the social scientific method limits the way environmental sociologists can engage in issues related to justice, much less actively advocate on behalf of communities seeking justice. In other words, environmental justice has experienced a *crisis of epistemology*.

I find the current discourse on of the most recent paradigm in environmental justice, *Ecological Modernization*, a classic example of this disconnect. Ecological Modernization engages in ideas about the environment-society interaction without a concomitant critique of the current economic and political system. Perhaps the most obvious change in the intellectual growth within the field of environmental sociology is its scale: the globalization of capital and environmental problems. Environmental sociologists have moved from micro-level studies of attitudes, and specific industries, and source of pollution to cross-national comparisons of environmental behavior and international governance (Riley, 2010). To *Green* the academy, there has to be key shifts in representations, theories, and pedagogies of environmental sociology or in the broader application of environmental studies in the liberal arts. One key addresses epistemology and the University merit system for tenure and the way the academy views public scholarship.

I believe that my work is a prime example of greening the academy through an emphasis on public scholarship which combines my activist principles with my academic training. I consider myself lucky; I work in an African American Studies department in a University which supports public scholarship.[6] It is beneficial to be located in a department which affirms multidisciplinarity. Furthermore, my department like other African American Studies departments across the nation was born out Black students' struggles in the 1970s. Here, there is an inherent commitment to justice.

To green the academy, then we have to *brown* the academy. In other words, pursuing cultural diversity is key to building intellectual diversity. The lack of diversity in environmental academic studies and organization led Dorceta Taylor to create MELDI, the Multicultural Environmental Leadership Development Initiative in 2002 at the University of Michigan. MELDI's goal is to foster minority presence in environmental professions through research and career development activities. Among its many accomplishments, MELDI serves as information resource for underrepresented students and professionals in environmental organizations. But this is merely the first step, not the last. We must also confront conventional notions of value-free research; we must accept our responsibility as intellectuals and bring questions of justice to the forefront of our work – not just sitting back hoping that our research will get into the right hands.

The success of political ecology, a discipline rising largely from the disciplines of environmental studies, geography and political science, presents a useful example of the ways in which environmental sociologists can reopen issues of justice and political economy. For instance, Forsyth (2008) explores the writings of Piers Blakie and his commitment to social justice and environmentalism. Forsyth notes that in the 1980s, Blaikie and his colleagues strayed from the structuralist-materialist-Marxian analysis of environmental and social change to embrace a "locally-determined, discursive, and participatory approach" in confrontation with environmental problems. Political ecology orientation also gave rise to discourse on sustainable development among environmental sociologists.

Jean-Guy Vaillancourt (2010) chronicles the differences and similarities in the writings of two leading authors in environmental sociology, Fred Buttel and Riley Dunlap. Their debates center on their varying points of departure as it relates to the primacy of the biophysical world in sociological constructions, the causes and consequences of environmental problems, and the adoption (or lack thereof) of a constructivist framework around the globalization of environmental problems. Vaillancourt characterizes Buttel's worries about economic elites who are likely to exploit globalizing discourse around sustainability and environmental problems to serve their own interest. This idea harkens back to Agarwal and Narain's premise (in Villaincourt, 2010) that the globalization of environmental issues is tantamount to neocolonialism. Environmental sociology would do well to reflect critically on claims of empiricism and discovery of social facts, and interrogate of power and the role of state in the creation of, and ability to solve environmental problems.

Zelezny and Bailey's (2006) article written in reaction to S&N's *Death of Environmentalism* correctly points out the gender differences in dimensions of environmentalism. Countering S&N's thesis that American society has grown more politically conservative, Zelezny & Bailey demonstrated that resurgent conservatism is a pattern seen mainly in American men. Women are inclined to have more progressive political positions on environmental issues. Furthermore, female environmental leaders are more likely to propose locally-based solutions to environmental problems.

Michelle A. Lueck (2007) offers a refreshing and critical view in the articulation of environmental sociological theories, most notably the treadmill of production and ecological modernization theory. The author suggests that these perspectives are unduly pessimistic and fails to offer "hope", particularly, collective hope: "Pessimism can easily become a dominant feature of environmental sociology, especially for those who desire social change" (Lueck, 2007, 255). For example, acceptable of the treadmill of production demands that the only solution is the overthrow of the capitalist system. And while the ecological modernization theory may seem more optimistic in contrast, its insistence that environmental problems are solved with technological innovations removes agentic action. Thus, both theories are problematic because both are utopian, and while they may inspire hope, the means to reach those goals are essentially unattainable by individual action.

In addition to challenges in the diversity of the environmental sociologists and other environmental professions, pessimism in articulating solutions to environmental problems, and the need for historicity in understanding nature-society interaction, the field should also consider the role of its scholars in relation to the larger public. The Academic Affairs Committee of the Syracuse University Senate published a white paper in response to Chancellor Nancy Cantor's institutional commitment to what she refers to as "scholarship in action."[7] After talks with several scholars, including myself, who situate their work among public or engaged scholarship, they categorized the following roles: the public intellectual/public communicator, the community partner-in-action, and the community-engaged teacher. (Phelps, 2007). Defining community-engaged scholarship as it relates to the University merit system on tenure and promotion is a critical step in acknowledging the salience of justice in environmental studies, and in higher education. The point of this chapter is not question the ideological commitment of environmental sociologists. Rather, it is a call for expansion in the ideological dimensions of the academy, so that justice is situated at the foundation of research and teaching.

NOTES

[1] For more information on those environmental justice campaigns: In 1995–1996, I worked homeowners associations in the San Francisco neighborhood of Bayview Hunters Point to halt the permit of a $250 million power plant proposed by energy giant AES Corporation. In the mid 1990's, Bayview was the home to over 27,000 residents, mostly African Americans. The area is also the city's main industrial corridor with a Federally designated Superfund site with the former US Naval Shipyard, a state Superfund site, two of the area's power plants, 58 reported underground leaking storage tanks, 325 underground petroleum-storage tanks, the municipal wastewater treatment facility, and 700 hazardous waste material sites. See the following for more information on the Bayview Hunters Point campaign: Edward Epstein, "S.F. Rebuffs Controversial Plan for Power Plant in Bayview", *The San Francisco Chronicle*, June 18, 1996; Pratap Chatterjee, "Environment: Natural Gas Produces "Dirty" Energy, say Studies", *IPS-Inter Press Service*, December 11, 1995; Staff writer, "San Francisco Committee Opposes S.F. Power Plant", *The San Francisco Chronicle*, June 7, 1996; Clarence Johnson, "Disputed S.F. Power Plant Exptex to Get 1st OK Neighbors worry about health issues", *The San Francisco Chronicle*, March 4, 1996; Clarence Johnson, "Bayview-Hunters Point Sick of Industrial Fumes", *The San Francisco Chronicle*, February 13, 1995.

[2] In the summer of 1996, I helped an organization called St. James Citizens for Jobs and the Environment campaign against the construction a plastics manufacturing complex by Shintech, a wholly owned Japanese subsidiary of Shin Etsu. The $700 million dollar chemical complex would have located less than two miles from the local elementary school. This proposed facility would add an annual estimated 600,000 pounds of airborne toxics and daily wastewater discharges of 8 million gallons into the neighboring Mississippi River. Like Bayview Hunters Point, this area known as Convent, Louisiana was host to number of chemical facilities prior to the Shintech proposal. Within a three-mile radius, there were over 5 operating plants in the Convent: Star Enterprise-Taxaco refinery, IMC-Agrico, Zen Noh Grain elevators and wood chip mill, and the Occidental chemical company. The fight to stop Shintech became national known as the "test case for environmental racism". For more information on the campaign against Shintech in Convent, Louisiana: Staff writer, "Conyers, Greenpeace: Shintech a national focus", *The Associated Press State & Local Wire*, August 28, 1998; Bill Dawson, "Shintech Chemical Plant plans shifted to new site", *The Houston Chronicle*, September 19, 1998; Vicki Ferstel, "Shintech becomes test case; EPA trying to apply new, vague order". *The Advocate (Baton Rouge, Louisiana)River Parishes Bureau*, September 12, 1997; Jim Yardley, "Proposed plant raises ire in Louisiana; Test case: Does plastics plant planned near black neighborhood violate; Clinton's edit against 'environmental racism", *The Atlanta Journal and Constitution*, September 1, 1997; John McMillan, "Groups clash over Shintech; Environmetalists halt jobs meeting", *The Advocate (Baton Rouge, Louisiana) River Parishes Bureau*, July 27, 1997; Staff Writer, National Desk, "Poor Residents in Louisiana Fight Plan for Chemical Site", *The New York Times*, May 12, 1997.

The nearly decade long campaign to halt the license of a uranium enrichment plant by URENCO, a consortium of American and European nuclear interests in the Northern Louisiana town of Homer, Louisiana. Plans for this nuclear project included bisecting a road between two historic and predominantly African American communities of Forest Grove and Center Springs – a plan that failed to acknowledge the existence of these two communities in the company's application. For more information, see Peter Shinkle, "Uranium Plant dropped", *The Advocate (Baton Rouge, Louisiana)*, April 23, 1998; Chris Gray, "LA. Uranium Project is Scrapped", *Times-Picayune (New Orleans, LA)*, April 23, 1998; Tom Meersman, "Utility project stirs charges of racial bias; A federal board has questions the selection of a Louisiana site for a nuclear-fuel enrichment plant by consortium that includes Minnesota's Northern States Power Co.", *Star Tribune (Minneapolis, MN)*, May 31, 1997; Peter Shinkle, "Race factor in denial of uranium plant", *The Advocate (Baton Rouge, Louisiana)*, May 13, 1997. Robert Bullard, Testimony of Dr. Robert D. Bullard Regarding Citizens Against Nuclear Trash's Contention, In the Matter of Louisiana Energy Services Docket No. 70–3070, US Atomic Safety and Licensing Board, May 27, 1997.

[2] See United Church of Christ 1987 publication: Toxic Waste and Race. This is the first national analysis of the relationship between race and environmental hazards. The report, was updated and released on its 25th anniversary: Robert D. Bullard, Ph.D., Paul Mohai, Ph.D., Robin Saha, Ph.D., Beverly Wright, Ph.D., *Toxic Wastes and Race at Twenty, 1987–2007: A Report prepared for the United Church of Christ Justice and Witness Ministries,* March 2007, retrieved from www.ucc.org/justice/pdfs/toxic20.pdf.

[3] My dissertation research focused on the four methodological debates that plagued environmental justice analysis: race versus class as the most significant predictor of environmental racism and injustice, snapshot versus longitudinal analyses of environmental injustice, the appropriate geographic unit for use in analyses, and the appropriate use of a comparison group in analyses. For more information, please consult the dissertation, Kishi N. Animashaun, *Racialized Spaces: Exploring Space as an Explanatory Variable in Environmental Justice Analysis,* August 2005, University of Michigan.

[4] In regards to the persistent methodological debates in environmental justice analysis, Weinberg wrote, "While we have contributed greatly to policymakers' understanding of exposure and environmental hazards we have by now largely exhausted the answers that current methods offer. We need to rethink the environmental justice project and to be more intellectually open and methodologically creative" – see A.S. Weinberg, "The environmental justice debate: A commentary on methodological issues and practical concerns" 1998, *Sociological Forum 13(1):25–32.*

[5] Activists of the environmental justice community also reacted to the Shellenberger and Nordhaus article. For more information see Lu Blaine's piece in Grist magazine in May 2005 entitled, "Ain't I an Environmentalist?" and *The Soul of Environmentalism: Rediscovering Transformational Politics in the 21st Century* published by Redefining Progress at www.rprogress/soul/soul.pdf.

[6] The top three journals in the field of sociology are American Journal of Sociology, Annual Review of Sociology, and British Journal of Sociology, respectively. The ranking of these journals are determined by a measure called the *journal impact factor,* as calculated by the ISI Web of Knowledge's Journal Citation Reports. – http://isiknowledge.com. The impact factor measures the number of times a particular journal's articles have been cited in the Journal of Citation Reports within the past two years. This measure is a critical ranking in the prestige of published articles in academia, and it is measure of merit for many academicians.

[7] The administration under Chancellor Nancy Cantor at Syracuse University has advocated and advanced the merits of public scholarship, or what is referred at Syracuse University as "scholarship in action". For more information, see Nancy Cantor's speech, *Scholarship and Action and the Expansive Mission of Higher Education,* January 23, 2007 at http://www.syr.edu/chancellor/speeches/1_07_address.pdf and her statement on Scholarship in Action at http://www.syr.edu/chancellor/vision/index.html. See the white paper produced from the Academic Affairs Committee of the University Senate of Syracuse University by Louise Wetherbee Phelps, *Learning about Scholarship in Action in Concept and Practice*, August 2007. *Imagining America,* a consortium of US higher educational institutions that affirm public scholarship has also produced a report supporting this type of scholarship within the university merit system: Julie Ellison and Timothy K. Eatman, *Scholarship in Public: Knowledge Creation and Tenure Policy in the Engaged University: A Resource on Promotion and Tenure in the Arts, Humanities, and Design,* 2008 at http://www.imaginingamerica.org/TTI/TTI_FINAL.pdf.

REFERENCES

Anderton, D. L. (1996). Methodological Issues in the Spatiotemporal Analysis of Environmental Equity. *Social Science Quarterly, 77*(3), 123–140.

Anderton et al. (1994a). Environmental equity: The demographics of dumping. *Demography, 31*(2), 229.

Anderton et al. (1994b). Hazardous Waste Facilities: Environmental Equity Issues in Metropolitan Areas. *Evaluation Review, 18*(2), 229–248.

Anderton et al. (1997). Environmental equity in superfund: Demographics of the discovery and prioritization of abandoned toxic sites. *Evaluation Review, 21*(1), 3.

Animashaun, K. (2002). Exploring a Theory of Racialized Spaces in the Environmental Justice Movement. Unpublished manuscript, University of Michigan-Ann Arbor.

Blain, L. (2005). Ain't I an Environmentalist? *Social Policy, 35*(3), 31–34.

Bullard, R. D. (1996). Environmental justice: It's more than waste facility siting. *Social Science Quarterly, 77*(3), 493–499.

Bullard, R. D., Mohai, P., Saha, R., & Wright, B. (2007). Toxic Wastes and Race at Twenty 1987–2007. New York: United Church of Christ Justice & Witness Ministries.

Buttel, F. H. (1987). New Directions in Environmental Sociology. *Annual Review of Sociology, 13*, 465–488.

Cantor, N. Scholarship in Action: Investing in the Creative Campus. Retrieved November 20, 2008, from http://www.syr.edu/chancellor/vision/index.html

_____(2007). Scholarship in Action and the Expansive Mission of Higher Education. Retrieved November 30, 2008, from http://www.syr.edu/chancellor/speeches/1_07_address.pdf

Chatterjee, P. (December 11, 1995). Natural Gas Plan Produces 'Dirty' Energy says Studies. IPS InterPress Services.

Cohen, M. J. (2006). "The Death of Environmentalism": Introduction to the Symposium. *Organization and Environment, 19*(1), 74–81.

Collins, Patricia Hill (2008). "Black Feminist Epistemology" in *Just Methods: An Interdisciplinary Feminist Reader* (editor, Alison M. Jaggar) Boulder: Paradigm Publishers.

Conyers, Greenpeace: Shintech a national focus. (August 28, 1998). The Associated Press State & Local Wire.

Davidson, P., & Anderton, D. L. (2000). Demographic of Dumping II: A National Environmental Equity Survey and the Distribution of Hazardous Materials Handlers. *Demography, 37*(4), 461–466.

Dawson, B. (September 19, 1998). Shintech Chemical Plant plans shifted to new site. The Houston Chronicle.

Dunlap, R., & Catton Jr., W. R. (1979). Environmental Sociology. *Annual Review of Sociology, 5*, 243–273.

Dunlap, Riley. 2010. The maturation and diversification of environmental sociology: from constructivism and realism to agnosticism and pragmatism. In *The International Handbook of Environmental Sociology*, edited by M. R. Redclift and G. Woodgate. Cheltenham, UK: Edward Elgar.

Ellison, J., & Eatman, T. K. (2008). Scholarship in Public: Knowledge Creation and the Tenure Policy in the Engaged University. Retrieved November 30, 2008, from http://universitysenate.syr.edu/academic/pdf/white-paper-nov-12-2007.pdf

Epstein, E. (June 18, 1996). S.F. Rebuffs Controversial Plan for Power Plant in Bayview. The San Francisco Chronicle, p. A1.

Farganis, J. (2000). Readings in Social Theory: The Classic Tradition to Post-Modernism (Third ed.). Boston: McGraw Hill.

Ferstel, V. (September 12, 1997). Shintech becomes test case; EPA trying to apply new, vague order. The Advocate.

Forsyth, T. (2008). Political ecology and the epistemology of social justice. *Geoforum, 39*(2), 756–764.

Foster, John Bellamy. (2000). *Marx's Ecology: Materialism and Nature*. New York: Monthly Review Press.

Gelobter, M., Dorsey, M., Fields, L., Goldtooth, T., Mendiratta, A., Moore, R., et al. (2005). The Soul of Environmentalism: Rediscovering Transformational Politics in the 21st Century. Oakland, CA: Redefining Progress.

Gray, C. (1998, April 23, 1998). LA Uranium Project is Scrapped. Times Picayune, p. C1.

43

Hannigan, J. A. (1995). Environmental Sociology. New York: Routledge.

Harding, Sandra (1987) *Feminism and Methodology.* Bloomington: Indiana University Press.

Johnson, C. (February 13, 1995). Bayview-Hunters Point Sick of Industrial Fumes. The San Francisco Chronicle, p. A1.

_____ (March 4, 1996). Disputed S.F. Power Plant Expect to Get 1st OK Neighbors worry about health issues. The San Francisco Chronicle, p. A13.

Krieg, E. J. (1998). Methodological considerations in the study of toxic waste hazards. *Social Science Journal, 35*(2), 191–201.

Lueck, M. A. M. 2007. Hope for a cause as cause for hope: The need for hope in environmental sociology. *American Sociologist, 38*(3), 250–261

McCarthy, Deborah & Leslie King (2005) "Introduction: Environmental Problems Require Social Solutions" in *Environmental Sociology: From Analysis to Action* (editors Leslie King & Deborah McCarthy). Lanham: Rowman & Littlefield Publishers, Inc.

McMillan, J. (July 27, 1997). Groups clash over Shintech; Environmentalists halt jobs meeting. The Advocate.

Meersman, T. (May 31, 1997). Utility project stirs charges of racial bias; A federal board has questions the selection of a Louisiana site for a nuclear-fuel enrichment plant by consortium that includes Minnesota's Northern States Power Co. Star Tribune, p. 1A.

MELDI (Minority Environmental Leadership Development Initiative). [date accessed June 6, 2011]. Available from http://meldi.snre.umich.edu/

Mills, C. W. (2000). The Sociological Imagination (40th Anniversary Edition ed.). New York: Oxford University.

O'Connor, James. (1989). "Uneven and combined development and ecological crisis". *Race and Class 30*, 1–11.

Phelps, L. W. (2007). Learning about Scholarship in Action in Concept and Practice (Report). Syracuse: Syracuse University – Academic Affairs Committee of the University Senate.

(No author). Poor Residents in Louisiana Fight Plan for Chemical Site. (1997, May 12, 1997). The New York Times, p. 8.

(No author). San Francisco Committee Opposes S.F. Power Plant. (1996, June 17, 1996). The San Francisco Chronicle, p. A22.

Rudy, A. P., & J. Konefal. 2007. Nature, sociology, and social justice: Environmental sociology, pedagogy, and the curriculum. *American Behavioral Scientist, 51*(4), 495–515.

Schlosberg, David. (2007). *Defining Environmental Justice: Theories, Movements, and Nature.* New York: Oxford University Press.

Schnaiberg, A., & Gould, K. A. (1994). Environment and Society: The Enduring Conflict. New York: St. Martin's Press.

Shellenberger, M., & Nordhaus, T. (2004). The Death of Environmentalism: Global Warming Politics in a Post-Environmental World. Retrieved November 15, 2008, from http://thebreakthrough.org/PDF/Death_of_Environmentalism.pdf.

Shinkle, P. (May 13, 1997). Race factor in denial of uranium plant. The Advocate.

_____ (April 23, 1998). Uranium Plant dropped. The Advocate.

Szasz, A., & Meuser, M. (1997). Environmental inequalities: Literature review and proposals for new directions in research and theory. *Current Sociology, 45*(3), 99.

United Church of Christ Commission for Racial Justice. (1987). Toxic Wastes and Race in the United States: A National Report on the Racial and Socioeconomic Characteristics of Communities with Hazardous Waste Sites. New York: United Church of Christ.

Vaillancourt, Jean-Guy. 2010. From environmental sociology to global ecosociology: the Dunlap-Buttel debates. In *The international handbook of environmental sociology, second edition*, edited by M. R. Redclift and G. Woodgate. Cheltenham, UK: Edward Elgar.

Weber, M., Gerth, H. H., & Mills, C. W. (1946). From Max Weber: Essays in Sociology. New York: Oxford University Press.

Weinberg, A. S. (1998). The environmental justice debate: A commentary on methodological issues and practical concerns. Sociological Forum, *13*(1), 25–32.

Woodgate, Graham. 2010. Introduction. In *The International Handbook of Environmental Sociology, Second Edition*, edited by M. R. Redclift and G. Woodgate. Cheltenham, UK: Edward Elgar.

Yardley, J. (September 1, 1997). Proposed plant raises ire in Louisiana; Test case: Does plastics plant planned near black neighborhood violate Clinton's edict against 'environmental racism'. The Atlanta Journal-Constitution, p. 08A.

Zelezny, L., & Bailey, M. (2006). A Call for Women to lead a different Environmental Movement. Organization & Environment, *19*(1), 103.

GREENING POLITICAL SCIENCE

TIMOTHY W. LUKE

The place of Nature, in political science, depending on how one sees environmental issues and Nature itself, is either very old and truly foundational or quite new and still evolving. In its older traditional forms, political discourse is complex. Nature inescapably can be regarded as the determinate condition of scarcity, necessity, and limits; or, with the coming of modernity, its newer modern forms cast it as potentially a realm of abundance, freedom, and possibility, depending on how humans think and act about creating "the wealth of nations." From Aristotle onward, and gaining strength with Rousseau, Locke, and Hobbes as well as Hume, Smith or Malthus, "the state(s) of Nature" cannot be ignored in politics. Yet, to observe its impact on political thought and action, it is crucial to not limit one's attention only to the narrow confines of political science as a discipline.

OVERVIEW

Indeed, Nature has been, from Aristotle to Rawls, a foundational explanation used by authorities for establishing who would rule and who should be ruled; what the characteristics and purposes of government are and are not; how states must be organized to protect themselves from all disorder whether domestic and foreign; where government could intrude in the economy, family, and society and where it should not; when rulers must act to attain prosperity, stability, and unity as well as never act to maintain those collective benefits; and, why governments of humans usually emerge, develop, expand, decline, or then expire, like the human beings they rule, or more unusually how human governments might develop, extend, deepen, and establish institutions of rule to check, slow or even suspend these allegedly natural cycles of life. In this tradition, Nature's dictates, laws or tendencies always are advanced as the defining justification, boundary condition, and ultimate cause behind determining the "who, whom" of power. Thus nature (in its philosophic usage) forms a pretext for philosophic naturalism.

Consequently, one often finds in the traditions of jurisprudence, political philosophy, law or public administration, a deeply rooted naturalism that spins theories and practices in a certain naturalistic manner, granting various powers, positions or privileges to some as well as denying them to others. These ethical scripts do persist today in constitutional thinking, legal traditions, and administrative techniques. Such clusters of knowledge antedate the environmental turn of thought; and, their conventions survive today in the design of constitutional arrangements,

S. D. Fassbinder, A. J. Nocella II and R. Kahn (Eds.), Greening the Academy:
Ecopedagogy Through the Liberal Arts, 47–62.

the conduct of legal practices, and the organization of administrative codes, but most of them typically are placed separately from today's environmentalism as the stuff of revered cultural heritage.

While these rich traditions must be acknowledged, they should not be the anchor lines for ascertaining the depth of greening in today's academy. With today's widespread and intense worries about the Earth's ecology, the processes of greening the academy in light of the modern environmental movement are accelerating. In political science, one can turn to the newer thematics, like those of green citizenship, environmental justice, green statism, natural capitalism, green urbanism, climate change, or green globalism. There certainly are strains of environmental political analysis that still cling to older texts like William Ophuls' *Ecology and the Politics of Scarcity* (1977) or Jared Diamond's *Collapse* (2005), whose neo-Malthusian and neo-Hobbesian visions of politics find some environmental followers whether it is during the hard times of the 1970s or the 2000s. However, during the more hopeful times of the 1950s–1960s, or even 1980s–1990s, many political thinkers have reimagined Nature in less harsh, essentialist or naturalistic terms. Important figures, like Murray Bookchin *Post-Scarcity Anarchism* (1971), Carolyn Merchant, *The Death of Nature? Women, Ecology, and The Scientific Revolution* (1980), Neil Smith, *Uneven Development* (1984), or even Christopher Manes, *Green Rage* (1990), all saw today's economy and society as very human constructs whose inequalities, irrationalities, and inconsistencies could be remade in better ways with the right green theories and practices. The promise of Earth Day in 1970 was based on rethinking humanity's relations with the environment after the whole world saw it from space during the Apollo moon missions from 1968 to 1973 as a verdant and vital sphere of life. Driven by this image, many thinkers have sought to develop public policies and political practices tied to protecting and preserving the Earth's abundance to benefit all forms of life rather than following hard naturalistic dictates driven by accepting and accommodating humans to the strictures of scarcity.

The changing qualities of the ecological crisis in the twentieth and twenty-first centuries are probably nowhere as pressing as with various articulations of environmental thinking across the general field of political science. With the swelling anxieties about the risks of global warming, climate change, widespread drought, water shortages, and dangerous pollution (Beck, 1992: Diamond, 2005), the Earth's ecologies have become central preoccupations for different cultural, economic, political, and scientific interests. Efforts to interpret, evaluate, and then act effectively on the basis of deepening worries about human depredations of the environment frequently are linked to their analysis by political scientists in policy studies, political theory or bureaucratic responses, especially given their perceived importance to assuring the survival and well-being of the Earth (Dryzek, 2000; Barry and Eckersley, 2005; Dobson and Bell, 2006; O'Neill, 2008).

As Dobson (2007, p. 73) contends, the common tactics of today's genuinely green political movements, or those grounded in a politics of ecologism, all come together at the same crossroads where the public must see: "the finitude of the planet, the need to restrict growth, the consequent need to reduce consumption and the necessity for calling into question the practices... that help reproduce the growth economy." These imperatives are perhaps true, but how, or even whether, a politics can be implemented to attain them is a major question. Nonetheless Dobson's perspective serves as a basic map of the political and intellectual contours of political studies of the environment. Indeed, the varying characteristics of political ideologies in today's global age perhaps show up nowhere quite as clearly as in the ideological discourses of political ecology.

GREENING POLITICAL DISCOURSE

Environmentalist agendas, therefore, have become a well-entrenched preoccupation over the past forty years in political science, and their various visions for political thought and practice each express a response to the present crisis and its seemingly ever more dire environmental circumstances (Gottlieb, 1993; Dowie, 1995; Luke, 1999a). There are many ways to map the diverse variants of environmental practices, politics, and policies (Luke 1997); but, for the purposes of this brief overview at this specific historical conjuncture, there are seven salient types worth noting as analytically distinct approaches—environmental justice, critical climatology, ecomodernization, green statism, natural capitalism, resource managerialism, and banal ecologism. Each of them, as Dobson would expect, has their own political map, social critique, and transformational program, which enable their proponents to espouse their special visions of political ecology

Their strategies for green change might endorse democratic or authoritarian responses, direct actions or legislative innovations, communitarian or bureaucratic responses, lifestyle alterations or regulatory interventions, environmental citizenship or ecological technocracy. Such transformational programs for meeting the challenges of a world beset by environmental crises, however, typically map out cultural, economic, and political strategies intent upon creating a more sustainable or resilient society. By accepting ecological scarcity, restricting consumption, slowing growth, and curtailing production, the ideology of ecologism holds the crises of environmental unsustainability and ecological collapse can be directly confronted and largely corrected.

A. Environmental Justice

The environmental justice movement is a critically important and highly active green political force. It arguably has its prefigurations in the pioneering works of Murray Bookchin, writing under the pseudonym of Lewis Herber (1962; 1965) and Rachel Carson (1962) in the 1950s and 1960s as they call into question the unexpected costs, unintended consequences, and negative feedbacks of coexisting with toxic chemicals, extensive pollution, and complex technologies. As one the first powerful resistances from below, the environmental justice movement found a major proponent in the work of Robert Bullard (*Dumping in Dixie* (1990).

Bullard and other voices in the environmental justice movement concentrate on issues of spatially unequally negative environmental impacts, especially those due to the racial, gender, and class inequalities whose unequal distributions lead to greater or less ecological ill-effects (Bullard, 1993). Pollution is found everywhere, but it is truly more common in specifically "polluted" locales. Where one finds racial minorities, ethnic outsiders, working class people, or poor women and children, it is clear that air, water, and soil pollution are far more common and serious. Racial majorities, ethnic elites, or rich people in general all tend to be living, working, and playing at locations where pollution is much less frequent and intense (Mellor, 1992; Salleh, 1997; Baumann, 2000).

Environmental justice politics typically focus upon localized inequalities and generalized imbalances in the workings of advanced industrial capitalism. Climate change or species endangerment often is an issue that more privileged groups express their apprehensions over, while they tend to be mum about a lack of adequate sewer facilities, clean drinking water, toxic soils, point-based air pollution, wood smoke pollutants or insufficient food. The greater visibility of environmental justice politics in the global world economy follows from runaway shops, job loss, and capital disinvestment plaguing some locations over others. And, as economic worries about sites with such problems increase, it is apparent the flight of jobs, businesses, and capital to poorer, less regulated and more underdeveloped new sites quickly compound themselves in serious ecological problems (Paehlke, 2003; Mol, 2003; Goldman, 2005).

In response to claims about environmental injustice, the powers that be frequently first engage in denial. Once they admit environmental racism or sexism may, in fact, exist, their responses vary (Benton, 1993). However, typically one might look to look to critical climatology for more global solutions, ecomodernization for growth strategies that address inequalities or green capitalism to find an ecological gospel of wealth which aught afford individual opportunities to escape both material poverty and environmental injustice (Bookchin, 1971).

B. Critical Climatology

One of the most visible variants of green politics today is critical climatology. With its focus upon the phenomena of global warming, which are lined to rapidly increasing levels of greenhouse gases like carbon dioxide, methane, nitrous oxide, chlorofluorocarbons or sulfur hexafluoride, critical climatology measures and monitors how human industrial activities are apparently causing environmental disasters along with economic growth. Rising levels of carbon dioxide produced by burning fossil fuels in automobiles, power plants, factories, home heating, and transport systems are singled out as the main cause of increasing atmospheric temperatures, melting glaciers, weather disruptions, and rising sea levels. While these phenomena were provisionally analyzed during the 1950s (Plass, 1956a, 1956b; Plass, 1959), and a sustained system of monitoring has been in place since 1958 at the Mauna Loa Observatory in Hawaii, they became popular concerns around 1990 in response to works by Bill McKibben, *The End of Nature* (1989) and Al Gore, Jr., *Earth in the Balance* (1992), which predicted severe consequences following from such radical climate change.

Al Gore, in particular, has spent much more time and energy since losing the 2000 U.S. presidential election, on the processes of climate change, and his *An Inconvenient Truth* (2006) movie and book have become the keystone for the arch of anxious policy responses to this meteorological conception of history. At the same time, a vast network of United Nations backed scientists in the Intergovernmental Panel on Climate Change (IPCC) and various national scientific centers, like the Pew Center in Washington, DC; the Tyndall Center in Cambridge or the PIK Center in Potsdam also have become central sites for anchoring the claims of critical climatology. To steer away from the doom carried aloft by carbon dioxide emissions, the critical climatologists prescribe lifestyle changes, regulatory interventions, and new green energy investments. Some of the program complements other ideological variants of political ecology (Vanderheiden, 2008a; 2008b).

Gore, Rajendra Pachauri, the IPCC, James Hansen and others are constantly challenged by doubters, but the Stern Report (2007) in the United Kingdom along with the Fourth Report of the IPCC (2007) have done much to legitimize the far-ranging program of critical climatology. Climate models have made some national governments and global firms rethink their contributions to the trends in global warming, but the deadlines for implementing materially significant changes often are pushed out from 2020 to 2035. More significantly, many regional, provincial, state, county and city governments have adopted policies to promote carbon neutrality along with other measures to adapt to, or possibly mitigate the trends toward disruptive climate change. Still, the pressing state of emergency that this green politics assumes can be characterized by the Rajendra Pachauri, the panel head of the fourth IPCC assessment report, who declared in 2007: "If there is no action before 2012, that's too late, there is not time. What we do in the next two, three years will determine our future. This is the defining moment" (Rosenthal, 2007, A1).

C. Ecomodernization

A third highly visible variant of green politics is the school of ecomodernization, which sees the looming challenges of the coming ecological collapse as the opportunity to simultaneously look beyond old wave "gloom and doom" environmentalism and move ahead to a more affirmative green political economy that will "break through" decades of deadlock in environmental policy (Commoner, 1971; Schnaiberg, 1980; Benton, 1994; Goldman, 2005). While prior forms of industrialization have disrupted the Earth's environment, ecomodernizationists place their faith in the inventive potential and ethical promise of modernization as an ethico-political project of more just and effective rationalization. Therefore, the project of modernization can advance and, indeed, attain even greater success simply by curbing waste, controlling excess, and curtailing externalities that past managerial philosophies and industrial design practices accepted as tolerable overhead costs.

There many proponents of ecomodernization, but the most vocal and visible ones today are Michael Nordhaus and Ted Shellenberger. Their works, "The Death of Environmentalism" (2004) and *Breakthrough* (2007), are dedicated to developing a "postenvironmental" politics centered on a comprehensive ecomodernization program. The ideological spin on ecologism asserts "when we called on environmentalists to stop giving the "I have a nightmare" speech, we did not mean that we should close our eyes to the increasingly hot planet, the destruction of the Amazon, or continued human suffering" (Nordhaus & Shellenberger, 2007, p. 240). Not unlike all modernizationist thinking, they claim "we should open our eyes to the multiplicity of ways we can see and experience the world. Global warming could bring drought, disease, and war–*and* it could bring prosperity, cooperation, and freedom" (Nordhaus & Shellenberger, 2007, p. 10). Ecomodernizationists, then, argue that the regulatory pressures imposed by certain countries and the market forces exerted through overall cost competition are causing "actual institutional transformations" in advanced industrial societies, and these changes should "no longer be interpreted as mere window dressing" (Mol, 1996, p. 303) as they were in the past.

Sophisticated high technology and astute capital investment combined with a new postindustrial social contract are ready to be integrated into existential decisions about the whys-and-wherefores of ecomodernization: "What kind of a country do we want? How can we achieve it? These questions implicitly contain a question about *investment*: How will Americans invest our wealth and our labor" (Nordhaus & Shellenberger, 2007, p. 10). To crack open the doors to ecologism's promised future, the worn-out brands of dead environmentalism must be forgotten. Fruitless environmentalism politics only "imagine solutions that seek to constrain" the economy and society as ecomodernization assets; the fruitful alternatives of ecologism seek instead to "unleash, human activity and economic growth" (Nordhaus & Shellenberger, 2007, p. 40). This basic reorientation towards capital-intensive, large scale, technology-centered, and quality growth based projects, therefore, can be counted upon to make green politics triumphant in its ecomodernizationist forms.

D. Green Statism

A fourth increasingly common articulation of green politics is green statism. Taking note of the alarm raised by critical climatologists, and yet becoming frustrated by the slow progress being made by ecomodernizationsts, green statism pushes fusing the thinking of ecologism with power of larger effective states. While the willingness to mobilize state power to rescue "Nature" from "Society" has been a frequent theme in many environmentalists' writings, ranging from William Opfuls (1977) to Lester Brown (1980), the particular angle that ecologism adds to green statism is the coercive decisionism lying at its heart. Whether it is species loss, global warming, severe drought, coastal flooding or economic collapse, contemporary green statism uses such conditions of crisis to declare a general state of emergency to correct ecological imbalances. A solid instance of such green politics at work is Robyn Eckersley's *The Green State* (2004).

Eckeresley's notion of green statism is rooted in a green public sphere of humans and nonhumans; and, for her, "the project of building the green state can never be finalized: inasmuch as it will lead to "a dynamic and ongoing process of extending citizenship rights and securing an inclusive form of political community (Eckersley, 2004, p. 16) to many of a global scale. Indeed, the brief for a green state would be to far more effectively and comprehensively "protect ecosystems and environmental victims (Eckersley, 2004, p. 16). Even though it is aware of the contributions of environmental science, ecomodernization or green business, the green state becomes critically important to enact, and then enforce "more ecologically responsible modes of state governance" (Eckersley, 2004, p. 15). Nonetheless, green statism ultimately means to empower experts rather than citizens. Even though it speaks about a public sphere and its democratizing possibilities, it is less clear that Eckersley and other green statists see, as Bookchin (1995, p. 232) advocates, an ecological politics able to "inculcate the values of humanism, co-operation, community, and public service in the everyday practice of civic life."

E. Natural Capitalism

A fifth articulation for green politics that also has won over many supporters is the odd school of natural capitalism. Developing more or less alongside critical climatology, ecomodernizationism, and green statism, natural capitalism provide a new vision of practicing local and global exchange by keeping the environment as well as the economy in mind. Natural capitalism is suspicious of the concentrated state power behind green statism and not entirely comfortable with the technocratic foci of ecomodernizationism (Hawken, Lovins, & Lovins, 1999). Instead it often looks to the smaller scale, quicker reacting, and broader engaged responses of business enterprises eager to leverage the full-spectrum of pressing environmental problems as new business opportunities in full accord with the world's actually existing capitalist economies. Buttel pinpoints the structural origins of natural capitalism's main concerns. That is, "just as there is a structural incentive for capital to externalize environmental and other costs onto the rest of society, there is also a capitalist logic of conservation and efficiency: (1998, p. 209).

Natural capitalists, therefore, essentially recast the market and its complex division of labor as an underleveraged asset (von Weizacker, Lovins, and Lovins, 1998). It has been stymied by short-sightedness, greed, and waste as the practices of concentrated ownership, planned obsolescence, big profits, and rapid return-on-investment distorted its traditional probity and rationality during the twentieth century. Consequently, the proponents of natural capitalism, like Paul Hawken, Amory Lovins, David Orr, Hunter Lovins or Ernest von Weizacker, seek to reimagine the Earth as an economy rather than a wilderness. Consequently, the environment is not merely a site; it is a system of services that to be fundamentally reimagined in terms of cost, benefit, asset, liability, gain, loss and value. Business and environment are seen not as opposing forces, but as being of one piece. The new business model is discernable in Nature, itself.

F. Resource Managerialism

A sixth significant permutation of political discourses about the environment can be found in the long-standing practices for a green politics embedded in resource managerialism. Political science as policy science, administrative science or decision science is more than comfortable with resource managerialism. Indeed, this approach to green politics has ridden along with the expansion of American state power since the era of Reconstruction (Croway, 1953; Vogt, 1947; Diamond, 2005). The formation of bureaus to conduct national geological surveys, map out national forests, delineate public from private lands, reclaim deserts with dams, and police Native American lands, territorial lands, and far-flung overseas commonwealths or colonies to maximize their resource productivity speak directly to the significance of resource managerialism as green politics in the U.S.A. (Gottlieb, 1993; Luke, 1997; Luke 1999b).

Resource managerialism often is dismissed as not being authentic green politics, because it appears to stand for a business as usual approach to existing economic and political problems. In fact, this interpretation usually is quite far from the truth. Beginning with panics in the nineteenth century about the loss of animal species, erosion of farmlands, depletion of forests, and exhaustion of mineral deposits, resource managerialism has sought to rethink many existing values and practices of industrial production, commercial circulation, and capital accumulation in order to meet the demands of mass consumption which was transformed into the narrow promise of industrial democracy (Benton, 1994). The politics of "more" drive the programs of endless economic growth launched in the nineteenth and twentieth centuries; hence, the institutional means of getting, keeping, and expanding access to fresh stocks of natural resources in order to manufacture more goods and services keeps the core precepts of industrial democracy alive (Commoner, 1971).

Thus, the conceptual articulation of resource environmentalism are an ideology that is, in fact, quite powerful. Resource managerialism allied with the popular and venerable beliefs of conservation during the Progressive Era, but it also validates deeper, more potent fundamentalistic environmental nationalism throughout the twentieth century (Vogt, 1947; Osborn, 1948; Croway, 1953; Carson, 1961; Ophuls, 1977; Brown, 1981; Dowie, 1995). Resource managerialism expresses a clear agenda for adapting to the political world. At the same time, it prescribes certain beliefs about the nation's economic condition, and propounds a strict program for political action to meet those conditions, while regarding them as institutionally vital truths (Gottlieb, 1993; Barry, 1999; Luke, 1999). Resource managerialism has always had an institutional propensity to affirm scientific expertise and technological acumen, and this tenor in its practices clearly does continue even today. Indeed, its backers highlight the changing face of green politics in this global age by privileging its corporate, scientific and nationalistic approaches to managing the Earth in an era of expansive globalization (Friedman, 2008; Beck, 2000; O'Neill, 2008).

G. Banal Ecologism

A seventh variant of green politics that has taken root and grown considerably over the past twenty years is the adoption, cooptation or mobilization of green affect, care or sensibilities in the conduct of everyday life itself. Whether it is in the realm of architecture, construction, design, farming, gardening, housing, clothing, management, planning, religion, technology, or urbanism, there is a fascinating, but also essentially, banal ecologism that nests in the thinking and practices of many producers, consumers, savers, commuters or everyday actors going about the conduct of their everyday biopolitical existence. Echoes of critical climatology, ecomodernizationism, green statism or natural capitalism clatter around the chambers of banal ecologism, but mostly this variant of ecologism narrows its sense of radical changes in human relationship with the non-human natural world by reimagining some ordinary sliver of human life in transformative terms.

A bit of this banality is displayed in a transnational energy corporation like British Petroleum (BP), using bright clean green and yellow product marketing pitches centered on sunflower images to reimagine its sales of energy goods and services in an ecological life "beyond petroleum." Other qualities of banal ecologism surface in widely available chapbooks for living lives of green tied to green activism, green commercialism, green consumerism, green residentialism or green suburbanism, like MacEachern (2008), *Big Green Purse: Use Your Spending Power to Create a Cleaner, Greener World*; Yarrow (2008) *How to Reduce Your Carbon Footprint: 365 Simple Ways to Save Energy, Resources, and Money*; and, Bach (2008), *Go Green, Live Rich: 50 simple Ways to Save the Earth (and Get Rich Trying)*. Such corporate-enablements for ecologism truly do believe everyday green agency pursued for its own sake will transform selves and societies in a manner that affirms like Dayton-Hundon's Target up-scale discount stores a pledge by all on Earth "To Love Your Mother." The banality of its ecologism, in turn, reduces the green dimension to the saving of energy, resources, and money.

Still, the most thorough-going vision of a green politics tied to banal ecologism is mapped out by the "c2c," or "cradle to cradle," green design credo of the architects William McDonough and Michael Braungart. In *Cradle to Cradle: Remaking the Way We Make Things* (2002), they offer new administrative design, manufacture, and technological alternatives to what they see as the flawed material metabolism of the Industrial Revolution, which rests on a take, make, waste cycle of economy. Rooted in "The Hannover Principles" for sustainable design as propounded by McDonough (1992) and others in the early 1990s, the "cradle to grave" vision of resource misuse is an inefficient, open, and unstable system for living. The "cradle to cradle" model creates closed loops of energy, material, information, and labor flows that eliminate waste by turning it into "nutrients" for other energy, material, information and labor flows in a new industrial revolution.

Ultimately, this green politics is rooted in the banal truism of "waste not, want not" to rethink the micro and macro dimensions of contemporary economies and societies. Rather than ecomodernization, this ecologism is essentially a bioeconomization of actually existing capitalism via "eco-efficiency." Such biomimicry turns waste into food, energy or material for other systems to the degree that waste disappears. With color-coded design protocols, cradle to cradle practice burrow through commodity chains in search of greater economy, efficiency, and ecology. Somewhat counter-intuitively, then, ecological scarcity disappears in the abundance of economic waste. The banal devotions of reduce, reuse, and recycle become a radical program of transformation that ultimately revalorizes consumption as a means to revitalize continuous production.

From intelligent power grids, green roofs, organic plastics to non-toxic materials, perpetual circulation, and lifecycle design, ecologism itself is turned the benchmark of individual prosperity, environmental health, and social equity. The mission to remake the way we make things, reframe the way things serve people, and reinvent the ways people and things make ecological, economic, and equitable connections is part of this literature. These texts ironically impress the banality as well as the radicalism of this green politics into the conduct of everyday conduct. In a way, it is a redirection of ordinary biopolitical life which is well-worth doing, although it is not clear that it is anywhere near as radical as its proponents suggest.

Having looked at green politics, which Dobson labels as ecologism, and surveyed its active basis for serving as an ideology (or some actionable rationality of power coupled with a conceptualized practicality for knowledge), one can see many dimensions of a transformative "ideology" behind his ecologism. Of course, Dobson's conceptual chapbook–now in its fourth edition–has taken great pains to show how ordinary "environmentalism" is not an ideology because of its managerialist, meliorist, and materialist fixation upon maintaining present values of production and consumption, but his case is overdrawn. Still, "ecologism" does work well as an ideology because its variants do have, an actively concentrated set of attributes, including: (a) an analytical description of society, or a mapping of reality for adherents to navigate around the political world; (b) fairly comprehensive prescription of/for a particular society with coherent cluster of beliefs about the human condition to sustain and reproduce that new social formation; and, (c) a complex program for political action that imagines how to get from the society of the present to a new order of the future that is being prescribed to improve and enhance it.

Green politics conducted within these elementary distinctions, therefore, crystallizes as both a mode of/for global thought production; and, the thought of/for a global mode of production. Such systems of reasoning are always contestable, and never completely closed or coherent; and, this remains true of politicized ideologies of "ecologism" as well as what many political scientists would regard as its environmentalist, conservationist, ecocentrist, or naturalist alternatives. Such ideological moves find expressions for possibilities latent in various economy and society formulae, like primitivism, agriculturalism, pastoralism, industrialism, post-industrialism/informationalism as well as ruralism, urbanism, nomadism. Nonetheless, in today's globalized, consumeristic, and materialist order, "ecologism" can operate as a normative ideal, a normalizing formation, and a norm-generalizing system. That strands of ecologism are legitimately circulated thought systems of/for a globalist model of liberal democratic capitalist production is reality that surfaces in many places. When even former Prime Minister, and now Lady Margaret Thatcher cynically or ironically can assert, "We are all environmentalists now," one can see why ecologism's partisans demand that its followers soon gain the correct green consciousness as true devotees of/for "ecologism."

Ecologism, therefore, has become–as ideology–and a code of responses to many political questions about "the present" and the manifold ways in which it becomes presented to us, taken as present by us, and then acted upon presently by us as "politics," "policies," and/or "practices." Whether it is environmental justice, critical climatology, ecomodernization, green statism, natural capitalism, resource managerialism, or banal ecologism, in these, and other forms, green politics finds itself working as an ideology. With these articulations, green politics can carry a coherent consistent code of beliefs about mapping reality, prescribing solutions for problems plaguing that reality, and programming political actions for transforming the present society into some greater future perfect green condition. While some continuities persist, many of green politics innovations for novelties in today's globalist order are quite distinctive.

H Greening Politics

Political thinking has addressed "the environment" in various guises and under different names since political thought first began; however, in its modern articulations within the U.S.A. after 1903, when the American Political Science Association was founded, much of its limited green disciplinary attention only has focused on the public policies of administering the environment as a storehouse of resources requiring astute and efficient management. The Progressive Era's creation of resource managerialist bureaux, policies, and techniques carried forward through the century with the New Deal, the Great Society and even into the Opportunity Society of the 2000s. At the same time, other dissident visions of the environment arose from the minorities rights, women's' rights, and consumers' rights struggles of the 1950s and 1960s as well as the more holistic ecological vision of the Earth expressed by Earth scientists during the Space Race between the U.S.A. and U.S.S.R. all of these diverse understandings of "the environment" in political science remain quite important today.

The issues of sustainability, resilience, and vulnerability all are connected to the environmental challenges faced by today's risk obsessed society, and they have been a major policy concern for a generation (WCED, 1987). Assessing, managing, and perhaps negating the serious future ecological risks that preoccupy many governments is a crucial challenge; but, for others, the effect of water shortages, global warming, hazardous wastes or ecosystem collapse already are now being experienced. Consequently, the degree of social vulnerability, loss of economic sustainability, or hope for cultural resilience as these adverse effects befall their populations are serious concerns that must be, and gradually are being, addressed by political analysis.

Political science in general has not focused tremendous attention on the environment per se, but it has been a focus of research in the areas of comparative politics or international relations. The success of many negotiations leading the Montreal Protocol and regulations to control chlorofluorocarbons in the 1980s (Litfin, 1994) lead some to believe concerted collective action at the global level could effectively address many other challenges as well. Whether it was climate change, water politics, industrial pollution or biodiversity conservation, many political scientists have spent decades espousing the merits of institution-building for a "global ecopolitics" (Pirages, 1978; Young, 1994; Wapner, 1996; Young, 2002; Lipschutz, 2003; Jasanoff and Martello, 2004; Barry and Eckersley, 2005; Conca, 2006; O'Neill, 2008). The more difficult recognition that many of these efforts tend to be exercises in symbolic summitry, disciplinary deadlock or misery mystification rarely is marked by political scientists, largely due to an enduring faith in liberal institutionalism or policy incrementalism. Nonetheless, it is increasingly apparent after years, and then decades of talk, of continued policy inaction and worsening ecological conditions (Sachs, 1993; Luke, 1997; Goldman, 2005) that these genres of research are not having much material influence outside of the academy.

These unfortunate tendencies in much of political science, however, still points towards an easy acceptance of politics as usual plus proclivities to take a new green wrapper, overlay, or wash on the issues. By and large, environmental politics in the U.S.A. are still characterized in fairly conventional 1960s and 1970s terms – saving the big outdoors, protecting endangered species, or stopping pollution. More recently, global warming terms of political discourse have become common, but even here fighting climate change is still focused on comparable goals – lessening CO_2 pollution, saving polar bears, and keeping Arctic ice formations intact. Despite its disciplinary label, political science is not terribly science-oriented or science-driven. Political worries about the environment, therefore, usually show up on the periphery of many electoral contests, regulatory concerns, media campaigns, judicial proceedings, or, now and then, direct action. By and large, environmental issues in the U.S.A. usually preoccupy Westerners more than Easterners, certain niche publics (like students, rural property owners, scientists, affluent suburban populations, or young people) or those worried about environmental justice issues (chemical plant sitings, rural landowners, underprivileged minorities or blighted inner city neighborhoods). Broader engagements from workers groups, big business, or central bureaucrats, like one tends to see more in Europe/Canada or Australia, are usually exceptional and short-lived. Saving the environment continues to be viewed as the obverse outcome of growing the economy. Political legitimacy and success are deeply rooted in economic growth, so pushing any ideas, interests or influences that might lessen growth typically is regarded with suspicion, if not hostility. Therefore, taking an environmentally-friendly stance in U.S. politics, as the Obama administration has discovered,, usually means finding some means of demonstrating how environmentalism actually promotes economic growth, provides more jobs or adds to national greatness. Otherwise, as the recent Bush administration illustrated, environmental politics are sidetracked, downplayed, and shortchanged in the general workings of the American state *per se* as well as the ordinary concerns of political science as an academic discipline.

Given the greater importance of economic growth, the project of greening politics might still leave the environment open for continued neglect where it serves as a space for lip service, add-ons or a means to other ends. The Great Recession of 2008–2009 only has reemphasized these tendencies. If green politics is to succeed today, ecomodernization, natural capitalism or banal ecologism are probably its best hopes. Hence, as President Obama's economic recovery plans are unveiled, green agendas get layered over industrial policy, jobs policy, energy policy, recreation policy, technology policy, and science policy. These more diffuse and decentered concerns are where "the environment" or "ecology" is finding their best political traction, but at least they seem to be gaining getting some solid forward traction after many years of mean-spirited neglect.

REFERENCES

Bach, D., & Rosner, H. (2008). *Go Green, Live Rich: 50 Simple Ways to Save the Earth (and Get Rich Trying.* New York: Broadway Books.

Barber, B. (1984). *Strong Democracy.* Berkeley: University of California Press.

Barry, J. (1999). *Rethinking Green Politics.* London: Sage.

Barry, J., & Eckersley, R (Eds.) (2005). *The Global Ecological Crisis and the Nation-State.* Cambridge, MA: MIT Press.

Barry, J., & Eckersley, R. (Eds.) (2005). *The State and Global Environmental Crisis.* Cambridge, MA: MIT Press.

Baumann, Z. (2000). *Liquid Modernity.* Cambridge: Polity Press.

Beck, U. (2000). *What is Globalization?* Oxford: Blackwell.

Beck, U. (1992). *The Risk Society.* London: Sage.

Benton, T. (Ed.) (1994). *The Greening of Marx.* New York: Guilford.

Benton, T. (1993). Natural Relations: Ecology, Animal Rights and Social Justice. London: Verso.

Bookchin, M. (1995). *From Urbanization to Cities: Towards a New Politics of Citizenship.* London: Cassell.

Bookchin, M. (1971). *Post-Scarcity Anarchism.* San Francisco: Ramparts Books.

Brown, L. (1981). *Building a Sustainable Society.* Washington, DC: W. W. Norton.

Bullard, R. (1990). *Dumping in Dixie: Race, Class and Environmental Quality.* Boulder, CO: Westview Press.

Bullard, R. (1993). *Confronting Environmental Racism: Voices from the Grassroots.* Boston: South End Press.

Buttel, F. H. (1998). "Some Observations on States, World Orders, and the Politics of Sustainability," *Organization and Environment* (11:3)

Carson, R. (1962). *Silent Spring*. New York: Houghton Mifflin.

Commoner, B. (1971). *The Closing Circle: Nature, Man, and Technology*. New York: Knopf.

Conca, K. (2006). Governing Water: Contentious Transnational Politics and Global Institution Building. Cambridge, MA: MIT Press.

Croway Jr, S. (1953). *Resources and the American Dream*. New York: Ronala Press.

Diamond, J. (2005). *Collapse*. New York: Viking.

Dobson, A. (2007). *Green Political Thought*. 4th ed. London: Routledge.

Dobson, A., & Bell, D. (Eds.) (2006). Introduction, *Environmental Citizenship*. Cambridge MA: MIT Press.

Dowie, M. (1995). *Losing Ground: American Environmentalism at the Close of the Twentieth Century*. Cambridge, MA: MIT Press.

Dryzek, J. (2000). *Deliberative Democracy and Beyond: Liberals, Critics, Contestations*. Oxford: Oxford University Press.

Eckersley, R. (2004). *The Green State: Rethinking Democracy and Sovereignty*. Cambridge, MA: MIT Press.

Goldman, M. (2005). *Imperial Nature: The World Bank and Struggles for Social Justice in the Age of Globalization*. New Haven, CT: Yale University Press.

Gore Jr. A. (2006). *An Inconvenient Truth*. Emmaus, PA: Rodale.

Gottlieb, R. (1993). *Forcing the Spring: The Transformation of the American Environment Movement*. Washington, DC: Island Press.

Hawken, P., Lovins, A.B., & Lovins, L.H. (1999). *Natural Capitalism*. Boston: Little Brown.

Herber, L. (1962). *Our Synthetic Environment*. New York: Knopf.

Jasanoff, S., & Martello, M.L. (Eds.) (2004) Earthly Politics: Local and Global in Environmental Governance. Cambridge, MA: MIT Press.

Lipschutz, R. D. (2003). *Global Environmental Politics: Power, Perspectives, and Practice*. Washington, DC: CQ Press.

Litfin, K. T. (1994). *Ozone Discourses: Science and Politics in Global Environmental Cooperation*. New York: Columbia University Press.

Luke, T. W. (1997). *Ecocritique: Contesting the Politics of Nature, Economy and Culture*. Minneapolis: University of Minnesota Press.

Luke, T. W. (1999a). *Capitalism, Democracy, and Ecology: Departing from Marx*. Urbana: University of Illinois Press.

Luke, T. W. (1999b). "Environmentality as Green Governmentality." *Discourses of the Environment*, ed. Eric Darier. Oxford: Blackwell, 1999. 121–151.

MacEachern, D. (2008). *Big Green Purse: Use Your Spending Power to Create A Cleaner, Greener World*. New York: Penguin.

Manes, C. (1990). *Green Rage: Radical Environmentalism and the Unmasking of Civilization*. Boston: Little Brown.

McDonough, W., & Braungart, M. (2002). *Cradle to Cradle: Remaking the Way Things Work*. New York: North Point Press.

McDonough, W. (1992). *The Hanover Principles: Design for Sustainability*. Charlottesville, VA: William McDonough & Partners.

McKibben, B. (1989). *The End of Nature*. Boston: Houghton Mifflin.

Mellor, M. (1992). *Breaking the Boundaries: For a Feminist Green Socialism*. London: Virago Press.

Merchant, C. (1980). *The Death of Nature? Women, Ecology and the Scientific Revolution*. New York: Harper and Row.

Mol, A.J.P. (2003). *Globalization and Environmental Reform*. Cambridge, MA: MIT Press.

Nordhaus, T., & Shellenberger, M. (2007). *Breakthrough: From the Death of Environmentalism to the Politics of Possibility*. Boston: Houghton Mifflin Company.

O'Neill, K. (2008). *The Environment and International Relations*. Cambridge: Cambridge University Press.

Ophuls, W. (1977). *Ecology and the Politics of Scarcity*. New York: W.H. Freeman.

Osborn, F. (1948). *Our Plundered Planet*. Boston: Little, Brown.

Paehlke, R. (2003). *Democracy's Dilemma: Environment, Social Equity and the Global Economy*. Cambridge, MA: MIT Press.

Pirages, D. (1978). *The Next Context for International Relations: Global Ecopolitics*. North Scituate, MA: Duxbury Press.

Plass, G. (1956a). Carbon Dioxide and the Climate. *American Scientist*, 44: 302–316.

Plass, G. (1956b). The Carbon Dioxide Theory of Climate Change, Tellus, vii, no. 2: 140–154.

Plass, G. (1959). Carbon Dioxide and the Planet. *Scientific American* (July): 41–47.

Rosenthal, E. (2007). "UN Report Describes Risks of Inaction on Climate Change," *New York Times* (November 17): A1.

Sachs, W (Ed.) (1993). *Global Ecology: A New Arena of Political Conflict*. London: Zed Books.

Salleh, A. (1997). *Ecofeminism as Politics: Nature, Marx, and the Postmodern*. London: Zed Books.

Schnaiberg, A. (1980). *The Environment: From Surplus to Scarcity*. New York: Oxford University Press.

Shellenberger, M., & Nordhaus, T. (2004). *The Death of Environmentalism: Global Warming Politics in a Post-Environmental World*. Accessed at www.thebreakthrough.org/images/Death_of_Environmentalism.pdf.

Smith, N. (1984). *Uneven Development. Nature, Capital and the Production of Space*. Oxford: Blackwell.

Stern, N. (2007). *The Economics of Climate Change*. Cambridge: Cambridge University Press.

Vanderheiden, S. (2008). *Atmospheric Justice: A Political Theory of Climate Change*. New York: Oxford University Press.

Vanderheiden, S. (Ed.) (2008). *Political Theory and Global Climate Change*. Cambridge, MA: MIT Press.

Vogt, W. (1947). The Road to Survival. London: Victor Gollancz.

von Weizacker, E, Lovins, A., & Lovins, H. (1998). *Factor Four: Doubling Wealth—Halving Resource Use: A Report to the Club of Rome*. New York: Kogan Page.

Wapner, P. (1996). *Environmental Activism and World Civic Politics*. Albany: State University of New York Press.

World Commission on the Environment (WCED) (1987). *Our Common Future: The World Commission on Environment and Development*. Oxford: Oxford University Press.

Yarrow, J. (2008). *How to Reduce Your Carbon Footprint: 365 Simple Ways to Save Energy, Resources, and Money*. London: Duncan Baird Publishers.

Young, O. R. (2002). *The Institutional Dimensions of Environmental Change: Fit, Interplay and Scale*. Cambridge, MA: MIT Press.

Young, O. R. (1994). *International Governance: Protecting the Environment in a Stateless Society*. Ithaca, NY: Cornell University Press.

GREENING PHILOSOPHY[1]

STEVEN BEST

THE CURRENT CRISIS

The current Kabuki theater of political drama in American culture, as it is plays before a televised audience, masks the fact that we live in an unprecedented era of social and ecological crisis. Predatory transnational corporations such as ExxonMobil and Maxxam are pillaging the planet, destroying ecosystems, pushing species into extinction, and annihilating Indigenous peoples and traditional ways of life. War, globalization, and destruction of peoples, species, and ecosystems march in lockstep: militarization supports the worldwide imposition of the "free market" system, and its growth and profit imperatives thrive though the exploitation of humans, animals, and the Earth (see Kovel 2002; Tokar 1997; Bannon and Collier 2003).

Against the mindless optimism of technophiles, the denials of skeptics, and complacency of the general public, I depart from the premise that there is a global environmental crisis which is the most urgent issue facing us today.[2] If humanity does not address ecological problems immediately and with radical measures that target causes not symptoms, severe, world-altering consequences will play out over a long-term period and will plague future generations. Signs of major stress of the world's eco-systems are everywhere, from shrinking forests and depleted fisheries to vanishing wilderness and global climate change.

Ours is an era of global warming, rainforest destruction, species extinction, and chronic resource shortages that provoke wars and conflicts such as in Iraq, Afghanistan, and Libya. While five great extinction crises have already transpired on this planet, the last one occurring 65 million years ago in the age of the dinosaurs, we are now living amidst the sixth extinction crisis, this time caused by human not natural causes. Human populations have always devastated their environment and thereby their societies, but they have never intervened in the planet's ecosystem to the extent they have altered the average temperatures and every interlinked ecosystem.

We now confront the "end of nature" where no natural force, no breeze or ripple of water, has not been affected by the human presence (McKribben 2006). This is especially true with nanotechnology and biotechnology. Rather than confronting this crisis and scaling back human presence and aggravating actions, humans are making it worse. Human population rates continue to swell, as awakening giants such as India and China move toward western consumer lifestyles, exchanging rice bowls for burgers and bicycles for SUVs. The human

S. D. Fassbinder, A. J. Nocella II and R. Kahn (Eds.), Greening the Academy: Ecopedagogy Through the Liberal Arts, 63–76.

presence on this planet is like a meteor plummeting to the Earth, but it has already struck and the reverberations are rippling everywhere.

Despite the proliferating amount of solid, internationally assembled scientific data supporting the reality of global climate change and ecological crisis, there are still so-called environmental "skeptics," "realists," and "optimists" who deny the problems, often compiling or citing data paid for by ExxonMobil. Senator James Inhofe has declared global warming to be a "myth" that is damaging to the US economy. He and others revile environmentalists as "alarmists," "extremists," and "eco-terrorists" who threaten the American way of life.[3]

There is a direct and profound relationship between global capitalism and ecological destruction. The capitalist economy lives or dies on constant growth, accumulation, and consumption of resources. The environmental crisis is inseparable from the social crisis, whereby centuries ago a market economy disengaged from society and ruled with its alien and destructive imperatives. The crisis in ecology is ultimately a crisis in democracy, as transnational corporations arise and thrive through the destruction of popular sovereignty.

The western environment movement has advanced its cause for over three decades now, but we are nonetheless *losing ground* in the battle to preserve species, ecosystems, and wilderness (Dowie 1995; Speth 2004). Increasingly, calls for moderation, compromise, and the slow march through institutions can be seen as treacherous and grotesquely inadequate. In the midst of predatory global capitalism and biological meltdown, "reasonableness" and "moderation" seem to be entirely unreasonable and immoderate, as "extreme" and "radical" actions appear simply as necessary and appropriate. As eco-primitivist Derrick Jensen observes, "We must eliminate false hopes, which blind us to real possibilities."

The current world system is inherently destructive and unsustainable; if it cannot be reformed or "greened": it must be transcended through revolution at all levels—economic, political, legal, cultural, technological, and, most fundamentally, conceptual. The struggles and changes must be as deep, varied, and far-reaching as the root of the problems.

A CRITICAL HISTORY APPROACH

To understand where the environmental movement must go, it is necessary to understand where it has been. To avoid serious mistakes in organizing future struggles, one must know what problems existed in the past and persist in the present. It is increasingly understood that environmental history must be a social history, one that works with a broad definition of "environment" that encompasses both wilderness and urban settings, as it examines how various groups fought environmental battles.

One can chart three main stages in the evolution of the US environmental movement: its beginnings in the 19th century, the rise of mainstream environmentalism in the 1970s, and the reaction against it and move toward more radical, democratic, and diverse positions and struggles. I will quickly lay these out and then suggest what a revolutionary environmentalism might look like. As one can see, the US environmental movement has been based on economic privilege, whiteness, and male-domination, but these limitations are being overcome in dynamic ways with the emergence of revolutionary environmentalism.

FIRST WAVE: 19TH CENTURY ORIGINS

One must look to the 19th century roots of modern environmentalism to understand why, in the US and elsewhere, the environmental movement is still comprised predominantly of middle or upper class white people.

The modern environmental movement emerged in England and the US in the mid-19th century, growing out of the concerns of the Romantics and conservationists. As industrialization and capitalist markets reshaped landscapes and societies, figures such as William Blake, William Wordsworth, Ralph Waldo Emerson, and Henry David Thoreau grew alarmed at the destruction of forests and countryside and degradation of human spirit in market relations and mechanistic worldviews. Following the lead of Jean-Jacques Rousseau who declared everything natural to be free and good (before corrupted by society), they praised nature as the antithesis to all that was rotten in modern life, and extolled the beauty and divinity of the wild.

Overall, the founders and pioneers of American environmentalism were white, male, elites; they advanced important new sensibilities within the mechanistic and anthropocentric frameworks of the time, and sparked the creation of environmental protection laws and national parks. Yet many were classist, racist, sexist, and misanthropic. Their emphasis on rugged individualism and solitary journeys into wilderness hardly encouraged social awareness or activism. They sought to preserve nature for their enjoyment, not for the benefit of the working classes and poor. Their understanding of "environment" was of a pristine wilderness, such as could be enjoyed exclusively by people of privilege and leisure.

Unfortunately, this elitist and myopic definition discounted the *urban* environment that plagued working classes. If one's definition of "environment" focuses on "wilderness" apart from cities, communities, and health issues, then it will exclude the plight and struggles of women, people of color, workers, children, and other victims of oppression who work, live, play and attend school in toxic surroundings that sicken, deform, and kill. It fails to see and draw connections between environmental and social problems, and thus ignores crucial issues of race, class, and gender, all of which must be integrated into an effective environmental movement of the future.

Environmental historians also have often reproduced these biases and blind spots in one dimensional narratives.[4] The standard environmental history moves from the Romantics and conservationists to 20th century pioneers such as Aldo Leopold and Rachel Carson, and climaxes with a sea of more white faces in the streets of the first Earth Day on April 22, 1970. Long before Rachel Carson, however, African-American abolitionists opposed the use of chemicals such as arsenic being used to grow crops. Women played a significant role in furthering the aesthetic appreciation of nature; Alice Hamilton was a pioneer of occupational health and safety; and Jane Addams' activism on oppressed people was inseparable from her push for better housing, working, and sanitation conditions.

Only recently did environmentalists themselves address the race, gender, and class biases of the movement. The elitist white biases of the 19th century movement resurfaced in problematic form in the 20th century, whether in Paul Ehrlich's book, *The Population Bomb* (1968), which demonizes people of color as mindless breeders, calls for forced sterilization, and invokes eugenic themes. Racism, reactionary, and elitist positions also informed the anti-immigration and misanthropic attitudes of Edward Abbey and Dave Foremen of Earth First!, or the often asocial perspective of deep ecology.[5]

SECOND WAVE: THE MODERN MAINSTREAM

Rachel Carson's book, *Silent Spring* (1963), is often credited with sparking the modern environmental movement. It captured the attention of the nation with its vivid prose and dire warning of the systemic poisoning effects of newly invented pesticides, especially DDT.

But the modern environmental movement did not arise because of Rachel Carson, or other key individuals such as Murray Bookchin and Barry Commoner. It emerged and sustained itself in the larger *social context* of the 1960s, as shaped by the struggles of the "new social movements" (radical students, countercultural youth, Black liberation, feminism, Chicano/Mexican-American, peace, anti-nuclear, and gay/lesbian/bisexual/transsexual).[6] These movements, in turn, arose amidst the turmoil spawned by the civil rights struggles of the 1950s.

Significantly, in the early stages of a social learning process, environmentalism was not initially embraced by new social movements and radicals. Blacks and a number of white radicals rejected environmentalism as a bourgeois concern, elitist and racist cause, and a dangerous diversion from the hard-won focus on civil rights and the Vietnam War. The political mindset was dominated by humanist and anthropocentric concerns, and even "progressive" figures and groups were unprepared to embrace an emerging new ethic that challenged human species identity as Lord and Master of the wild. As they began to take shape in the 1960s, environmental concerns were— and mostly remain—"enlightened anthropocentric" worries that if people do not better protect "their" environment, human existence will be gravely threatened.

As the new social movements began to wane, however, and various types of pollution became concrete and crucial issues for communities, environmentalism became a mass concern and new political movement. At the turn of the decade in 1970 the future of the environmental movement seemed bright. Riding the crest of 1960s turmoil and protests that were beginning to wane, environmentalism became a mass concern and new political movement. The first Earth Day on April 22, 1970 drew 20 million people to the streets, lectures, and teach-ins throughout the nation, making it the largest expression of public support for any cause in American history. In this "decade of environmentalism," the US Congress passed new laws such as the Clean Air Act, and in 1970 President Nixon created the Environmental Protection Agency. Some environmental organizations such as the Sierra Club (founded by John Muir in 1892) existed before the new movement, but grew in members, influence, and wealth like never before. The larger groups—known as the "Gang of Ten"—planted roots in Washington, DC, where they clamored for respectability and influence with politicians and polluters.

The movement's insider/growth-oriented recipe for success, however, quickly turned into a formula for disaster. Many battles were won in treating the symptoms of a worsening ecological crisis, but the war against its causes was lost, or rather never fought in the first place. Potentially a radical force and check on capitalist profit, accumulation, and growth dynamics, the US environmental movement was largely a white, male, middle-class affair, cut off from the populist forces and the street energy that helped spawn it. Co-opted and institutionalized, in bed with government and industry, mindful of the "taboo against social intervention in the production system" (Commoner), defense of Mother Earth became just another bland, reformist, compromised-based, single-interest lobbying effort.

Increasingly, the Gang of Ten resembled the corporations they criticized and, in fact, evolved into corporations and self-interested money making machines. Within behemoths such as the Wilderness Society, the Environmental Defense Fund, and the Sierra Club, decision-making originated from professionals at the top who neither had, nor sought, citizen input from the grassroots level. The Gang of Ten hired accountants and MBAs over activists, they spent more time on mass mailing campaigns than actual advocacy, and their riches were squandered largely on sustaining bloated budgets and six-figure salaries rather than protecting the environment. They brokered compromise deals to win votes for legislation that was watered-down, constantly revised to strengthen corporate interests, and poorly enforced. They not only did not fund grassroots groups, they even worked against them at times, forming alliances instead with corporate exploiters. Perversely, Gang of Ten organizations often legitimated and profited from greenwashing campaigns that presented corporate enemies of the environment as benevolent stewards and beacons of progress.[7] Like their 19th century predecessors, they too were largely white, male, middle-class, promoting environmentalism as a single-issue cause, aloof from problems related to race and class. They became a part of the problem rather than the solution. New forms of struggle evolved from necessity.

THIRD WAVE: DIRECT ACTION, GRASS ROOTS, AND ALLIANCE POLITICS

The emerging groups of the third wave of US environmentalism were profoundly dissatisfied with a mainstream environmental movement that was corporate, careerist, compromising, and divorced from the complex of social-environmental issues affecting women, the poor, workers, and people of color.

Some groups worked through legal channels at the grass roots level, attacking corporations and effecting change in ways that the mainstream organizations could or would not do. Others viewed the state as irredeemably corrupted by the influence of money and corporate interests, with some turning to sabotage and direct action tactics. These include Paul Watson and the Sea Shepard Conservation Society (Watson 2002), the Animal Liberation Front (Best and Nocella 2004), Earth First! (Foreman 1991; Manes 1990; List 1993; Scarce 1990; Foreman and Haywood 2002; Taylor 1995), and the Earth Liberation Front (Rosebraugh 2004; Best and Nocella 2006; Akerman 2003; Pickering 2002; Taylor 2006). Still others sought to build new kinds of alliances and link environmentalism to social justice movement. These tendencies include ecofeminism, the environmental justice movement, the international Green movement, Native Americans in the u.s. (Churchill 1993), southern groups such as the Zapatistas (Leon 2001), Black liberation groups such as MOVE, and the alter-globalization movements building alliances against global capitalism, such as were dramatically visible in the Battle of Seattle in 1999 (Danaher and Burbach 2000; Welton and Wolf 2001; Solnit 2004; Yuen, Burton-Rose, and Katsiaficas 2004).

One of the most significant forms of environmentalism took the form of a broad social movement that promoted alliances, inclusiveness, and diversity. A critical part of the grassroots revolution was the "environmental justice" movement that engaged environment, race, and social justice issues as one complex. Building on a long and sordid US tradition of racism and discrimination, corporations and polluters targeted the poor, disenfranchised, and people of color to produce and discard their lethal substances. To protect their communities from *real* "eco-terrorism," Native Americans, Asian Americans, Blacks, and Hispanics organized and fought back, proving that marginalized did not mean powerless and that environmentalism did not only have a white face. Acknowledging the importance of defending the wilderness, the environmental justice movement sought to build a multi-issue, multiracial environmental movement.

Similarly, the alter-globalization movement recognizes global capitalism as the common enemy of world peoples. As dramatically evident in the 1999 "Battle of Seattle," among dozens of heated battles around the world thereafter, "anti-" or "alter-globalization" groups recognized their common interests and fates, and formed unprecedented kinds of alliances (Brecher, Costello, Smith 2000; Kahn and Kellner 2006). The interests of workers, animals, and the environment alike were gravely threatened in a new world order where the WTO could override the laws of any nation state as "barriers to free trade." Global capitalism was the common enemy recognized by world groups and peoples. Bridging national boundaries, North-South divisions, different political causes, and borders between activists of privileged and non-privileged communities, alter-globalization movements prefigured the future of revolutionary environmentalism as a global, anti-capitalist/anti-imperialist alliance politics, diverse in class, race, and gender composition.

REVOLUTIONARY ENVIRONMENTALISM

In the last three decades, there has been growing awareness that environmentalism cannot succeed without social justice and social justice cannot be realized without environmentalism. To be sure, defending forests and protecting whales are crucial actions to take, for they protect evolutionary processes and ecological systems vital to the planet and all species and peoples within it. Yet at the same time, it is also critical to fight side-by-side with oppressed peoples in order to address all forms of environmental destruction and build a movement far greater in numbers and strength than possible with a single-issue focus. Such a holistic orientation can be seen in the international Green network, the u.s. environmental justice movement, Earth First! efforts (as initiated by Judi Bari) to join with timber workers, alter-globalization channels, Zapatista coalition building, and often in the communiqués and actions of ALF and ELF activists. Examples of broad alliance politics are visible also in recent efforts to build bridges among animal, Earth, and Black liberationists and anti-imperialists (Best and Nocella 2006). These various dynamics are part and parcel of the emergence of global revolutionary environmentalism.

There are key similarities between what has been called "radical environmentalism"—which includes social ecology (Bookchin 1986), deep ecology (Tobias 1984; Sessions and Devall 1985), ecofeminism (Diamond and Orenstein 1990), Earth First!, and primitivism (Zerzan 2002)—and what I term "revolutionary environmentalism."[8] Among other things, both approaches reject mainstream environmentalism, attack core ideologies and/or institutions that have caused the ecological crisis, often adopt spiritual outlooks and see nature as sacred, reject the binary opposition separating humans from nature, and in many cases defend or adopt illegal tactics such as civil disobedience or monkeywrenching (Abbey 2000). However, a key distinguishing trait of revolutionary environmentalism is that it supports and/or employs illegal tactics ranging from property destruction for the purpose of economic sabotage to guerilla warfare and armed struggle, recognizing that violent methods of resistance are often appropriate against fascist regimes and right-wing dictatorships. Revolutionary environmentalism seeks to counter forces of oppression with equally potent forms of resistance, and uses militant tactics when they are justified, necessary, and effective. With the advance of the global capitalist juggernaut and increasing deterioration of the Earth's ecological systems, ever more people may realize that no viable future will arise without militant actions and large-scale social transformation, a process that requires abolishing global capitalism and imperialism, and would thereby embrace revolutionary environmentalism.

As evident in the communiqués of the ALF and ELF, as well as in the views of Black liberationists, Native Americans, anarchists, and anti-imperialists, many activists are explicitly revolutionary in their rhetoric, analysis, vision, actions, and political identities. Revolutionary environmentalists renounce reformist approaches that aim only to manage the symptoms of the global ecological crisis and never dare or think to probe its underlying dynamics and causes. Revolutionary environmentalists seek to end the destruction of nature and peoples, not merely to slow its pace, temper its effects, or plug holes in a dam set to burst. They don't act to "manage" the catastrophic consequences of the project to dominate nature; they work to abolish the very hierarchy whereby humans live as if they were separate from nature and pursue the deluded goal of mastery and control. The objectives thought necessary by revolutionary environmentalists cannot be realized within the present world system, and require a rupture with it.

Revolutionary environmentalists recognize the need for fundamental changes on many levels, such as with human psychologies (informed by anthropocentric worldviews, values, and identities), interpersonal relations (mediated by racism, sexism, speciesism, ageism, classism, homophobia, and elitism), social institutions (governed by authoritarian, plutocratic, and corrupt or pseudo-democratic forms), technologies (enforcing labor and exploitation imperatives and driven by fossil-fuels that cause pollution and global warming), and the prevailing economic system (an inherently destructive and unsustainable global capitalism driven by profit, production, and consumption imperatives). Revolutionary environmentalists see "separate" problems as related to the larger system of global capitalism and reject the reformist notion of "green capitalism" as a naïve oxymoron. They repudiate the logics of marketization, economic growth, and industrialization as inherently violent, exploitative, and destructive, and seek ecological, democratic, and egalitarian alternatives.

As the dynamics that brought about global warming, rainforest destruction, species extinction, and poisoning of communities are not reducible to any single factor or cause—be it agricultural society, the rise of states, anthropocentrism, speciesism, patriarchy, racism, colonialism, industrialism, technocracy, or capitalism—all radical groups and orientations that can effectively challenge the ideologies and institutions implicated in domination and ecological destruction have a relevant role to play in the global social-environmental struggle. While standpoints such as deep ecology, social ecology, ecofeminism, animal liberation, Black liberation, Native American autonomy and liberation, and the ELF are all important, none can accomplish systemic social transformation by itself. Working together, however, through a diversity of critiques and tactics that mobilize different communities, a flank of militant groups and positions can drive a battering ram into the structures of power and domination and open the door to a new future.

Thus, revolutionary environmentalism is not a *single group*, but rather a *collective movement* rooted in specific tactics and goals (such as just discussed), and organized as multi-issue, multiracial alliances that can mount effective opposition to capitalism and other modes of domination. I do not have in mind here a super-movement that embraces all struggles, but rather numerous alliance networks that may form larger collectives with other groups in fluid and dynamic ways, and are as global in vision and reach as is transnational capitalism.[9] Although there is diversity in unity, there must also be unity in diversity. Solidarity can emerge in recognition of the fact that all forms of oppression are directly or indirectly related to the values, institutions, and *system* of global capitalism and related hierarchical structures. To be unified and effective, however, anti-capitalist and anti-imperialist alliances require mutual sharing, respectful learning, and psychological growth, such that, for instance, black liberationists, ecofeminists, and animal liberationists can help one another overcome racism, sexism, and speciesism.

New social movements and Greens have failed to realize their radical potential. They have abandoned their original demands for radical social change and become integrated into capitalist structures that have eliminated "existing socialist countries" as well as social democracies in a global triumph of neoliberalism. A new revolutionary force must therefore emerge, one that will build on the achievements of classical democratic, libertarian socialist, and anarchist traditions; incorporate radical green, feminist, and Indigenous struggles; synthesize animal, Earth, and human liberation standpoints; and build a global social-ecological revolution capable of abolishing transnational capitalism so that just and ecological societies can be constructed in its place.

ECOLOGICAL DEMOCRACY OR BARBARISM: TOWARD A EVOLUTIONARY
FOURTH WAVE OF ENVIRONMENTALISM

Windows of opportunity are closing. The actions that human beings now collectively take or fail to take will determine whether the future is hopeful or bleak. The revolution that this planet desperately needs at this crucial juncture will involve, among other things, a movement to abolish anthropocentrism, speciesism, racism, patriarchy, homophobia, and prejudices and hierarchies of all kinds. In a revolutionary process, people throughout the world will reconstitute social institutions in a form that promotes autonomy, self-determination of nations and peoples, decentralization and democratization of political life, non-market relations, guaranteed "rights" for humans and animals, an ethics of respect for nature and all life, and the harmonization of the social and natural worlds.

To conclude, I want to raise the question: Is there a direction or coherence in the history of environmentalism? We believe there is, along three main lines:

1. *Broadening* of the scope and meaning of environmentalism: whereas the first two waves of u.s. environmentalism were predominantly white, male, and middle class in composition and outlook, and were rooted in a dualistic concept of the "environment" defined in terms of physical wilderness divorced from urban and social environments, the environmental movement since the 1970s has become increasingly diversified and broadened. "Environmentalism" today is defined and shaped by a host of groups and perspectives, and is inseparably linked to social issues and struggles.

2. *Connecting* the various branches of a social-environmental movement: the last few decades show a deepening awareness that all liberation struggles are interconnected, such that no one is possible without the others, thereby leading

to the concept of "total revolution" that unites in one struggle human, animal, and Earth liberation. *Igniting a Revolution: Voices in Defense of the Earth* (Best and Nocella, 2006) shows the diversity of the new politics and tendencies toward making new connections and alliances.

3. *Radicalizing* political struggle: analysis of modern environmentalism in the u.s. and elsewhere reveals a dialectic whereby increasingly radical forms of struggle emerge when necessary, when a prior strategy proves inadequate and effective for protecting the Earth. Thus, the legal-based tactics of mainstream environmentalism, which turned ecology into just another bureaucratic interest movement, ultimately gave rise to more militant tactics involving direct action, sabotage, arson, and armed struggle. The future of environmental politics is unpredictable, but in this accelerated and desperate stage of ecological crisis and biological meltdown, radicals will defend the Earth "by any means necessary."

Revolutionary environmentalism is based on the realization that *politics as usual just won't cut it anymore.* We will always lose if we play by their rules rather than invent new forms of struggle, new social movements, and new sensibilities. The defense of the Earth requires immediate and decisive: logging roads need to be blocked, driftnets need to be cut, and cages need to be emptied. But these are defensive actions, and in addition to these tactics, radical movements and alliances must be built from the perspective total liberation.

A new revolutionary politics will build on the achievements of democratic, libertarian socialist, and anarchist traditions. It will incorporate radical green, feminist, and Indigenous struggles. It will merge animal, Earth, and human standpoints in a total liberation struggle against global capitalism and its omnicidal grow-or-die logic.

Radical politics must reverse the growing power of the state, mass media, and corporations to promote egalitarianism and participatory democratization at all levels of society – political, cultural, and economic. It must dismantle all asymmetrical power relations and structures of hierarchy, including that of humans over animals and the Earth. Radical politics is impossible without the revitalization of citizenship and the re-politicization of life, which begins with forms of education, communication, culture, and art that anger, awaken, inspire, and empower people toward action and change.

This is a pivotal time in history, a crossroads for the future of life. Windows of opportunity are closing. The actions that human beings now collectively take or fail to take will determine whether the future is hopeful or bleak. While the result is horrible to contemplate, our species may not meet this challenge and drive itself into the same oblivion as it drove countless other species. There is no economic or technological fix for the crises we confront, the only solution lies in radical change at all levels.

Clearly, there is no guarantee that *Homo sapiens* will survive in the near future, as the dystopian visions of films such as *Mad Max* or *Waterworld* may actually be realized. But nor is there is any promise that revolutionary environmentalism can or will arise, given problems such as the factionalism and egoism that typically tears political groups apart and/or the fierce political repression always directed against resistance movements.

Amidst so many doubts and uncertainties, there is nonetheless no question whatsoever that the quality of the future—if humanity and other imperiled species have one—depends on the strength of global resistance movements and the possibilities for revolutionary change.

NOTES

[1]   Much of this article was taken from the Introduction co-authored with Anthony J. Nocella II in *Igniting a Revolution: Voices in Defense of the Earth* (Best and Nocella 2006), which was republished in *Green Theory and Praxis* journal retrieved from http://greentheoryandpraxis.org/journal/index.php/journal/article/view/15/16, Vol 2, No. 2, 2006.

[2]   The claim that we currently are witnessing an advanced ecological "crisis," upon which the argument for revolutionary struggle rests, means that there is an emergency situation in the ecology of the Earth as a whole that needs urgent attention. If we do not address ecological problems immediately and with radical measures that target causes not symptoms, severe, world-altering consequences will play out over a long-term period. Signs of major stress of the world's eco-systems are everywhere, from denuded forests and depleted fisheries to vanishing wilderness and global climate change. As one indicator of massive disruption, the proportion of species human beings are driving to extinction "might easily reach 20 percent by 2022 and rise as high as 50 percent or more thereafter" (Wilson 2002). Given the proliferating amount of solid, internationally assembled scientific data supporting the ecological crisis claim, it can no longer be dismissed as "alarmist;" the burden of proof, rather has shifted to those "skeptics," "realists," and "optimists" in radical denial of the growing catastrophe to prove why complacency is not blindness and insanity. For reliable data on the crisis, see the various reports, papers, and annual *Vital Signs* and *State of the World* publications by the Worldwatch Institute. On the impact of *Homo sapiens* over time, see "The Pleistocene-Holocene Event," http://rewilding.org/thesixthgreatextinction.htm. On the serious environmental effects of agribusiness and global meat and dairy production/consumption systems (which include deforestation, desertification, water pollution, species extinction, resource waste, and global warming), (Robbins 2001).

[3]   For elaboration of the position of corporate interest, US. law enforcement, and others that spawn the propaganda that the ELF and Earth First! are "ecoterrorists," see Long (2004), Arnold (1997), and Lewis (2005).

[4]   For an example of a standard, single-focus narrative on the history of u.s. environmentalism (Nash 1967). To read an alternative, far broader account that links environmental and social history by including the fight for safe working and living conditions and the struggles of women, labor, and others (Gottlieb 1993). Marcy Darnovsky (1992) notes that "Too sharp a focus on wilderness blurs the environmental significance of everyday life...In limiting their scope as they do, the standard [environmental] histories contribute to still-widespread associations of the environment as a place separate from daily life and innocent of social relations" (p. 28).

[5]   far and away, the harshest critic of deep ecology, Earth First!, and primitivism—all reviled as being racist, misanthropic, mystical, irrational, and atavistic—is social ecologist Murray Bookchin (Bookchin 1995). Although Bookchin makes a number of important points against these movements, he often takes statements out of context and fails to account for the diversity and competing divisions within groups, such as existed in Earth First! between the "wilders" (e.g., Dave Foreman and Christopher Manes) and the social-oriented "holies" (e.g., Judi Bari and Darryl Cherney). For critiques of Bookchin's one-dimensional readings of deep ecology and Earth First!, see Taylor's article "Earth First! and Global Narratives of Popular Ecological Resistance"in *Ecological Resistance Movements: The Global Emergence of Radical and Popular Environmentalism* (Taylor 1995) also see Taylor's essay, "The Religion and Politics of Earth First!" (1991).

[6]   For a historical and critical analysis of new social movements Boggs (1987).
[7]   For examples of greenwashing and "environmental" groups serving the cause of corporate propaganda (Dowie 1995; Rampton and Stauber 1999).
[8]   It is critical to point out that contributors to this volume use different terms to talk about similar or the same things; thus, in addition to "revolutionary environmentalism," one will also see references to "radical environmentalism," "radical ecology," or "revolutionary ecology." It is natural that different people discussing new ecological resistance movements will use different terminology, and we did not attempt to impose our own discourse of "revolutionary environmentalism" on any of the authors, although some do use the term "revolutionary environmentalism." While there is general consensus on the need for a militant resistance movement and revolutionary social transformation, we leave it to the reader to interpret and compare the different philosophical and political perspectives.
[9]   In 1996, for instance, the Zapatistas organized a global "encuentro" during which over 3,000 grassroots activists and intellectuals from 42 countries assembled to discuss strategies for a worldwide struggle against neoliberalism. In response to the Zapatistas' call for an "intercontinental network of resistance, recognizing differences and acknowledging similarities," the People's Global Action Network was formed, a group explicitly committed to anti-capitalist, anti-imperialist, and ecological positions (see http://www.nadir.org/nadir/initiativ/agp/en/index.htm). For more examples of global politics and networks that report on news, actions, and campaigns from around the world, covering human rights, animal rights, and environmental struggles, see *One World* (http://www.oneworld.net/), *Protest.Net (*http://www.protest.net/), and *Indymedia* (http://www.indymedia.org/en/index.shtml).

REFERENCES

Abbey, E. (2000). *The monkey wrench gang*. New York, NY: HarperCollins Publishers Inc.

Akerman, G. A. (Winter, 2003). *Beyond arson? A threat assessment of the Earth Liberation Front*. Terrorism and Political Violence, Vol. *15*, No. 4.

Arnold, R. (1997). *Ecoterror: The violent agenda to save nature, the world of the Unabomber*. Bellevue, WA: Free Enterprise Press.

Bannon, I., & Collier, P. (Eds.) (2003). *Natural resources and violent conflict: Options and actions*. Washington, DC: The World Bank.

Brecher, J., Costello, T., & Smith B. (2000). *Globalization from below: The power of solidarity*. Cambridge, MA: South End Press.

Best, S. (January 2006). "Senator James Inhofe: Top terrorist threat to the planet," IMPACT Press, Issue 59, 2006 (http://www.impactpress.com/articles/winter06/bestwinter06.html).

Best, S., & Nocella, A. J., II. (Eds.) (2006). *Igniting a revolution: Voices in defense of the earth*. Oakland, CA: AK Press.

Boggs, C. (1987). *Social movements and political power: Emerging forms of radicalism in the west*. Philadelphia, PA: Temple University Press.

Bookchin, M. (1995). *Re-enchanting humanity: A defense of the human spirit against anti-humanism, misanthropy, mysticism, and primitivism*. London, UK: Cassell.

Bookchin, M. (1986). *The modern crisis*. Philadelphia, PA: New Society Publishers.

Churchill, W. (1993). *Struggle for the land: Indigenous resistance to genocide ecocide and expropriation in contemporary North America*. Monroe, ME: Common Courage Press.

Danaher, K., & Burbach, R. (Eds.) (2000). *Globalize this! The battle against the World Trade Organization and corporate rule*. Monroe, ME: Common Courage Press.

Darnovsky, M. (October–December, 1992). *Stories less told: histories of US environmentalism*. Socialist Review. Vol. *22* No. 4. pp. 11–54.

Diamond, I., & Orenstein, G. F. (Eds.) (1990). *Reweaving the world: The emergence of ecofeminism*. San Francisco, CA: Sierra Club Books.

Dowie, M. (1995). *Losing ground: American environmentalism at the close of the twentieth century*. Cambridge, MA: MIT Press.

Ehrlich, P. R., & Ehrlich, A. H. (Eds.) (1990). *The population explosion.* New York, NY: Simon and Schuster Inc.

Foreman, D. (1991). *Confessions of an eco-warrior.* New York, NY: Harmony Books.

Foreman, D., & Haywood, B. (2002). *Ecodefense: A field guide to monkeywrenching.* Chico, CA: Abbzug Press.

Foster, J. B. (2005). *Organizing ecological revolution.* Monthly Review. Vol. 7 Num. 5; http://www. monthlyreview.org/1005jbf.htm.

Gottlieb, R. *Forcing the Spring: The Transformation of the American Environmental Movement.* Washington, DC: Island Press, 1993.

Indymedia. http://www.indymedia.org/en/index.shtml. June 1, 2006.

Kahn, R. (August, 2005). *From Herbert Marcuse to the Earth Liberation Front: Considerations for revolutionary ccopedagogy.* In Green Theory and Praxis: A Journal of Ecological Politics. CA: Fresno. Fresno State University, Political Science Department.

Kahn, R., & Kellner, D. (2006). *Resisting globalization.* In The Blackwell Companion to Globalization, Ed. by G. Ritzer, Malden, MA: Blackwell Publishers.

Kovel, J. (2002). *The enemy of nature: The end of capitalism or the end of the world?* New York, NY: Zed Books Ltd.

Leopold, A. (1949). *A sand county almanac.* New York, NY: Oxford University Press.

Lewis, J. (2005). Statement of John Lewis, Deputy Assistant Director, Federal Bureau of Investigation. Oversight on Eco-terrorism specifically examining the Earth Liberation Front ("ELF") and the Animal Liberation Front ("ALF"), U.S. Senate Committee on Environment & Public Works, May 18, 2005. Online at: http://epw.senate.gov/hearing_statements.cfm?id=237817 (accessed: 6/21/2005).

List, P. C. (1993). *Radical environmentalism: Philosophy and tactics.* Belmont, CA: Wadsworth Publishing Company.

Long, D. (2004). *Ecoterrorism.* New York, NY: Facts on File, Inc.

Nash, R. *Wilderness and the American Mind.* New Haven: Yale University Press, 1967.

Manes, C. (1990). *Green rage: Radical environmentalism and the unmaking of civilization.* Boston, MA: Little, Brown and Company.

Merchant, C. *Radical Ecology: The Search For a Livable World.* New York: Routledge, 1992.

McKribben, B. (2006). *The end of nature.* New York, NY: Random House Trade Paperbacks.

Nash, R. *Wilderness and the American Mind.* New Haven: Yale University Press, 1967.

Nocella, A., II & Walton, M. J. (2005). *Standing up to corporate greed: The Earth Liberation Front as domestic terrorist target number one.* Green Theory and Praxis: A Journal of Ecological Politics. CA: Fresno. Fresno State University Political Science Department.

One World UK (2011). *One World.* Retrieved May 22, 2006 from http://www.oneworld.net/.

Pickering, L. J. (2002). *The Earth Liberation Front: 1997–2002.* NY: South Wales. Arissa Publications.

Ponce de León, J. (Ed.) (2001). *Our word is our weapon: Selected writings subcomandante insurgente Marcos.* New York, NY: Seven Stories Press.

Protest.net (2011). Retrieved June 2, 2006 from http://www.protest.net

Rampton, S., & Stauber, J. (1999). *Toxic Sludge is Good For You!* Monroe, MN: Common Courage Press.

Robbins, J. (2001). *The food revolution: How your diet can help save your life and our world.* Berkeley, CA: Conari Press.

Rosebraugh, C. (2004). *Burning rage of a dying planet: Speaking for the Earth Liberation Front.* New York, NY: Lantern Books.

Scarce, R. (1990). *Eco-warriors: Understanding the radical environmental movement.* Chicago, IL: The Noble Press, Inc.

Solnit, D. (Ed.) (2004). *Globalize liberation: How to uproot the system and build a better world.* San Francisco, CA: City Light Books.

Speth, J. G. (2004). *Red Sky at Morning: America and the crisis of the global environment.* New Haven, CT: Yale University Press.

Taylor, B. R. (November–December 1991). *The religion and politics of Earth First!.* The Ecologist. Vol. 21 Num. 66.

Taylor, B. R. (Ed.) (1995). *Ecological resistance movements: The global emergence of radical and popular environmentalism.* Albany, NY: State University of New York Press.

Taylor, B.R. (2003, Winter). *Threat assessment and radical environmentalism.* Terrorism and political violence, Vol. *15*, No. 4.

Taylor, B.R. (2005). *Encyclopedia of religion and nature.* http://www.religionandnature.com/ern/sample. htm. London: UK. Thoemmes.

Taylor, H. (April 2006). *The radical environmental movement: Incorporating empire and the politics of nature.* In Green Theory and Praxis: A Journal of Ecological Politics. CA: Fresno. Fresno State University, Political Science Department.

Tokar, B. (1997). *Earth for sale: Reclaiming ecology in the age of corporate greenwash.* Boston, MA: South End Press.

Watson, P. (2002). *Seal wars: Twenty-five years on the front lines with the harp seals.* Toronto, ON: Key Porter Books.

Welton, N. and Wolf, L. (Eds.) (2001). *Global uprising: Confronting the tyrannies of the 21st century.* Gabriola Island, BC: New Society Publishers.

Yuen, E., Burton-Rose, D. and Katsiaficas, G. (Eds.) (2004). *Confronting capitalism: Dispatches from a global movement.* Brooklyn, NY: Soft Skull Press.

Wilson, Edward (2002). *The duture of life.* New York, NY: Knopf.

Zerzan, J. (2002). *Running on emptiness: The pathology of civilization.* Los Angeles, CA: Feral House.

GREENING ECONOMICS

MIRIAM KENNET AND MICHELLE GALE DE OLIVEIRA

INTRODUCTION TO THE CONCEPTS AND COMPETING FRAMEWORKS IN GREEN ECONOMICS

"If the bee disappears off the surface of the globe, then man would only have four years of life left," attributed popularly *to* Albert Einstein:*(Lean and Shawcross 2007).Colony Collapse Disorder is leading to bee losses at 30%. One third of the world's agricultural production relies on the European Honey Bee Apis mellifera. Climate change has forced the once common great yellow bumblebee (bombus distinguendus) to now cling only to the north of Scotland."* (Savage:2009: 15)

This year, the City of London and many other cities, saw mass demonstrations against the role of casino banking and the damage caused by capitalist economics speculators to the rest of society. St Paul's Cathedral was closed for the first time since the Second World War as protesters surrounded it. Nowhere has this frustration been more evident than in Egypt with the significance of the Arab Spring movement which was actually focused on (and largely unknown outside Egypt) the hideous corrupt backhanders, President Mubarak extracted from every single economics transaction made in the country.

> Meanwhile, Egyptian courts have charged former President Hosni Mubarak with corruption and sentenced in absentia his former finance minister, Youssef Boutros-Ghali, to 30 years in prison on charges of corruption and embezzlement of public money.

> Frustration with cronyism and corruption is a key grievance of those protesting in the streets in Libya, Syria, and Yemen as well. (Levey, BBC 2011).

The protests, this year, have had far reaching effects, from the "Indignants" in Spain, to the *Occupy Wall Street* movement in the financial district of New York, USA.

WHAT IS WRONG WITH MAINSTREAM ECONOMICS AND HOW WE ARE CHANGING IT TOGETHER

Occupy Wall Street, which began in September 2011, is a large scale and significant protest and movement at the heart of the financial sector in many cities in the USA and is supported by over 50% of Americans. Its slogan is "we are the 99%" which is the described as the difference in wealth between the very richest who are regarded

S. D. Fassbinder, A. J. Nocella II and R. Kahn (Eds.), Greening the Academy: Ecopedagogy Through the Liberal Arts, 77–106.

as causing and benefiting from the boom which led to the current "great economic contraction and downturn." Ordinary people around the developed world are being forced to pay for it with austerity measures, possibly the last denouement of a failing capitalist system which is turning on finances of "*the people*" to bail them out. The focus of the protest is against the power and influence of corporations, corporate greed and the banks as international corporations and the revolving door between them, the financial sector. Governments are powerless in the face of enormous funds these banks and corporations wield, which are mainly composed of the misappropriation of ordinary people's money in the name of shareholding and trickle down wealth theory. The Green Economics Institute also point out the revolving door between the large energy companies, media corporations and governments. Add to this mix, which is predicated on inequalities, the complete and disastrous corruption of representative democracy and its impotence in the face of a hollowed out western economy outsourced to countries with low human rights standards and slave labour conditions in a race to the bottom. The Green Economics Institute argues for a reinstatement of local or regional production, investment and reduction in the volumes of trade and volumes of speculative investment, and an increase in its quality and standards and a reversal of this "Global shift" in world trade and financial flows.

In 2012, the Earth Summit RIO + 20 will focus on the *Green economy and rethinking growth*. This chapter will explore how the above mentioned problems and characteristics of the current global economics system are all related. It will investigate how a Green Economy is one of the only solutions for creating a global economy providing social and environmental justice and which can help us to avoid a dangerous swing towards protectionism and "me first" solutions to a challenging era for human kind. Although complex and new, it is one of the solutions that have managed to really gain ground with governments around the world. It is also remarkable as this is a very radical solution that has arisen almost entirely from activist and campaigners, almost entirely green activists! Its stance is creating nothing less than a new world order! It no longer accepts that men own 99% of the world's assets or control the corridors of power and money. Its contribution amongst other things has been to create a climate in which it is now considered time to put a woman at the head of the IMF and world global financial institutions and to create an economy where the resources of the world, the global commons are truly shared and where nature and other species are given legal standing and the care and understanding to play their role on the earth.

Our system of capitalism and neoliberal economics has for the past 60 years encouraged and measured itself according to the paradigm of ever increasing economic growth fuelled by speculation and consumption, (and overconsumption) as well as capital betting on ever increasing GDP in developed countries. With the repeal (1999) of the Glass-Steagall Act – the final regulatory firewall to prevent speculation with the ordinary public's money was removed so that the economy became the stock for this huge betting ring. This capitalist investment was based on an ideology of an ever increasing growth, consumption and consumer and government's vociferous demand pegged to increase so much so that it used up much of the worlds resources and natural capital and started to eat up most of the world's economic capital.

Ever more inventive and complex instruments were created to bolster up ever more needy GDP growth. Many of these instruments were not even understood by the traders themselves. Unnoticed this casino capitalism started to extrude far beyond the real economy of the mature economies and of more developed countries, who began outsource their entire sections of their economies, especially production activities and such repetitive jobs as call centres and with them any social and environmental standards. This led to ever cheaper labour costs, a race to the bottom, and the only means to continue to satisfy this hungry machine was for it to use a form of slave labour from countries with very low standards of ethics or CSR or social provision. This became the cheapest form of labour on the planet and we now have more slaves on the planet than at any time in history. Far from abolition, the capitalist casino economy has been driven by commodities such as sex, war, guns, and car industries. These all make huge amounts of money and feed the capitalist machine.

However this very unpleasant machine itself is starting to implode with austerity measures being imposed on such ancient economies as Greece and such developed economies as Ireland, and formerly rich countries such as Iceland. The resultant unrest has been experienced from outside the European Commission's Charlemagne Building at the heart of Europe, into the streets of Greece and young people are protesting all over Europe from Spain to Italy about the drastic fall in jobs and living standards.

This machine, this capitalist system had at the head of its main institution, the IMF, a man well known for taking sexual advantage of women, with a string of affairs and coercion behind him. It seemed that this mainstream global economic machine was comfortable with a testosterone driven image and a driven and selfish raison d'etre. Nothing else mattered except neoliberal GPD growth and ever increasing expansion. The annual bounty of the entire planet (some even say 2 planets worth of bounty) was eaten up and destroyed in the Lust for Greed and Greed for Lust and testosterone driven, (and lots of it) economic gain. The saying went around that "If Lehman Brothers had been Lehman sisters, the banking crisis would not have happened." The Deputy Prime Minister in the UK raised the issue of gender imbalance and unequal pay and influence in the financial sector in Parliament as being a factor in the cause of the current economic crisis.

All that has changed – the machine was exposed for the unpleasant entity it was and now there is a woman in the role, and the IMF- the former imposer of austerity measures on others has reached the limit of its own excesses and can't raise enough bail out funds to stop the rot.

Whilst this denouement of capitalism has been going on, there have been stirrings of what is really driving the world economy.

Table 1. Miriam Kennet October 2011

2. Environmental Economics Umbrella			
←--→			
Spectrum of responses to the environmental imperative			
Capitalism	Ecological economics		Nationally managed solutions And economies
Austerity Neo liberal More free trade	Avoid		Green Growth China Green 5 year plans
Resource economics	Reduce, reuse, recycle, repair substitution The commons		Green Stimulus Packages
CSR	Deep Ecology		Green Quantitive Easing
Triple Bottom Line	The economics of gender		Green Investment Parts of Asia
Carbon trading and Kyoto	Anthropocene economics and the economics of global environmental change		Green Venture Capital Green Patents
Green Jobs			
Green Growth	Green Economics Mixed diverse and inclusive and progressive solutions • Life style changes • regulation • rationing where necessary • some market activity • incentive-carrot and stick • some techno fixes • social and environmental justice driver • economics for global environmental change • Substitution • Contraction and convergence	Green Economy	Green New Deal Keynesian stimulus
	Heterodoxy		

THE ENVIRONMENTAL ECONOMICS UMBRELLA: THE GREEN ECONOMY BEGINS TO STIR

As with the dinosaurs before them, a small tiny and seemingly insignificant movement began to stir about 16 years ago. This is slowly and quietly now threatening the very survival, dominance, and logic of the capitalist machine. Green is the new black and the green dialogues which.are being regarded as the way forward- the design of the economies of the twenty first century. Now most countries have greens in at different levels of government and with national influence following a range of policies but all offering to provide green jobs, as it is one of the fastest growing sectors in most economies.

The green economy is a fascinating place at present with several competing dialogues currently going on under the labels of pro-growth, anti-growth, limits to growth, green growth, austerity, life style changes, techno-fixes and many more. Some of these prevailing ideas will be introduced and discussed here. Even the credit rating agencies may be including environmental risk in a countries credit rating. As with many human activities these ideas and competing dialogues are fiercely debated.

THE GREEN GROWTH SCHOOL: THE WOLF IN SHEEP'S CLOTHING

Masquerading as green economics -(which is actually based on social and environmental justice and a concern to benefit all people everywhere, other species, nature, the planet and its systems) -is the idea of Green Growth–which is the business and main stream backlash and the skewing of the concept to mean the opposite to what is intended. It follows from green consumerism- the idea you can have your cake and eat it at the same time. The Green Growth School advocates a bit of greening and environmental greenwash around the edges and maintaining control and doing Business as Usual. Here we find the fascinating (but alarming) alliance of the Price Waterhouse Coopers heading up WWFs initiative on green economy and entire alliance of companies and some larger corporate NGOs allowing the agenda to be set to "green the economy" with business, and they mean business, corporate or capital – or capitalism – depending on your own point of view. In any case, this occurs within an alliance which is similar in structure to that of the World Council of Business and Sustainable Development? We found such an alliance at the Copenhagen COP 15 conference where every single NGO registered in the USA had come via the WCBSD. The World Council of Business and Sustainable Development is an alliance of all the worlds largest businesses and the voice of its capital (and it is designed to keep things that way whilst tweaking some environmental greenwashing). There is no room for dissenting voices, as all the little USA NGOs signed up without checking.

Green growth theory is powered through the London School of Economics, the OECD, the Korean Government and United Nations Environment Programme, and its theory is that green is good for growth, and growth is good for green. Stern

delivered a speech in October 2009 arguing that the world will see the fastest growth it has ever seen in the next 50 years and that this will fund the environmental clean up.

In fact it is probable that green companies are the main companies that will probably last but that is not the rationale of green economics and it misses its most important parts. This view, which I documented in my paper (Kennet 1997), I called the *wolf in sheep's clothing* (Kennet 1997, p. 182) – it makes all the right noises but misses the guts of the changes. This view differs little from the Friedmanite theory of the firm, as the most important entity and at all costs its survival must be assured. However, measuring "social and environmental bads" is introduced by environmental economics into this view and although it is in effect a red herring, actually delaying underlying structural change, its performance is probably better than doing nothing at all.

GREEN NEW DEAL AND KEYNESIAN STIMULUS

The most popular alternative at the moment in Europe and with the European greens (Green European Foundation) is the Keynesian green stimulus Green New Deal which largely wants to switch consumption from market laissez faire capitalism to a more managed green public project based approach for public works and infrastructure. This is called the Green Deal in the USA and in Korea and Europe, the Green New Deal. However its meaning can vary, for example the UN includes for example the manufacture of more cars, albeit ones using ecotechnology or what purists might call a techno fix. This is in part the impetus for carbon storage and sequestration and for carbon scrubbers and green tech and those products that use rare earth metals mainly sourced from China. This view argues that a programme of cuts and austerity won't work and that a technological evolution in the economy has always worked well before and so advocates that a stimulus of spending and green quantitative easing are the answer, without the need for lifestyle changes.

One particular Green New Deal proposed (Elliot et al. 2009) a sample of £10 billion in green quantitative easing invested in the energy efficiency sector, which could:

- Create 60,000 jobs (or 300,000 person-years of employment) while also reducing emissions by a further $3.96MtCO_2e$ each year;
- This could also create public savings of £4.5 billion over five years in reduced benefits and increased tax intake alone;

A sample of £10 billion in 'green quantitative easing' invested in onshore wind could:

- Increase wind's contribution to the UK's total electricity supply from its current 1.9 per cent to 10 per cent Create over 36,000 jobs in installation and direct and indirect manufacturing This is a total of 180,000 job-years of employment -. Create a further 4,800 jobs in the operations and maintenance of the installed capacity and other related employment over the entire 20 year lifetime of the installation (equivalent to 96,000 job-years)

- And, if this directly replaced energy from conventional sources, it could decarbonise the UK economy by 2.4 per cent – reducing emissions from the power sector by up to 16 $MtCO_2e$ each year. This corresponds to a £19 billion reduction in environmental damage.
  Or, a sample investment of £10 billion could:
- reskill 1.5 million people for the low-carbon skills of the future, bringing 120,000 people back into the workforce, and increasing the earnings of those with a low income by a total of £15.4 billion.
- A £50 billion programme in 'green quantitative easing' in the short term to rebuild the economy. Next, planning must begin for all of the new forms of bond finance detailed in the Group's report to ensure the long-term stable funding needed for the long-term transformation.

Measures on tax that are explicitly designed to re-gear the UK economy and transform energy infrastructure:

- Tax incentives on green savings and investment, so that future ISA tax relief – costing more than £2 billion a year – is only available for funds invested in green savings
- A general tax-avoidance provision to end the abuse of tax allowances. A Financial Transaction Tax, commonly known as a "Tobin Tax". Such a tax, applied internationally at a rate of about 0.05 per cent has the potential to raise more than £400 billion a year.

New savings mechanisms that support the greening of the economy now, create thousands of new jobs and guarantee stable returns into the future:

- Green bonds
- Local authority bonds, Carbon linked bonds, to align investment returns with carbon A new publicly owned 'Green New Deal Investment Bank' to allocate the capital provided by green quantitative easing, and new bank lending to government:
- Green New Deal Investment Bank, a publicly owned bank to hold and disburse capital provided by 'green quantitative easing'. It will be used exclusively to fund companies and projects designed to accelerate the transition towards a low carbon economy.
- Treasury Deposit Receipts, like those issued during the Second World War, a mechanism whereby banks were forced to use their ability to create credit to lend to government.

THE GREEN ECONOMY SCHOOL

This year 2012 the UN RIO + 20 global conference is entitled *Green Economy rethinking growth*. The world is taking up this challenge. Their definition of the

green economy is according to the United Nations General Secretary (2012) for the first Preparatory Meeting of the UNCSD identifies four strands:
United Nations definition of a Green Economy would:

a. end market failure and the internalization of externalities.
b. proceed from a systemic view of the economic structure and its impact on relevant aspects of sustainable development.
c. social goals (jobs, for example) and examines ancillary policies needed to reconcile social goals with the other objectives of economic policy.
d. the macroeconomic framework and development strategy with the goal of identifying dynamic pathways towards sustainable development" 2012 Earth Summit 2012.

(2011 United Nations Policy Options Proposals for Rio + 20).

a. Getting prices right, including removing subsidies, valuing natural resources and imposing taxes on things that harm the environment (environmental "bads") in order to internalize externalities, support sustainable consumption and incentivize business choices;
b. Public procurement policies to promote greening of business and markets;
c. Ecological tax reforms based mainly on the experience of European countries; The basic idea is that shifting the tax base away from "good" factors of production such as labour to "bad" factors such as pollution will allow for a double dividend: correcting environmental externalities while boosting employment;
d. Public investment in sustainable infrastructure (including public transport, renewable energy and retrofitting of existing infrastructure and buildings for improved energy efficiency) and natural capital, to restore, maintain and, where possible, enhance the stock of natural capital. This has particular salience within the current recessionary context, given the need for public expenditure on stimulus packages;
e. Targeted public support for research and development on environmentally sound technologies, partly in order to compensate for private underinvestment in pre-commercial research and development, and partly to stimulate investments in critical areas (such as renewable energy) with potentially high dynamic scale economies, and partly to offset the bias of current research and development towards dirty and hazardous technologies;
f. Strategic investment through public sector development outlays, incentive programmes and partnerships, in order to lay the foundation of a self-sustaining process of socially and environmentally sustainable economic growth;
g. Social policies to reconcile social goals with existing or proposed economic policies (2011 UNEP).

THE LOWER GROWTH SCHOOL

The foundations of this approach can be found in Malthus (1817) and issues raised by Hardin (1968) in *The Tragedy of the Commons*. The debate also questions the root of technological fixes to ecological problems and, one might argue, Environmental Economics and Corporate Social Responsibility.

In *The Limits to Growth* (1972), Meadows argues that rapidly diminishing resources force a slowdown in industrial growth due to a rise in the death rate and a decrease in food supply and medical services. Despite greater material output, the world's people will be poorer than they were. This collapse occurs because of non-renewable resource depletion. Growth would be stopped well before 2100, caused by overloading of the natural absorptive capacity of the environment. These models were influential, and Meadows suggested the use of technology to circumvent problems.

Rachel Carson's book *Silent Spring* (1962) shows the devastating effects of chemicals on the natural world. She highlights the effects on bird's eggs which led to a silent spring. Carson writes that the obligation to endure gives us the right to know and to stop using such chemicals. This genre is also featured in such books as *Chemical Children* by Mansfield and Munro (1987) and Paul Ehrlich's article on the dangers of an increasing population, *The Population Bomb* (1969).

UK Government departments have started exploring staff's capacity to deal with today's crises, plunging into changed economic and ecological problems. Surprisingly, this has opened radically new ground, focusing on economic management through The Green Economics Institute. Radical approaches such lower-growth economics, degrowth economics and Redefining Prosperity are being taught and discussed in government departments as they gain in popularity as an approach. Important work under the banner of Redefining Prosperity has been done by Kennet and Heinemann (2008), Victor (2008), and Anderson (2008), with Jackson leading the Sustainable Development Commission in this area Serge Latouche, whose focus is not dissimilar to the work of Green Economics, is the leading thinker in this movement.

GREEN ECONOMICS AND REALITY – UNRAVELLING THE SOVEREIGN WEALTH FUNDS AND DEBT IN A POST OIL PHASE

Sovereign wealth funds started slopping capital whizzing around the world and with national banks becoming exposed to debt, in an unregulated way, and property hopelessly overvalued in many countries, then the die was cast for a global economics catastrophe perhaps on a scale never seen before and almost impossible to unravel.

The new problem today is that capital has morphed into this new form due to the herd spending and several countries investment, and a stubborn arch dependence on fossil fuel economies. Much of the worlds capital has already taken flight into a few major economies creating a small number of ultra powerful sovereign wealth funds, a kind of power oligopoly and unfortunately most of them (with the sole exception of

Norway) have horrific human rights standards. Failure to understand this important structural change in capital and capitalism means the inability to either reverse this situation or to change or improve it.

GREEN ECONOMICS AND LIFESTYLE CHANGES

On the other hand a "green economics agenda" argues for a life style change which provides less consumption, less resource use and alternatives to the consumption patterns and high mass consumption of Rostow of the Kennedy administration – the main economics policy paradigm of the last 60 years.(Jorion2011) It argues for lower growth – in developed countries-contraction and convergence for everyone. This view allows for degrowth shifts to be included, as it reduces overall economic activity and lowers GDP and typically the GINI coefficient and other measures of well being go up in advanced economies, above a certain level of satisfaction of the basic physical requirements of living. The emphasis on growth as an end itself disappears. The alleviation of poverty, education of everyone especially girls, the participation in democracy, the halting of climate change and sea level rise and the halting of biodiversity loss are all important aims of such an economy. The equality within and between countries and between generations becomes much more interesting in such an economy. This method allocates more to less developed countries and less to more developed countries.

Green Economics intrinsically is supportive of the *Contraction and Convergence*, based on the principle proposed by Aubrey Meyer of the Global Commons Institute initially for reducing global carbon emissions by a consensus of contracting larger emitters and expanding emitters who are not using enough. This elegant solution is based on social and environmental justice and so is attractive to green economists. It has been adopted as a principle for carbon by the UNFCC. As economists, green economists also regard it as a key idea to implement a green economy. In practise less developed countries can still grow to meet in the middle range of basic living standards but those over consuming countries need to contract to meet in the middle to ensure that there is enough to go round.

The role of the commons, ownership of air, water and soil is important as well as resources that we all need to live. The substituting of carbon increasing private goods such as cars for public goods with the replacement by the commons such a publicly owned and lower carbon train transport is important. The promoters of green economics also recommend slow travel as a change in lifestyle and of ways of reconstituting economic life – using bicycles and walking more within the community are also features with prominent green economists taking the *No Flight Pledge*. In particular green economics changes the emphasis away from capital intensive gadget driven short life produced goods for consumption and capital accumulation economics, with demand artificially stimulated by advertising and marketing, towards more labour intensive longer term durable and sustainable goods. The taxation system would offer short-term disincentives for social and environmental "bads" and encourage with incentives "goods" and the protection and creation of the global commons. It argues for home production for local and smaller scale needs where necessary and remaining within the limits to growth and the limits of the planet's resources and an awareness of the total supply chain and the manner and place of production as well as how what we consume is produced. Green Economics deals with social and environmental justice and the provisioning for the needs of all people everywhere, nature, other species, the planet and its systems.(Kennet and Heinemann 2006). It integrates the physical environment and its data into a real economy perspective together, with social science, to create an economics discipline fit for purpose for the 21st century. More recently it is clear it is intensely practical having first expanded in the governments of many countries and the attempt to implement it around the world.

It has thus been called the economics of doing, the economics of caring and the economics of sharing-sharing with each other, sharing with other species and sharing the planet and its resources (Kennet 2010). The other strands of policies which do form an integral tool kit for a green economy-include regulation, techno fixes, incentives, and taxation. Even in some cases rationing of use where it benefits the community. Green Economics is about doing more with less and in some cases avoidance and finding an alternative.

Reuse, reduce, recycle, repair are also useful aspects of policies. Green Economics is an inclusive discipline, for all people everywhere, especially women, minorities, people with special needs, and those hitherto without a voice, nature, other species, the planet and its systems as beneficiaries rather than throw away imputs to the economics sausage machine. It is NOT about the greatest happiness of the greatest number. It seeks to value everyone and everything on the planet. It seeks to enhance and allow flourishing rather than to destroy, as mainstream economics sometimes does as is claimed a predestined "inevitability in economics mainstream logic."

THE DEVELOPMENT OF THE DISCIPLINE: SOME ASPECTS OF THE GREEN ECONOMICS ANALYSIS OF THE NEED FOR CHANGE

Table 2. Intellectual ideas surrounding Green Economics Miriam Kennet (2011)

Heterodox economics Umbrella	Green Movement Philosophy and Theory	Environmental economics Umbrella	Degrowth
Neo keynsian economics		Welfare Economics	Lower growth
		Environmental Economics School	
Marxist school		Ecological Economics	Eco socialism
Austrian school		Feminist Economics	Zero carbon
		Development Economics	

Green Economics	Limits to growth
Inclusion, all people everywhere, women, minorities, people with special needs, other species, nature, the planet and its systems. An economics of inclusion and sharing. The rights responsibilities and impacts of everyone and everything on the planet	

In particular two umbrella terms are relevant here, firstly the heterodox schools of economics containing elements from the Neo-Keynesians, the Austrian, and Marxist schools but also increasingly a home for the Green Economics school and to an extent the ecological economics schools.

Additionally, although confusingly, the umbrella term of Environmental Economics does contains the ecological economics school and the green economics schools, the specific term environmental economics when used to describe a school itself (as opposed to the terms use as an umbrella term), has been criticised for being too close to the mainstream, neo liberal and business as usual methodology and in that sense lacking ambition for radical change.

In 1989, after the fall of the Berlin Wall, capitalism seemed to be unrivalled in its ascendency and to have won the political and moral battle for the future of economics. Governments and banks allowed themselves to believe that the era of cycles of boom and bust was actually well and truly behind them and that we had moved into a period of continued economic growth and ever expanding GDP which could last forever. They believed that a deregulated international, free trade, consumption driven, capitalist economy would always continue to deliver ever-expanding growth led by Anglo-Saxon stock markets.

We were personally worried about this, as we clearly saw behind this facade certain facts and truths and problems which were not being addressed at all. Firstly all the economics models were very one dimensional and ignored reality in favour of a certain mathematical and statistical, purism and elitism. The main problems seemed to us to be:

    a. One fifth of humanity was still starving in life threatening poverty (Sachs 2005) even through this period of unparalleled plenty- and this seemed to question the distributive theory of economics.

    b. Climate change was ratcheting up and sea level was rising and the evidence from the latest IPCC scientific consensus appeared to suggest this was largely anthropocentric and we thought the increase in carbon was caused by a consumerist, fossil fuel, car driven economy which needed amending.

    c. This capitalist economy was very uneven and unequal and consisted largely of intrafirm trade, behind closed doors which even then, had a turnover larger than many countries and it also seemed to be driven by unelected invisible power elites and to be leading to catastrophic decline of the worlds natural capital. In fact this process has now resulted in an oligopoly of world capital power resting in a tiny number of sovereign states' wealth funds able to mobilise and dominate the entire globe's resources at will. They include such entities as the oil states in the middle east- (This latest trend began in Kuwait) and in Singapore, Norway and above all in China, with the BRICS coming up the rear -Brazil, India and Russia, all accelerating fast in terms of their trade and a group of CIVETS also doing well – Cambodia, Indonesia, Vietnam, Egypt and Turkey and South Africa. Whilst on the other side, the PIGGS and–the Euro zone, are struggling as they have bought products and moved production to these newer countries, to such an extent as to hollow out their economy and are unable to refinance their enormous debts. The world's largest economy the USA has even fallen into this trap and now is unable to call the tune when trading for example with the owner of much of its debt China. As a result, downgrades of many of the more developed economies have occurred recently in the credit ratings agencies such as Standard and Poor. This is a warning that dumping our social, environmental and production standards comes back to haunt us. What goes around really does come around!

d. We never believed that the boom could continue in a world of finite resources.
e. Miriam Kennet had watched the developments in China from the start when she was involved in putting in the telecoms infrastructure in the early 1990s and saw the few were benefiting at the expense of the many and it was becoming more unequal.
f. She noticed the Global Shift (Dicken 2009) and the rapid changes in the balances of trade and huge outsourcing as the west grew more lazy and arrogant (like the fall of the Roman Empire identified by Gibbon in the 20th century). She was alarmed by the developed economy as it outsourced its core activities and practised social and environmental dumping, just at the very time that explicit standards were rising legally, (with lots of talk about environmental and social improvement). The reality was rather different -and happening a long way away. For example the contents of mobile phones contain a mineral that is largely mined by children in the DRC Congo and is the cause of wars and serious genocide in DR Congo and Rwanda, which would horrify many of the mobile phone users if they stopped to think about it. It is solving such dynamics and making the public aware of their own responsibility and actions, as well as and changing and shifting such trade flows that is the stuff of green economics. This double speak-standards, normative books and speeches were happening but on the quiet the energy was being put into hiding all the dirty linen in poorer and less developed countries. We now know this included borrowing from them to the extent that the USA is largely in debt to such countries completely. The hollowing out of western economies and companies seemed to Kennet an unsustainable economics system and one doomed to failure. On the other hand the human rights were being eroded in the

production of unnecessary luxury goods to an alarming rate. This is happening whilst in many other countries, in Africa for example were left out altogether or condemned to produced commodities whose benefit went to corrupt and brutal power elites. These are put in place and propped up by greedy western and developed economies that shipped our minerals or oil or anything of value. Life expectancy for example in Nigerian is still a shocking 30 years, even though its rulers stash away millions in Swiss bank accounts and amongst the richest in the world.

The mainstream pathway advocated by western and more developed nations and Countries' Financial Ministers was and still is for the western unlimited accumulation of goods often with little real benefit or intrinsic value. An example might be shoes in the west, for example shoes made in China. Stateless migrant women workers make these in sweatshop factories from the countryside whose papers do not give permission for their children to join them, or live with them or get an education. In its search for cheap goods the West fails to question the human rights of the producer.

g. Biodiversity was falling and species extinction was becoming very serious and expensive and 7 times more expensive than the cost of climate change. (Sukhdev 2009, Stern 2006).

CHARACTERISTICS OF A GREEN ECONOMY

In the early 1960s and 1970s, the tide began to turn and competing economics alternative platforms began to arise, insisting on a change of focus. These new disciplines were based on a concern for social and environmental commitments, and a reappraisal of economics foundations for human and planetary welfare.

This began to lead to reforms within academic economic theory and social practise, such as the Corporate Social Responsibility movement (CSR) developed by O'Carrol, Environmental Economics, and Sustainable Development Economics developed by Chichilnisky.

THE NEED FOR CHANGE IN THE ACADEMY

The academy initially greeted these movements with hesitant interest and many have now found their way into mainstream economics teaching and are popular with students.

These movements although useful are simply not radical enough to solve today's problems. Just as economics in the time of Adam Smith was initially aimed at countering the Industrial Revolution poverty of English cities, as Keynesian economics was constructed to avoid the horrors of a Great Depression and a Third World War, today's economics must be essentially and fundamentally committed to today's crises.

This time, economics must focus on halting environmental and social injustice, and must restructure and or replace the entire system. Therefore, the aim of the Green Economics Institute, of Miriam Kennet and Volker Heinmann and Michele Gale D'Oliveira has been to theorize, produce, and mobilize such a discipline – a "green economics" and it has en route received much resistance from the " high priests " of main stream economics who have the most to loose from this shifted paradigm.

Policymakers, academics, and leaders in business alike have arrived at a realization that we are on a collision course between Ecology and the Economy. Necessarily, Greening the Economy is regarded as one of the only ways to tackle the economic recession and environmental catastrophe. But in order for theory to become practise, Environmental Economics and Green Economics must gain visibility in economics departments and business schools. Mainstream economics resists a surprising level of new thinking – even in the face of enormous market failures and economic meltdowns. Yet students, policy makers and the general public have embraced the Green Economics strand of Environmental Economics and are hungry for change, demanding that it be reflected in the Greening of the Academy, both in business schools and economics departments. Even advisors to the Bank of England regard Green Economics as one of the more healthy areas of the economy.

Green Economics requires an emergent and transformative pedagogy and the democratic participation of all people everywhere, an inclusion of previously unheard voices, and "lived practise" (Turk 2010). Refusing to be reduced to a set of definitive principles or timeless truths, it represents a dynamic, expansive, praxis-based economics. Exactly for this reason, Green Economics has been described as "the economics of doing."

METHODOLOGY OF GREEN ECONOMICS AND ENVIRONMENTAL ECONOMICS

A methodological and philosophical transformation needs to challenge the core of what we think of as economics. We can learn from Leonardo da Vinci (1452–1519) believed that it was important to understand the connections between the "art of science" and the "science of art." His argument was that his success in one field was due to his understanding of another field. In his case, this was anatomy and art.

The scientific discovery of interconnectedness was a key to the emergence of the New System Theory in the late 20th century, a theory that led to the discipline of Holism led in the UK by the Schumacher College. This discipline addresses and links traditions that are foreign to each other. It has no desire to be centralised, over-organised or hierarchical. In this sense, Green Economics and its development is in fact one of the most holistic and multidisciplinary economics the world has ever seen. There is no human activity, no part of the planet that is not of interest to Green Economics; it is the very economics of interconnectedness. Green Economics is based in a web network of like thinking innovators from 48 countries and all walks of life. As "the economics of doing" (Kennet 2009) – integrative, participatory, and dynamic – Green Economics is a distinct aspect of greening the academy in implementation, discipline and philosophy. Crucial to the teaching and implementation of Green Economics is an understanding of methodology. Mainstream economics reduces reality by application of simplistic mathematical concepts that make the world appear more precise than it actually is. Commoner (1971:97, 213) warned how modern technology caused intensifying "assaults on the environment, creating a debt to nature ultimately leading to ecosystem collapse." Mainstream economics remains focused on an infinite growth assumption, and the belief that supposedly innate and uninfluenced consumer preferences should inform economic decision-making. As far as consumption is concerned, infinite growth contradicts scientific findings of ecologists (particularly climate change experts) and psychologists. In response, Green Economics chooses to reflect the world's interconnectedness by utilizing both verbal reasoning and narrative description in addition to quantitative methods. To study mainstream economics today a student is required to to be first qualified in mathematics. A green economics approach is much more mixed.It does not see mathematical formulae as the only solution to the world's problems. Indeed the use of mathematics and econometrics to solve the world's problems has been likened to *"using a power drill to dust a window"*-(2007) by Tony Lawson Head of Econometrics at Cambridge University, in our International Journal of Green Economics. We proposed that a complete rethink is required in our economics constructs.

Green Economics has been heavily influenced by Feminist theory and the idea of other voices, seeing this as lacking within Environmental Economics which continues in the tradition of the mainstream. While the mainstream concerns itself with competitive production and exchange in markets, the economy is underpinned by millions of people, (especially women) involved in care, reciprocity, and direct production every day. Their work is completely ignored in GDP figures, balance sheets, economics discussions and text books. One of the main contributions of Green Economics is the notion that production does indeed occur in the home or "oikia," rather than simply by homo economicus or rational economic man. It also points out the links between oikia–economics and ecology. Indeed, the Greek root of the word "economics" refers not to the office or factory but to the home: the site of physical, affective and mental production (Feiner 2003). Important feminist influences have warned against theories that legitimise a single gendered homo-economicus version or "story" of reality, ignoring and excluding "gynaika ekonomika" from the public economic sphere. Feminist methodologies allow us to understand the way in which the foundations of a discipline are laid and then expose them as particular and and needing to change.

Table 3. Foundation Concepts in Green Economics. Miriam Kennet © (October 2011)

Economics theories predicated in a capitalist environment			Economic theories situated in alternatives Radical/ participation/ Anti-materialism	Changed bases for economics activity Holistic (Bloom), Green/ philosophy
Economic	Environmental	Social	Socially responsible investment (SRI Henderson)	Subsistence economy (Mies) The love Economy (Henderson) Ecofeminism (Shiva)
Austerity packages and structural adjustment programmes imposed by World Bank/MF	Environmental economics (Pearce)	Welfare economics (Sen. Pigou)	Parecon (Albert) 60s communes economics	Ecosocialism (Kovel)
	World Council of Business and Sustainable Development		Green Economics	
Green Market economy Heinrich Boell Foundation	Corporate social responsibility (O Carroll, Bowen)	Development economics Myrdal, Sen,	Anti-Development (Shiva)	Buddhist economics (Schuhmacher)
Lower growth (Jackson and Anderson)	Green Fiscal Commission (Ekins)	Stakeholder theory (Freeman)	Degrowth (Latouche)	Deep Ecology (Naess)
Market solutions Green Growth (Stern LSE OECD)	Lower Carbon Economics carbon trading Chichilnisky	Tripple Bottom Line Elkington	Anti-globalisation (Gramsci)	Industrial ecology (Korhonen)
Green Deal (Obamah and Chicago School)	Greening the Economy (Sukhdev Kennet)		Arab spring 5 star movement in Italy and others	

(Continued)

Table 3. (Continued)

Green Accounting Sarkozy, Stiglitz, McGlade	Sustainable development Economics (Brundtland and Chichilnisky	Feminist (Henderson, Mies)	Ecological economics (Daly, Boulding, Martin Alier, Costanza)
	Green New Deal Green Keynsianism	Green Economics (Miriam Kennet, Mayer Hillman, Volker Heinemann, Paul Ekins, Michael Jacobs)	
	Development Economics (Sussex University)	Global commons and contraction and convergence (Aubrey Meyer)	Progressive economics (Volker Heinemann)
	Green New Deal	ending corporate tax evasion (european greens, Kennet, green economics and UNCUT movement)	Anti globalisation movements (Green Party England and Wales, Mike Woodin, Caroline Lucas, New Internationallist)
	Decent Work and Green Jobs (International Labour Organisation)	Slow movement	Transition towns movement

Green Economics is an interdisciplinary economic field, which integrates, explores, and transforms while encouraging democratic participation in the economic re-evaluation and restructuring process. There has been a marked watershed of momentous happenings both economically and in the natural world. For the first time, mainstream policy-makers are recognizing that humankind could become the first species to destroy itself and its planetary home. More importantly, these mainstream policy-makers also realize that this destruction constitutes a choice – and that by altering behaviour, this tragedy can still be averted. Thus, Green Economics has emerged as *the* economics story and as one of the few alternatives to austerity packages. It has dovetailed with the launch of the Keynesian Green New Deal and the TEEB by the UN and EU, the Stern Report's sequels.. Green Economics has featured in the most unexpected of quarters – from the headline story at the European Business Summit and its launch by the United Nations. The discipline has been launched around the world, with the UK-founded Green Economics Institute opening its doors in South America, Africa, and Asia. Its popularity comes from the widespread realisation that the mechanisms for planetary and human-species desecration are embedded, justified and driven by the current system of economics and the realisation other choices and trajectories are now both possible and desirable.

Mainstream economics has become completely divorced from the purpose of provisioning for the needs of all humanity, all other species, the biosphere, and the planet itself (Kennet and Heinemann 2006). Mainstream economics always had a more narrowly focused approach. Today, however, policymakers are noticing that just as the mechanism for destruction is embedded in the current system, the mechanism for altering behaviour can be found in another system, that of Green Economics.

FOUNDATIONAL DISCIPLINES AND CONCEPTS IN GREEN ECONOMICS

Environmental and Ecological Economics

Environmental economics has been used as a powerful umbrella term for several strands of economics, which seek to enhance, challenge or replace the mainstream. In universities, these generally include Environmental Economics itself, along with Welfare Economics, Ecological Economics, lower growth economics, lower carbon economics, degrowth economics, and development economics. Further, it includes many other iterations of pluralist/holistic or Heterodox Economics Thus the umbrella covers any perspective that challenges the mainstream. This section will discuss a number of theorists and schools in this arena, with a fundamental role in the genesis of the umbrella concept of Environmental Economics.

First, this section will focus on a several key contributors to the creation of Environmental Economics as a discipline, specifically Barbara Ward, Kenneth Boulding, and Herman Daly. It will then broaden the picture with the creation of sustainable development as a sub-discipline and the "Limits to Growth" perspective.

An avid supporter of what came to be known as Sustainable Development, Barbara Ward advocated economic justice for developing countries. Along with René Dubos, she wrote the first book on the subject, titled, *Only One Earth – The Care and Maintenance of a Small Planet* (Ward 1972). Her work in this field was decisive in the formation of non-mainstream platforms in Environmental Economics, and helped to lead the way in the early days of the global environmental awareness movement.

Another important figure in the development of Environmental Economics was Kenneth Boulding. Author of the famous "Spaceship Earth," Boulding wrote much on sustainability, pushing academia to recognize that economics only exists within nature, and that Earth must be protected. There was a concern that the colonies of his day would eventually be "pried off" of the edges of Europe's sinking environmental and economic lifeboat (Boulding 1978: 302). These prophets of early Environmental Economics encouraged new platforms to break with mainstream thinking patterns, and left a vast literary legacy to Environmental Economics. Garret Hardin. Hardin 1974) added to these ideas in his famous essay about lifeboat economics. However the main difficulty was that the methodology continued to be that of mainstream economics and measurement of the problems rather than avoidance.

Ecological Economics

An important subset of the Environmental Economics umbrella, Ecological Economics regards the economy as a subsystem of a larger global finite ecosystem – similar to Kenneth Boulding's description in "Spaceship Earth" (1966). Vitally, Ecological Economics recognises the interdependencies of the economic, social and ecological spheres, with the market being brought in only after equity and sustainability considerations are met, and only as a facilitator of the efficient allocation of resources. Markets are never used as an arbiter of (1) the equitable distribution of income and wealth creation or (2) the ecologically sustainable rate of resource use. Ecological Economics takes a major step toward reform, giving due attention to the complexity, value incommensurability and uncertainty in economy-ecology relations. However, it remains predominantly human-centred, with some ecological economists recognizing bio-centrism. This suggests an economy that takes into account the intrinsic values and needs of other species besides maximising human sustainable well-being. In all, a re-humanized discipline is needed whose emphasis is less biophysical, more economic and institutional, and incorporates intrinsic values while restructuring economics with holistic, inclusive and long-term aims at its core (Barry 2006).

The Ecological Economist Herman Daly had a tremendous impact on the field of Environmental Economics, breaking from the mainstream in many ways over the course of his career. Daly's contributions included his model of the "Steady State Economy" (1993), which involved his addition of biophysical and moral aspects to J.S. Mill's (1848) "Stationary State" model. Further, Daly radically broke from mainstream tradition with his "Means Ends Spectrum." This model describes economic growth – or the production of more goods and services – to satisfy "intermediate ends" as being finite, explaining that technology cannot always be depended upon to solve resource scarcity. Importantly, Daly stated that the trivial wants of some people do not take precedence over the basic needs of others (Hussen 2004:258). Finally, Daly with other radical economic authors rejected the sustainable development movement, viewing it as a euphemism. As development requires economic growth, and growth requires resource exploitation, development cannot be sustainable. He was one of the first theorists to promote the "zero-growth economy," which would have a tremendous impact on the field of Environmental Economics and eventually Green Economics.

Critique of Sustainable Development Economics

In 1987, the United Nations World Commission on Environment and Development (UNCED) issued the Brundtland Report, establishing sustainable development as a discipline. The report defined sustainable development as *"meeting the needs of the present without compromising the ability of the future to meet its needs."* Realising that economic development was environmentally unsustainable, this approach insists that the solution is accelerated growth rather than lower growth and development. Further, the Brundtland Report argues for a more enlightened globalisation to reach "sustainability" standards and to resolve environmental degradation. Set upon the presumption that chronic poverty is the root of environmental degradation, the Report points to sustainable growth as key to eradicating starvation, homelessness, disease, and other problems facing developing countries. Arguably, sustainable growth, then, would alleviate political, social, and economic pressures which ultimately endanger the environment, creating equitable and just societies which protect the environment while simultaneously developing. Acknowledging that many nation states are weaker than global corporations, sustainable development argues in favour of benevolent corporations being the agents of global problem-solving. Finally, with Stakeholder Theory, (Freeman 1994), Stakeholder engagement (Andrioff & Waddock 2002) (Curzon 2009) and Corporate Social Responsibility (O Carroll 1979, 1993), the instrumental methodology is designed to provide significant competitive advantage for the firm when a subset of ethical principles (trust, trustworthiness and cooperation) is operationalised. Chichilnisky (who is now a green economist) in fact developed the concept of the school of economics of sustainable development. In all these fields people move from one field to another in their writing (as many do) of these fields overlap in the middle but are substantially different at the margins.

Despite the popularity of *sustainable development* in Environmental Economics circles, many Green Economists mistrust the integration of corporate interests into the umbrella discipline. Corporations are seen as undemocratic, unelected, uniform, lacking in transparency and being the fundamental causes of the environmental and social crisis. In privatising natural assets, corporations behave as unbridled, uncontrolled, and unaccountable, representing the full destructive force of neo-liberal economics. Indeed, Milton Friedman (in Bakan 2004:35) himself argues that the socially responsible corporation would be "immoral." Green Economics questions how the corporation's short-term interest involves implementing equity and environmental justice through this managerial "environmentalist" approach. Dobson (2005) and Springett (2005 and 2006) criticize sustainable development's short-term techno-fixes which remain subject to the neo-classical paradigm, while simultaneously hijacking environmentalism and the language of "sustainability" (Welford 1993 and 2007).

But as in any critique, sustainable development is complex and cannot be definitively labelled. At one level and one end of the spectrum, the paradigm embodies corporate aims to capitalize on environmental and social justice, or "green-washing," noted in its proximity to Corporate Social Responsibility and Stakeholder Theory. Alternatively, at the opposite end of the spectrum of its advocates, sustainable development is sincerely embraced by veritably green and progress-minded organizations, such as ICLEI and the Sustainable Cities Movement. Without a doubt, sustainable development has had a tremendous effect on the development of Environmental Economics as a discipline. Still, its ambiguous aims and unclear scope have led to a false dawn of environmental and social solutions as it fails to reform the current paradigm and instead has been used to reinforce it by unscrupulous big business corporations.

As noted earlier, the Brundtland Commission's work on sustainable development also led to the growth perspective's predominance within Environmental Economics. First, the growth perspective assumes the potential of green and sustainable growth to secure environmental justice through the eradication of poverty via a trickle down of wealth. Second, this view states that consumption is natural to human beings, who will always require and desire more products. Thus, through this paradigm, the capitalist economic system becomes fiercely consumerist, creating products that consumers believe they need in order to live "the good life." At the same time, consumers learn generationally that the capitalist system cannot function without high growth, and this learning becomes an accepted truth. Part of this led to the high mass-consumption theories that have resulted in the conditions which created the unsustainable and reckless borrowing to feed the property boom, bubble and subsequent current downturn and the economic collapse as commodities, debt and natural resources are exhausted or become too expensive to continue to exploit. This is currently affecting Spain, Ireland, and the USA in particular. The environmental and social reality of our world demands the protection of both ecological and human resources, but in order to change this behaviour, global society must be offered alternatives – alternatives which Environmental Economics and sustainable development in particular have been unable to deliver.

Deep Ecology

Deep ecology, as a more radical school, has a major role in the future development of economics. Greening the academy will depend on insights from this school. In accordance with deep ecology principles, Green Economics argues that nature has its own intrinsic value, which it extends to animals based on the ethics of Singer's *Practical Ethics* (1994). Singer argues for the rights of all sentient beings, and Green Economics extends this argument to all life forms. Similarly, Leopold (1997) and Arne Naess (1995), founder of deep ecology, argue for the preservation of the biosphere, geological and biological systems, and all life forms for their own sake – not merely for human benefit. Criticising the *"shallow anthropocentric technocratic environmental movement," they charge that its values lie in an over-simple concern for pollution, resource depletion, and the health and affluence of people in the developed countries* (Sessions 1995: xii).

SHARING THE PLANET WITH OTHER PEOPLE AND OTHER SPECIES

Thus, Green Economics combines deep ecology with an anthropocentric equity ethic, seeking to preserve the natural lifeforms and systems. Greening the Academy will require a deeper, broader, intensified economics, one that connects with the realities of our world today.

Green Economics aims for every person to maintain comfortable living standards without exploiting other people or resources. The question is – what does "comfortable" mean, in a world with less land to live on due to sea level rise, 9 billion people in it. The resources need to be shared amongst the 99% of people who are currently disposed by the richest 1% who own most of the wealth. The idea in green economics is that all people everywhere, nature, other species, the planet and its systems become beneficiaries of the green economy rather than throw away inputs to a system which does not regard them as more than resources with no intrinsic value. A good example is that of a battery chicken – whose entire existence is used and abused for the cheapness when bought and eaten momentarily, without thought or consideration, by the eventual consumer. A green economics perspective argues that its wrong to consume other species -or other sentient species at all- and the deep ecological perspective argues that the chicken has its own rights and intrinsic value just to enjoy being a chicken and that these are immutable and must be provided- in life and in death. It is an open question then after that discussion as to whether it is even right to consume a chicken as food. In all events battery production of other species is regarded in green economics as "wrong" under any and all circumstances.

GREENWASHING

Similarly other species must not be misused, as in some opportunist abuses of even the Kyoto Protocol, to abuse and factory farm animals for their slurry- as happened in Mexico where large companies. In one case for example, Smithfield Industries, in the USA, outsourcing its dirty work, could claim spuriously under the guise of environmentalism that it was saving CO_2, and then could pollute the local Mexican water so badly that swine flu was able to flourish and spread from the area. In this sense, the growth perspective is rejected as dangerous and unnecessary.

THE COSTS OF THE CURRENT CRISIS: THE NEED FOR SOCIAL AND ENVIRONMENTAL JUSTICE

Environmental Economics stands at a turning point in global environmental and economic history. Never before has such a combination of environmental, social, and economic changes led to a crisis of this magnitude. Corporate Social Responsibility and market-based sustainable development theories were gradually being received as palpable reforms to mainstream paradigms.

Greening the academy will require Environmental Economics to substantially evolve and recognize today's most urgent problems. Our planet is changing drastically, and academia must race to process its new challenges. Today, the Earth is experiencing the 6th ever mass species extinction, while climate change is accelerating at a rate that terrifies scientists. Planetary conditions have worsened beyond the rim of experts most pessimistic conclusions. Experts warn that we may see the disappearance of Arctic ice sheets. The Stern Report (2006) shows climate change as the single worst market-failure in world history and thought initially to be a unique and dismal failure of the capitalist system– and incredibly now succeeded by the even more catastrophic ecosystems failure and the huge costs of biodiversity loss. These alone are predicted to be seven times greater than climate change costs according to ecological economics measurements emerging from a new report by the United Nations Environment Programme (Sukhdev 2008). Indeed, these economic costs outpace any previous human dilemma as their scope is truly global and affects our very survivability, underlining the reality that economics has always been engrained in the natural world. Economists may tend to forget this fundamental fact, but the mainstream is now quite literally being "brought back to earth."

Today, Environmental Economics needs to assume a deeper meaning. The discipline must undergo both soul-searching and radically change away from the mainstream economic system which has excused hardship, pain and misery for some, while others enjoy wasteful and unprecedented riches. Such inequity is criminal and unethical. Of Planet Earth's 6.5 billion people, one fifth of the world's human population do go to bed hungry every night and live in morbid poverty (Sachs, 2005). Environmental Economics must take this reality to heart – *if one fifth of cars crashed and one fifth of aeroplanes fell out of the sky as a result of faulty design, the response would be to immediately return to the drawing board, reworking the system's design.* (Kennet, 2007).

Our economics system has long been out of balance with nature. It has long been out of balance with people's needs. Greening the academy will be the first step in opening society to integrative and effective solutions to our current environmental and economic crises.

The placing of boundaries in economics is an intensely political act, with the reminder that the notion of free choice applies only to those with the economic power and freedom to apply it (Kaul, 2003). Of particular importance to the greening of the academy is women's economic inequality. This is often represented in unequal pay which results in unequal poverty. Green Economics theory seeks to correct mainstream economics' perspective of gendered economic injustice. With such knowledge, the commoditisation of labour and of the individual, addressing the effect of an uncaring supply chain to fuel greater consumption, resource depletion, increasing hardship and inequality is rejected by a green economics approach. Such inequalities, especially gendered inequalities and exclusion are in fact rejected by green economics at its core rather than as a subsequential logic and this innovation makes green economics unique... We took the gender equality issue as our primary response to the New Scientists question of what we thought would make the most difference today. Green Economics is clear that reducing gender inequality, by educating and empowering girls in the political system, will also reduce the birth rate, and thus the population and solve many of today's problems. It will also right many inequalities, and unequal societies do not do as well. It is fascinating that the empowerment of women has been at the heart of many protests in the Arab Spring. Even such hugely wealthy countries as Saudi Arabia have finally agreed to give women the vote (it seeming monstrous that this is still not the case today!). It has also been a factor in protest in Iran, in Tunisia, (although half the judges in Tunisia are women) and in Afghanistan. Women the world over are fed up with receiving medieval treatment and lack of opportunity, of education and of human rights.

THE ROLE OF NATURE AS A BENEFICIARY IN A GREEN ECONOMY

The role of nature itself is also intrinsic to relearning economics and the greening of the academy. Climate change has forced us to remember our role as temporary visitors on Earth rather than its owners or stewards, and leads to a rethinking of our position in the universe. Green academies will teach this to society, to untwist the environment from mainstream economics' stranglehold. Now, rather than using science to control nature, our scientific knowledge will provide us with the capacity to live within it and respect it and to understand our role and responsibility within it. Humanity cannot underestimate the importance of replacing outdated survival strategies, including techno-fixes and environmental overshoot, and wrongly limiting ourselves to mitigation and adaptation in dealing with climate change. Reversal and reduction must start to feature in our calculations and our lifestyles. Innovation will be vital to converting the economic system, creating sustainable lifestyles to exist within the planet's means comfortably but differently.

Over the last few hundred years, mainstream economics has tamed and used nature as an expendable given resource, and has only valued resources once they have become scarce or exhausted. Green Economics, in contrast, seeks an economics of abundance, rather than scarcity, and comprises both the natural and social sciences, making a distinction between values and costs. The mainstream, treats nature (the planet's life support machine) as abundant and limitless and therefore has exploited and consumed it as a "free good" and unlimited resource. The main stream however only values scarcity. Making nature scarce would be calculated by mainstream economists as increasing its value! This is of course a completely crazy and suicidal logic! In spite of the academic trend regarding environmental issues, business schools in universities actually represent the planet's entire life support system in such a fashion. Therefore green issues and environmental change should start to form the core of the academy rather than the other way round. Business is actually a subset of the earth, and nature underpins the world economy and so greening the academy is a vital step in the move to survivability and the implementation of reality in our academy as a whole.

Today, nature has become visibly fragile and "scarce." Goldsmith (2005) shows that Environmental Economics attempts to adjust neo-liberal economics to the needs and costs of nature. However, this only works if the adjustments are small. Should it seek to adjust to nature's entire carrying capacity, the discipline of economics must clearly be rewritten in order to include and account for the whole adjustment. Such complete rethinking and rewriting is the work of Green Economics with its completely changed philosophy, ontology and methodologies.

THE ROLE OF GREEN ECONOMICS IN GREENING THE ACADEMY

As a crucial aspect of greening the academy, Green Economics supplies an integrative, participatory and dynamic teaching approach in conjunction with the appropriate economic foundations for our time. Holistic and interdisciplinary, Green Economics is both a natural and social science that chooses appropriate tools for each problem from its wide portfolio of methodologies. Fundamentally incorporating progressive ideas into scientific thinking and methodology, this discipline is open and able to explore new ideas that may radically change our perspective. This chapter will come to a close contending that Green Economics inherently combines a scientific as well as a social science approach. In the past decades, neo-classical economics has misappropriated a narrow interpretation of Darwinism in order to justify its version of capitalism, thus advancing the power of the strongest and fittest, while preserving inequalities. Green Economics, as the economics of doing and sharing, provides a dynamic and transformative idea, focusing equally on practice as well as theory. Refusing to accept the status quo, this discipline has managed to resist the static fate of other paradigms, and cannot be reduced to simple -"isms", "timeless truths" or stagnant principles. Thus, Green Economics seeks to reintegrate economics and science, addressing injustices by focusing on a broader reality than possible through mainstream economic methods.

It works by Greening the Academy through a participative, democratic and a truly green approach. Green Economics grew out of an alternative style of networking much like the Arctic Monkeys, rejecting the conventional Institutional approach and linking innovators and campaigners directly to each other. In that sense it is a very contemporary movement, which is agile and active and it is available to those outside the mainstream "priesthood of economics." It was born during of an age of Facebook and LinkedIn and web applications and as such can comfortably incorporate the aspirations of young people, and those who want change directly, especially for example those in Africa, and Egypt and is active at the very heart of their current calls for change... This is an exciting prospect as we move into a year when the global focus is on *the Green economy: Rethinking growth* and its GDP driver and into an era where we try and allow the earth's resources to flourish in abundance, and where we move towards an economics for all people everywhere, nature, the planet and its systems. It is therefore vitally important to ensure that we create an economics which is progressive in all its activities and which provides social and environmental justice as well as caring, sharing and doing (Kennet et al., 2011). We need an economics of hope for the 21st century even in the face of climate change, sea level rise, land depletion and any other challenges the world brings us. That sharing must be about sharing the earth with other species and with each other in an inclusive way for the benefit of everyone and everything on the planet. That is the message of green economics and the work of Greening the Academy.

REFERENCES

Anderson, V. (2008). Victor Anderson's opinion piece on the economic growth and the economic crisis. *Prosperity without growth.* Retrieved August 10, 2009 from http://www.sd-commission.org.uk/publications.php?id=832.

Andrioff, J., & Waddock, S. (2002). Unfolding stakeholder engagement. In Andrioff, J. et al. (Eds.), *Unfolding Stakeholder Thinking: Theory, Responsibility, and Engagement.* Sheffield: Greenleaf Publishing Ltd.

Moon, B.K. (2007, December 3). Time for a new green economics: a test for the world. In Bali and Beyond. *Washington Post.* Retrieved August 10, 2009 from http://www.washingtonpost.com/wp-dyn/content/article/2007/12/02/AR2007120201635.html

Barry, J. (1999a). *The environment and social theory.* London: Routledge.

BBC (2011). Occupy London in Protest. Retrieved October 16th 2011 from http://www.bbc.co.uk/news/world-asia-pacific-15319924.

Boulding, K. (1966). The economics of the coming of spaceship earth. In H.E Daly *Towards a steady state economy,* San Francisco W H Freeman and Company 1973.

Brundtland, G. H. (1987). *Our common future.* World Commission on Environment and Development OUP 1–11.

Carson, R. (1962). *Silent Spring.* New York: Houghton Mifflin.

Carroll, A.B. (1993). *Business and Society: Ethics and Stakeholder Management.* Cincinnati OH: South-Western.

Carroll, A.B. (1979). A three-dimensional conceptual model of corporate social performance. *Academy of Management Review, 4*(4), 497–505.

Commoner, B. (1971). *The Closing Circle: Nature, Man, and Technology.* New York: Knopf.

Daly, H. (1974, May). The economics of the steady state. *American Economic Review (Papers and Proceedings), 64*(2), 15–21.

Dobson, A. (2000). *Green Political Thought.* London: Routledge.

Ehrlich, P. (1969). *The Population Bomb.* New York: Ballantine.

Feiner, S. (2003). Reading neo-classical economics towards an erotic economy of sharing. In D. Barker and E Kuiper (Eds.), *Towards a feminist philosophy of economics* (pp. 180–193). New York: Routledge.

Freeman, E. R. (1984). *Strategic management: A stakeholder approach.* Boston: Pittnan.

Goldsmith, E. (2005). Rewriting economics. Retrieved January 17th, 2006 from www.greeneconmics.org.uk.

Gramsci, A. (2006). Some theoretical and practical aspects of economism. Retrieved January 17, 2006 from http://marxism.halkcephesi.net/Antonio%20Gramsci/prison_notebooks/modern_prince/ch07.htm.

Elliott E., et al. (2009). Green New Deal Group demands. Retrieved 23rd October 2011 from http://www.greennewdealgroup.org .

Hardin, G. (1968). The Tragedy of the Commons. *Science, 162,* 1243–1248.

Henderson, H. (2006). Growing the green economy – globally. *International Journal of Green Economics, 1*(3) (2007), 276.

Hussen A. (2000). *Principles of environmental economics.* London: Routledge

Jorion, P. (2011). *Le capitalisme a l'agonie.* Paris: Fayard.

Kaul, N. (2003). The anxious identities we inhabit positivisms and economics understandings. In Kuiper and Barker (Eds.), *Towards a feminist philosophy of economics* (pp. 194–210). London: Routledge.

Kennet, M. (1997). Green Backlash strategies. In Kennet, M., & Scott Cato, M. (Eds.), *Green Economics Beyond Supply and Demand to meeting peoples needs*, London: Green Audit.

Kennet, M. (2007). Editorial Progress in Green Economics: ontology concepts and philosophy. Civilisation: the lost factor of reality in social and environmental justice. *International Journal of Green Economics, 1*(3), 225.

Kennet, M., & Heinemann, V., (2006). Green economics setting the scene. *International Journal of Green Economics,* V *1*(1), 68–102.

Kennet, M., & Heinemann V. (2008). The second opinion piece for the Redefining Prosperity, third seminar "Confronting Structure – achieving economic sustainability. Sustainable Development Commission UK Government Independent Watchdog Paper 10 11 208. *Prosperity without growth.* Retrieved August 10, 2009 from http://www.sd-commission.org.uk/publications.php?id=772.

Kennet, M. (2008). The Economics of Doing No 13 e : 51 Green Economics for European Green Activists Berlin December 2007 Green European Foundation: The Green Economics Institute European Commission.

Kennet, M. (2009). Green Economics and Pedagogy, Developing Teaching Green Economics. In *Proceedings of the 4th Annual Green Economics Conference*, Oxford University Part 1: 118. London: The Green Economics Institute.

Kennet, M. (2010). *A Green Economics Reader.* London: The Green Economics Institute.

Kennet, M, et al. (2011). *A Handbook of Green Economics: A Practitioners Guide.* London: The Green Economics Institute.

Lean, G., & Shawcross, H. (2007, April 15th). Are mobile phones wiping out our bees? *The Independent.* Retrieved August 10, 2009 from http://news.independent.co.uk/environment/wildlife/article2449968.ece.

Meyer, A. (1995). *Contraction and Convergence.* London: The Global Commons Institute.

Leopold, A. (1997). *A Sand County Almanac.* Oxford: Oxford University Press.

Levey, S. (2011). Fighting Corruption After the Arab Spring: Harnessing Countries' Desire to Improve their Reputations for Integrity. Retrieved October 16, 2011 from http://www.foreignaffairs.com/articles/67895/stuart-levey/fighting-corruption-after-the-arab-spring.

Meadows, D. et al. (1972). *The Limits to Growth: A report for the Club of Rome's Project on the Predicament of Mankind.* (2nd Ed.) New York: Universe Books.

Mies, M. (1998). *Patriarchy and Accumulation on a World Scale.* New York: Palgrave Macmillan.

Mies, M. (2007). Patriarchy and accumulation on a world scale revisited. *International Journal of Green Economics, 1*(3), 268.

Mill, J.S. (1848). *Principles of Political Economy.* London: D. Appleton & Company.

Mansfield, P., & Munro, J. (1987). *Chemical Children.* London: Ebury.

Naess, A. (1995). *Deep ecology for the 21st century.* Boston MA: Shambhala Publications.

Savage, P. (2009). A bee in our bonnet. You bet: The plight of the bumble bee. In *Roundabout* RG8 R and A. (13–15).

Salleh, A . (Ed.) (2009). *Eco sufficiency and global justice.* London: Pluto.

Sachs, G. (2005). *The end of poverty How we can make it happen in our lifetime.* London: Penguin.

Sessions, G. (1995). Deep ecology for the 21st century Shambala Publications.

Singer, P. (1994). The defence of animals. In Singer (Ed.), *Ethical Studies: Practical ethics in Bowie Business Ethics.* Nelson Thornes.

Sukhdev, P. (2008). *TEEB Interim Report.* Geneva: UNEP.

Springett, D. (2006). Managing the narrative of Sustainable Development "discipline" of an inefficient concept. *International Journal of Green Economics. 1*(1), 50.

Stern, N. (2007). *Stern Review. The economics of climate change.* Cambridge: Cambridge University Press.

Turk, J. (2010). Green Economics Methodology. In *A green economics reader.* London: Green Economics Institute.

United Nations Earth Summit (2011). *Workshops, Meetings, and Events.* Retrieved October 16th 2011 from http://www.earthsummit2012.org/workshops-meetings-and-events.

Victor, P. (2008). *Managing without Growth: Slower by Design.* Cheltenham UK: Edward Elgar.

Ward, B., & Dubos, R. (1972). *Only one earth: the care and maintenance of a small planet.* 1st Ed. New York, Norton.

Waring, M. (2009). Policy and measure of woman. In A. Salleh (Ed.), *Eco-sufficiency & Global Justice: Women Write Political Ecology* (pp. 165–179). London, UK: Pluto Press.

Welford, R. (2007). Examining discussing and suggesting the possible contribution and role of Buddhist economics for corporate social responsibility. *International Journal of Green Economics, 1*(3), 341.

Wheat, D.I. (2009). Teaching Economics as if Time Mattered. In J. Reardon, ed. *The Handbook of Pluralist Economics Education* (pp. 69–90). London: Routledge.

GREENING GEOGRAPHY

DONNA HOUSTON

INTRODUCTION

One of the central concerns of the discipline of geography is the study of human-environment relationships over time and space. Geography is one of several disciplines that have played a key role in investigating diverse environmental issues such as the impacts of agriculture, mining, development, globalization and urbanization on the earth's systems and processes. Geographers have also influenced wider social, political and philosophical debates that ask questions about: what is environment and what is our human place in it? As a consequence, there is no one particular moment in geography's disciplinary history where an environmental consciousness took shape to spark an "ecological turn" toward green thinking, politics and philosophy. If anything, the "environment" is such a pervasive concept for geographers that it is often in danger of becoming overdetermined and representing too many different ideas and realities. As the geographers Kay Anderson and Bruce Braun (2008, p. *xi*) succinctly state, "natural environment, built environment, perceptual environment, virtual environment: generations of geographers must have surely wondered what, or where, environment is *not*."

My purpose in writing this chapter about "environmental geographies" is to reflect on how environment and nature have been understood, narrated, studied and theorized by geographers since its formation as an academic discipline in the late nineteenth century. However, I do not provide a chronological account of the evolution of environmental ideas in geography. Such a task would be cumbersome and only serve to emphasise my opening remarks. Instead, I set out three key "environmental moments" within English-speaking academic geography that reflect some important debates that geographers have had over the past century about what constitutes environment and about how human-environment relationships are understood and represented.

The first of these moments covers the period of the late-nineteenth and early twentieth centuries and focuses on the relationship between environment and empire. I include this section because the legacies of imperialism and colonialism on environmental thinking in geography (and indeed in many other disciplines) have cast long shadows into the present. The second "environmental moment" discussed in this chapter represents a period of critical reflection that began during the later half of the twentieth century and which continues to influence contemporary academic geography. This moment describes how geographers engaged with the

S. D. Fassbinder, A. J. Nocella II and R. Kahn (Eds.), Greening the Academy:
Ecopedagogy Through the Liberal Arts, 107–120.
© *2012 Sense Publishers. All rights reserved.*

task of critiquing and decolonising disciplinary knowledge draw on a range of critical perspectives to rethink human-environment relations; such as Marxism, feminism, poststructural and postcolonial theories. In this section the subfields of critical environmental geography (also called nature-society geographies) and political ecology are introduced. The final "environmental moment" focuses on the recent emergence of *more-than-human* perspectives in Geography that do away with any clear distinction between separate categories of humans and environment (Whatmore 2002). *More-than-human* geographies grapple with the question of how agency might be redistributed across the human-environment interface. *More-than-human* thinking in contemporary Geography co-exists with critical environmental geographies and political ecology and each of these perspectives has contributed to lively interdisciplinary scholarship on ecological politics and philosophy. I conclude this chapter with a reflection on how recent work in this enlarged context of "environmental geographies" is connected to the broader project of fostering dialogue between the humanities and sciences and "greening" the academy in a climate of change.

ENIVRONMENT, GEOGRAPHY, AND EMPIRE

For over a hundred years, the relationship between the physical ('natural') environment and the capacity of human beings to influence (or be influenced) by it has been an important topic for geographers. It is a topic that has shaped the discipline's beginnings as a University subject in the late nineteenth century; and it is reflected in the knowledge produced through Geography's early engagement with exploration and empire (Livingstone 1992; Driver 2001; Castree 2005). Geographers played a significant role in the practices of empire as explorers, chroniclers, collectors and cartographers of new territories (Driver 2001). Key field techniques such as the topographic survey, mapping and detailed regional descriptions of "exotic" people, climates, plants and animals were central to the development of the geographic enterprise (Livingstone 1992; Driver 2001). These empirical accounts of exploration and discovery provided the groundwork for territorial conquest and resource colonization and were used to bolster claims of Enlightenment and the idea that Europeans brought culture and civilization to the "savage wilderness" of the New World (Driver 2001).

ENVIRONMENTAL DETERMINISM

The relationship between academic geography and the science of exploration and empire produced a field of knowledge that mobilized environmental narratives in particular ways. By the late nineteenth and early twentieth centuries, "the environment" served as a major integrative concept in Geography that brought together social and natural phenomena in one field of study (Castree 2005). Environmental thinking by geographers at this time often conflated the social and natural in ways that were highly problematic. For example, geographical historian David Livingstone (1991; 1992) shows how the perceived superiority of European culture produced a colonial quasi-science that attempted to link racial characteristics to climate. Influenced by the popularity of Darwin's *On the Origin of Species* (published in 1859), geographers sought to understand the spatial distribution of human racial characteristics and apply these to a scale of human evolutionary development. Livingstone argues that this created a "moral economy" of climate – where tropical and desert climes were thought to produce inferior humans on the grounds that human evolution stagnated (or even degenerated) in hot, harsh environments (Livingstone 1991, p. 429).

These explanations not only served as a basis for the justification of the violent acquisition of territory and the forced labour of slaves and indentured migrants; but also contributed to the emergence of a geographical science that integrated the study of nature and human nature (Castree 2005, p. 57). This focus on the relationship between humans *and* environment was what made geography unique from other disciplines such as biology and geology that also undertook naturalistic inquiry (Castree 2005). But this integrative science was largely descriptive and heavily influenced by social Darwinism – a mode of thought that located cultural practices in evolutionary biology. Darwin's evolutionary biology was particularly influential to William Morris Davis' (1899) development of his cycle-of-erosion model to explain the development of landforms. Ellen Churchill Semple published *Influences of Geographic Environment* in 1911, an expansive example of "scientific racism" that attempted to casually explain environmental influences on human physiology, culture and migration (Peet 1985). Semple's environmental determinism was fundamentally tied to the idea of modern progress, where the "fittest" states exploited their natural advantage. Semple's work reinforced the idea that human consciousness and action is a reflection of the intent of nature; which argues Richard Peet (1985, p. 321) in turn, bolstered the ideological claims of imperialism and capitalism.

Alternative Environmental Perspectives

Of course, not all geographers during this period were social Darwinists. Scholars as Peter Kropotkin and George Perkins Marsh in particular offered quite radically different versions of geography to those of Davis and Semple (Olwig 1980). Though pursuing very different political agendas, the Russian anarchist geographer Kropotkin and American conservationist Marsh eschewed deterministic explanations of environmental influences on culture (Livingstone 1992, p. 258). Kropotkin's study of people and landscapes in northern Siberia combined ethology, ethnography and detailed historical and empirical work (Robbins 2004, pp. 17–20). In 1902 he published *Mutual Aid: A Factor in Evolution* where he argued that mutual cooperation between species was a central mechanism in natural selection (Robbins 2004, p. 18). Kropotkin was particularly critical of social Darwinism that viewed hierarchy, competition and domination as a key aspect of evolutionary success – arguing instead for a form of social cooperative anarchism based on mutual and sustainable relationships between people and environment (Robbins 2004, p. 20). George Perkins Marsh was also concerned about the impacts of unsustainable human activity on the earth's ecosystems. He published *Man and Nature* in 1864, which he described as "a little volume showing that whereas (others) think that the earth made man, man in fact made the earth" (cited in Olwig 1980, p. 37). Marsh was particularly concerned with interconnected effects of degrading ecosystems (for example how deforestation can effect water quality in lakes and rivers). Marsh's work inspired the US conservation movement and is credited with creating the impetus for the establishment of the US Forestry reserves in 1873 (Olwig 1980, p. 38).

Both Kropotkin and Marsh were important environmental thinkers but their insights were not really taken up in geography until the latter part of the twentieth century. However, after World War One, the rise to prominence of cultural ecology and the Berkeley School of Geography lead by Carl Ortwin Sauer (1925–1959) discredited the claims of environmental determinism. The Berkeley School was influential in shaping environmental research that took a historical approach to understanding human and cultural influences on landscapes. Sharply critical of environmental determinism, Sauer's approach was to study the *interaction* between culture and environment through the diffusion of material culture that acted upon and transformed environments over time. The "cultural ecology" traditions of Kropotkin, Marsh and Sauer would later form inspiration for critical environmental geographies and political ecology.

GEOGRAPHY'S RETREAT FROM NATURE?

Despite the refutation of environmental determinism within geography – it was a popular and powerful doctrine that produced lasting effects. The "moral geographies of empire" reinforced Enlightenment binary distinctions between civilization and savagery, culture and nature, light and dark that persisted well into the twentieth century (Livingstone 1991; Driver 1992). The tendency to see evidence of human social structures (capitalism, patriarchy, imperialism) in the natural world remained an unchallenged assumption underpinning the production of geographical knowledge for much of the twentieth century. Even the Berkeley School with its focus on cultural ecology in the agrarian landscapes of the developing world tended to emphasise notions of nature as pre-modern and representative of a simpler way of life (FitzSimmons 1989). Thus, modern academic geography inherited two problems that left an enduring legacy on environmental thinking within the discipline. The first is the academic tradition that emerged out of imperial relationships with the rest of the world and which developed a set of largely descriptive field techniques and imbued these with moral explanations about the relationship between nature and human nature. Environmental determinism made evident the empirical and theoretical difficulties of making holistic and integrative claims about the relationship between people and environment. In practice, its sweeping claims proved to be narrow, inward looking and politically objectionable (Tuner 2002a).

The second problem geographers inherited related to a retreat from "environmental thinking" within academic geography. Environmental determinism – though discredited – created conditions for the "jettisoning" of nature from geography (Peet 1985; FitzSimmons 1989; Castree 2005). Geographers distanced themselves from any idea that the environment might serve as an integrative or unifying concept for bringing together diverse disciplinary themes. As a consequence, while the environment remained an object of study for geographers for much of the twentieth century, it rarely was the focus of critical inquiry and theoretical development within the discipline. Ironically in the 1970s and 1980s when global environmental crises prompted calls for greater attention to human-environment relationships and a focus on integrative approaches to environmental problems such as ecological sustainability – the discipline of geography was largely absent from the scholarly and political debate (Turner 2002).

CRITICAL GEOGRAPHIES: NATURE-SOCIETY AND POLITICAL ECOLOGY

Geography throughout the twentieth century did not end its focus on human-environment relationships, but it did become a discipline that eschewed the environment as a unifying concept (Beaumont and Philo 2004; Demeritt 2009). Richard Peet (1985) has argued that this lack of theoretical attention to the political dynamics of environment is one of the enduring after-effects of imperialism and environmental determinism. For some geographers, the lack of an integrative focus on environment as something that holds the many divergent strains of geography together in one discipline constitutes something of a missed opportunity. Some geographers have worried that this has meant geography (as a discipline broadly engaged with human-environment relations) has not demonstrated leadership in interdisciplinary scholarly, policy and public debates about environmental sustainability and climate change (Turner 2002; Zimmerer 1997). This is further compounded by the development of academic specialisations within geography, which by the mid-twentieth century, had become firmly entrenched in a substantial divide between "human" and "physical" approaches (Beaumont and Philo 2004). Geographers leaning towards the physical sciences developed an environmental geography focused on earth systems and processes; and human geographers have focused on regions, culture, economics, politics, space and urban worlds.

There is of course more to be said here in terms of the real and perceived impacts of progressive specialisation within the discipline on the production environmental geographies (see Demeritt 2009). But what I am tracing in this chapter is the development of environmental thought in geography that contributes more broadly to the greening of the humanities and social sciences. The remainder of this section is devoted to a discussion of the second "environmental moment" that emerged in geography during the 1980s that reflects a critical turn in geographical theory and research. This era sparked a renewed interest in nature and environment – but this time in a context of understanding the historical, economic, political and ideological underpinnings of these concepts. This has produced a diverse set of theoretical and ontological understandings about the constitution of nature and society and has revitalised environmental themes within human geography in particular.

I follow two key developments that continue to flourish in present geographical scholarship. The first is the development of political ecology as a sub discipline and the second is the proliferation of critical environmental geographies (also called nature-society geographies). In recent years, there has been quite a bit of blurring of the boundaries between critical environmental and political ecology perspectives. This is because both these specializations share a commitment to making connections between social and environmental justice through careful critical analyses of political struggles over the environment.

"The Matter of Nature" in Geography

In 1989 Margaret FitzSimmons published a paper in *Antipode: A Journal of Radical Geography* titled "The Matter of Nature." She argued that while geographers had developed a dynamic and nuanced set of theories around space, the same could not be said about nature. It was not that geographers had not been producing groundbreaking work on the politics of the environment – Michael Watts had published his seminal work on political ecology *Silent Violence: Food, Famine and Peasantry in Nigeria* in 1983 and Neil Smith had published *Uneven Development: Nature, Capital and the Production of Space* in 1984. What FitzSimmons identified was a distinct lack of rigorous disciplinary debate amongst geographers about the social and ideological constitution of nature. She cited several reasons for this absence. The first reason pertained to the development of specialisations, which tended to separate nature out from culture. For example, urban geographers at the time tended to focus on the social, economic and spatial formation of cities – paying little attention to the essential ecologies that support their function. FitzSimmons also argued that the legacies of environmental determinism also played a role in under-theorizing nature in geography. But another important reason for the under-theorization of nature, FitzSimmons observed, was because the "naturalness" of nature hides its social construction. FitzSimmons' arguments echoed the sentiments of the literary critic Raymond Williams who famously wrote in his essay "Ideas of Nature" that "nature contains, though often unnoticed, contains an extraordinary amount of human history" (1980, p. 67).

FitzSimmons' essay is marked an important turn back towards environmental thinking in human geography. It was published at a time of great critical reflection within academic geography. In the late 1980s and early 1990s, geographers became increasingly sensitive to how the production of geographical knowledge (past and present) was implicated in relationships of power (Driver 1992, p. 23). They turned their attention to the production of power and knowledge in "geographical imaginations" and how such imaginations produced cultural and political difference (Gregory 1990). Geographical work in this vein uncovered hidden and previously unexplored assumptions about some of the founding ideas in geography. Margaret FitzSimmons' essay drew attention to the idea that nature is not given but socially constructed through discourse and power to reflect certain Western visions of the world; which are then enacted through regimes of planning, management and development. The ideological critique of nature in geography has produced a large volume of environmental scholarship that covers a range of themes from subaltern political struggles over resources; the social production of environmental inequity; to the political constitution of discourses of nature in conservation and wildlife management.

Political Ecology

Political ecologists working at the intersections of landscape change, development and subaltern studies have made a key contribution to understanding how human-environment relationships are implicated in politics and power. The early political ecology of the 1980s and 1990s analyzed "unequal power relations, conflict and 'cultural modernization' under a global capitalist political economy as key forces in reshaping and destabilizing human interactions with the physical environment" (Walker 2005, p. 74). For example, Piers Blaikie and Harold Brookfield's (1987) book *Land Degradation and Society*, examined the interaction between rural land users in developing countries and environmental deterioration. Blaikie and Brookfield argued that while it was important to understand environmental factors leading to land degradation (such as droughts, soil composition and floods etc), it was equally significant to understand the impacts of political, economic and historical processes in exacerbating poverty, marginalization and unsustainable land management practices. Political ecologists such as Blaikie and Brookfield argued that the unequal integration of rural land users into global markets frequently worked to undermine traditional ecological knowledge and the adaptive capacities of local people to their environments (Walker 2005, p. 74).

Early political ecology posited environmental struggles over landscapes and resources as central to understanding human-environment relations. Political ecologists undertook a major critique of modern Western development regimes and drew attention to the frequently devastating impacts of these on Third World landscapes, ecologies and livelihoods. What was significant about such work was the emphasis on the interaction between biophysical and social processes in the making of environmental problems and subsistence crises. This work highlighted the profoundly unjust, invisible and often contradictory objectives of environmental research programs that often claim to be preserving or conserving environmental values, while at the same time creating conditions in which Indigenous people are denied access to lands and resources.

Perhaps as a consequence, political ecology in geography has tended to lean towards highlighting the politics of environment (Demeritt 2009). This move is exemplified in the collection of essays that appeared in Michael Watts and Richard

Peet's (1999) edited collection *Liberation Ecologies: Environment, Development and Social Movements*. The "new" political ecology, as it has come to be called, emphasizes the role of social movements in shaping environmental agendas and how power and knowledge is embedded in local struggles over land and resources (Peet and Watts 1996). This work is particularly attentive to Indigenous and popular environmental movements engaged in cultural struggles against modern development practices and draws on insights from poststructural theory challenge the foundational truths of science, modernity and rationality (Escobar 1996). More recently, political ecologists have enlarged their field of research to extend beyond the rural forests and agrarian landscapes of the developing world – to explore a whole range of environments as contested arenas of discourses, politics and entitlements (Watts and Peluso 2001; Swyndegdow et al., 2006). It is here that a lot of common ground can be found with a broadly defined field of critical environmental geography.

Critical Environmental (Nature-Society) Geographies

Margaret FitzSimmon's call to bring "the matter of nature" back into geography marked a critical and cultural turn in environmental thinking. Falling under the broad umbrella of "nature-society", geographers incorporated postcolonial, cultural, actor-network theory (ANT) and the sociology of scientific knowledge (SSK) perspectives into their work on environment (Castree and Braun 2001). Indeed, as nature-society perspectives in geography became theoretically diverse, so too did the types of environmental research undertaken by geographers. Starting with the idea that nature and environment are socially constructed and historically situated (though never reducible to human thoughts and actions alone), much of this work emphasized how nature is "remade" through politics, political economy, discourse and culture (Castree and Braun 2001). Questions of power and justice remain central to "nature-society" geographies that explore how people and environment are mutually constituted through production and consumption. Public controversies over issues such as the labeling of genetically modified foods, environmental disasters such as the gas leak at a Union Carbide factory that in 1984 killed 3000 people in Bhopal India, and unruly transspecies epidemics such as the BSE ("mad cow disease") outbreak in the United Kingdom in the 1990s highlight the entanglement of people and environment. Geographers have turned their attention to the contingencies and complexities of contemporary environmental problems and how they challenge underlying assumptions that humans and environment occupy separate spheres.

Rethinking Nature-Society Relations

A big part of critical environmental and nature-society geographies therefore is to critically rethink ideas about environment, nature and wilderness and how these ideas have historically supported the domination of the nonhuman in Western culture. For example, representations of wilderness and "the wild" as places of pure, undefiled and nonhuman nature have excluded non-European cultures and knowledges about habitable worlds (Cosgrove 1995). Bruce Braun's (1997) exploration of the "buried epistemologies" found in contemporary struggles over the temperate rainforests in the Pacific Northwest is an excellent example. He argued that both extractive industries and environmentalists (while on different sides of the resource development debate) drew on social constructions of nature as "pure" and "external". Such perspectives that regard nature as external to human communities (either as a resource or asset to be preserved) marginalize Indigenous histories and understandings of nature where humans and environment are not separate from each other but intimately connected through a whole web of relations (Braun 1997, p. 25). What Braun's study demonstrated was how nature comes to *matter* in various cultural, physical, and historical registers.

This idea of how nature and environment come to matter (in both a material and discursive sense) has also been taken up by urban geographers in recent years. They have illuminated the "nature-society" dialectic of cities that points to the ways in which environment, far from being external to urban production or the raw stuff upon which communities are built, is intrinsically a part of urban life (Swyngedouw 2006). Work in this area has tackled a variety of issues such as the sedimentation of environmental racism and injustice in communities of color (Pulido, Sidawi and Vos 1996); human-animal interactions at nature-culture borderlands of cities (Wolch 1998); and the production of hybrid urban natures and technologies in the everyday life of cities (Swyngedouw 2006). Geographical research in this vein has sought to write nature back into accounts of how cities work and how "urban natures" are made and experienced by different collectives over time and place. Increasingly, the idea that the material and cultural fabric of our everyday lives is made up of lively encounters between humans and nonhumans have begun to take shape in geography (Whatmore 2002; Braun 2006). Such perspectives pose the question: how do we come to understand our experience of living in a world shared with others? (Anderson and Braun 2008, p. *xviii*)

Much recent work in geography on rethinking natures and cultures has already anticipated a world in which firm distinctions between human and nonhuman no longer hold sway. One of the most evocative aspects of environmental studies in geography is that its theoretical and philosophical insights emerge out of individual and collaborative engagements with the living world. It is this insight that there is a material recalcitrance to living and non-living things that exceeds our capacity to know and represent them has underpinned geographical work across the "human" and "physical" divide (Smith 1984). Despite such understandings, getting beyond the "nature-society" duality has also proven to be a much thornier issue than ever imagined. Thus, while many critical takes on environmental geographies have painstakingly unpacked Enlightenment traditions that posit nature and culture in an unequal hierarchy of power and knowledge, they still tend to evoke themes of "construction', 'interaction', and 'interrelation" between something called *nature* and something called *society* (Castree 2005, p. 226). The final part of this chapter explores the possibility of an environmental studies that eschews this distinction altogether and explores the ways in which environmental geographies might engage with the pressing ecological challenges of the twenty-first century.

"More Than Human" Geographies

More-than-human geographies illustrate a shift from "dualistic" to "relational" approaches to thinking about and doing environmental geographies (Braun 2008, p. 1). Relational thinking across the nature-society interface has been nurtured in geography's various subfields (see previous sections) for some time. However, *more-than-human* perspectives constitute a mode of enquiry that not only critiques categories such as "society" and "environment" but also redistributes participation across human and nonhuman collectives (Whatmore 2002; Anderson and Braun 2008). This has important implications for how scholars in the humanities and social sciences engage with and tell stories about environment. We might indeed ask, what happens to environmental studies if the term "environment" gets taken out of the picture, and instead comes to be represented by assemblages, networks, collaborations, actants, performances, and co-fabrications? (Braun 2008, p. 1).

Relational thinkers in geography have utilized diverse approaches in tracing this complex issue (see Castree 2005, pp. 223–241). Sarah Whatmore (2002; 2006), for example, draws on the work of Bruno Latour, Donna Haraway and Isabel Stengers in her writing on hybrid or *more-than-human* geographies. *More-than-human geographies* constitute an enlarged field of environmental relations that explore associations and connections between things – for example – wildlife, bodies, technologies, politics, governance, affects, natures and economics (Whatmore 2002). The important idea here is the recognition that new vocabularies and practices might need to be developed to explain the complexity of human-environment relationships. Sarah Whatmore and Lorraine Thorne (1998) in their work on the spatial formations of elephant wildlife exchange, explore the ethics of conservation practices by looking at how elephants are caught up in captive breeding programs in zoos and in wildlife management in national parks. Such practices challenge the idea that nature is external to us – Whatmore and Thorne draw attention to this fact by examining how elephant agency and being becomes entangled in networks of scientific intervention, conservation funding, care and neglect.

More-than-human approaches seek to displace the idea that human "being" is ontologically separate and situated in an external environment. In this regard, human subjects are not autonomous from environment; rather they *inhabit* hectic and often unruly corporeal worlds that exert their own material agencies. Influenced by Latour's (1993) advocacy for the rights of objects or "parliament of things" (all that we categorise under the schema of modernity as "nonhuman" including plants and animals), *more-than-human* geographies refuse to make subject-object distinctions that do not acknowledge the hybridity of matter. Such perspectives encourage environmental scholars to move beyond questions of how "the environment" is talked about and constructed in discourse. Rather, they amplify the many different senses and registers through which humans and nonhumans interact. There exist many examples in the world of efforts to rethink the more-than-human environment including the reclaiming of marshes and wetlands to improve water quality and mitigate floods in cities; household sustainability initiatives; the growing acceptance and use of traditional ecological knowledge in environmental management regimes and local and regional struggles to transform degraded environments. While this list is far from exhaustive, what these different instances register is the recognition of the "ontological pluralism" of humans and nonhumans as well as a multiplicity of environmental stories, histories, practices and relations that make up the material fabric of our everyday lives (Howitt and Suchet-Pearson 2003).

Sharing the World with Others

More-than-human approaches thus infuse a different politics and ethics to environmental studies: one that is attuned to themes such as vitalism and conviviality (Binghman and Hinchliffe 2008; Braun 2008). Themes of vitalism and conviviality help to shape engagements with the living world where "different forms of life are constituted through what circulates between them" (Anderson and Braun 2008, p. *xviii*). In other words, vitalism and conviviality encourage scholars to consider things such as the vibrant material worlds of a disused urban lot where micro-ecologies are shaped by the activities of children and animals, or, the imaginative geographies of environmental justice activists working to transform accumulative material histories of unsustainable land use in their localities.

The question, then, of how are we to live in a world shared with others does not disregard the varied philosophical, empirical and practical work that makes up contemporary environmentalisms. Neither does it imply that we have somehow moved beyond the injuries and injustices of race, class and gender in the making of environmental politics. But what it does do is open up different possibilities for understanding how "living environmentalisms", as Giovanna Di Chiro calls them, are made through the "worldly and laborious engagements with the fleshy realities of socio-ecological interdependence" (Di Chiro, 2008, p. 279). The focus on the worldly work of assembling environmental knowledges and practices emphasises a renewed commitment to ontology and "ways of doing." This has key implications for the ways in which twenty-first century academics might engage with human and nonhuman communities, and with each other in interdisciplinary border-work (Di Chiro 2008).

ENVIRONMENTAL GEOGRAPHIES AND ANTHROPOCENE PEDAGOGIES

By way of a conclusion, I want to suggest that contemporary environmental geographies have much to offer an interdisciplinary project of greening the academy. In the last two sections in particular have demonstrated a proliferation of

117

environmental themes in geography that are not easily contained in one relatively short book chapter. The proliferation of environmental thinking in geography (and also in other academic disciplines) demonstrates the complexity of environmental issues and problems and our individual and collective responses to them. The stories about environmental thinking in geography that I have chosen to tell in this chapter are reflective of both the pitfalls and possibilities for understanding and rethinking human-environment relations. Environmental thinking in geography began with according a great deal of agency to environmental influences on human society – but in a way that was ultimately highly anthropocentric and which reflected particular ideologies and aspirations connected to capitalism and imperialism. The environment is a difficult concept to grasp because in Western cultures, it often is treated as a mirror through which our social formations and desires are reflected back to us.

As we contemplate environmental thought and action in the twenty-first century, we are confronted with the reality of visible and present climate change that is likely to worsen dramatically. The Nobel Prize winning atmospheric scientist has proposed that we are currently living in the Anthropocene – a new geologic era of our own making that may yield a permanent geologic record of human-induced environmental change (2002). The implications of the Anthropocene are slowly being taken up in the humanities and social sciences (Lorimer 2008; Rose and van Dooren 2011) as we grapple with the social, political and ethical dimensions of climate change, declines in biodiversity and cascades of extinctions. Contemporary environmental thinking in geography highlights two compelling realities of life in the Anthropocene: (1) that the environment is a contested political terrain where geographies of uneven development continue to play out and (2) that the environment is more-than-human and has its own stories that are not reducible to human interests and concerns.

The "greening" of academic thought within the university has been pretty good at recognising the first reality. While there is still a long way to go, academic scholarship across the humanities and social sciences has highlighted different ontological perspectives on green thinking and which can be found in literature, film, philosophy, art, city planning and classroom pedagogies to name but a few. Understanding that the environment is a contested political terrain means coming to terms with the past and particularly how Western cultural logics about nature and environment have produced a separation between nature and culture that has reinforced colonizing relationships. The project of "decolonising" these relationships recognises that the violent suppression and exclusion of alternative environmental knowledges – particularly the traditional ecological knowledge of Indigenous peoples has contributed to deepening social and environmental crisis (Grande 2004; Rose and Robin 2004). Challenging western scientific cultures of "expert knowledge" within the academy highlights an urgent need to think more deeply about animate and interconnected ecologies and the ways in which we are all implicated in them.

This brings us to the second reality: that environment is not and never has been a wholly human construction. With this insight comes the understanding that greening the academy is not just an ideological and philosophical project – but also a material one. Universities, like all modern institutions, are entangled in ecological relationships at different geographical scales. In recent years, many universities have instigated sustainability initiatives that focus on green architecture, reducing waste and energy consumption; promoting walking, cycling, car sharing and public transportation; and supporting ethical food choices, community gardens, fair trade products and local produce. But perhaps there is more to be said about the "ecosystem services" that universities perform. As spaces of cultural knowledge, many university campuses have historically supported extensive grounds that include arboretums, lakes and streams that serve as markers of enlightenment and colonial privilege. Yet, many such university campuses are also located in transformed urban environments and often provide much needed green space for local children as well as biological niches for other species. The ethics and politics of the "more-than-human" university play out in other ways too. The housing of animal laboratories on campuses is a deeply contested issue where questions about ethics towards other species has become central to debates about animal emotions, suffering and calls in to question the quality of data yielded from stressful experimental situations (xxx).

Pedagogies in the Anthropocene illuminate complex ecological stories about what it means to be human in the present moment. These stories challenge us to think critically about how humans have transformed the biosphere and how this necessitates an urgent need for more sustainable relationships across scale, place, time, and with the living/dying world. In exploring these themes, geographers have made an important contribution to the broader project of situating the humanities and social sciences in political/ecological terms. Contemporary environmental geographies help to shape emerging environmental stories that inform pedagogies in the Anthropocene. At the same time, Anthropocene pedagogies are also in and of the world and require an engagement with material life in all of its permutations if we are to confront serious changes to the ways in which we think and act in a climate of change. The environment, after all, is where we live.

REFERENCES

Anderson, K., & Braun, B. (2008). Introduction, in Kay Anderson and Bruce Braun (Eds.), *Environment*, Hampshire UK and Burlington USA: Ashgate.

Blaikie, P., & Brookfield, H. (1987). *Land Degradation and Society*. London and New York: Methuen.

Bingham, N., & Hinchliffe, S. (2008). Reconstituting Natures: Articulating Other Modes of Living Together, *Geoforum, 39*, 83–87.

Braun, B. (2008). Environmental issues: inventive life, *Progress in Human Geography*, 1–13.

Beaumont, P., & Philo, C. (2004). Environmentalism and Geography: The Great Debate? In John A Matthews and David T Herbert (Eds.), *Unifying Geography: Common Heritage, Shared Future*, London and New York: Routledge.

Castree, Noel. (2005). *Nature*, London and New York: Routledge.

Castree, N., & Braun, B. (2001). *Remaking Reality: nature at the millennium*. London and New York: Routledge.

Di Chiro, G. (2008). Living Environmentalisms: Coalition Politics, Social Reproduction and Environmental Justice, *Environmental Politics, 17*(2), 276–298.

Escobar, A. (1996). Constructing Nature: elements for a poststructural political ecology in Richard Peet and Michael Watts (Eds.), *Liberation Ecologies: environment, development, social movements,* London and New York: Routledge.

Fitzsimmons, M. (1989). The Matter of Nature. *Antipode, 21*(2), 106–120.

Houston, D. (2008). Crisis and Resilience: Cultural Methodologies for Environmental Sustainability and Justice, *Continuum: A Journal of Media and Cultural Studies, 22*(2), 179–190.

Howitt, R., & Suchet-Pearson, S. (2003). Contested Cultural Landscapes in Kay Anderson, Mona Domosh, Steve Pile and Nigel Thrift (Eds.), *Handbook of Cultural Geography,* London: Sage Publications.

Latour, B. (1993). *We Have Never Been Modern,* New York: Harvester Wheatsheaf.

Livingstone, D. (1992). *The Geographical Tradition: Episodes in the History of a Contested Enterprise,* Oxford UK; Cambridge USA: Blackwell.

Peet, R., & Watts, M. (Eds.). (1996). *Liberation Ecologies: environment, development, social movements,* London and New York: Routledge.

Pulido, L., Sidawi, S., & Vos, R. O. (1996). An Archaeology of Environmental Racism in Los Angeles, *Urban Geography, 17*(5), 419–439.

Rose, D. B. (2004). 'The Ecological Humanities in Action: An Invitation', *Australian Humanities Review,* Issue 31–32, April.

Smith, N. (1984). *Uneven Development: Nature, Capital and the Production of Space,* New York: Blackwell.

Swyngedouw, E. (2006). Circulations and Metabolisms: (Hybrid) Natures and (Cyborg) Cities, *Science as Culture, 15*(2), 105–121.

Turner II, B.L. (2002). Response to Thrift's "The future of geography", *Geoforum, 33,* 427–429.

Walker, Peter A. (2005). Political Ecology: Where is the Ecology? *Progress in Human Geography, 29*(1), 73–82.

Whatmore, Sarah. (2002) *Hybrid Geographies: Natures, Cultures, Spaces,* London: Sage.

Whatmore, Sarah. (2006). Materialist Returns: Practising Cultural Geography in and for a More-than-Human World, *Cultural Geographies, 13,* 600–609.

Willems-Braun, Bruce. (1997). Buried Epistemologies: The Politics of Nature in (Post)colonial British Columbia, *Annals of the Association of American Geographers, 87*(1), 3–31.

Wolch, Jennifer. (1998). Zoopolis, in Jennifer Wolch and Jody Emel (Eds.), *Animal Geographies: Place, Politics and Identity in the Nature-Culture Borderlands,* London and New York: Verso.

GREENING HISTORY

EVA-MARIA SWIDLER

What is sometimes termed the 'discovery of history' by other disciplines has, in the last couple of decades, unleashed a torrent of self-examination and philosophical reflection in the intellectual world. The historical analysis of the particular division of scholarship into the various disciplines, the study of the historical evolution of each profession and its place in the social and political constellation, the consideration of the rise and fall of different vocabularies or discourses or understandings as part of a larger social history and cultural trajectory, the causal connection of new paradigms of understanding to changing political and economic forces–all these kinds of historicizing projects have liberated academics from the positivism which reigned mid-20th century, and opened the door for sophisticated discussions of theory, epistemology, truth-claims, relativism. The discovery of history provided the antidote to the simple and multiply layered positivist myth that objective data speak transparently and yield the single truth.

The ultimate irony, then, is that history is the hold-out to this epistemological discussion. Allan Smith has a relatively benign description of history's relationship to the philosophy of knowledge: "substantial numbers of practicing historians remain relentlessly uninterested in fundamental questions concerning the status of the knowledge they produce," though he goes on two pages later to claim more harshly that historians have an 'active hostility' to epistemological discussions.[1] Oliver Daddow, in his article "Still No Philosophy Please, We're Historians" also uses milder terms such as 'rank indifference' and 'collective apathy' describing history's attitudes towards theory.[2] Others such as Keith Jenkins more jarringly call history 'intellectually backward' and 'rabidly anti-theoretical.'[3] Smith proposes that historians don't want to undercut their own legitimacy, and therefore view any questioning of empirical research as a fundamental threat. He also speculates that this theory-aversion has deep roots in the psychological profiles of those who are attracted to become historians–history attracts those who have uncomplicated notions of truth and representation, he says. A connection that the standpoint theory of knowledge construction could make between these 'uncomplicated' (perhaps 'transparent' would be a helpful term here) notions of research and the sociological and political profiles of historians seems more productive than a resort to personal psychology. But however viewed, the curious result is that history departments have no specialists in theory, as say anthropology or political science or sociology departments do, and in fact generally have no courses in theory at all. (Perhaps

S. D. Fassbinder, A. J. Nocella II and R. Kahn (Eds.), Greening the Academy:
Ecopedagogy Through the Liberal Arts, 121–140.
© 2012 Sense Publishers. All rights reserved.

a capstone course for majors in 'methodology' might address a few philosophical ideas; or then again perhaps not.)

In this essay, I will argue that the sociological origins of professional historians, rooted in the discipline's particular position within the academy, combine with a lack of theoretical, intellectual self-consciousness to promote a subfield of environmental history which is highly influenced by its academic parent, and which is therefore a peculiarly conservative field within the environmental disciplines. Solutions to this self-reinforcing dynamic lie in affirmative steps to increase the diversity of practitioners, as well as in cultivating insight into the ways that history writing in general is influenced by power and helps to reproduce power and sustain the status-quo. In order to ask what political, economic, or cultural forces shape the way history is written and how written history sustains the political economy, the discipline must acknowledge the social creation of historical knowledge. An essential first step will be to comprehend how theory fits into the production of historical knowledge; history must see itself as an epistemological venture. Similarly, the taboo within the discourse against any appearance of advocacy can only be broken when historians give up their attachment to empiricism and are willing to locate themselves within the social world. That is, environmental history will only be able to break out of its relative isolation within environmental studies and offer its considerable skills to the interdisciplinary field when it historicizes itself and its theories. Towards that goal, I offer these opening thoughts.

An umbrella field known as 'environmental history' came into being in the early 1970s, as did so many other environmental disciplines. Naturally, historians have studied the non-human world and the relationships of humans to it for as long as history has been studied, under rubrics such as 'forest history', or 'the Annales school', for instance. These earlier formulations of the field were driven by pre-Earth Day dynamics, however. In the early 1970s, environmental history, whether the branch concerned with the history of cultural concepts of the environment or the branch concerned with the history of actual human-nature interactions, took its place among a wave of increasingly significant revisionist schools of history, including social history, women's history, African-American history, and labor history. Thus, in its inception, environmental history was part of a broader radical attempt to reconceptualize history from a variety of grassroots perspectives. In somewhat later terminology, the historians of these waves were attempting to deconstruct the Grand Narrative that had been so painstakingly constructed in the previous century of professionalized history.

Each of these new movements in history was generated by the admission of new categories of students into the previously exclusive academy. Social history (the study of history as driven by social groups and social conflicts rather than by the actions of great individuals and leaders) and labor and working class history coalesced in the 1960s as members of the lower classes made their way into college through the G.I. bill and the college loans available in the later decades of the 20th century. Similarly, women's history and Black history drew interest a few years later, as women and people of color were, in some proportion at least, increasing in the ranks of historians as a benefit of the civil rights and women's movements. The parallel for environmental history was that it, too, was driven by the political dynamics and agenda of a mid-century movement, in this case the environmental one; typical topics included a U. S. focus, wilderness and parks, a history of the American environmental movement, and preoccupations with figures such as John Muir or Aldo Leopold. But being defined as a separate strand of history from all of these other 'new' interpretive ventures, all of which could be and were lumped together under the broader rubric of 'social history', both shaped and weakened environmental history. Practitioners of social history in all its variations shared that fundamental understanding of the historical dynamics of change mentioned above, i.e. they saw history as driven by social groups rather than by great individuals, and as driven by conflict rather than consensus. But despite environmental history's shared origin from a movement of the 1960s or 70s, it shared neither of these premises.

Instead, the vast majority of pre-eminent practitioners of the first decades of environmental history were white men, resembling the practitioners of the old mainstream history, with whom they often shared the preoccupation with leading great figures and the cultural rather than political economic causes of change. (That the chosen great figures and cultures of study were also white and male, as in mainstream history, went unremarked.) To this day, environmental historians frequently see themselves as in direct competition with all of social history, while social historians of gender or race or the working class operate at worst in benign parallel to each other, and at best in varying degrees of cooperation and integration with each other. To be fair, from the other side, social historians often see environmental historians as in direct competition with them, as well. The crucial question is how this strange state of affairs came to be, and therefore whether and how this divergence between social and environmental history can be overcome to create the synthesis of human and natural studies that environmental studies has as its necessary core.

In a typical historian's fashion, I want to protect myself preemptively from criticism. What follows, in necessarily only a few pages, are the broad outlines of the discipline as I see it. Indeed there are the exceptions, subtleties and complications that historians so adore. And indeed, as we shall review in the conclusion, there are hopeful changes afoot. But, (here I am referring in a historian's fashion to a great name in the field to cover myself for the sin of having a clear opinion), Donald Worster notes that, "Historians seem to have trouble with any large explanation, or perhaps any explanation at all..."[4] So in a decidedly untypical move for a historian, this depiction of the past and present, if not the future, is laid out without timidity and without further apology or qualification.

At the root of the problem of this divorce of environmental from social history is the nature of the discipline of history itself. As a professional field, history has been rightly and continuously lambasted for decades as "the conservative discipline par excellence," in Hayden White's oft-quoted words first published over 40 years ago.[5]

It is difficult, on many levels, to quantify the politics of those who choose to enter history in preference to other social sciences and humanities. To a certain extent there is a chicken and egg question which is a moot point; whether conservatives like history and then create a historical narrative in keeping with their views, or whether history as philosophically constituted is somehow inherently conservative and thus attracts like-minded students, the result is the same, and the cyclic dilemma of largely conservative historians writing conservative works continues.

While we cannot easily draw a depiction of the landscape of the political outlooks of historians, this conservatism is directly correlated with the sociological profile of historical practitioners. Sidestepping the question of how the perceived political alignment of history might be a factor in creating that profile, The American Historical Association notes merely that it cannot tell whether history as a field attracts a disproportionate number of white men or whether history as it is structured actively drives others away, and even in 2005 writes, "the discipline has an unusually limited appeal to women and minorities." The only undergraduate college fields which are whiter are construction, mechanics, agriculture, theology, and education. Among all humanities and social science Ph.D.'s awarded in 2000, only political science had fewer women and only English had fewer minorities, putting history in an overall last place in terms of diversity.[6] When we go on to observe that not surprisingly a disproportionately high number of those already reduced women and minority historians are entering the social history specialties of women's and African-American history, creating either disciplinary refuges or ghettos depending on your view, we can get a sense of the highly homogenous profile of the rest of the historical profession, environmental history unfortunately included.

As supporters of affirmative action have frequently pointed out, the purposeful introduction of diversity into a profession does not merely benefit the previously excluded groups and individuals, it greatly benefits and strengthens the profession itself, bringing entirely new methodologies, insights, questions, and systems of operation. Accordingly, environmental history as done by historians has suffered from, among other things, the narrow political and sociological profile which it inherits by virtue of its location in history departments.

As an overwhelmingly white and relatively male specialty within an already 'conservative discipline par excellence,' environmental history has been preoccupied with establishing itself as a legitimate field in the eyes of those conservative disciplinarians. Much of Black and women's history on some level assumed that it would be suspect to the historical establishment and was therefore willing to take a confrontational stand. Unlike those specialties, environmental history has yearned for acceptance and integration. Environmental history journals abound with articles taking stock of the field, considering why it has failed to make incursions into textbooks and the Grand Narrative. Environmental history conferences buzz with discussions of why the field hasn't achieved some kind of elusive 'arrived' status within the profession. These are important and relevant questions, of course, but not the only ones. There are no similar discussions about environmental history's participation and status, or lack thereof, in wider environmental studies or public environmental policy, or its absence from interdisciplinary approaches like food systems studies, or its invisibility in the public consciousness and the best-seller lists where the *biologist* Jared Diamond is the public intellectual writing environmental history.

As an outgrowth of the discipline of history, environmental history naturally inherits history's weaknesses–its political positioning in the academy, its student recruiting profile, the disciplinary institutional forces such as the particular tenure requirements and funding formats which ultimately determine professional success or failure. Unlike the social history upstarts, who attempted some political challenges and made some allies in women's studies, African-American studies, and labor and American studies, and thus have maintained some threads of a radical political discourse, environmental history largely accepted the pre-existing intellectual structure of the field of history, with that combination of Great Man figures and explanations rooted in the primacy of culture rather than political economy. (The trends in the last couple of decades of an increasingly de-radicalized social history are clearly beyond my scope here, but may offer more instruction on the conservatizing influence of maintaining residence within a history department.) Despite its roots in the rebellious social and political movements of the 1960s and 70s, and the actual allegiance of many if not all of its practitioners to some kind of an environmentalist agenda, environmental history did and does not look to those political comrades for strength, but instead has looked to the mainstream of history for affirmation. Thus the weaknesses of environmental history's liberal, white and male social origins have been amplified, and it has gotten mired in the conservative swamp of history departments.

Accordingly, environmental history has inherited the intellectual weakness of the parent discipline, along with its sociological profile. While musings on the future of the field are common, musings on historical theory and its impact on how environmental history is and can be written are minimal. One cluster of sophisticated and provocative writings which *has* emerged is around the concepts of wilderness and nature, with William Cronon as a main founding figure.[7] The discourse proposed that a couple of the favored topics of environmental historians, wilderness and nature parks in the 20th century in particular, were in fact formulated and defined in the context of certain class and racial concerns. An important and useful self-examination and discussion ensued. But the somewhat paradoxical final result for the discipline from this promising start seems to have been a retreat from even the low level of environmental advocacy that environmental historians engaged in. (Despite their roots in the environmental movement of the 1960s, in their allegiance to the mainstream of the historical discipline, environmental historians have often aspired to 'objectivity' or the appearances thereof, and been averse to anything that might be perceived as 'taking sides'; see more below.) Environmental historians engaged in this discourse on race, class and environmentalism, and in the discourse on ideas of nature in general, have settled on a new version of objectivity, seemingly satisfied with describing the range of various possible cultural attitudes towards the non-human world, and ending in a bemused, post-modern style relativist paralysis that allows no environmentalist position at all.

The rest of the environmental history field seems instead to have moved forward directly without this detour in continuing a highly traditional (for history) empiricist research agenda as a preemptive response to attacks from other historians on environmental history for not being 'objective' enough. As a personal example of the fetishism of data, a theoretical article of mine was rejected in 2008 by a reviewer at a flagship environmental history journal as "not scholarly work at all" specifically *because* it "had no empirical basis." (Interestingly, that article was accepted for publication in a scientific journal which obviously had no qualms about the lack of empirics. I received several supportive and interested emails from soil scientists from Israel to Mexico to India in the wake of its appearance in print.)[8]

So the field of history continues to generally operate on its practical research level from an outmoded and conservative philosophical tradition of empiricism which sees no need to discuss epistemology or theory, believing that objectivity is possible, desirable, and self-evidently produces truth. The corollary to this operating platform, also politically conservative, is that advocacy of any kind compromises that desirable, indeed essential, objectivity. And indeed, environmental history as a body studiously avoids advocacy. In fact, it avoids advocacy so assiduously that it eschews any involvement in policy formation or current commentary at all, lest it be seen to be partial. Lone voices such as Stephen Pyne attend conferences and may beg historians to become involved in U.S. Forest Service decision-making councils to offer historical insight, and Stephen Dovers may write articles rooting for historians to participate in public discussions and debates, but the calls are so far unheeded.[9] In 2007, in a step of seeming progress 30 years after its formation, the American Society for Environmental History formed an advocacy process. But so far the one and only advocacy position issued by the American Society for Environmental History has been to oppose the closure of the EPA's libraries; after all the advocacy branch is charged with pronouncing only "on matters directly relevant to the practice of history such as insuring continued access to documents and archival materials" because "when we as a society start advocating on matters outside our professional expertise, we risk losing professional credibility," although the organization notes that it "encourage(s) members to consider joining societies that do take advocacy roles."[10]

One interesting exception to historians' virtual ban on public involvement comes from the military-diplomatic field of history, whose practitioners have a particularly unshakeable faith in their own objectivity, and seem to draw on their sense of self-evident expertise to freely make policy recommendations; they often move in and out of military, espionage and government positions without comment or aspersions from others in the discipline. Presumably the highly official nature and politics of their public work somehow laves it of the connotations of partisanship.

A final consequence of environmental history's inward directed gaze, looking only within history for confirmation of its viability and validity as a field, has been its general failure to engage in the multiple new interdisciplinary discussions of environmental issues. For instance, food and agriculture systems issues have sociologists, ethnobotanists, agronomists, economists and geographers working together, with nary an environmental historian in sight. In sustainability fora, historians have till recently been rarely in evidence, despite the central contribution that history should have to make to a study which specifically examines the viability of systems over time spans. (Happily, the 2011 annual professional conference of environmental historians had as its theme 'History and Sustainability', one of the bright signs of a possible turn within the profession, or at least an emerging struggle for its heart. Unfortunately, as a counter to that optimistic sign, the conference took place in Arizona despite the pressure from a number of members to honor a call for a boycott of the state in response to its recent passage of anti-immigrant laws.) In environmental studies departments, historians are notable mostly by their minimal presence among the numerous anthropologists, geographers and economists, as well as scientists. They sometimes seem to be outnumbered here even by art professors.

Although beginning to engage with environmentally focused researchers from other disciplines will not alone effect a cure for the demographic profile of environmental historians and the intellectual consequences of that profile, it can spur some self-examination, as well as offer an infusion from others of well-developed and generative theories of human-nature interaction. Given the unexamined nature of theory among historians as a whole, interactions with others who do discuss theory might legitimize such discussions within history as well as prevent an unnecessary re-invention by historians of the theoretical wheel. And in looking forward to the kinds of changes that can help environmental history to move away from its history-centered self-conception and instead to position itself among the other environmental disciplines, beginning to think and talk explicitly about the social theory inherent in each of its various historical accounts can begin the overdue process of the academic integration of environmental history into interdisciplinary environmental knowledge.

Despite history's preference for thinking that it operates without theory, a number of theoretical approaches can in fact be deduced from a survey of the literature of environmental history. Firstly, there are a few environmental historians who operate from a traditional intellectual history set of principles, in which new ideas cause social change. The majority of work being written today, however, falls into other patterns; modernization theory, biological determinism, and various forms of economism, in which institutions (such as 'capital' or 'the market') self-realize, are the most prominent among them. Modernization theory is heavily promoted in readers and textbook kinds of contexts, and is the environmental history version of what history calls "the rise of the West." We can represent it here with one of its most famous current volumes, *Something New Under the Sun: An Environmental History of the Twentieth Century World* by John McNeill, the current president of the American Society for Environmental History as of this writing in 2011.[11]

Something New Under the Sun brings together massive documentation, but aside from a brief mention of competition among states, companies and individuals as the driver of the world's current ecological strategy on p. xxiii, the thrust of the body of the book is actually a single argument. The modernizationist interpretation runs thus: (1) environmental change is due to economic growth, (2) economic growth is due to population growth and more productive technology and (3) technological change is the result of human ingenuity.

Population and naturally ingenious technology as the root causes of humanity's relationship with nature leads to fairly predictable solutions for the current ecological crisis. McNeill writes on page 359 of that book, "My interpretation of modern history suggests that the most sensible things to do are to hasten the arrival of a new, cleaner energy regime and to hasten the demographic transition toward lower mortality and fertility."

A comprehensive, well-written and politically much less conservative but theoretically similar synthesis, *A Green History of the World: the Environment and the Collapse of Great Civilizations* by Clive Ponting, predated McNeill's book by a decade. It, too, attributes environmental destruction to population density and technology, and therefore concludes in its final paragraphs that the twofold challenge is to find environmentally sustainable "means of extracting from the environment... food, clothing, shelter and other goods", and controlling rapidly rising human population.[12] Another recent technologically-driven volume by a prominent environmental historian is *Children of the Sun*, by Alfred Crosby, with its chapters chronologically and thematically organized by energy technology.[13]

These modernizationist understandings of the roots of human environmental problems yield some very practical politics, which center around population control programs and 'appropriate technology.' Anyone familiar with the ecological state of the world will certainly take as given that both human numbers and the specifics of current human technology are highly problematic; the theoretical and historical question remains whether these factors are so-called independent variables, or products and reflections of other social and political realities. In the world of environmental studies, analyses and critiques of modernization theory and its allied technological determinism, of which these volumes are straightforward examples, abound, so I will go no further here.

Among environmental historians there is perhaps an even more popular explanation than the traditional modernizationist account for the shape of the contemporary world. This is the biological thesis set forward most notably by the aforementioned Alfred Crosby in the widely read and cited *Ecological Imperialism: The Biological Expansion of Europe, 900–1900*. Crosby argues that the real reason Europeans have triumphed over the rest of the world, expanding their race's biological boundaries and thereby cultural boundaries as well, is because 'their' flora and fauna (germs included) have excelled in colonizing the globe. On closer reading, though, Crosby's argument is not that a truly random allocation of superior nature to the European continent explains European success. Instead, it emerges that European species are better at being around people through lots of practice; when (non-tropical) colonies become populated, of course those species which have coevolved with humans, i.e. European species, flourish.[14]

This version of history gives the credit but also the responsibility for colonial triumph to disease and ecology rather than to human choice and aggression. As the book jacket says, "the Europeans' displacement and replacement of the native peoples in the temperate zones was more a matter of biology than of military conquest." This argument implies that the colonial arrangement of the globe was a natural one; it implies that Europeans have merely acted in a 'natural' way, just as other species do, in attempting to expand their biological realm into the rest of the world (he even calls the settler-colonialist states the 'Lands of Demographic Takeover'); and it fosters the colonial myth of the empty landscape awaiting human settlement. This last point may need a line or two of clarification. *Ecological Imperialism* argues that once an area became noticeably settled with humans, European species were the more fit species to cope with the humanized landscape, as they were *the* species which had evolved under pressure from humans. The corollary is that if European species were so successful at invading new territory after white settlement, then the species living there, in New Zealand or North America, for instance, had *not* co-evolved with humans.

The fact is, of course, that species in the lands of European colonial settlement *had* co-evolved with humans, but with their *own* humans and *their* patterns of land use. Indigenous species flourished in indigenous humanized landscapes, but European species flourished when those landscapes became not newly humanized, but newly Europeanized, with European systems of cultivation, crop rotation, transportation, or settlement, establishing European parameters and European ecological niches. And those landscapes became Europeanized, thus secondarily allowing the establishment of European species, through political decisions and actions, not through the superior biological hardiness of European species.

So although Crosby's work purports to move the catalyst of change from the human to the natural world, from the human imperialists to the plant, animal, and germ ones, the argument nevertheless rests on assumptions about the character of human societies, European and 'native' respectively. Underlying the ecological imperialism argument is the premise that only Europeans really humanized their landscape, while 'native' landscapes were still part of nature. Native (natural, that is) species therefore fell prey to European (human-adapted, that is) species once landscapes were *really* settled with people (white people that is). Critiques of anti-moral, racially-driven theories such as this one are also abundant, so we will go no further down this path, either.

Nature in the form of climate rather than biology has also been proposed as the cause of historical change, usually by non-historians. We might look here at archaeologist Stephen Mithen's *After the Ice: A Global Human History 20,000–5000 B.C.* or at *The Recurring Dark Ages: Ecological Stress, Climate Changes, and System Transformation* by the sociologist Sing C. Chew. Historians as well as many others from across the humanities and social sciences will generally find the straightforward environmental determinism here unconvincing, necessitating no further critique.[15]

Finally we come to perhaps the most popular set of historical theories in environmental history, those revolving around what is uncritically called 'the economy.' The economy is here generally taken to have a self-evident definition, roughly paralleling the cash nexus in the modern world. Although it also might explicitly be defined as the system for the production, circulation and distribution of goods and services, 'the economy' notably excludes goods and services not included in the cash nexus today, such as those included under the rubric of 'housework.' This school interprets the history of the political, social and ecological state of the world as a result of the automatic workings of an economic system, without reference to either humans or to power, and therefore without reference to struggle. The driving forces of history, the actual actors, in economistic accounts are structures like 'the market', or processes like 'the accumulation of capital.' Fundamental is the idea that the 'economy' is indeed an independent realm, not merely one face of the larger constellation of power relations in society. Only if so conceptualized can the economy be seen as an independent driver of change. Thus 'the economy' consists of logics, structures and processes, not people. 'Economic causes' are therefore the unfolding of internal logics, not the results of the intentions or desires of either individuals or classes of people, and very certainly not the result of struggles between and among classes or other groups. And while in this model the superhuman economic structure is the *deus ex machina*, the arena defined as 'the economy' overlaps closely with that part of the social world in which white men, particularly powerful ones, are the main actors on stage: in the contemporary world, these would be financiers, merchants, industrialists, policy makers and even traditional factory workers, rather than the economically invisible 'informal' laborers, housewives or subsistence farmers. In fact, economistic analyses typically mention neither class, race nor gender struggles anywhere in their discussions of economy and history, an interesting and peculiar fact given that often these authors conceive of themselves as at least liberal if not radical.

Paradoxically, although many historians have adopted a paradigm in which the economy so-conceived is the source of dynamism and change, in fact economism is anti-historical in the kinds of explanations it produces. It eliminates people and their volition, it eliminates conjunctures and specificities, in favor of an inexorable and inevitable unfolding structural, superhuman logic. Many accounts of historical environmental change written by non-historians as well as historians themselves might be classified within this paradigm; many world-systems writers, for instance, fall here, posing the world-system, rather than humans, as the actor and agent of change. Contrasting the economic structure of explanation with a historian's, Deborah Fitzgerald, a historian of technology at MIT, argued at the 2003 annual conference of the American Society for Environmental History that "the history of agriculture has been written by economists," who have therefore written it as though it had an inevitable outcome. Historians, she said, have the task of rewriting that history as though instead choices were made, and as though the outcome was not predetermined.[16]

In fact, in many instances 'economic' explanations are tautological and not really explanations at all. In Fitzgerald's essay "Accounting for Change: Farmers and the Modernizing State," she writes that the commonplace interpretation of the transformation of American farms from small, animal powered, lightly capitalized entities to large, mechanized enterprises geared towards the international market is an economic interpretation. She points out however that, "while an economic interpretation aptly describes most farms in 1940,...it certainly does not explain why farmers changed their minds and their practices....The observation that it happened is not the same as an explanation for how and why it happened."[17]

While many environmental historians have been distracted by the economy or the market away from consideration of how and why the economy or the market is constructed the way that it is, historians of technology can provide insight. Just as the power relations and struggles in larger society create particular physical technologies, the dynamics of society create the social technologies of economic markets, money, or finance. What historian David Noble says of technology in general applies well to the economic devices in particular. He points out that although it is seemingly self-evident that technology emerges from society, not the other way around, modern Americans have come to think that technology shapes them. "...(I)t has served at once as convenient scapegoat and universal panacea–a deterministic device of our own making with which to disarm critics, divert attention, depoliticize debate and dismiss discussion of the fundamental antagonisms and inequities...." It "at once is the vehicle and mask of domination."[18]

Theoretical reflection on questions like these, i.e. questions of the socially produced nature of markets, or the extent of the embeddedness or independence of the economy from larger society, is clearly necessary to properly evaluate historical explanations which rest on particular answers to those questions. Unfortunately, historians' reluctance to engage in theoretical discourse shuts down these discussions, and once again environmental history suffers as well.

Richard White points out in his insightful historiographical article "The Nationalization of Nature" that multiple levels of analysis are essential for good environmental history. Looking at the trajectory of environmental history writing he argues that "environmental histories, it seems, parallel the history of the state.... When writing about eras of strong or living states, environmental historians make their histories state-based. When writing about eras with few or weak states or those when the state seems to be in decline, historians write in other frames than that of the nation." This dynamic explains the use of relatively global perspectives on environmental history for the pre-modern past, the present and the future, but a national framing for the 18th, 19th and 20th centuries, especially in U.S. history writing.[19]

The thrust of White's argument, however, is that many scales of analysis are relevant. Moving from one scale to another changes the array of problems under examination and "each scale reveals some things while masking others," though there may be better and worse choices according to what problems we want to examine. History "does not have to choose between the local, regional, national, and transnational but can establish shifting relationships between them."[20]

But, reflecting the passing of interest in the political, environmental history has come to regard the market and commodification as 'the great engine for modern environmental change,' often superseding explanations based on international, national or regional politics. Also superseded are explanations based on the politics of fracture within these realms–that is, superseded are those social history categories of class, race and gender which drive national and regional politics. Looking away from humans and their lives and struggles instead to the realm of supposedly disembodied and institutional forces like the market or the economy for explanation, environmental historians have missed the point where social history integrates with, indeed is essential for, good environmental history. In postulating that the market, or 'the economy', is an ultimate explanation, rather than part of that which needs to be explained by reference to the society which constructs economies and markets, environmental historians do indeed set themselves up as in competition with social history. Instead of analyzing the dynamics of social power at work in the environmental depredations effected through the market, environmental historians want to stop their discussion once they get to the word 'market.'

William Cronon's classic works of U.S. environmental history, *Changes in the Land* and *Nature's Metropolis*, might well be classified here. In *Changes in the Land*, Cronon describes 'the integration of New England ecosystems into an ultimately global capitalist economy'–in brief, commodification's effect on the landscape, or as he titles his final chapter, "That Wilderness Should Turn a Mart." Similarly, Cronon's *Nature's Metropolis* describes the imprint of the capitalist grain trading city of Chicago on its far-flung hinterlands, beautifully implicating urban finance in the structure of rural life and nature, compellingly weaving a single landscape from what are usually posed as the opposing domains of city and countryside. Nevertheless, *Nature's Metropolis* envisions agricultural, technological and transport decisions and myriad other facets of the rural world as nothing more than impositions on the country by the logic of rational, capitalist economic thinking–the mark of the market. (The book incidentally also participates in another common modernizationist model of the mutual accommodation of nature and the farm in premodern times, only to be replaced by the dynamic of degradation under capitalism.)[21]

Newer works in American environmental history, written 20 years after *Changes In The Land*, often still find the commodification of nature to be the most compelling available fundamental cause of ecological change. Ted Steinberg's *Down to Earth: Nature's Role in American History* "argues that the transformation of nature (e.g. soil, trees, water) into a commodity is the primary driving force behind changes in American history," according to its cover. (I *do* advocate actually reading books, but find cover summaries to provide public confirmation and validation of my own summaries.) Richard Tucker's *Insatiable Appetite: The United States and the Ecological Degradation of the Tropical World* similarly links American consumer demand for tropical agricultural commodities to destruction in the Third World.[22]

One of the classics of environmental history, *Rivers of Empire*, written by a virtual environmental history 'founding father' Donald Worster, considers the evolution of irrigation in the arid West. Although Worster is highly critical of capitalism, its agriculture, and its ecological destructiveness, he follows most of environmental history in his interpretation of the logic of capitalist decision making. He, unlike a chorus of contemporary, non-historian, critics of federal policy in the West, does not see economic irrationality at work. He does not see the scope of financial subsidies to agriculture and ponder the conundrum of why it is subsidized at all and specifically why it is subsidized in the way that it is. (Social history!) Therefore he does not make a link between whatever motivates the subsidization and structuring of farming and the eventual ecological consequences of agriculture. Instead, he, like so many others in history, accepts at face value capitalism's claims about itself: that its workings naturally and inevitably reflect a market-based drive for efficiency even if at the expense of other values. According to him, a sufficient explanation is that the irrigation system is "imposed...and induced to run, as the water in the canal does, in a straight line toward maximum yield, maximum profit."[23]

In environmental history's defense, this 'economism' which is so prevalent at the moment is paralleled in other discourses as well, notably in the preoccupation with economic 'globalization' as the explanation for all modern phenomena. Imperialism, neo-colonialism, racism, national politics expressed in foreign policy–these are not the sources of world conflict or the sources of globalization itself; everything is attributable to the cancerous, self-expanding, alive market. But although environmental history has company in this explanatory trope, it is not absolved of its responsibility as a self-examining intellectual discipline to make its theories visible and debated. In so doing, it might discover weaknesses, and might discover an awful lot of common ground with its erstwhile social history 'competitors.'

Here, environmental history might also find theoretical grounds for advocacy. It is only with a comprehension that individual and group human agency has created, shaped, and can and will in the future alter the market, society, and thereby the environment, that environmental historians could become advocates for humans to make *other* demands and choices than those they make now.

And finally, we come to the question of how environmental history has engaged with science, which, to add one more tough assessment, has been minimally. Importantly, the natural sciences too, in their own way, have discovered history in recent years just as the humanities and social sciences did. Unfortunately, the essential historicity of all of nature itself, which is exactly the grounds on which environmental history can integrate with the natural sciences, is erratically incorporated into environmental history's discourse. Although there is a general sense within environmental history that ecological theory has radically changed in the last decades, often historians rest their descriptions and understandings of human impact on an understanding of succession theory generally discarded in the science world. Ecologists and geographers are eagerly reconceptualizing the important role of chance and specificity in determining any given state of nature. In other words, scientists have reintroduced possibilism into the path that nature takes, and rejected determinism. A given setting might take any number of trajectories in terms of flora, soil, hydrology etc., depending on specifics and synchronicities: a piece of land might become one ecosystem or another depending on whether there is a heavy storm immediately following a fire, for example, eroding soil or washing away certain seed sources. The trajectory taken might well permanently open some ecological doors while permanently closing others.

That is, many ecologists now argue that we cannot understand why a landscape is the way that it is without knowing its history–meaning its 'natural' or non-human history, at least as much as its human history. While many ecological scientists are happily adopting historical thinking, historians themselves most commonly continue to envision a human impact on a timeless nature, in which nature has cyclic dynamics of its own, but no ongoing history of its own. For historians but not for scientists, nature only becomes historical when humans enter it, most often white male humans in fact, leaving non-whites in the neverland of 'prehistory'.[24]

Not only environmental history as traditionally defined but also social history can participate in a historical understanding of nature. If we start with a proposition that the gender, class or racial dynamics of history create the way in which a society, or parts of a society, interact with, create, recreate, or destroy nature, then social history is as much a part of the explanations for why nature is the way that it is today as biochemistry is. (For instance, it might become clear that the racial history of the Southern Tenant Farmers' Union is needed to explain the state of soil in the U.S. South, and therefore the long-term or even permanent ecological fate of abandoned farm fields there.) Not only could historians enter into this newly-defined historical ecology with some comfort, they can clearly make a wonderful case that understanding the discipline of history is now fundamental to the emerging historicized framework of the natural sciences. Environmental history could offer its particular disciplinary insights as essential to not only environmental studies at large, but ecology as well.

However, so far in this instance, environmental history seems to be acting more like a stereotypical humanities discipline than a social science, avoiding engagement with research which contains numbers or scientific terminology as somehow beyond its capacities; this is in all likelihood one reason why historians are still largely operating on outmoded scientific ideas.

I've focused so far on the hardships, limits, and problems environmental history has both encountered and produced in its work of incorporating nature into history and history into nature. There are successes too, and bright spots, and signs of change, all of which can be cultivated.

To start with our most recent topic, the integration of science and history, we have not only the turn towards history of scientists themselves presenting an opportunity, but a wealth of already existing interdisciplinary literature, albeit not written by historians. Archaeologists and geographers in particular have done much work in this area, predigesting some of the scientific work which might be more formidable to science-unaccustomed historians. Environmental historians can use these as departure points for their own work. Additionally, European environmental historians, acknowledged but poorly integrated into the general American discourse, are more comfortable with science and can provide some entrés for us. A real integration of history and science would provide the intellectual groundwork for social movements to integrate social concerns with environmental ones, as they must if either are to be really addressed.

On another important front, a recent (August 2008) article in the journal *Environment and History* by another grand homme of the environmental history field, J. Donald Hughes, points out kindly that historians are sometimes accused of being light on theory, and advocates for environmental historians to take up that challenge. While the theory that Hughes goes on to suggest as fitting subject matter revolves around the integration of culture and nature, and history and science, and not around the hidden theories of history itself, it is a wonderful public proposition nevertheless.[25] Dissident historians have long bemoaned the lack of historical theory and then gone on to write their own; the problem thus is not that there is no sophisticated historical theory to start the discussion, it is just that we have to allow that discussion to take root and evolve. This can be an incredibly difficult political task, or a simple one; that will be up to us.

Sustainability is beginning to raise its head in environmental history as well. In addition to the already mentioned sustainability theme of the ASEH conference of 2011, which succeeded in inspiring what was to my mind a remarkably uncharacteristic set of panels and papers covering topical issues such as the Gulf oil spill, water privatization, and climate change, there is a history and sustainability project at Cambridge University, which has held a colloquium at Cambridge and one at Harvard. Entering into this territory will open other cans of theoretical worms, such as just what 'sustainable' means, but if environmental history can keep and expand its new theoretical foothold, history should eagerly and righteously insert itself into the thick of sustainability studies.

The integration of social and environmental history has made a recent start as well. A 2006 article in the *Journal of Social History* entitled "Common Ground: Integrating Social and Environmental History" noted that social historians are known for their willingness to engage in social action and advocacy, and called for social historians to engage with environmental history and work on current environmental problems.[26] In September of 2008, a conference on integrating social and environmental history was held in Paris. One of the two organizers was Stephen Mosley, the author of the just-mentioned article, so it remains to be seen whether the larger communities will take up the project. It also remains to be seen whether a claim will be made that integration has happened by re-labeling work done in the current, often conservative, vein of cultural histories of views of nature, histories of science, etc. (as some of the papers at the Paris conference seemed to be) or whether an new integration of methodologies and basic assumptions about cause and effect will actually come to pass. One important factor will of course be politics; social historians in both the past and present have in general operated from a more radical political departure point than environmental historians. The success or failure of this integration will have as much to do with how politics in the academy and the discipline proceed as anything else. Nevertheless, we have a beginning to bringing together social and environmental history, another essential process for the field.

If we choose to pursue connections outside our discipline, we might be greatly aided here by a sister field which history often ignores, perhaps as a more radical competitor: American Studies. The Environment and Culture Caucus of the American Studies Association has as its mission to "further work that reflects historical and cultural analysis of environmental issues and concerns, and [to] hope to demonstrate the relevance of environmental scholarship to the central issues of race, class, gender, sexuality and colonialism...."[27]

As environmental history, hopefully, comes to terms in the ways we're discussing with the fact that there are politics and theory inherent in any of its interpretations, perhaps we will be willing to break away from the pack and begin to participate in policy and public responsibility. So far in this country, forays into policy are still pretty well untrod by environmental historians. For instance, The Environmental History and Policy Program of the Center for Contemporary History and Policy at the Chemical Heritage Foundation in Philadelphia had, in July of 2011, six paid and volunteer staff. The disciplines from which they hailed were: science and technology studies, urban anthropology, business administration, public policy, arts administration, and sociology. In other words, despite the title's announcement of a history program at a history center, no staff were actually environmental historians in the sense of having trained as historians. Rather than reflecting poorly on the program, this absence of historians reflects, I would argue, on the aversion to policy and advocacy that the discipline of history has promoted and perhaps even enforced.[28]

As John Tosh noted in a paper for the relatively new project titled History and Policy, "Applied history does not stand in good odour with the historical profession. By a longstanding prejudice its practitioners are thought to sacrifice their objectivity as scholars and to flout the accepted norms of historical reasoning."[29] Yet History and Policy is attempting to break that prejudice, and environmental historians need to be in the forefront of a movement towards applied history, or policy participation, as environmental conditions on the planet reach further crises. We can both hope and campaign for a revision of the spirit and letter of the ASEH advocacy project which currently restricts itself to ensuring archives.

A successful undertaking of all of these transformations (an overt embrace of theory in environmental history, a new willingness to engage in policy issues, an integration of environmental history with social history, and greater interactions with disciplines outside of history such as American Studies or Environmental Studies) might lead us as a result to one last transformation which addresses what I argue are the very roots of environmental history's peripheral standing among environmental disciplines: diversity.

While environmental history has in just the most recent years made strides in increasing the number of women authors, speakers and officials in its organizations, it remains male at a roughly 2:1 ratio by my estimate, and resolutely white.[30] (In this American culture averse to discussions of class, one can only speculate about the class origins of practitioners in the field.) A wider diversity of historians will yield a positive feedback loop of an increasing diversity of views, opening the door and welcoming a yet more diverse population of students. The ASEH began a Diversity Committee in 2007, hoping to address the problem of such a homogenous constituency, and perhaps it can do so. A rising number of papers, panels and historians specialize in environmental justice as a way of integrating social and environmental issues. Sometimes paternalism creeps into the discourse of environmental justice, assuming against all the wider evidence that issues of nature preservation, wilderness, and biodiversity are purely white male issues, and that poor people, women, and people of color can only be engaged in environmental concerns on matters of self-interest. Nevertheless the environmental justice agenda has done wonders to broaden environmental history's outlook.

But I would argue that the basis of all environmental history's weaknesses is the inherited problem of history's character as an overall discipline, and the impact of those inherited politics and timidity on the environmental specialty within history. We environmental historians certainly cannot remake history as a discipline, but we can become known as a specialty within the department that is open and desirable for women and minorities, the way social history is. To build such a reputation, we must not merely post metaphoric notices that we are equal opportunity historians, hoping to keep our 'respectability' with the mainstream of the profession; we must speak publically, loud and clear, to the environmental issues that women, people of color and the working classes know to be important, and we must welcome them when they do so too. Then and only then will we find diversity and strength, and only with that diversity and the intellectual power that it creates can we bring what history has to offer to the table of the larger environmental discourse.

NOTES

[1]   Allan Smith, "History and Theory: A Comment," *Rethinking History 9*, no. 4 (Dec. 2005): 485, 487.
[2]   Oliver Daddow, "Still No Philosophy Please, We're Historians," *Rethinking History 9*, no.4 (Dec. 2005): 494.
[3]   Keith Jenkins, *Rethinking History* (London: Routledge, 2003), xvii.
[4]   Mark Harvey, "Donald Worster," *Environmental History 13*, no.1 (January 2008): 150.
[5]   Hayden White, "The Burden of History," *History and Theory 5*, no. 2 (1966): 112.
[6]   For these and other interesting demographic observations by the American Historical Association's assistant director for research, see Robert B. Townsend "The Status of Women and Minorities in

the History Profession, 2002," *Perspectives* April 2002, http://www.historians.org/perspectives/issues/2002/0204/0204pro1.cfm; Robert. B. Townsend, "Rising Tide of History Undergraduates Contrasts with Declining Ph.Ds.: But Demographics of History Students Quite Different from Other Fields," *Perspectives*. Dec. 2005, http://www.historians.org/perspectives/issues/2005/0512/0512new2.cfm; and Robert B. Townsend, "The Status of Women and Minorities in the History Profession, 2008," *Perspectives* Sept. 2008, http://www.historians.org/perspectives/issues/2008/0809/0809new1.cfm

[7] William Cronon's essay "The Trouble With Wilderness; or, Getting Back to the Wrong Nature" in *Uncommon Ground: Rethinking the Human Place in Nature*, ed. William Cronon (New York: W. W. Norton & Co., 1995), 69–90 is often considered to have ignited this discussion.

[8] See Eva Swidler, "The Social Production of Soil," *Soil Science 174*, no.1 (Jan. 2009): 2–8.

[9] Stephen Dovers, "Sustainability and 'Pragmatic' Environmental History: A Note from Australia," *Environmental History Review 18*, no. 3 (Fall 1994): 21–36, and "On the Contribution of Environmental History to Current Debate and Policy," *Environment and History* 6 (2000): 131–150.

[10] ASEH Executive Committee, "Advocacy Guidelines," *ASEH*, March 2007, http://aseh.net/about-aseh/policies-and-guidelines/copy_of_advocacyguidelines.pdf

[11] John R. McNeill, *Something New Under The Sun: An Environmental History of the Twentieth Century World* (New York: W.W. Norton and Company, 2000).

[12] Clive Ponting, *A Green History of the World: The Environment and the Collapse of Great Civilizations* (New York: Penguin Books, 1991), 407.

[13] Alfred Crosby, *Children of the Sun: A History of Humanity's Unappeasable Appetite for Energy* (New York: W. W. Norton Co., 2006).

[14] Alfred Crosby, *Ecological Imperialism: The Biological Expansion of Europe, 900–1900*, (Cambridge: Cambridge University Press, 1986).

[15] Stephen Mithen, *After the Ice: A Global Human History 20,000–5000 B.C.* (Cambridge, MA: Harvard University Press, 2006). Sing C. Chew, *The Recurring Dark Ages: Ecological Stress, Climate Changes, and System Transformation* (Lanham, MD.: AltaMira Press, 2006).

[16] Deborah Fitzgerald, "A Plurality of Ruralities: A Roundtable of Environmental Approaches to Agricultural History" (presentation, annual convention of the ASEH, Providence, RI, March 26–29, 2003).

[17] Deborah Fitzgerald, "Accounting for Change," in *The Countryside in the Age of the Modern State: Political Histories of Modern America*, eds. Catherine McNicol Stock and Robert D. Johnston (Ithaca and London: Cornell University Press, 2001), 189.

[18] David Noble, *Forces of Production: A Social History of Industrial Automation* (New York: Alfred Knopf, 1984), xi.

[19] Richard White, "The Nationalization of Nature," *Journal of American History 86*, no. 3 (Dec., 1999): 977.

[20] Ibid., 983.

[21] William Cronon, *Changes in the Land: Indians, Colonists and the Ecology of New England* (New York: Farrar Strauss and Giroux, 1983) and *Nature's Metropolis: Chicago and the Great West* (New York: W.W. Norton, 1991).

[22] Ted Steinberg, *Down To Earth: Nature's Role In American History* (New York: Oxford University Press, 2002). Richard Tucker, *Insatiable Appetite: The United States and the Ecological Degradation of the Tropical World* (Berkeley: University of California Press, 2000).

[23] Donald Worster, *Rivers of Empire: Water, Aridity and the Growth of the American West* (New York: Oxford University Press, 1985), 6.

[24] For one example of historicized ecology by scientists, see Dave Egan and Evelyn Howell, eds., *The Historical Ecology Handbook: A Restorationists' Guide to Reference Ecosystems* (Washington D.C.: Island Press, 2001). For one example by a geographer, see Emily W. B. Russell, *People and the Land Through Time: Linking Ecology and History* (New Haven: Yale University Press, 1997).

[25] J. Donald Hughes, "Three Dimensions of Environmental History," *Environment and History 14*, no.3 (August 2008): 319–30.

[26] Stephen Mosley, "Common Ground: Integrating Social and Environmental History," *Journal of Social History 39*, no. 3 (Spring 2006): 915–933.

27 "Environment and Culture Caucus," *The American Studies Association,* 2011, http://www.theasa.net/caucus_environment/.

28 "Policy Center Staff," *Chemical Heritage Foundation,* 2011, http://www.chemheritage.org/research/policy-center/staff.aspx.

29 John Tosh, "In Defense of Applied History: The History and Policy Website," *http://www.historyand policy.org/papers/policy-paper-37.html.*

30 The ASEH does not track the demographics of its membership, I was told in an email exchange with the membership director.

GREENING ANTHROPOLOGY

BRIAN MCKENNA[1]

"The earth [is] ... the common property of the human race ... but the landed property ... has dispossessed more than half the inhabitants of every nation of their natural inheritance ... and thereby created a species of poverty and wretchedness that did not exist before ... I am pleading for ... a revolution in the system of government ... revolutions [of] justice ... [for] the persons thus dispossessed."

- Thomas Paine, American Patriot (1796)

What Thomas Paine wrote over two centuries ago is more apropos than ever today. Amidst the terror of neoliberalism (Giroux 2004, 2011b, Bauman 2006, Collins et al., 2008, Harvey 2010) world-historic catastrophes unfold, from the financial meltdown of 2008 to the BP Gulf oil disaster of 2010. These events were built on massive infrastructures of deception and illusion: the necessary illusions of unchecked power.

War forebode these traumas. The Nuremberg Protocols were ignored (Mandel 2005) in a mad rush for oil as the United States invaded Iraq under false pretenses. Tens of thousands died. Millions were scarred for life as the U.S. devolved into a torture state (Giroux 2011a). It was a "public engagement" from above, spawned by neoconservatives and strongly supported by a reliable friend: the academy.

Several U.S. universities were active participants in the war including my alma mater, Michigan State University. Peter McPherson, MSU's President, was recruited by President Bush to oversee Iraq's economic restructuring in 2003. Standing with the imperial rulers of an occupying army, McPherson (the former head of USAID) worked to impose his political and economic vision on a captive nation (McKenna 2003).

"If you don't do enough to create a political constituency for privatization now," he told Fortune Magazine, "then it will get killed in the cradle" (Kahn 2003, McKenna 2003).

For his free market zeal, one of McPherson's own team members accused him of believing in an "ideological nirvana," according to Kahn (Kahn 2003).

Back home on MSU's campus, there were no public protests or teach-ins about the war nor about the activities of MSU's President. McPherson returned home, after a six month leave of absence, to a hero's welcome. Tenured faculty were, by and large, publicly silent.

S. D. Fassbinder, A. J. Nocella II and R. Kahn (Eds.), Greening the Academy: Ecopedagogy Through the Liberal Arts, 141–160.

I worked as a local environmental journalist (and applied anthropologist) at the time, 2001–2004, and wrote several articles about connected McPherson's neoliberal work abroad with his neoliberal work at home, focusing on his anti-environment activities. When his good friend Vice president Cheney came to campus to deliver the graduation MSU address in 2002, I wrote a column, *"King McPherson's New Throne* (2002) in which I reported McPherson's recent appointment to chair the Department of Energy's powerful external advisory committee and asked him to help release 15,000 pages of minutes from Cheney's secret energy industry meetings.

Later, when the MSU President served in Iraq, I wrote *"Who is Michigan's Empire Man?"* (2003) and catalogued a series of his anti-green activities. McPherson energetically supported General Motors in intimidating Lansing's Westside citizens (encompassing about 4,000 households) by pressuring them – as part of a Lansing State Journal petition to which he lent his signature – not to file an air pollution appeal as was their right under the Clean Air Act (McKenna 2002a); he agreed to let MSU police infiltrate a registered campus student group, United Students Against Sweatshops (since renamed Students for Economic Justice), who were concerned about the World Trade Organization and unfair labor practices; and he refused to abide by a democratic MSU student referendum in March 2003 that supported a proposed $5-per-semester tax to pay for renewable energy on campus. These connections "could have been a teachable green moment of epic proportions for the faculty" (McKenna 2003). But was not.

ECONOMIC TRANSCENDENCE

In the midst of the United States' world-wide dispossession, a burgeoning movement seeks to "green the campus," a development that could theoretically challenge the corporatization of the university and help reclaim democratic life (Sullivan 2010, Barlett and Chase 2004). Across "new landscapes of inequality" (Collins et al., 2008), colleges and universities are awash in civic engagement initiatives, public-private partnerships and campus sustainability programs. The American Association for Sustainability in Higher Education founded in 2006, defines sustainability "in an inclusive way, encompassing human and ecological health, social justice, secure livelihoods, and a better world for all generations." These efforts could seriously challenge the status quo.

And yet, at MSU, and at campuses around the country, the levels of critical civic engagement about "sustainability" is a pittance of what it could be. Anthropologist Peggy Barlett is at the forefront of the movement and helped found Emory University's Office of Sustainability in Atlanta. She identifies a paradox in a profession, anthropology, that is honors holism in theory but defers from holism where they work: the campus. "For ... anthropologists [our] loyalty [is] to the place we did our fieldwork, " she said, "we're experts on Papua New Guinea or sophisticated about Paris. There's no prestige in being knowledgeable about the particular town or bioregion where our university may be located. This attitude transmits to our students a notion that, well you don't have to know anything about where you are to be a successful person and a knowledgeable citizen. In this particular era, that's a dangerous habit" (Wells 2011).

Anthropologists – and all academic workers – are at a crossroads. They must determine what it means to "green the academy" in an era of permanent war, "green capitalism," and the neoliberal university (Sullivan 2010). As Victor Wallis makes clear, "no serious observer now denies the severity of the environmental crisis, but it is still not widely recognized as a capitalist crisis, that is, as a crisis arising from and perpetuated by the rule of capital, and hence incapable of resolution within the capitalist framework (Wallis 2010). Anthropologist Merrill Singer concurs, calling for "an eco-nomic transcendence of the capitalism mode of production (Singer 2010: 128).

A THREATENING SCIENCE

"When practiced properly," David Price reminds us, "anthropology is a threatening science (Price 2004:29)." Anthropologist Laura Nader concurs. Plunder, she says, is a chief dynamic of our times. The Latin American novelist Eduardo Galeano captures the zeitgeist. "Plunder, internal and external, was the most important means of primitive accumulation of capital, an accumulation which, after the Middle Ages, made possible a new historical stage in world economic evolution (Mattei 2008)." Primitive accumulation – wars, violence, enclosures and privatization – is a chief means by which capitalism appropriates the commons.

Primitive accumulation and ethnocide are ongoing. This is especially evident in one of my focal areas: Indians of North America (McKenna 2011, 2006b). The Bullfrog Film *Homeland: Four Portraits of Native Resistance* (2005) illustrates the continued destruction of the Indian commons (see also Biolsi 2004, Oswalt 2009). Gail Small, a member of the Northern Cheyenne Indian Tribe in Lame Deer, is profiled. "You put in 75,000 methane gas wells around our reservation, you take our ground water, pollute our air, destroy our rivers, the Cheyenne here will probably not be able to survive. We'll have a wasteland here. That's what's at stake here. Where will the Cheyenne go?"

Where indeed? Human beings are treated as so much waste in this age of disposability (Giroux 2011). The earth has become the *private* property of a human cabal. Can reason and democracy alter the neoliberal capitalist tide and rescue the commons?

This article surveys the wide breath of green anthropological activity, both theoretical and applied, in ecological and environmental realms (e.g. conservation, biodiversity, ethnobotany, water security, and eco-cities). The amount of material is vast, so much so that Les Sponsel, a leader in the field, exclaims, "no one can keep track of it all."

I focus on four pressing areas of critical green practice in anthropology with which I am involved: backyard anthropology (Johnston 2001), critical public pedagogy (Sandlin 2009), activist applied anthropology, and the political ecology of health.

A GREEN COMMONS?

Universities are a kind of commons, an essential bulwark for creating an alert democracy to address these monumental social problems. But today, as indicated above, universities are fast becoming capitalist knowledge factories (Aronowitz 2000), a central tier of Eisenhower's feared "military industrial academic complex" (Giroux 2007).

Can greening the academy help reverse the neoliberal cataclysm? Will it educate for "revolutions of justice?" Anthropology asks these questions in its theories, ethnographies and classroom curricula. As such, its fundamental green message is radical (Singer 2010, Johnston 2007, Anderson 1969). Anthropology charts the long view of our species detailing the prehistory of primitive communism (constituting vast millennia of species history) to primitive accumulation which is our lot today (Merchant 2005).

Every semester I show the film *N!ai, The Story of a !Kung Woman* in my Introduction to Anthropology class. Filmed by ethnographer John Marshall, on and off over 28 years, the film documents the hunter and gatherer Bushmen of Botswana, who only required 2–3 days per week for subsistence procurement. They ate 105 plant species from the local ecology which constituted 60–70% of their diet (the mongongo fruit and nut being a staple) and also hunted an occasional giraffe for most of their 20,000 year-old adaptation (and transformation) of their environment. The film then portrays the Kung San's colonization as they were cast onto reservations, stricken with tuberculosis and pressured into the South African Army of the apartheid era. In just one generation under the South Africans they were victims of ethnocide and some would argue genocide (Robbins 2008).

Afterwards I discuss the work of Marshall Sahlins who in his classic *Stone Age Economics* (Sahlins 1972) calls the Kung's 20,000 year type of social organization "the original affluent society." I contrast Kung society with American students' everyday lives, mired in student debt, part-time jobs and unknown futures.

"There it is," I say, "Primitive communism versus primitive accumulation, all in one hour of viewing." "Who are the primitives?" I ask.

How green is anthropology? What gains have been made? What limitations constrict its movement and application to real world scenarios? What is my vision? I address each of these in this chapter. Indeed the gains are enormous.

In 1996 the Anthropology and Environment section of the AAA (http://www.eanth.org/) was established to catalogue the gains and advance green anthropology. Anthropologist Barbara Johnston was a key activist in forming the subdiscipline, working as "disciplinary organizer," serving on task forces, committees, writing reports, booklets and books, responding to community demand for this work. Its mission, is, in part, to "coordinate a discipline-wide collaborative effort that would renew anthropology's commitment to holism, to reach beyond our own field to incorporate research and practitioners from other disciplines," according to Johnston. It has not come close to accomplishing that high standard, however it is a valuable group with 678 members (as of June 2011). It has journals (*Human Ecology, Journal of Ecological Anthropology, Ecological and Environmental Anthropology*), anthologies and textbooks, publisher's series, specialists, activists, programs, and courses; and an excellent listserv (see above website for access). It has searchable archives which is an indispensible scholarly resource. As of June 2011 the EANTH list had 1513 subscribers.

But three key questions loom. First, how does anthropology, ostensibly a science of holism, reconcile the overspecialized practice it has largely become (Harvey 2009) with the widespread call to speak plainly for the educated lay public beyond academia? (Eriksen 2006) Second, how does anthropology reconcile its limiting context within the military-industrial-academic complex" on the one hand with the liberating movement to radically green the academy – and the country – on the other (Johnston 2007)? And third, how does anthropology situate itself with respect to a failed neoliberal ideology – in which capitalism has proven unsustainable – given anthropology's long standing commitment to defend Indigenous peoples, democracy and the commons (Singer 2010)?

MAKING ANTHROPOLOGY HOLISTIC

Splitting and the Overcoming of Splitting

The last person to write a chapter describing "green anthropology" for a general readership was William Balee, in 1996. In *Greening the College Curriculum* (Collett and Karakashian 1996) Balee's job was to discuss the "vast subject matter" of environmental/ecological anthropology up to that time. Befitting his own expertise, Balee focused on his specialty, forest ecology.

"Jungle is as much a myth as Tarzan is," Balee explained. "The ecologist who tries to study undisturbed communities (such as a virgin forest) is likely to spend his whole life trying to find one!" These aphoristic statements draw attention to the "pristine myth," which has served as justification for colonization of North America (Denevan 1996). Perhaps no greater case of normative blindness (i.e., how culture renders the obvious invisible) exists in America than Cahokia, the third largest structure in pre-capitalist North America. It was a city of about 20,000 people in a region that had over 50,000. The Mississippian peoples had departed around 1300, probably after an ecological catastrophe, but left behind nearly a hundred great structures including Monks Mound, at 100 feet high and 785,000 cubic yards, the largest pyramid north of Mexico. It took over 200 years to build. Existing today on the outskirts of St. Louis, Cahokia was seen as empty land with the mounds left behind by the Lost Tribes of Israel. Certainly Indians could not have created it! Manifest Destiny required this view (Pauketat 2010).

One would think that this is pretty significant scholarship that deserved a wider distribution. That's what Charles Mann (2005) thought after hearing Balee talk "about anthropogenic forests—forests created by Indians centuries or millennia in the past." Said Mann, "it was a concept I'd never heard of before." He reflected, "Gee, someone ought to put all this stuff together, I thought. It would make a fascinating book." He waited but nothing happened. So he finally wrote it. His resulting book, *1491* became a national bestseller (Mann 2005).

Why didn't Balee write that book? In fact, it is a common story in anthropology: a lack of urgency to communicate with the public. This has become a crisis. The 2009 American Anthropology Association annual meeting was titled, "The End/s of Anthropology," expressing worry about the profession's future. Unlike other disciplines, anthropology has not produced many public intellectuals. It suffers from the challenge of "public engagement" and is groping for strategies, models and ideas. The conference asked its 12,000 members "What is the relevance of anthropology in today's world?" The relevance is enormous, particularly its "green" contributions. But relatively few academics, citizens, nor even anthropologists are aware of the scope. One reason is that anthropology has become a "social siLence" (Tett 2009, McKenna 2011). Anthropologist Gillian Tett, the Managing Director of the Financial Times, said as much in a blistering speech at the 2010 AAA meetings (McKenna 2011). The author of the bestselling *Fool's Gold* (2009) which recounts how she predicted the 2008 meltdown, argues that anthropologists need to project themselves more forcefully into the culture. "Anthropologists are well trained to absorb information, not project it. They have to emit."

Public pedagogy and journalism are not new ideas in anthropology (Eriksen 2006). Franz Boas, Margaret Mead, Ashley Montague, Louis Leaky, Marvin Harris and, more recently David Mayberry Lewis, producer of the Millennium book (1992) and TV Series on PBS were active public communicators. Boas, one of the founders of U.S. anthropology, was adamant about marshalling civic voice against injustice. He developed the methodology of historical particularism (i.e., that cultures are to be studied diachronically and in depth) and was a tireless advocate for "cultural relativity' (i.e., that cultures should be analyzed on their own terms). He became an outspoken critic of racism. As Price describes it, "Boas and his students saw it as their duty to bring this perspective to the streets, newspapers, radio broadcasts, and government agencies (Price:34)."

What happened then? Read on.

OUR GREEN BODIES

We are Animals, with Culture

There are four classic branches within anthropology: physical (or biological), cultural, linguistics, and archaeology. Today applied anthropology is usually added as the "fifth field." Anthropologists are required to study the basics of the first four areas in graduate programs. All five branches have abiding environmental/ecological foci, and yet they have generally become isolated from one another.

Even within ecological/environmental anthropology there are divisions, subfields and splits. There are four main approaches within "ecological anthropology," including cultural ecology, historical ecology, political ecology and spiritual ecology, which developed historically in that order. Within these groupings there are a number of topical subfields and/or methods including ethnobotany, medical ecology, primate ecology, systems ecology, ethnoecology, behavioral ecology, information ecology, human ecology, forest ecology, aquatic ecology, arctic ecology and more. Other evolving subfields from across anthropology as a whole include, prehistoric ecology, bioarcheology, cognitive anthropology, Darwinian evolutionary ecology, and the political ecology of health. A special note must be made about scholars who pursue ecological approaches within the broad field of American Indian and Indigenous studies.

Let's look at the five major branches in order to consider the interstices of each of the various anthropological approaches and subfields. This allows us to see where ecological/environmental approaches to anthropology can be observed.

First, a word about terminology: Sponsel defines ecological anthropology as the exploration of how culture influences the dynamic interactions between human populations and ecosystems in their habitat through time. He views environmental anthropology as an applied dimension of ecological anthropology; others like Michael Dove prefer to see it as a more recent development replacing ecological anthropology.

For an excellent overview of the subdiscipline, with references, consult Sponsel's webpage (http://www.soc.hawaii.edu/Sponsel/).

From a *biological (or physical) anthropology* perspective, humans are "green" in their very being. We are all extensions of the Earth. We are culture bearing animals, descended from the trees, the result of biocultural evolution. That is, humans are nature, albeit a nature that we have had a hand in sculpting. Our large craniums (in juxtaposition to our Australopithecine ancestors) are dialectically related to the freeing of our hands and subsequent tool use. Our species' history is borne of material struggle, we now have the capacity to make meaning, learn, plan and cooperate. We both adapt to and transform our environments, culturally, biologically and politically. Our black, white, red, and brown skin colors are related to the latitudes we've traversed in and out of Africa beginning over a hundred thousand years ago.

Cultural anthropology is about making connections, revealing hidden assumptions, teaching about human diversity and subaltern cultures, uncovering origins (of humans, the state, one's landscape, oneself) and resisting oppression. There are a number of outstanding ecological ethnographies. *One is Priests and Programmers* by Stephen Lansing (1991) which argues that temple priests in Bali regulated irrigation networks for the rice farming system based on cooperative spiritual principles. These were undermined by the Western Green Revolution (Nazarea 2006). Another important work is *Against the Grain* (2008) an edited volume in honor of Pete Vayda. His methods of "event ethnography," and the "actor centered approach" are in many ways similar to the methods of investigative journalists. Tim Ingold is widely touted in the field for important scholarly contributions like *The Perception of the Environment* (2000) in which he theorizes about the ethnography of everyday pedestrian movements and how something as simple as walking binds time and place in people's experience, relationships and life-histories. Ingold was influenced by anthropologist Gregory Bateson in books like *Steps to an Ecology of Mind* (1972). Bateson posited the mind as an immanent part of the whole interconnected system of organism-environment relations not as something confined in our bodies against nature "out there." Bateson left a mark on ecological anthropology influencing many, including Roy Rappaport and E.N. Anderson who, in books like *Ecologies of the Heart* (1996) argues that the emotional side of humanity is more basic than the mind. There are a number of excellent readers that span the field including Dove and Carpenter's *Environmental Anthropology: A Historical Reader* (2005) and Carrier and West's *Virtualism, Governance and Practice: Vision and Execution in Environmental Conservation* (2009). There is a debate within anthropology concerning the degree to which anthropologists ought to advocate for "ecological rights" versus those who think that they shouldn't. I take up this issue later, below.

Archaeology reconstructs the cultures and environments of prehistoric peoples through analyses of artifacts, fossils, natural and material remains. Bioarchaeologists and paleopathologists can tell us much about prehistoric health, nutrition, environments and even inequality based on investigation of remains like plants, teeth, skeletons and coprolites (hardened human feces). Archaeologists are the ones who provide evidence for how civilizations in ancient Sumer and the American Southwest, failed due to ecological destruction. Charles Redman was a trailblazer in this realm with his *Perspectives on Southwestern Prehistory* (1991). For an excellent textbook on this area, I refer readers to Hornborg and Crumley's *The World System and The Earth System: Global Socio-Environmental Change and Sustainability Since the Neolithic* (2006). Another valuable text is Crabtree and Campana's *Exploring Prehistory: How Archaeology Reveals our past* (2005). See reference section for American Anthropological Association link to best archaeology and environmental student Fieldschools (AAA 2011).

Linguistic anthropology investigates how people classify local flora, fauna and landscapes. It captures the referential contexts for how people explain illness symptoms, medicine, herbology, and treatments. This has enormous theoretical and practical implications. Michael Halliday was a founder of social semiotics who has had a profound impact on ethnolinguistics. For example, his analysis of "economic growth," described how its English language metaphoric association with notions of large, tall, and good provides "growth with a positive connotation when in fact it has severely negative ecological consequences (see, Jones 2010). Elois and Brent Berlin (1996) collected ethnobotanical data over seven years to reveal Tzeltal and Tzotzil Maya's in-depth knowledge of gastronomic illness and treatment. A recent article in the *Annual Review of Anthropology* summarizes the methodologies used to analyze environmental discourses including discourse analysis, ecolinguistics and ecocritical linguistics (Mühlhäusler and Peace 2006). Eugene Hunn's *A Zapotec Natural History: Trees, Herbs, and Flowers, Birds, Beasts, and Bugs in the Life of San Juan Gbëë* (2008) is an excellent portrait of the linguistic power of an Zapotec Indian community located in the state of Oaxaca. Anthropologist Daniel Moerman constructed the world's most complete inventory of Native American Ethnobotany. The searchable database is available at (http://herb.umd.umich.edu/). Moerman devoted 25 years to the task of gathering together the accumulated ethnobotanical knowledge on more than 4000 plants. More than 44,000 uses for these plants by various tribes are documented here. The database contains thousands of details on foods, drugs, dyes and fibers of Native American Peoples, derived from plants. Moerman is an Emeritus Professor from my campus, the University of Michigan-Dearborn. One of his former students developed a brochure identifying Native American plants on campus. The Environmental Interpretive Center sponsors walks based on it, as do I.

The fifth discipline of *applied anthropology* has grown exponentially since academic jobs have become scarce. One could make the argument that most anthropologists referenced in this article do applied work to one degree or another and indeed, there are rampant debates within the discipline about what constitutes "applied" or public work (Ervin 2005). The *Society for Applied Anthropology Newsletter* under the editorship of Tim Wallace is a quarterly publication that provides timely articles on this valuable work (http://www.sfaa.net/newsletter/newsletter.html). A leader in environmental applied anthropology is Barbara Johnston. She works as a tireless bridgewalker between NGOs, citizen groups, governments and the academy. Her new book *Life and Death Matters: Human Rights, Environment and Social Justice (2011, 2nd edition)* is essential reading (see also Johnston 1994). In the wake of Japan's Fukushima nuclear disaster, Johnston has written articles for the *Bulletin of the Atomic Scientists, CounterPunch, Truth-out.org*, the *SFAA Newsletter* Johnston (May 2011) as well as appearing on television. Another bridgewalker is David Cassagrande who mines the interstices between ecological theory, human cognition and public policy. His groundbreaking work with interdisciplinary teams on medical botany among the Tzeltal Maya and rural communities on the Mississippi floodplain demonstrate that community resilience is more determined by equal distribution of information rather than the complexity of information (Cassagrande 2007). I have worked as a "data democratizer" myself a medical school evaluator, Executive Director of the environmental organization LocalMotion ("better health through fewer toxins,") and public health worker. As a government environmental health official, I conducted an environmental health assessment for county government in Mid-Michigan, a 300 page work on water, air and food that was eventually suppressed. Later it was released by Public Employees for Environmental Responsibility (PEER 2001, McKenna 2002).

ANTHROPOLOGY'S GREEN HISTORY (ABRIDGED)

From Forests and Pigs to Bombs and Revolution

In his "green curriculum" article Balee cited three major figures in the history of ecological anthropology, Julian Steward, Roy Rappaport and Eric Wolf. Steward is a seminal figure who is important for breaking with armchair evolutionary theorists and inventing the method of "cultural ecology" (a term he coined) in his work with the Shoshoni Indians in the American Southwest (Steward 1955). He investigated how a culture adapted and achieved what he called "homeostasis" in a given ecology through ones material culture (pots, tools, baskets etc.). Rappaport advanced ecological theory in *Pigs for the Ancestors* (1968) where he argued that the Tsembaga Maring of Papua New Guinea regulated their culture through the ritual slaughter of pigs (McKenna 2009).

Later Steward's student Eric Wolf broke with Steward and the systems theory of Rappaport. Wolf argued that cultural ecology had to become synthesized with political economy in order to account for the dialectical relationships between global and local forces. He critiqued Steward's notions of an isolated, bounded population as the unit of analysis and critiqued ideas that humans primarily seek adaptations to environments to achieve homeostasis. Wolf helped to establish the field of "political ecology." He asked, famously, "If there are connections everywhere why do we persist in turning dynamic, interconnected phenomena into static, disconnected things?"

In this light, other connections are relevant. Steward served as an expert witness for many years with the Department of Justice. Laura Nader charges that "Steward's social evolutionary theory became a matter of legal and political significance, a theory that legitimized the denial of Indigenous rights to collectively hold lands (Nader 2008:104)." By depicting the Northern Paiutes as too primitive to be organized (thus going against the Boasian tradition) he assisted the state in depriving them of lands, she said. Price argues that Steward self-censored much of his Marxist theory because it was dangerous at the time (Price 2004). One influential scholar who openly did build on Marx was Marvin Harris whose *Rise and Anthropological theory* (1968, 2001) and *Cultural Materialism* (1979) are fundamental readings still.

Ecological anthropology has advanced tremendously since Steward. Much of the groundwork that supported the creation of the subdiscipline, in 1996, took place at the epoch changing United Nation's Rio de Janeiro Conference on the Environment (Rio Earth Summit) in 1992. Many anthropologists were active participants including a large contingent who advocated for Indigenous rights issues. Darrell Posey organized a parallel event at the time called the Earth Parliament, a fifteen-day assembly of Indigenous and minority groups. The strategy worked, influencing the main assembly to forge an agreement at the Rio Summit to "not carry out any activities on the lands of indigenous peoples that would cause environmental degradation or that would be culturally inappropriate." Many anthropological luminaries were involved in the two-week proceedings including Linda Raben, a former member of the AAA Committee for Human Rights. She worked at the Rainforest Foundation at the time. Another was Mexican anthropologist Lourdes Arizpe, the former Director of the Institute of Anthropological Research at the National University of Mexico (a major environmental anthropology prize is named after her). Others included Pam Puntenney (2005, 2008), Terrence Turner and Emilio Moran (2010) who represented the AAA's environmental task force established by former AAA President Roy Rappaport. Mary Elmendorf, a winner of the prestigious Malinowski Award by the Society for Applied Anthropology attended as a delegate. Elmendorf was a recipient of the Nobel Peace Prize (along with CARE) and the person primarily responsible for educating the World Health Organization to address women's issues.

Anthropology may have produced legions more of these activist environmental anthropologists, were it not for the encroachments of the U.S. government. In a magnificent work of scholarship anthropologist Davis Price drew on more than 30,000 pages of FBI and government memoranda released under the Freedom of Information Act which described dozens of activist anthropologists who were prosecuted during the Red Scares of the 1940s and 1950s (Price 2004). Price showed that it was not Communist Party membership or Marxist beliefs that attracted the most scrutiny but the levels of public action, particularly around racial justice. He argues, "McCarthyism took a large chunk out of American anthropology—a chunk so deep it continues to affect and limit the scope and approach of anthropology today" (Price 2004:33).

This may be a factor why few anthropologists are familiar with the work of political ecologist James O'Connor. Anthropologist Barbara Johnston worked closely with O'Connor in forming the influential environmental journal *Capitalism, Nature, Socialism*. In O'Conner's powerful and prescient book *Natural Causes, Essays in Ecological Marxism* (Guilford Press: 1998) he argues that the dynamics of capital revolve around not one, but two central contradictions. The first involves the traditional understanding of the contradiction between capitalism's productive forces and its productive relations. Capitalism's relentless motions to accumulate and "grow" come up against the necessary contradictions of overproduction, underproduction and worker unrest. The second contradiction of capital addresses the ecological crises of our times. It arises from the way capital limits itself by impairing its own social and environmental conditions, using nature as both "tap and sink." O'Connor is tough on traditional Marxists for undertheorizing the role of ecology. But he is equally tough on most (liberal) ecologists for not reading enough political economy and Marx.

Similarly, in this age of privatization, one would expect that more environmentalists would be familiar with the groundbreaking work of anthropologist Bonnie McCay. Her research refutes the underpinnings of Garret Hardin's popular Malthusian thesis in "Tragedy of the Commons." Hardin, an ecologist, promoted a very pessimistic view of human nature, one ideologically supportive of capitalism. In analyzing an Old English commons Hardin asserted that each individual herdsman would selfishly add more cows to his herd while overgrazing the commons whose grass he would

151

take for "free." Since each herdsman would do this, overgrazing resulted and the commons was damaged or destroyed. McCay drew upon her ethnographic fieldwork with Newfoundland fishing communities to demonstrate how they successfully managed common-pool resources in sustainable ways. She and her colleagues in books like "The Question of the Commons" (1987) and Enclosing the Commons (2002) document how communities can act as stewards with broader social interests beyond self-serving interests. "Common property" does not mean equality of access. It means systems of obligations, rights and duties to protect shared resources.

When it comes to the commons, few places seem more obvious a place to work together than the growing campus sustainability movement. It is a "common ground." A leader in this movement is Peggy Barlett, an anthropologist at Emory University. Barlett conducts Sustainability Across the Curriculum Workshops for the Association for the Advancement of Sustainability in Higher Education. She has greatly advanced the theory and practice of the greening movement on campus (Wells 2011).

A number of anthropologists are active in this bridgewalking work. In fact the two universities who have created formal schools of sustainability (Arizona State University and the University of South Florida) did so with the drive of anthropologists (Wells 2011).

Carl Maida is a partner in a community-based participatory research project, Community Action for a Renewed Environment (CARE) Program–Reducing Toxic Risks, funded by the U.S. Environmental Protection Agency. His recent book, *Sustainability and Communities of Place* (2007) explores sustainable development as a local practice, worldwide. For the past two decades anthropologist Sam Beck (2009) has directed the New York City Urban Semester Program at Cornell University where he connects students' medical experiences with diverse urban ecological issues.

There is continued debate about the best approaches for campus involvement. Should anthropologists, in the words of one campus organizer, "simply tell the 'truth' or let the 'truth' dazzle gradually?" (McKenna and Darder 2011) A leading anthropologist in the sustainable campus movement takes the latter view telling me that anthropologists often refrain from getting involved in sustainable campus initiatives "because we're disciplinarily trained to be very critical." She argued that "That stance is bad for forging good working relationships with non-academic partners, the heart of culture change work. And it makes it hard to accept the messy realities of compromise. Power structures are only changed in incremental struggles that are not fun and require us to give up control. Anthropologists are not so good at long-term dialogue with leaders to help them see a different way, let alone organizing to shift the legal or grassroots structures that bind corporate (or academic) leaders."

Other anthropologists take a more urgent view of social change strategies, reflecting "the 'truth' should thunder mightily" approach. See more on this below.

Thousands of ecological/environmental anthropologists wrestle with these issues of public voice. They are involved in conservation, ecotourism, sustainable urban development, sustainable agriculture, sustainable forestry, and sustainable fisheries initiatives around the world. In a 2011 message to EANTH listserv nine leading environmental anthropologists, including its current President, Paige West, provided links to their websites to improve public accessibility about their applied work. I provide links in the reference section to each one: Dan Brockington, University of Manchester (2011), Bram Buscher (2011), Wolfram Dressler, University of Queensland (2011), Rosaleen Duffy, University of Manchester (2011), Robert Fletcher, National Peace Academy (2011), Jim Igoe, Dartmouth College, Katja Neves, Concordia University (2011), Sian Sullivan, Birbeck College (2011) and Paige West, Columbia University (2011).

THE GULF BETWEEN MEDICAL ANTHROPOLOGY AND ENVIRONMENTAL ANTHROPOLOGY

Medical doctors tend to ignore the environmental etiologies to illness and disease. Are anthropologists reproducing this divide? Cecil Helman, in the most popularly read medical anthropology textbook, neglected environmental health for years. His recent 2007 book expounds on environmental issues but presents them mostly as an "add on" (i.e. he does not integrate them well with clinical medicine) largely reproducing the restricted clinical gaze of biomedicine (McKenna 2008).

For over three decades Ann McElroy and Patricia Townsend have bridged disparate fields by developing the concept of "medical ecology." In 1977 they noted that no one had "pull[ed] all this work together in a coherent field of study," bridging disparate fields. Their fifth of their book Medical Ecology in Ecological Perspective (2009) is an exceptional compendium of wide ranging literature and is extremely well written. It should be required reading for all anthropologists.

In a similar fashion, critical medical anthropologists Merrill Singer and Hans Baer have begun to integrate more environmental literature into their work, including *Global Warming and the Political Ecology of Health* (2008) and *Killer Commodities* (2008) (where I wrote a chapter on sunscreen). Others include Janice Harper whose critique of development in Madagascar and asthma in Houston continues to develop the political ecology of heath model. Elizabeth Guillette (1998) found that children from two similar towns nestled in the Yaqui Valley, one of Mexico's largest agricultural areas, demonstrated strikingly different neurological capabilities as a result of differential exposure to pesticides. One town was beholden to pesticides since the 1950s while the other town opted for traditional farming and shunned pesticides. Children exposed to pesticides lacked energy, were saddled with significant learning disabilities, and had coordination problems.

Similarly, environmental anthropologists need to work more closely with epidemiologists, as I have with Devra Lee Davis. It is estimated that ten million cancers over the last thirty years were entirely preventable, most having environmental etiologies as contributing factors (Davis 2007, McKenna). Davis today is bringing widespread attention to the dangers of cell phone use (Davis 2010).

A DISCIPLINARY DEBATE

Analysts, Advocates, Mediators or Troublemaking Anthropology?

Barbara Johnston argues that applied anthropologists can play four different roles: analysts, advocates, mediators, and troublemakers (Johnston 2001). She warns that "[W]hen environmental justice work involves advocacy and action – confrontational politics – a number of professional bridges are burned. ...'Cause-oriented' anthropology suggests people who make trouble. Troublemakers are celebrated in this discipline when their cause succeeds and justice prevails. But often 'justice' is elusive, success is hard to gauge, and action results in unforeseen adverse consequences." (Johnston: 2001, 8).

Johnston has never held a full time academic job and that is perhaps one reason she has been effective as an activist/troublemaking anthropologist (see also Johnston 2011, 2001). Johnston's recent edited work *Half-Lives & Half-Truths, Confronting the Radioactive Legacies of the Cold War*, (2007) details the ethnographic (and often advocacy) work of fourteen anthropologists researching the consequences of the first nuclear age, from the Marshall Islands to the former Soviet Union. As Laura Nader, a contributor, notes, "over the past fifty-plus years, relatively few American anthropologists or the American Anthropology Association have voiced opposition to this [Marshall Islands] destruction." (p. 304) Nader critiques the scores of anthropologists who worked in the Pacific, like Margaret Mead, but never spoke up about the nuclear testing. She calls this a normative blindness of the profession. At the same time Mead is very important for how she popularized anthropology and worked as a border-crossing intellectual.

Much of the profession is only now learning now about historical practitioners of this important work. Earle Reynolds was a physical anthropologist who moved his family to Hiroshima to work as a biostatistician for the Atomic Bomb Casualty Commission's Pediatrics Department in 1951 (Price 2008). The more he learned about the devastation and the physical and psychological horrors endured by the Japanese, the more he became convinced that the nuclear arms race had to be stopped. He understood that his work was to survey the bodies of Hiroshimans to predict casualties in a later nuclear war. He quit and became a world renowned activist, sailing his boat into nuclear testing areas to draw attention to the issue. He received letters of support from around the world, even from Martin Luther King Jr., but his colleagues in the American Anthropology Association came to regard him as "a dangerous outsider" (Price 2007: 62). Anthropologist David Price used FOIA requests to learn to what extent Reynolds' actions were monitored by the state. He was closely watched. Moreover, as Price notes, "Reynold's activist-applied anthropology radically unhitched mission from employment. His story illustrates how applied research can unleash knowledge that bears a weight of uncomfortable responsibility–a responsibility that if acted upon can lead anthropologists to take duty bound actions...[that endanger] their careers. That it seems unusual to consider the outlaw Reynolds an applied anthropologist tells us more about the ethical banality we encounter in our work in mainstream applied anthropology than it does about Reynolds (Price 2007:70)."

Yet critical education is the basis of anthropology even though civic minded anthropologists can find themselves at risk simply for doing what they were hired to do: investigate a given external issue. Ted Downing, former SFAA President (1985–87), experienced this and more. In 1995, Downing wrote an evaluation report describing the severe social and environmental impacts likely to be suffered by Chile's Pehuenche Indians from a proposed dam project underwritten by the World Bank. After his report was censored Downing demanded that the World Bank publicly disclose his findings. The Bank responded by threatening "a lawsuit garnering Downing's assets, income and future salary if he disclosed the contents, findings and recommendations of his independent evaluation." We do not have a good accounting of how often this happens to anthropologists, but we need to learn more about this and teach these lessons to our students. In any case, resisting censorship is, as Downing says, "good applied" anthropology.

Environmental anthropology's future depends on "good applied anthropology." Efforts must be made to dramatically expand the work of these key issues in the discipline: (1) bridging the divide between environmental/ecological and medical anthropology, (2) restoring the holistic connections between the four fields, (3) exploring the phenomenological and religious meanings of environmental and ecological landscapes, (4) expanding the theoretical power of the political ecology of health, (5) learning from archaeologists who are holistic by default, (6) reflexively critiquing the field of anthropology so as to better recognize how state repression continues to limit inquiry, (7) educating academic anthropologists about the perils and possibilities of applied environmental work, (8) overcoming self-censorship and public timidity, (9) adopting theories and practices from ecological socialism and (10) developing new strategies of applied/activist anthropology centered around journalism, sustainable campus initiatives, critical public pedagogy and others, yet unnamed.

IN MY IMAGINATION UNIVERSITY

Many universities boast area studies programs that critically investigate the political ecology and culture of specific regions of the world, like Africa, Latin America, or Asia. It's common for these programs to house perspectives that are critical of capitalism. But usually the only sector of the university that studies corporations in an in-depth manner is the Business College, though that's rarely critical. University scholars are not taking full advantage to investigate what Ralph Nader calls "the most animistic entity known to man," the corporations. They are treated like persons! Consider Dow Chemical. It is the 42nd richest company in the world. With revenues of $57.5 billion in 2008, Dow Chemical is worth more than 65% of the world's countries (124 nations), according to World Bank statistics. It's like having a foreign country in your own backyard! Were that Dow could be studied like a foreign country, like it deserves.

I began writing about Dow Chemical after I made a disturbing connection on Michigan State University's campus one day. Dow is a major corporate funder of MSU. In 2001 it merged with Union Carbide and began to receive international rebuke for its refusal to assist the victims of Union Carbide's 1984 Bhopal disaster, the worst industrial accident of all time. Interestingly, a few months later, in the Spring of 2002 Dow co-sponsored a seminar series at MSU's Detroit College of Law, called, "Creating Sustainable Cities in the 21st Century." On March 19th the talk was titled, "Abandonment of the Cities." I noted to myself that there was no mention that day of the irony that Dow Chemical had abandoned the city of Bhopal. Moreover, there were no protests even though MSU had an active sustainability program. A few days later I wrote about it as a local journalist did (I was then an adjunct at MSU) and then wrote a number of stories about them (McKenna 2002, 2003, 2004, 2005, 2009).

I propose three areas for publically engaged anthropologists in their work to "green the academy." First, as critical scholars they can lead interdisciplinary team efforts to investigate local hometown corporations in fine ethnographic detail. Secondly, they can lead their students to research and write a critical environmental histories of their own town or city, carefully documenting how seven local actors (media, medicine, corporations, public health, community groups/unions, environmental groups, and universities) interact to enhance or disturb health. Third, they can join campus sustainability groups (and reach out to serve on Ph.D. committees outside of their departments) and steer them more forcefully towards critical anthropological knowledge and eco-socialist models as they work to ethnographically detail the culture, resources and power dynamics of the university in reclaiming it as a democratic public sphere.

If one looks squarely at reality they would have to concur with Ralph Nader who famously asserted at an American Anthropological Association conference in 2001 that "anthropologists need not go to all Four Corners of the globe to deconstruct the ideologies of corporate power." For example, he noted, "General Motors has more rights than most U.S. citizens. The most animistic, inorganic institution in the world is the modern corporation ...it's given the constitutional right to remain silent. He said that "studying up means getting behind those images."

The two contradictions of capitalism are on full display. In "greening the academy," anthropologists need to educate citizens about this holistic, cross-cultural, and necessarily radical (or root) view of reality. As critical intellectuals, anthropologists are in a position to forcefully critique – in public – their own cities, hometowns (and universities), diagnosing how issues of culture, resources and power impact local health and environment. Anthropologists need to bring the full weight of anthropological knowledge, insight and methodologies to wider audiences. And they need to rethink how to cast these activities as a continuation of the sentiments expressed in the unfinished American Revolution. The green movement provides an important space for anthropologists to engage in Thomas Paine's "revolutions of justice." As CUNY anthropology professor David Harvey states it, "The capitalist class will never willingly surrender its power. It will have to be dispossessed" (Harvey 2010).

NOTE

[1] I would like to thank several anthropologists for generously contributing their time to reviewing this article and making valuable contributions: Les Sponsel, Barbara Johnston, Colleen Boyd, Peggy Barlett, Carl Maida, Sam Beck and Gene Anderson, and Pamela Puntenney. All errors are my own.

REFERENCES

Adorno, T. (1998). *Critical Models, Interventions and Catchwords.* NewYork: Columbia University Press. American Anthropological Assn. Fieldschools (www.aaanet.org/profdev/fieldschools/)

Anderson E. (2010). *The Pursuit of Ecotopia: Lessons from Indigenous and Traditional Societies for the Human Ecology of Our Modern World.* Westport, CT:Praeger.

Anderson, E. N. (1996). *Ecologies of the Heart: Emotion, Belief and the Environment.* New York:Oxford University Press.

Baer, H., & Singer, M. (Eds.) (2008). *Killer Commodities: Public Health and the Corporate Production of Harm.* New York:AltaMira.

Baer, H., Singer, M., & Susser, I. (2003). *Medical Anthropology and the World System.* Westport, CT: Praeger.

Balee, W. (1996). Anthropology, In *Greening the College Curriculum, A Guide to Environmental Teaching in the Liberal Arts.* Collett and Karakashian eds.

Barlett, P., & Chase. G, (Eds.) (2004). *Sustainability on Campus: Stories and Strategies for Change.* Cambridge, Mass.: MIT Press.

Bateson, G. (1972). *Steps to An Ecology of Mind.* Chicago: University of Chicago Press.

Bauman, Z. (2006). *Liquid Fear.* Cambridge: Polity.

Beck, S. (2009). Introduction: Public Anthropology, *Anthropology in Action, 16*(3), 1–4.

Berlin, E.A., & Berlin, B. (1996). *Medical ethnobiology of the Highland Maya of Chiapas, Mexico: the gastrointestinal diseases.* Princeton, N.J.: Princeton University Press.

Biolsi, T. (Ed.) (2004). *A Companion to the Anthropology of American Indians.* Malden, MA: Blackwell.

Brockington, D. (2011). Environmentalism and Conservation Website (http://environmentalismand conservation.wordpress.com/).

Boyd, C. (2009). You See Your Culture Coming Out of the Ground Like a Power: Uncanny Narratives in Time and Space on the Northwest Coast. *Ethnohistory, 56*(4), 699–731.

Buscher, B. (2011). The Critical Side to Conservation and Energy website. http://brambuscher.com/

Carrier, J.G., & West, P. (Eds.) (2009). *Virtualism, Governance and Practice: Vision and Execution in Environmental Conservation (Studies in Environmental Anthropology and Ethnobiology)* New York: Berghahn Books.

Casagrande, D. et al. (2007). Problem and opportunity: Integrating anthropology, ecology, and policy through adaptive experimentation in the urban American Southwest. *Human Organization, 66*(2), 125–139.

Clay, P. M., & Olson, J. (2008). Defining "Fishing Communities"; Vulnerability and the Magnuson-Stevens Fishery Conservation and Management Act. *Human Ecology Review, 15*(2), 143–160.

Collins, J., di Leonardo, M., & Williams, B. (2008). *New Landscapes of Inequality, Neoliberalism and the Erosion of Democracy in America.* Santa Fe: SAR Press.

Crabtree, P., & Compana, D. (2005). *Exploring Prehistory:How Archaeology Reveals our Past.* McGraw Hill: Boston.

Crumley, Carole, (Ed.) (2001). *New Directions in Anthropology & Environment: Intersections.* Walnut Creek, CA: AltaMira.

Denevan W.M. (1996). *Pristine Myth,* in Encyclopedia of Cultural Anthropology, David Levinson and Melvin Ember, eds., New York, NY: Henry Holt and Co. 3:1034–1036.

Dove, M., & Carpenter, C. (Eds.) (2005). *Environmental Anthropology: A Historical Reader*. Malden, MA: Blackwell.

Downing, T. (2008). See website for professional profile and writings at www.ted-downing.com

Dressler, W. (2011). Politics, Environment and Development website http://wolframdressler.com/

Duffy, R. (2011). Conservation Politics Website. http://conservationpolitics.wordpress.com/

Ervin, A. (2005). *Applied Anthropology: Tools and Perspectives for Contemporary Practice*. 2nd. Boston: Allyn and Bacon.

Elmendorf http://www.uflib.ufl.edu/spec/manuscript/guides/Elmendorf.htm

Eriksen, T. H. (2006). *Engaging Anthropology, The Case for a Public Presence*. Berg Publishers.

Fletcher, R. (2011). Cultural Dimensions of Ecotourism and Conservation website http://ecotourism conservation.wordpress.com/

Freire, P. (1970). *Pedagogy of the Oppressed*. New York: Seabury Press.

Giroux, H. (2011a). American Democracy Beyond Casino Capitalism and the Torture State. *Truthout*, May 16.

Giroux, H. (2011b). *The Twilight of the Social: Resurgent Politics in an Age of Disposability?* Boulder: Paradigm Publishers.

Giroux, H. (2010). *Zombie Politics and Culture in the Age of Casino Capitalism* (Popular Culture and Everyday Life) New York: Peter Lang Publishing.

Giroux, H. (2007). *The University in Chains: Confronting the Military-Industrial-Academic Complex*. Boulder: Paradigm Publishers.

Giroux, H. (2004). *The Terror of Neoliberalism*. Boulder: Paradigm Publishers.

Guillette, E. (1998). An Anthropological Approach to the Evaluation of Preschool Children Exposed to Pesticides in Mexico. *Environmental Health Perspectives*, V.106:347–353.

Haenn, N., & Wilk, R. (2005). *The Environment in Anthropology: A Reader In Ecology, Culture, and Sustainable Living*. New York: New York University Press.

Harris, M. (2001, 1969). *The Rise of Anthropological Theory, A History of Theories Of Culture*. Walnut Creek: Alta Mira.

Harris, M. (2001, 1979). Cultural *Materialism, The Struggle for a Science of Culture*. Walnut Creek: Alta Mira.

Harvey, D. (2010). *The Enigma of Capital: And the Crises of Capitalism*. Oxford:Oxford University Press.

Harvey, D. (2009). *Cosmopolitanism and the Geographies of Freedom*. New York:Columbua University Press.

Hornborg, A., & Crumley C.L. (Eds.) (2006). *The world System and the Earth System–Global socioenvironmental change and sustainability since the Neolithic*. Left Coast Press, Walnut Creek, CA.

Igoe, J. (2010). The spectacle of nature in the global economy of appearances: Anthropological engagements with the spectacular mediations of transnational conservation. *Critique of Anthropology* Dec. 23, vol. 30, no. 4: 375–397.

Igoe, J. (2011). Spectacle of Nature website. (http://spectacleofnature.wordpress.com/)

Ingold, T. (2000). *The perception of the Environment: Essays on livelihood, dwelling and ill*. London: Routledge.

Johnston, B. (2011). *Life and Death matters, Human Rights, Environment and Social Justice* (2nd edition) Walnut Creek,CA: Left Coast Press.

Johnston, B. R. (Ed.) (2007). *Half-Lives & Half-Truths, Confronting the Radioactive Legacies of the Cold War*. Santa Fe: School for Advanced Research Press.

Johnston, B. R. (2001). Anthropology and Environmental Justice: Analysts, Advocates, Mediators, and Troublemakers. In *New Directions in Anthropology and Environment: Intersection*. Carole Crumley, ed. Lanham: AltaMira.

Johnston, B.R., & Young, J. (Eds.) (2001). Backyard Anthropology and Community Struggles to Reclaim the Commons? Lessons from the SFAA Environmental Anthropology Project. *Practicing Anthropology*.

Johnston, B. R. (Ed.) (1994). *Who pays the price? The Sociocultural Context of Environmental Crises*. Island Press:Washington DC.

Jones, A. (2010). Michael Halliday: An Appreciation. *International House Journal of Education and Development* (28), 13–16.

Kahn, J. (2003). Making Iraq Safe For Capitalism Can a U.S. Treasury team build a free-market economy in a war-torn land? July 7.

Lansing, S. (1991). *Priests and Programming: Technologies of Power in the Engineered Landscape of Bali.* Princeton: Princeton University Press.

Maida, C. (Ed.). (2007). *Sustainability and Communities of Place.* New York: Berghahn.

Mandel, M. (2005). Nuremberg lesson for Iraq war: it's murder. *Commondreams.org,* Retrieved from http://www.commondreams.org/views05/0830-33.htm

Mann, C. (2005). *1491: New Revelations of the Americas Before Columbus.* New York: Knopf.

Mattei, U., & Nader, L. (2008). *Plunder, When the Rule of Law is Illegal.* Hoboken NJ: Wiley-Blackwell.

May, S. (2008) Ecological Crisis and Eco-Villages in China, Pulse of the Planet Series. *Counterpunch* November 21–23. Accessed at http://www.counterpunch.org/2008/11/21/ecological-crisis-and-eco-villages-in china/

Mayberry-Lewis, David (1992). *Millennium: Tribal Wisdom and the Modern World.*

McElroy, Ann & Patricia K. Townsend (2009). *Medical Anthropology in Ecological Perspective* (fifth edition). Philadelphia: Westview.

McKenna, B. (2011). Staging a Christopher Columbus Play in a Culture of Illusion: Public Pedagogy in a Theatre of Genocide. In Special Edition of *Policy Futures in Education.* McKenna, B. & Darder, A. (Eds.) December, Volume 6.

McKenna, B. (2011). Bestselling Anthropologist 'Predicted' the Financial meltdown of 2008. *Society for Applied Anthropology Newsletter, 22*(1), 21–25.

McKenna, B. (2010). Exposing Environmental Health Deception as a Government Whistleblower: turning critical ethnography into public pedagogy. Policy Futures in Education. Volume 8 Number 1 2010. See:

McKenna, B. (2010). Half-Lives & Half-Truths, Confronting the Radioactive Legacies of the Cold War. Barbara Rose Johnston, editor. Santa Fe: School for Advanced Research Press, 2007. x + 326 pp. *Medical Anthropology Quarterly.*

McKenna, B. (2009). Dow Chemical's Knowledge Factories: Action Anthropology in Michigan's Company Town Culture." *Anthropology in Action, Journal for Applied Anthropology in Policy and Practice.* Volume 16, Number 2, Summer 2009, pp. 39–50 (12).

McKenna, B. (2009). Pigs for the Ancestors, American Style *Society for Applied Anthropology Newsletter, 20*(3), pp. 16–20.

McKenna, B. (2008a). The Anthropology of Censorship: "Yes, But ..." The Heggenhougen Challenge. Society for Applied Anthropology Newsletter 19(3) August. pp. 15–19.

McKenna, B.(2008b). Higher Ed's 'Civic Engagements Dumbed Down: Conjuring Freire in Dearborn. *CounterPunch.*

McKenna, B. (2006a). Great Lakes for sale! Michigan's Odawa Indians lead anti-Nestle fight. *The Free Press, Speaking Truth to Power since 1970.* April 22 See: http://freepress.org/departments/display/3/2006/1935

McKenna, B. (2006b). Native Resurgence Spurs Home, Giving Thanks to America's Indians, *CounterPunch,* November 24.

McKenna, B. (2003a). Who is Michigan's Empire Man? Big Ten University President Does Bush's Bidding. *Free Press.* August 18.

McKenna, B. (2003b). Education for What? A Chronicle of Environmental Health Deception in Lansing, Michigan, *Cooley Law Review,* Volume 20: 2, pp. 1 to 54.

McKenna, B. (2002a. Environmental Data Suppression in Lansing: Why Did They Do it? *From the Ground Up* (published bi-monthly by the Ecology Center, Ann Arbor, MI), Vol. 33, #4, December/January, pp. 15–17.

McKenna, B. (2002b). The Hollister/GM Offensive: Fear and Profits versus the Peoples' Health," *The City Pulse,* May 1, pp. 1, 6, 7.

McKenna, B., & Darder, A. (Eds.) (2011). In Press. The Art of Public Pedagogy: *Should the 'Truth' Dazzle Gradually or Thunder Mightily?* Special Edition of **Policy Futures in Education,** 9(6).

Merchant, C. (2005). *Radical Ecology: The Search for a Livable World* Moran, E. (2010). *Environmental Social Science: Human Environment Interactions and Sustainability.* Oxford, UK: Wiley/Blackwell.

Mühlhäusler, P., & Peace, A. (2006). *Annual Review of Anthropology* Vol. 35: 457–479.

Nazarea, V. (2006). *Cultural Memory and Biodiversity.* Tuscon: University of Arizona Press.

Neves, K. (2011). Engaging New and Unexpected Environmentalisms website. (http://web.me.com/katja. neves_graca/Katja_Neves/Welcome.html)

O'Connor, J. (1998). *Natural Causes, Essays in Ecological Marxism.* New York:Guilford.

Paine, T. (1796). *Agrarian Justice Common Sense*, Great Ideas Series, Penguin Books, London, England, 2004.

Pauketat, T. (2009). *Cahokia: Ancient America's Great City on the Mississippi.* New York:Viking.

Price, D. (2004). *Threatening Anthropology McCarthyism and the FBI's Surveillance of Activist Anthropologists.* Durham, NC: Duke University Press.

Public Employees for Environmental Responsibility (PEER) (2001). *The Story of Water Resources at Work, Ingham County, Michigan,* Washington, D.C., 130 pages, September 19.

Puntenney, P. (1995). Solving the Environmental Equation: An Engaging Anthropology. *NAPA. 15*(1), 4–18.

Puntenney, P. (1998). The Business of a Sustainable Career: Environmental Anthropology. *NAPA Bulletin* 8 JAN.

Rappaport, R. (1968). *Pigs for the Ancestors: Ritual in the Ecology of a New Guinea People.* New Haven, CT:Yale University Press.

Redman, C. (1991). *Perspectives on Southwestern Prehistory.* Denver:Westview.

Robbins, R. (2008). *Cultural Anthropology: A Problem-Based Approach.* Belmont, CA:Wadsworth.

Roberts, C. (2007). *The Unnatural History of the Sea.* Washington, DC: Island Press/Shearwater Books.

Sandlin, J., Schultz, B., & Burdick, J. (Eds.) (2009). *Handbook of Public Pedagogy, Education and Learning Beyond Schooling.* New York: Routledge.

Sahlins, M. (1972). *Stone Age Economics.* Piscataway, NJ: Aldine Transaction.

School for Field Studies (http://www.fieldstudies.org/index.cfm)

Singer, M. (2009). *Introduction to Syndemics, A Critical Systems Approach to Public and Community Health.* New Jersey: John Wiley & Sons.

Singer, M. (2010). Eco-nomics: Are the Planet-Unfriendly Features of Capitalism Barriers to Sustainability? *Sustainability, 2,* 127–144.

Sponsel, L. (2001). Do Anthropologists Need Religion, and Vice Versa? Adventures and Dangers in Spiritual Ecology. *In New Directions in Anthropology and Environment: Intersections.* C.L. Crumley, ed. pp. 177–200. Walnut Creek CA: AltaMira Press.

Sponsel encyclopedia http://www.eoearth.org/article/Ecological_anthropology).

Steward, J. (1955). *Theory of Culture Change: The Methodology of Multilinear Evolution.* Urbana:University of Illinois Press.

Sullivan, S. (2010). Green Capitalism, and the cultural poverty of constructing nature as a service Provider," *Radical Anthropology,* 18–27.

Sullivan, S. (2011). Engagements with Nature, Culture and Capitalism website. (http://siansullivan. wordpress.com/about/)

Townsend, P. K. (2009). *Environmental Anthropology: From Pigs to Policies.* Long Grove, IL:Waveland.

Wallis, V. (2010). Beyond Green Capitalism. *Monthly Review* 61:9. http://monthlyreview.org/2010/02/01/beyond-green-capitalism

Walters, B. et al. (2007). *Against the Grain: The Vayda Tradition in Human Ecology and Ecological Anthropology.* Lanham, MD: Alta Mira.

Wells, E. C. (2010). Anthropology, Sustainability, and Higher Education: An Interview with Peggy Barlett. *Society for Applied Anthropology Newsletter, 21*(4), 18–22.

West, P. (2006). Conservation Is Our Government Now: The Politics of Ecology in Papua New Guinea (New Ecologies for the Twenty-First Century). Durham, NC:Duke. See her webpage at: (http://bc.barnard.edu/~pwest/index.html)

Wolin, S. S. (2008). *Democracy Inc., Managed Democracy and the Specter of Inverted Totalitarianism.* Princeton: Princeton University Press.

GREENING COMMUNICATION

TEMA MILSTEIN

At this time of mounting human-induced ecological crises, the ways people communicate about nature have far reaching reverberations. Communication scholars engaged with ecological issues often assert that "what we say is what we see" (Cantrill & Oravec, 1996, p. 1) and what we see, or perceive, shapes how we behave ecologically. Communication scholars are especially concerned with the ways language, symbols, messages, interaction processes, and more broadly defined forms of discourse inform human perceptions of and practices within the natural world.

In the past 25 years, environmental communication emerged as a subfield within the communication discipline, yet the subfield is also a metafield that necessarily cuts across disciplines. The merging of communication foci and nature-human subjects has broadened and theoretically diversified environmental studies, providing a much-needed lens on the social meaning-making aspects of nature-human relations. For instance, in looking at communication research on environmental activism, one can begin to see how a communication lens provides an especially effective way to identify and critically analyze both the symbolic (language) and material (practice) aspects of ecological relations – in this case, those of eco-advocacy. Examples of such studies illustrate how activists engage potentially sympathetic outsiders via "toxic tours" of environmentally, racially, and socio-economically marginalized communities, opening up possibilities for critical and unified interpretation and advocacy (Pezzullo, 2007); how governments and corporations use discursive strategies to exclude Indigenous peoples and perpetuate the disproportionate targeting and devastation of them and their lands to maintain nuclear production processes (Endres, 2009); how activists initiate widely televised image events, such as the occupation of old growth trees marked for logging, to confront profit motive-driven industrialism with popular expression of community and ecological needs (DeLuca, 1999); or how recent globally networked actions calling for political response to mitigate climate crisis used strategic and performative communication to articulate ways forward and successfully used local action to buoy the climate crisis movement (Endres, Sprain & Peterson, 2009).

In order to illustrate communication studies' importance in a broad-based liberal arts approach to the environment, this chapter shows the range of valuable interpretations emanating from the field. To contextualize these interpretations, I also outline the origin and growth of the greening of the communication discipline. In addition, I describe current trends, looking at recent disciplinary conversations

S. D. Fassbinder, A. J. Nocella II and R. Kahn (Eds.), Greening the Academy:
Ecopedagogy Through the Liberal Arts, 161–174.
© *2012 Sense Publishers. All rights reserved.*

about scholars' ethical roles as environmental advocates and describing the early emergence of ecologically informed communication theory. Finally, I discuss future directions and possibilities for the field, including increased internationalization, intercultural conversation, and interdisciplinary collaboration.

CURRENT INTERPRETATION WITHIN THE FIELD

Environmental communication comprises two core assumptions. First, the ways we communicate powerfully shape our understandings of nature. Second, these understandings inform how we relate with and within the living world. In this way, scholars see communication as not merely reflecting but also as producing and naturalizing particular human relations with nature. Many studies also include a third assumption that our representations of nature are *interested*. In other words, representations of nature are not neutral, but instead informed by particular contexts and interests, often in ways we are unaware, directing us to see nature through particular lenses while also obscuring alternative ways of perceiving nature (Milstein, 2009a).

One of the discipline's key additions to the field of environmental studies has been the focused investigation of human-nature relations as both materially and symbolically constructed. Informed by poststructuralism, and in conversation with contemporary transdisciplines and orientations (such as science studies or ecofeminism), many environmental communication scholars view human symbolic traffic and human relations with the material world as intricately entwined. Scholarly explorations of this notion serve to bridge the humanities, social sciences, and natural sciences by paying close attention to the intersections of perception, meaning production, and practice, pointing to ways that "natural and cultural systems help shape each other and are radically consequential for each other" (Carbaugh, 1996, p. 40).

A goal of many critical environmental communication scholars is to identify, critique, and raise awareness about the ways in which environmental discourses reflect and reproduce a particular political economy of interests. In addition, many scholars explore and theorize about ecologically sustainable or restorative discourses, finding these persist or can be created or revitalized in cultures and communities. In this way, scholars are interested in illustrating ways that symbols, meanings, and/or discourses might allow for different socio-environmental views and inform different actions. In the following, I provide several examples to briefly illustrate the orientations and topics within the range of environmental communication work.

Examples of studies that look at discursive elements of consumerism include: A study of TV advertisements for Hummers and fast food that demonstrates ways corporations, to sell products and resist moves toward sustainability, activate perceived "threats" to masculinity posed by environmental and animal rights movements (Rogers, 2008); a study that looks at ways the meat industry uses discursive strategies such as "speaking" animals to construct a benevolent image for itself in advertisements that informs meat eaters to think about animals in ways that tacitly endorse cruel and environmentally destructive industry practices (Glenn, 2004); and a study that analyzes the evangelical movement to curb SUV driving and finds the campaign offers potential for stimulating sustainable environmental action yet also reproduces framings of mastery that perpetuate exclusion and control of both nature and other humans construed as inferior (Hendry & Cramer, 2005).

Examples of studies that look at how communication helps frame human relations with other animals include: An examination of ways endangered species proponents' strategic rhetoric about the uniqueness of orangutans and their rainforest habitat, the precariousness of their continued existence, and the timeliness for immediate action in the face of threats, may work to ally foreign audiences but may not do the same for Indonesians living alongside the species (Sowards, 2006); and an investigation of how contemporary Western zoo conservation discourses reproduce particular human relationships with nature and stand in the way of zoo abilities to work as agents for systemic ecocultural change (Milstein, 2009b).

Examples of studies that look at environmental discourse in pop culture or in culture-specific everyday talk include: An analysis of how dissonance in audience reactions to the documentary *Grizzly Man* was rooted in the film's disconfirmation of human faith in the nature/culture binary via the protagonist's death in becoming prey, or "pieces of meat," and object rather than subject (Schutten, 2008); and an examination of the ways members of a particular Indigenous culture speak of "listening" to nature, a cultural form of communication that supports a highly reflective and revelatory mode of being that opens one to relations between human and nonhuman forms (Carbaugh, 1999).

Other examples illustrate the role of communication and interdisciplinary theory in planning or evaluating the effectiveness of public participation in environmental decision making: One recent study by communication scholars examines participant feedback about multi-stakeholder processes regarding contentious environmental issues and highlights the roles of collaborative learning and stakeholder access, standing, and influence (Walker, Senecah & Daniels, 2006); another draws from the sociological tradition of Anthony Giddens to investigate ways environmental public participation can benefit from structuration theory and parallel systems thinking (Norton, 2007).

These examples merely scratch the surface of environmental communication research. They begin to illustrate, however, the range of work emanating from the field. The breadth and diversity of approach and topic are perhaps all the more remarkable when one considers the field's youthfulness.

THE EMERGENCE OF ENVIRONMENTAL COMMUNICATION

Environmental communication broke the surface of the communication discipline in the mid-1980s in the United States. Scholars often cite the 1984 publication of Christine Oravec's generative rhetorical study as definitively introducing environmental communication to the wider communication discipline. In this study, Oravec analyzed the discourse of early 1900s preservationists and conservationists, as each group represented opposite sides of a controversy over whether to build a dam in a highly regarded natural site in North America. Oravec illustrated how conservationists won — and the dam was built — by appealing to a "progressive" view of the "public" and its relationship to nature. The debate's outcome signaled the defeat of one view of society — the preservationist view that the intact beauty of nature serves the nation as an organic whole. The outcome also signaled the rise of the conservationist view of progressivism, in which the material needs of individuals determine the uses of nature, a view that is still a dominant discursive force in the way environmental decisions are made today.

A number of environmentally dedicated and methodologically diverse scholars started publishing in the 1980s, leading to remarkable growth in the field in the following decade. American scholars formed the Conference on Communication and Environment in 1991, a biennial interdisciplinary conference that brings together scholars who hold nature and communication as central to their work. From this meeting emerged the Environmental Communication Network (www.esf.edu/ecn/), which harbors a well-utilized listserv and a web site with links to bibliographies, sample courses, journals, undergraduate and graduate programs, and a newsletter for scholars, graduate students, and practitioners.[1]

Meanwhile, parallel growth was taking place internationally. The Europe-based International Association for Media and Communication Research founded its Environmental Issues, Science and Risk Communication working group in 1988, which began by focusing on media and environmental issues and now includes a broader spectrum of concerns regarding public understanding, media constructions, political discourses, and the environmental roles of pressure groups, new media, and activism. In 1990, a small group of award-winning journalists founded the Society of Environmental Journalists with the mission to advance public understanding of environmental issues by improving quality, accuracy, and visibility of environmental reporting; the international membership includes some 1,500 journalists and academics. In 2008, the European Communication Research and Education Association founded its Science and Environment Communication section to help provide core contributions to current debates about scientific and environmental problems and issues of democracy, citizenship, and power.

In 1996, US scholars created what became the division of Environmental Communication at the National Communication Association, establishing the field's legitimacy within the larger discipline and providing scholars a national platform. The 1990s also saw the publication in North America and Europe of key books examining communication and the environment (See Cantrill & Oravec, 1996; Cronon, 1996; Darier, 1999; Davis, 1997; DeLuca, 1999; 1999; Harvey, 1996; Herndl & Brown, 1996; Killingsworth & Palmer, 1992; Muir & Veenendall, 1996; Myerson & Rydin, 1996). By the mid-1990s, the more prominent communication journals began to publish environmental communication research on a regular basis (S. Depoe, 1997).

The past decade has brought the field increased participation and legitimacy. The US-based *Environmental Communication Yearbook* began publishing in 2003 and its 2007 transformation into a quarterly published academic journal, *Environmental Communication: A Journal of Nature and Culture* (Routledge), marked the coming of age of the field. Other interdisciplinary journals dedicated to issues of communication and environment began publication, including the Australia-based *Applied Environmental Education and Communication* (Taylor and Francis) in 2001 and the Germany-based *International Journal of Sustainability Communication: Research and Practice for a Sustainable Future* in 2007.

Whereas courses in environmental communication used to be a rarity, student interest and demand, as well as more Ph.Ds. graduating with a focus in environmental communication, have led to more departments offering undergraduate and graduate classes focusing on ecological issues. Presses began to publish textbooks in 2006 (Corbett, 2006; Cox, 2009) and new textbooks continue to be introduced (e.g., Hendry, 2010). While some departments still lack professors specializing in environmental communication, many now have at least one or two with environmental foci. In addition, some departments are beginning to market themselves as providing environmental communication among their emphases. Many faculty also affiliate with interdisciplinary sustainability programs at their universities, helping students across campus expand beyond techno-scientific elements to articulate the socio-cultural and communicative elements of environmental issues.

CURRENT TRENDS AND FUTURE DIRECTIONS IN ENVIRONMENTAL COMMUNICATION

Ethical Imperatives: Advocacy and Application

Environmental communication scholarship is not only engaged in intellectual exploration of social-ecological issues, but also often in seeking to bring about positive transformation. These efforts can range from scholars articulating via theory and research how communication helps to shape and shift nature in an effort to illustrate and raise awareness in and beyond the academy, to explicitly activist research in which theory is directly applied to particular situations in an effort to help enact social or political change.

Along these lines, recent conversations have been particularly interested in scholars' ethical roles. Environmental communication scholar Robert Cox (2007), three-time president of the Sierra Club (2007–2008, 2000–2001, & 1994–1996), has argued the subfield is a "crisis discipline" as it deals either directly or indirectly with pressing life-and-death issues such as climate crisis, endangered species, and toxic pollution. Much as the discipline of conservation biology strives to illustrate and explain biological elements of ecological collapse in an attempt to halt and reverse collapse, Cox and others claim environmental communication scholars have an ethical duty not only to try to explain but also to help change societal elements that cause ecological collapse. One could also use as an example restoration ecology, which both studies and applies notions of beneficial human intervention to help restore healthy ecological relations. Many argue environmental communication is or should be similarly restorative, uniquely focusing on and putting forth notions of beneficial human discursive interventions.

Though some argue that articulating scholarship as advocacy might not be especially effective or appropriate (Senecah, 2007), many, driven by the urgency to address communication's perceived environmental failures and healing possibilities, not only examine and critique discourses, but also engage their scholarship directly by facilitating or taking part in public processes, sharing critiques with discourse producers, and/or offering alternative discourses more conducive to sustainability. Still others choose research sites and approaches that ensure they are not merely observers but also advocates in their case studies, reflecting upon, contributing, and practicing discursive interventions.

Using communication research to help societies consider and transform human-nature relations seems inevitable as well as highly advisable, and, indeed, communities, organizations, and movements are calling for such work. A brief personal research example may help illustrate the usefulness of communication scholarship to such public endeavors:[2] I recently responded to calls from The Wilderness Society, Conservation Voters of New Mexico, and local US Southwest cultural and academic organizations to raise awareness about marginalized ecocultural ways of perceiving and practicing human relations with nature. We formed a collaborative community-based participatory action research project to attempt to identify and illustrate varied Southwest Hispanic environmental meaning systems. These efforts were focused not only on interpreting different ways of communicating relations with nature, but also on what advocates described as helping these communities "rewrite themselves into the land." Our findings pointed to Hispanic participants valuing a sense of *relations-in-place,* which constitutes nature as a socially integrated space that provides the grounding for human relations, and differs from dominant Western discourses that constitute nature as an entity separate from humans (Milstein, Anguiano, Sandoval, Chen & Dickinson, in press). Some organizations we collaborated with intend to use the study's findings to confront and sway pro-industry politicians who have long justified voting records by arguing they represent their "anti-environmentalist" Hispanic constituents. In the process, the organizations hope to identify ways of advocating for these communities' ecological values and needs by creating persuasive messages that accurately reflect Hispanic constituents.

Ethical ecological advocacy extends to pedagogy. Communication faculty teach students to critically reflect on human-nature relations by exposing them to different ways of communicating, helping them select language that matches their views of what needs to be done in the world, and pointing out ways to powerfully and persuasively use such language in their own environmental communication. Cox's (2009) textbook, now in its second edition, also emphasizes opportunities for students to apply their growing knowledge of principles of environmental communication to their campuses and communities. Using "Act Locally!" chapter exercises, students, for instance, interview local environmental groups about forms of communication the groups use to pursue missions, investigate types of communication in public environmental hearings in their community, count and characterize news stories in local media on environmental issues and examine effects on audiences, and design campus-based environmental campaigns that use appeals and messages to create demand and mobilize support to hold decision makers accountable.

ECOLOGICAL THEORY: NATURE AS CO-COMMUNICANT

In research, some scholars are exploring the notion that communication *mediates* human-nature relations and that this process is a connecting force. At first, mediation theory appears much like a material-symbolic discursive approach, understanding human discourse as informing views and actions toward nature. However, mediation theory also questions how nature's communication might mediate human-nature relations. Mediation is concerned, therefore, with the interactivity of ecological co-presence – the ways humans symbolically mediate views of and actions toward nature and the ways that all of nature "speaks" (Milburn interview with Donal Carbaugh, 2007) shaping and shifting living knowledge and interconnecting beings.

A mediation framework attempts to sensitize us to, and move us away from, modernist framings of nature as a passive, mute, detached object – framings used not only in Western culture at large but also in the majority of research in the humanities, social sciences, and physical sciences. Even studies that are explicitly critical of such conventional framings often stop at the step of illustrating and critiquing anthropocentric and hierarchical articulations of human-nature relations. Therefore, mediation, a nascent, demanding, and promising heuristic move in the field of environmental communication, is an attempt to both incorporate and move beyond critique to begin to posit an ecologically inspired ontological framework.

Scholars who are working toward these emergent directions argue that one must be cautious not to view nature as merely another text to decode and, instead, to view the notion of nature communicating as a nuanced way to articulate agency beyond the human world, to situate nature as an active subject in determining the ways we sense and perceive the world. Some have turned to existing theory, such as phenomenology, to attempt to stitch the human corporeally and perceptually back into the fabric of the Earth (Abram, 1997; Kinsella, 2007). Others have worked to articulate a materialist theory of communication in an effort to overcome nature objectification in constitutive theories (Rogers, 1998). Still others have created a framework for balancing the twin objectives of studying how the word and the world speak in order to design research that serves a diversity of peoples, eco-parts, and processes (Carbaugh, 2007). And then there are those who have empirically illustrated and critiqued how people of Western cultures discuss nature "speaking" in ways that bring people in touch with nature and inspire people to learn about and protect nature, yet can also be used to justify particular commercial endeavors

(Milstein, 2008). Still others argue the voices of nature, or the "extrahuman," must be included not only in everyday communication but also in democratic practices (Peterson, Peterson & Peterson, 2007).

AN INTERNATIONAL, INTERCULTURAL & INTERDISCIPLINARY FUTURE

If current growth is any indicator, the field will likely continue to experience great expansion and diversification with new energy and voices due to the widely recognized necessity of effective communication skills and analysis for today's ecological questions, problems, and policies. The vibrancy of this expansion depends upon further internationalization and more interdisciplinary and intercultural dialogue. The global topic of human-nature relations demands such moves, and such moves would further strengthen environmental communication's theoretical rigor and applicability.

Recently, Steve Depoe (2008), editor of the journal *Environmental Communication: A Journal of Nature and Culture*, convincingly argued that scholars have spent the past 25 years building the field of inquiry's cornerstones and the next logical step was "the creation of an international organization that brings more coherence, visibility, and impact to what scholars and practitioners are doing around the world" (p. 2). When this book went to press, scholars were actively working toward this goal by forming the International Environmental Communication Association (IECA) (http://environmentalcomm.org/).

The need to improve cross-talk among European and American-based scholars is apparent in the lack of Western hemispheric intellectual dialogue in most studies. For instance, ecolinguistics scholars, based largely in Europe, Australia, and Canada (see www.ecoling.net and www-gewi.uni-graz.at/ecoling), specifically focus on issues of communication and sustainability. Yet, though ecolinguistics research significantly overlaps with much US-based environmental communication research, only a few scholars from either camp explicitly interact with the other in their work.

Collaboration among global North, global South, and Indigenous scholars perhaps is even more imperative. Such discussions will generate valuable studies and ideas that speak to broader intercultural audiences and situations. Drawing on more truly global scholarship will expand options for rethinking our world and lead to better scholarly critiques. Along these lines, Piyush Mathur (2008) at the American University of Nigeria critiques what he characterizes as an inward looking US-based body of environmental communication scholarship, arguing such practices stand in the way of worldwide-informed or oriented intellectual traditions, robust critiques, or meticulous and ambitious thinking – in the end, limiting the field's theoretical savvy.

The richer international dialogue hoped for in the formation of the IECA goes hand-in-hand with more interaction with practitioners and more interdisciplinary conversations. Global South interdisciplinary scholars and practitioners who speak directly to issues of communication and sustainability yet who communication scholars have been slow to engage include philosopher Arturo Escobar (who has published political ecology work on discourse in Colombian Pacific rainforest communities); self-"deprofessionalized" agronomist Julio Valladolid and anthropologist Frédérique Apffel-Marglin (who have published work on ecological conversation, cosmovision, and the nurturing of biodiversity in Andean campesino communities in Peru); and physicist and activist Vandana Shiva (who has published prolifically on discourse, neoliberal globalization, ecojustice, and agricultural biodiversity in India).

In addition, scholars who represent some of the disciplines under the humanities' scrutiny, such as the natural and physical sciences and the legal and policy-focused disciplines, would benefit from closer dialogue with communication scholars to use their insights to better examine, explain, and critique the environmental discourses in which they take part. Working together in some investigations also allows communication scholars to better understand the contexts, drives, and frameworks of the discourses we sometimes critique. Scholars would also benefit from closer dialogue with other critics, such as cultural geographers and environmental literature scholars, so as to better co-build and strengthen theory via interdisciplinary critique, providing contrast to the separately generated, maintained, and utilized theory that disciplinary lines tend to promote.

A rich and careful development of the budding theory of mediation outlined above, for example, depends on such interdisciplinary conversations. Communication scholars are trained to examine human communication and, therefore, in their explorations of ways nature "speaks" are able to focus on ways humans perceive, articulate, represent, and reproduce nature communicating. These explorations, however, would be nourished were they in closer dialogue with scientific perceptions of ways nature communicates ecologically and biologically, or with psychology's notions of the emotional elements of mediation, or legal notions of the rights of elements of nature.

Other fields need communication scholars to help in their efforts to educate and communicate their messages – one recent example of an interdisciplinary effort that reflects such needs is an edited book titled *Creating a Climate for Change: Communicating Climate Change and Facilitating Social Change* (Moser & Dilling, 2007) that organized interdisciplinary academics and practitioners to examine the communication challenges associated with climate crisis and social change and offered practical suggestions on ways to communicate climate change more effectively to facilitate societal response.

Universities can and must support such interdisciplinary moves by backing the increasingly popular rhetoric of interdisciplinarity with structural and financial support and incentives for such endeavors. In addition, grant-giving institutions need to expand their focus beyond the natural sciences, law and policy sciences, and beyond positivist social science research. Calls and criteria for grant proposals should be written in ways that are also receptive to the value of critical and cultural approaches to looking at environmental issues. As I've detailed in this chapter and as others have in other chapters in this book, the range of interdisciplinary work can be extremely useful for contemporary environmental questions and endeavors. Part of this entails more scholars taking the risk of standing in the traditional gap between theory and practice, as well as building transdisciplinary bridges (Senecah, 2007).

Scholarly collaboration is only one aspect of creating increasingly relevant and informed transdisciplinary work. In addition, we need to encourage communication students to cross disciplines during their education and encourage students from the natural and physical sciences and the policy and legal sciences to extend their learning to environmental communication if they are to critically and successfully communicate as and to the next generation of world leaders. Universities also must create campus-wide curricula and programs for interdisciplinary environmental learning; some have begun to do such work. For instance, a biology professor at the University of New Mexico recently led efforts to form a Sustainability Studies Program that organizes affiliated faculty from the humanities, social sciences, and natural and physical sciences to offer an interdisciplinary and service-oriented minor; the University of Utah offers an innovative Environmental Humanities graduate program; James Madison University supports a first-year general education learning community that combines classes in communication, writing, and critical thinking with a focus on environmental topics and service; and University of Texas El Paso's Communication Department started an MA program in 2008 in Environmental Communication and social change with classes in Indonesia, Mexico, China, and the US in Indonesian, Spanish, Chinese, and English in conjunction with an NGO called Rare (www.rareconservation.org) based in Washington, DC.

There is high interest among students for these sorts of interdisciplinary and intercultural offerings, yet some students are also restricted from such choices by university disciplinary structures. As an example, I teach a graduate course titled "EcoCulture: Humans and the Environment" that attracts students from departments of Communication, Fine Arts, American Studies, Cultural Studies, Education, Anthropology, and Architecture and Planning. In the class, the liberal arts, fine arts, social sciences, and policy makers of the future are represented, yet notably the scientists of the future, who largely dominate environmental studies, are not. This is likely due to a problematically inward looking scientific curriculum at the graduate level in most universities.

The reality is our curricula have not caught up to what our students care about or need in order to be active participants and leaders in social or political environmental change. Often, students are creating their own interdisciplinary degrees if they have the freedom to do so. As educators, we have a powerful opportunity provided by these students who are pushing our diverse fields to dialogue; in turn, we can give students the opportunity to discover their interdisciplinary niche. Environmental communication offers a highly applicable entry into both such introductory and advanced interdisciplinary environmental studies learning.

IN CLOSING

Environmental communication has matured at a rapid pace in the past 25 years. The field forges an important path into understanding human relations with and within their ecosystems. I've outlined the ways interpretations in the field rest upon the assumption that the ways we communicate powerfully affect our perceptions, definitions, and practices of "the environment."

Current trends in environmental communication reflect our times of ecological crisis and rapid changes in human-nature relations. Some argue that environmental communication scholars are public advocates for the environment through their research and related work. Others are providing early articulations of an ecologically informed theory of communication, positioning nature as co-present, active, and dynamic force in human-nature relations. Both trends point to restorative directions in the realms of research, methodology, theory, application, and publicly useful scholarship.

The future potency of the field depends upon increasingly international, intercultural, and interdisciplinary conversations that are scholar driven, university supported, and which benefit students. As ecologically oriented scholars around the globe in the humanities, social sciences, and natural and physical sciences forge more open channels of discussion, we can create more fertile, reciprocal networks of knowledge. In the process, we can create increasingly helpful work that illustrates, questions, and remakes the place of the human within the ecosphere.

NOTES

[1]   At press, the newly formed International Environmental Communication Association (http://environmentalcomm.org/) planned to take on many of these services.

[2]   While communication work is relevant and important in today's advocacy for the environment, some organizations overlook communication perhaps because of a lack of familiarity with the discipline. This perhaps points to the need to publicize communication scholarship, and particularly environmental communication scholarship, more widely beyond academics and to work more closely with practitioners. For instance, the United Kingdom branch of the World Wildlife Federation recently began work to try to identify and circumvent discursive barriers public figures encounter when they try to broaden environmental public debates beyond narrow pre-occupations with short-term economic arguments. The organization is also working to identify stories people tell themselves about who they are, or the 'myths we live by,' to learn whether environmental problems can be tackled from within constraints imposed by today's dominant myths, and is looking at possibilities of creating new, more ecologically beneficial myths (www.wwf.org.uk/core/ge_0000004945.asp, accessed November 28, 2008). While WWF-UK is working with psychologists and marketing executives in these endeavors, they appear to have overlooked the seemingly obvious choice of communication scholars.

REFERENCES

Abram, D. (1997). *The Spell of the Sensuous: Perception and Language in a More-than-Human World.* New York: Vintage Books.

Cantrill, J. G., & Oravec, C. L. (Eds.) (1996). *The Symbolic Earth: Discourse and Our Creation of the Environment.* Lexington: University Press of Kentucky.

Carbaugh, D. (1996). Naturalizing communication and culture. In J. G. Cantrill & C. L. Oravec (Eds.), *The Symbolic Earth: Discourse and Our Creation of the Environment* (pp. 38–57). Lexington: University Press of Kentucky.

Carbaugh, D. (1999). "Just listen": "Listening" and landscape among the Blackfeet. *Western Journal of Communication, 63*(3), 250–270.

Carbaugh, D. (2007). Quoting, "the Environment": Touchstones on Earth. *Environmental Communication: A Journal of Culture and Nature, 1*(1), 64–73.

Corbett, J. B. (2006). *Communicating Nature: How We Create and Understand Environmental Messages.* Washington, Covelo, London: Island Press.

Cox, R. (2007). Nature's "crisis disciplines": Does environmental communication have an ethical duty? *Environmental Communication: A Journal of Culture and Nature, 1*(1), 5–20.

Cox, R. (2009). *Environmental Communication and the Public Sphere* (2nd ed.). Thousand Oaks, London & New Delhi: Sage.

Cronon, W. (Ed.). (1996). *Uncommon Ground: Rethinking the Human Place in Nature.* New York: W.W. Norton & Co.

Darier, E. (Ed.). (1999). *Discourses of the Environment.* Oxford: Blackwell.

Davis, S. (1997). *Spectacular Nature: Corporate Culture and the Sea World Experience.* Berkeley: University of California Press.

DeLuca, K. M. (1999). *Image Politics: The New Rhetoric of Environmental Activism.* New York: Guilford.

Depoe, S. (1997). Environmental Studies in Mass Communication. *Critical Studies in Media Communication,* 368–372.

Depoe, S. P. (2008). The prospect ahead. *Environmental Communication: A Journal of Nature and Culture, 2*(1), 1–2.

Endres, D. (2009). The Rhetoric of Nuclear Colonialism: Rhetorical Exclusion of American Indian Arguments in the Yucca Mountain Nuclear Waste Siting Decision. *Communication and Critical/ Cultural Studies, 6*(1), 39–60.

Endres, D., Sprain, L., & Peterson, T. R. (Eds.). (2009). *Social Movement to Address Climate Change: Local Steps for Global Action.* Amherst, NY: Cambria Press.

Glenn, C. B. (2004). Constructing Consumables and Consent: A Critical Analysis of Factory Farm Industry Discourse. *Journal of Communication Inquiry, 28*(1), 63–81.

Harré, R., Brockmeier, J., & Mühlhäuser, P. (1999). *Greenspeak: A Study of Environmental Discourse.* Thousand Oaks, Calif.: Sage Publications.

Harvey, D. (1996). *Justice, Nature and the Geography of Difference.* Cambridge, MA: Blackwell.

Hendry, J. (2010). *Communication and the Natural World.* State College, PA Strata Publishing.

Hendry, J., & Cramer, J. (2005). The logic of colonization in the 'what would Jesus drive?' anti-SUV campaign. *The Environmental Communication Yearbook, 2,* 115–131.

Herndl, C. G., & Brown, S. C. (Eds.). (1996). *Green Culture: Environmental Rhetoric in Contemporary America.* Madison: University of Wisconsin Press.

Killingsworth, M. J., & Palmer, J. S. (1992). *Ecospeak: Rhetoric and Environmental Politics in America.* Carbondale and Edwardsville: Southern Illinois University Press.

Kinsella, W. J. (2007). Heidegger and Being at the Hanford Reservation: Standing reserve, enframing, and Environmental Communication theory. *Environment Communication: A Journal of Nature and Culture, 1*(2), 194–217.

Mathur, P. (2008). Gregory Bateson, Niklas Luhmann, and Ecological Communication. *The Communication Review, 11*(2), 151–175.

Milburn interview with Donal Carbaugh, T. (2007). Donal Carbaugh. *Ecologue, Winter,* 1–2.

Milstein, T. (2008). When whales "speak for themselves": Communication as a mediating force in wildlife tourism. *Environmental Communication: A Journal of Nature and Culture, 2*(2), 173–192.

Milstein, T. (2009a). Environmental communication theories. In S. Littlejohn & K. Foss (Eds.), *Encyclopedia of Communication Theory* (pp. 344–349). Thousand Oaks, CA: Sage.

Milstein, T. (2009b). 'Somethin' tells me it's all happening at the zoo:' Discourse, power, and conservationism. *Environmental Communication: A Journal of Nature and Culture, 3*(1), 24–48.

Milstein, T., Anguiano, C., Sandoval, J., Chen, Y. W., & Dickinson, E. (in press). Communicating a "new" environmental vernacular: A sense of relations-in-place. *Communication Monographs*, 1–31.

Moser, S. C., & Dilling, L. (Eds.) (2007). *Creating a Climate for Change: Communicating Climate Change and Facilitating Social Change.* Cambridge, New York, Melbourne, Madrid, Cape Town, Singapore, São Paulo: Cambridge University Press.

Muir, S. A., & Veenendall, T. L. (Eds.) (1996). *Earthtalk: Communication Empowerment for Environmental Action.* Westport: Praeger Press.

Myerson, G., & Rydin, Y. (1996). *The Language of Environment: A New Rhetoric.* London: UCL Press.

Norton, T. (2007). The structuration of public participation: Organizing environmental control. *Environmental Communication: A Journal of Nature and Culture, 1*(2), 146–170.

Oravec, C. L. (1984). Conservationism vs. preservationism: The public interest in the Hetch-Hetchy controversy. *Quarterly Journal of Speech, 70*, 444–458.

Peterson, M. N., Peterson, M. J., & Peterson, T. R. (2007). Environmental communication: Why this crisis discipline should facilitate environmental democracy. *Environmental Communication: A Journal of Nature and Culture, 1*(1), 74–86.

Pezzullo, P. C. (2007). *Toxic Tourism: Rhetorics of Pollution, Travel, and Environmental Justice.* Tuscaloosa: The University of Alabama Press.

Rogers, R. A. (1998). Overcoming the objectification of nature in constitutive theories: Toward a transhuman, materialist theory of communication. *Western Journal of Communication, 62*(3), 244–272.

Rogers, R. A. (2008). Beasts, Burgers, and Hummers: Meat and the Crisis of Masculinity in Contemporary Television Advertisements. *Environmental Communication: A Journal of Nature and Culture, 2*(3), 281–301.

Schutten, J. K. (2008). Chewing on the Grizzly Man: Getting to the meat of the matter. *Environmental Communication: A Journal of Nature and Culture, 2*(2), 193–211.

Senecah, S. L. (2007). Impetus, mission, and future of the Environmental Communication Commission/ Division: Are we still on track? Were we ever? *Environmental Communication: A Journal of Nature and Culture, 1*(1), 21–33.

Sowards, S. K. (2006). Rhetoric of the perpetual potential: A case study of the environmentalist movement to protect orangutans. *The Environmental Communication Yearbook, 3*, 115–136.

Walker, G. B., Senecah, S. L., & Daniels, S. E. (2006). From the forest to the river: Citizens' views of stakeholder engagement. *Human Ecology Review, 13*(2), 193–202.

GREENING LITERATURE

COREY LEE LEWIS

It is both an over-used cliché, and a significant truism, that the pen is mightier than the sword.

Of course, one can always argue that this is not the case, that in any instance of conflict, physical force will triumph over intellectual ability. However, this distorts the larger, more complex reality: the fact that, although the soldier has the power to wield a gun, the politician with a pen has the power to wield the soldier. Both military orders and civilian laws—which must be followed by soldiers and citizens alike—are given in "pen." Recent cases of U.S. military personnel torturing prisoners of war in Abu Ghraib, Guantonomo Bay and other C.I.A. Black-Op sites, serve as a good example of this phenomenon. While the soldiers who beat, electrocuted, and tortured their victims are each responsible for the pain (and occasional deaths) they caused, those in the Bush administration who wrote the now infamous "Torture Memo" which sanctioned such horrific behavior are responsible for the fate of, not a few individual prisoners, but thousands. The same is true with regard to environmental problems. For example, the owners of Peabody Energy, the world's largest coal company, are responsible for emitting thousands of tons of Sulfur-dioxide into the atmosphere each year. However, as heads of the E.P.A., Christine Whitman and Mike Leavitt, along with other members of the Bush administration, are responsible for the increased emissions of, not just a few power plants, but hundreds. Their Clear Skies Initiative which undermined 30 years-worth of environmental law, actually increased the amount of sulfur-dioxide, mercury and other pollutants such plants can emit. In both cases, the pen or policy is clearly mightier, more capable of doing damage, than the sword, gun, or toxic industry.

We often fail to recognize the power of the pen because we mistake direct action for effective action simply because its results are generally more tangible and immediate. Similarly, we tend to conflate indirect action with ineffective action because its results take longer and are more subtle. This problem of perception has often marginalized some of our most effective, long-term strategies for creating the cultural change necessary to address environmental problems, strategies that, although subtle and indirect, yield powerful and lasting results. Because we have often focused on immediate or short-term change, much of the environmental movement has focused on reacting to environmental disasters and improving environmental policies, without a concomitant effort to changing mainstream cultural beliefs and practices While direct action strategies—such as tree-sitting and cleaning up oil spills, and policy based efforts like endangered species protection

S. D. Fassbinder, A. J. Nocella II and R. Kahn (Eds.), Greening the Academy:
Ecopedagogy Through the Liberal Arts, 175–184.
© *2012 Sense Publishers. All rights reserved.*

and clean air and water laws—are of vital importance, we often fail to recognize the need for, and efficacy of, long-term and indirect strategies for cultural change such as those provided by environmental literature, arts, and humanities. Although subtle and indirect, our popular media and literature often function as broader and stronger forces for cultural change then many of our more direct activist strategies.

Contrary to the common assumption that prevails today, public policy does not direct culture, but rather reflects it. Laws do not change individual or collective behavior; they merely crystallize the behaviors already accepted or denied by mainstream hegemonic culture. Conversely, literary and artistic works do not simply reflect the values of their authors; they also direct the attitudes of their audiences. A people's literature, then, might be viewed as a stronger force in shaping their society than their public policy. Such a perspective leads me to contend: People are not governed by their laws, but by their literature.[1] Or, in less poetic but perhaps more precise terms, the hegemonic beliefs and behaviors of a people are guided more strongly by their larger cultural narratives—and the texts that sustain or alter them— than by any set of public policies.

Most political efforts make the assumption that changes in policy create subsequent changes in culture, that one can change a people's values and behaviors through a top-down, policy-based approach. Unfortunately, however, this confuses cause with effect. When viewed from an anthropological perspective—when seen on a much longer time scale—it becomes clear that the policies of a people reflect their common values, attitudes, and behaviors much more than they direct them.

Take for example, the abolition of slavery in the U.S. Since the passage of the Emancipation Proclamation in 1863, slavery has been considered both illegal and immoral by mainstream American society. However, a cultural shift in hegemonic attitudes toward slavery preceded and caused the subsequent shift in policy. The Emancipation Proclamation itself did not *cause* American views of slavery to change, rather it *reflected* changes that had already taken place.

This cultural shift—which ultimately caused the change in policy—was itself created by antebellum literature. Early American authors, like freed slave Ottobah Cugoano, or "John Stuart," clearly changed the public's perception of, and attitude toward, slavery. In works like "Thoughts and Sentiments on the Evil and Wicked Traffic of the Slavery and Commerce of the Human Species" Cugoano argues passionately and pragmatically against slavery in 1787, almost a century before the practice became abolished. Other works from former slaves, such as Olaudah Equiano and Ukawsaw Gronniosaw, demonstrate that a cultural shift was taking place in the margins of society long before it took place in mainstream culture and public policy.

By 1852 the paradigm shift happening on the margins made it to the mainstream as evidenced by the reception of Harriet Beecher Stowe's *Uncle Tom's Cabin*. Not only was this the best-selling book of the 19th century, selling over 300,000 copies, but it also fueled the abolitionist movement and is recognized as having started the civil war. Abraham Lincoln, himself, is often noted for having observed of Stowe

"So this is the little lady who started this big war"(Stowe, p. 203). Thus, the public policy which outlawed slavery in the U.S. can accurately be viewed as in part a byproduct of abolitionist literature. In this case, literature *directed* public perception until public policy finally *reflected* those same values.

Literature, in general, is always already involved in this role of either supporting a particular hegemonic belief, or of subverting and replacing it. And works like Stowe's, specifically, are composed with the explicit intention of changing culture; they are, in environmental poet Gary Snyder's terms, engaged in "mythopoetics"— the attempt to change the operational myths and narratives of a culture, and thus the individual and collective values and behaviors of its members, through the strategic use of literature (*Real*). Our canon of environmental literature similarly is replete with texts which were composed specifically to shift hegemonic beliefs and behaviors and create revolutionary cultural change. The necessity of using such a strategy when seeking long-term cultural change was recognized by Antonio Gramsci in "Socialism and Culture," where he wrote, "every revolution has been preceded by an intense labor of criticism, by the diffusion of culture and the spread of ideas amongst the masses of men who are at first resistant... who have no ties of solidarity with others in the same condition." (12). David Korten likens this process of individual and collective transformation to forest succession, where an entire landscape is eventually and permanently changed through a pattern of emergence and displacement. Drawing on Kenneth Burke's concepts of "identification," Korten and others note the efficacy literature has to create powerful counter-narratives to those driving environmentally destructive societies, stating simply that in order for us to successfully respond to our current environmental crisis, "The key is to change the stories by which we define ourselves" (18). Stories, a people's literature, their guiding cultural narratives, exert either a beneficial role in their ecology, evolution and survival, or a deleterious one. This recognition stands as a central tenet of ecocriticism, and as an important insight for the environmental movement to take into the 21st century.

In this article I hope to demonstrate this close connection between literature and socio-political landscape by providing a historical survey of environmental texts and the emergence of ecocriticism as an academic discipline, alongside the evolution of the American environmental movement itself. Like Stowe and other antebellum abolitionists, the modern environmental movement has many literary predecessors whose work served as seminal starting points for larger paradigmatic shifts that have ultimately ended in the formation of new public policy. Upton Sinclair's novel *The Jungle* (1906) has long been credited with establishing the current Food and Drug Administration and a number of child labor and work-place-safety laws. The novel powerfully exposes the horrific health and safety conditions in Chicago's meat packing industry and caused President Theodore Roosevelt to throw his breakfast sausage out the window of the Whitehouse. The passage of both, the Pure Food and Drug Act and the Meat Inspection Act of 1906, were a direct result of the novel. Similarly, Rachel Carson's *Silent Spring* (1962) is recognized as having led to the banning of DDT pesticides in the U.S. only a decade later. Likewise, John Muir's many early essays on forest preservation led directly to the passage of the Forest Reserve Act in 1891, while his acclaimed *Mountains of California* (1897), was published in the same year the Forest Management Act was passed, which established our entire National Forest Preservation System; And Muir, himself, founded the Sierra Club, America's oldest and most well-known environmental organization. This short sampling of intentionally mythopoetic works illustrates well the process of cultural evolution whereby literary texts *reflect* the values of a marginalized group, transmit those values to the mainstream, and ultimately *direct* the formation of new hegemonic beliefs and policies—policies that now reflect the recently-shifted values of mainstream culture.

The American tradition of environmental literature has been intentionally political, and often subversive, from its very origins. Whether its authors were pro- or anti-conservation, the most common feature uniting American works of environmental literature is their mythopoetic—culturally transforming, or political—nature. Some of the earliest examples in the colonies took the form of promotional tracts that detailed, in exaggerated enthusiasm, the fertile and wild nature of the new world. Thomas Hariot's "A Briefe and True Report of the New Found Land of Virginia" (1588), is a typical example. In addition to describing the abundant natural wealth of the region, the vast stores of wildlife, timber, and mineral resources, Hariot claims that the ground is so fertile and climate so benign that a man can plant enough corn in "lesse then foure and twenty houres of labour, as shall yeeld him victual in a large proportion for a twelvemoneth" (Jehlen 74). John Smith's "A Description of New England" (1616), and William Wood's *New England's Prospect* (1634) offer similarly enthusiastic descriptions of the new world's riches. For these early writers, the expansive American landscape acted as an unlimited storehouse of both natural and symbolic resources. Their work had a significant impact on the number of immigrants moving to these shores, and directed many of the colonist's early environmental attitudes and perceptions.

Unlimited wealth and opportunity, whether it was natural or cultural, became a reoccurring theme in such promotional pieces. Thomas Jefferson's "Notes on the State of Virginia" (1781), and Hector St. John de Crevecour's "Letters from an American Farmer" (1782), provide typical examples of the time. Crevecour praises the natural abundance of his farm and contends that there is no better station in life than that of "an American farmer possessing freedom of action, freedom of thoughts, [and] ruled by a mode of government which requires but little from us" (Jehlen 975). Linking American political freedoms and economic opportunities to the physical freedom and sustenance provided by the rich American environment was common throughout our literary tradition. Historians, philosophers, and nature writers alike, from Frederick Jackson Turner and Joseph Wood Krutch to Wallace Stegner and Roderick Nash have always seen a direct connection between the character and vitality of the natural landscape and the character and vitality of its people.

This influence of the natural American landscape—as well as its nature writers—on mainstream culture is demonstrated best during the 1800's through the works of what many consider to be the holy trinity of early American nature writers: Emerson, Thoreau and Whitman. Ralph Waldo Emerson has long been recognized as one of America's most influential philosophers thanks to his development of Transcendentalism. First expressed in *Nature* (1836), transcendentalism linked the individual's knowledge of the divine with the divinity of nature, and thus revalued the natural world both physically and spiritually. Henry David Thoreau based much of his philosophy on Emerson's work, but evolved a much stronger political edge. His writings from "Civil Disobedience" (1849) to *Walden* (1854) consistently argue for the autonomy of nature and the individual, especially when they conflict with governmental or industrial power. In *Walden*, for example, Thoreau uses his observations of ants engaging in warfare to critique both the Mexican-American War and slavery, a critique that carried over to Thoreau's status as a tax resister. Social and environmental activists alike, from Mahatma Gandhi and Martin Luther King Jr. to John F. Kennedy and David Brower, have all credited Thoreau as one of the major influences on their lives and political efforts. Similarly, in *Leaves of Grass* (1855), Walt Whitman offers poetic praise for the natural landscape of America as well as her most common, and often most marginalized, citizens. By the time he died in 1892 *Leaves of Grass* had gone through nine editions, and still stands today, alongside *Walden*, as one of the most recognized works of American literature.

As the American frontier closed and the passenger pigeons and bison disappeared, our literary tradition became increasingly outspoken in its defense of non-human nature and more openly political in its purposes. While many of the 20th century's earliest nature writers like Mary Austin and Ernest Seton Thompson openly criticized increasing urbanization and the loss of wild habitat, the strongest calls for reform and revolution began around the middle of the century. In 1947 for example, Marjorie Stoneman Douglas published *The Everglades: River of Grass,* which exposed and vehemently criticized the destruction of Florida's fragile and exotic swamps. Concurrently, in the Midwest, forester and wildlife manager Aldo Leopold outlined his now famous "Land Ethic" in *A Sand County Almanac* (1949), arguing that human ethics must also be applied to the entire community of life, including the soil, that supports and sustains us. Paul Ehrlich's *The Population Bomb* was published in 1968, and the first Earth Day held in 1970. Shortly thereafter S. Godlovitch built on Leopold's eco-centric ethics to launch the Animal Rights movement with the publication of *Animals, Men and Morals: An Inquiry into the Maltreatment of Non-Humans* (1972). And three years later, Ernest Callenbach published *Ecotopia* (1975), in which California, Oregon and Washington secede from the union to start their own environmentally sustainable society, a move that has been mirrored by forest activists in the pacific northwest who have blockaded roads to timber sales and established "free state" zones to defend their local forests from federal officials and private loggers with barricades and their bodies.

As the 20th century began to turn toward the 21st and environmental problems continued to compound, American authors adopted more directly political strategies for their work. In *The Book of Yaak* (1996), Rick Bass argues passionately for the protection of the Yaak Valley, and includes the names and addresses of those who have the power to either protect the valley or let it get logged; in several places Bass confronts readers directly, asking, "Am I explaining it clearly? Is anyone please angry enough to write a letter? To write fifty letters, or five hundred" (p. 112). This explicit engagement with activism, the use of the literary text as a lobbying tool, is best exemplified in the emerging tradition of "Testimony" books. The first of these, *Testimony: Writers of the West Speak On Behalf of Utah Wilderness* (1996), was compiled by Stephen Trimble and Terry Tempest Williams in cooperation with the Utah Wilderness Coalition, and sent to every member of congress, in addition to selling widely all over the country. Similar efforts followed, including *Arctic Refuge: A Circle of Testimony* (2001), and *Wild Nevada: Testimonies on Behalf of the Desert* (2005), both of which were distributed in the same overtly political manner. And although politicians still debate whether or not to drill for oil in the Alaskan National Wildlife Refuge, thanks to efforts like these, the majority of American's are now strongly opposed to it; and in the silver state, an additional 558,000 acres of Wilderness were designated in 2006, in response to efforts like the publication of *Wild Nevada*. Such a direct synthesis of art and activism demonstrates the increasing manner in which literature is being used as a lobbying tool by contemporary environmental authors.

In addition to seeing a remarkable increase in the number of activist-oriented literary texts, this period has also enjoyed significant growth in activist-authored publications such as Julia "Butterfly" Hill's *The Legacy of Luna* (2000), which tells the story of her 2-year tree-sit to save Luna, an old-growth redwood, and the surrounding heritage forest from Maxxam Pacific's chainsaws. Similarly, EarthFirst!'s founder, Dave Foreman, published his *Confessions of an Eco-Warrior* in 1991, exposing the devastation of western public lands by logging, mining and grazing interests and detailing the legal and illegal efforts of citizens to defend against them. Such calls for direct action—efforts aimed at both civil disobedience and secret sabotage—have continued to escalate in frequency and intensity in the 21st century. As Gary Snyder prophetically wrote in 1992,

> The USA slowly lost its mandate
> In the middle and later twentieth century
> It never gave the mountains and rivers,
> Trees and animals
> A vote.
> All the people turned away from it. (*No* 250)

One of the most distinguishing features of both the new activism and the new activist literature of this time is the consistency with which the legitimacy of government authority is questioned and cast aside. Both, calls for, and acts of, illegal resistance have increased exponentially during this period. In *Endgame* (2006), for example, Derrick Jensen calls for readers to dismantle not only the dams killing our fish and rivers, but the entirety of civilization itself. Jensen outlines in some detail how a small group of saboteurs—he names the Blackout Brigade, but which is very similar to the existing Black Bloc—could bring down the entire electrical grid in the U.S. As the 20th century turned toward the 21st, American nature writers turned from celebrating the natural wonders of our land and lamenting their loss, to finally doing something about it. Not only are we currently seeing more calls for environmental reform, but also more for all out revolution.

Just as antebellum African-American writers were able to move their calls for revolution from the margins to the mainstream, contemporary writers of color, as well as women writers, have succeeded in raising their voices above the oppressive din of white mainstream culture. Since the 1970s, the emergence of the environmental justice movement, as a political force, has paralleled the growth of green literature by authors whose ethnicity or gender had traditionally been silenced. In 1977 Leslie Marmon Silko published her widely acclaimed novel *Ceremony*, which unflinchingly explored the environmental and imperial racism connecting the uranium mines on her ancestral lands and the Indian soldiers sent off to war with the Japanese victims of the bombs made from those mines. Two decades later, Linda Hogan published *Mean Spirit*, which explores the similarly devastating effects of another form of resource extraction from Native lands; this time it's oil, and the Osage are the victims of colonizing oppression. Other important works from Native American authors of this time period include Louise Eldrich's *Tracks* (1988), Joy Harjo's *She Had Some Horses* (1983), and Winona Laduke's *Last Standing Woman* (1997).

Latino and African American writers, likewise, have been gaining prominence in the traditionally "white" literary canon, with writers like Rudulfo Anaya, in his work *Bless me, Ultima* (1972), powerfully chronicling their own experiences of place and race amidst white colonizing culture. Such depictions of traditionally marginalized cultures have had a significant impact on mainstream culture; this is demonstrated by the wide reception of T.C. Boyle's *Tortilla Curtain* (1996), which exposes rampant American racism against Latinos during the same period when debates regarding "illegal" immigration have reached their socio-political peak. Similarly, Toni Morrison's 1987 Pulitzer Prize winning novel, *Beloved*, a modern re-telling of traditional slave narratives, won critical acclaim and was made into a mainstream movie starring Oprah Winfrey. Another example of how writers of color have gained widespread social relevance can be found in the works of African American poet and activist Audre Lorde. In addition to her many other works, *Zami: A New Spelling of My Name* (1982), launched an entirely new literary genre known as "biomythography," which links the personal experience to the collective in a powerfully mythopoetic manner. Although an extremely short sampling of environmental texts by authors of color, these pieces have had a tremendous impact on both, the American literary tradition and our larger political landscape.

In response to the growing literary and cultural significance of American environmental authors, the field of ecocriticism, or literary ecology, was established in 1993 with the founding of ASLE: the Association for the Study of Literature and Environment, and the election of Scott Slovic as its first president. That same year *ISLE: Interdisciplinary Studies in Literature and Environment*, the field's first professional journal was founded by Patrick Murphy, and today it has an international reception, while ASLE has affiliates in Korea, Japan, the U.K., and Australia. In 1996 Cheryll Glotfelty and Harold Fromm published *The Ecocriticism Reader*, the first critical anthology in the field, which was followed soon after by *Reading the Earth: New Directions in the Study of Literature and Environment* (1998), and *The Greening of Literary Scholarship* (2002).

Although ecocriticism gained prominence in the 1990's, it actually emerged in the 1970's alongside the environmental movement itself. First coined in 1978 by William Reuckert, the term Ecocriticism refers to the practice of studying environmental themes in literature as well as the role literature plays in the ecology of the human species; as such, this interdisciplinary field is concerned with the intersections between literature and culture—with the ways that one directs the other. Annette Kolodny's *The Lay of the Land* (1975) for example, explores how the feminization of the natural world in early American literature led to its definition as "inexhaustible-mother", or "always-available-whore," thus leaving it open for our history of rampant exploitation. In 1985 Frederick Waage published his seminal work *Teaching Environmental Literature: Materials, Methods, Resources,* firmly establishing what would become one of the field's strongest emphases: teaching. Since that time a number of environmentally themed textbooks and anthologies for teaching creative writing, composition, and literature have been produced including such works as *Being in the World* (1993), *A Forest of Voices* (1995), *Literature and Environment: An Environmental Reader* (1999), and the classically canonical *Norton Book of Nature Writing* (2002).

Because of the interdisciplinary and pedagogical emphases found in ecocriticism, it has been successful, through works like *Greening the College Curriculum* (1996), in extending its insights across a variety of departments on college campuses. Similarly in *The Campus and Environmental Responsibility* (1992), David Orr and David Eagan call not only for a greener curriculum, but for greener campuses as well, colleges that strive for sustainability in all of their practices from transportation and food purchasing, to construction and energy use. Thus, the cumulative effects of this field have been felt in every discipline, leading to the creation of environmentally themed courses in fields as disparate as art, psychology, political science, journalism and even economics.

Together these ecocritics are fomenting a slow revolution in the academy, a dawning recognition that, as David Orr observes, "Ultimately, the ecological crisis is a crisis of education" (p. 9). These scholars are reinvigorating environmental studies by developing a variety of interdisciplinary manners for re-introducing environmental values back into environmental education, arguing as I do, in *Reading the Trail: Exploring the Literature and Natural History of the California Crest* (2005), that it is not enough to teach students *about* the environment; we must also teach them *in* and *for* the environment (p. 215). Other field-based ecocritics such as John Tallmadge in *Meeting the Tree of Life* (1997), Ian Marshall in *Storyline* (1998), John Elder in *Reading the Mountains of Home* (1999), and the contributors to Hal Crimmel's landmark collection *Teaching Students in the Field* (2003), all agree. Each develops, and advocates for, a truly interdisciplinary form of environmental studies that synthesizes both the environmental sciences and humanities, as well as classroom and field-based instruction; by engaging with the ethical dimensions of environmental literature and using field-based strategies in instruction, this new form of environmental education strives not only to impart environmental knowledge, but also to change students' environmental perceptions, values and actions.

Ultimately it is the absence of ecological knowledge and ecocentric values that enables and perpetuates environmental violence and destruction. The first, and most vital step in destroying the earth, or any form of life, is to define it as having little value other than as an exploitable commodity. It is this definition—and the pen that writes it—rather than any particular form of degradation, that poses the greatest threat and holds the most destructive power.

In short, the pen will always be mightier than the sword, because the pen wields the power of the people, the collective power of culture and hegemonic belief. A people's literature both reflects and directs collective values and perceptions, as well as their individual beliefs and behaviors. Their laws, on the other hand, in the best of cases merely crystallize the morés of the mainstream, and in the worst promote only the interests of the ruling elite. Since the very beginning, American environmental authors have been calling for reform and revolution, pushing people past the limits of their present policies and perceptions, showing that ideas can be as powerful as actions and words as effective as weapons. Today we see an increasingly strong link between our literary tradition and our environmental movement, a growing recognition that we need both authors and activists, both personal and policy-based change.

In the end, we are restricted more by the boundaries of our imaginations than by those of our bodies, less by the limit of the law than by what the pen proscribes as possible or impossible. Ultimately, we find freedom, or are held hostage, not by the sharpness of the sword, but by the power of the pen.

NOTES

[1] "Literature" here is being used, in accordance with Cultural Studies Theory, which expanded our understanding of "texts" to include a range of communicative products of human culture including but not limited to journalism, film, television, visual art, performance art, creative writing and the literary arts.

REFERENCES

Bass, R. (1996). The Book of Yaak. Boston: Houghton Mifflin Publishers.

Gramsci, A. (1977). "Socialism and Culture." *Antonio Gramsci: Selections from Political Writings (1910–1920)*. London: International Publishers, 1977).

Jehlen, M., & Warner, M. (Eds.) (1997). *The English Literatures of America*. New York: Routledge.

Korten, D. (2006). *The Great Turning: From Empire to Earth Community*. San Francisco: BK Press.

Orr, D. (1996). "Reinventing Higher Education." *Greening the College Curriculum: A Guide to Environmental Teaching in the Liberal Arts*. Collett, J. & Karakashian, S. (Eds.). Washington D.C.: Island Press.

Snyder, G. (1992). *No Nature: New and Selected Poems*. New York: Pantheon Books.

Snyder, G. (1980). *The Real Work: Interviews and Talks, 1964–1970*. McLean, S. (Ed.). New York: New Directions.

Stowe, C., & Stowe, L.B. (1911). *Harriet Beecher Stowe: The Story of Her Life*. Boston: Houghton Mifflin Publishers.

GREENING DIS-ABILITY

ANTHONY J. NOCELLA II

INTRODUCTION[1]

This chapter is the first essay ever to connect together ecology, dis-ability, and animal advocacy, couched in terms of interlocking social constructions and the interwoven web of interdependent global life. Both concepts of "the natural world" and "disability" will be viewed here as socially constructed entities. I suggest that for the current global ecological crisis to transform into a more sustainable global community, including nonhuman animals, the field of environmental studies needs to engage in a discussion of colonization and domination. Next, I explain and deconstruct the meaning of disability. I critically examine environmentalism and environmental studies from an anti-oppression perspective. Finally, I demonstrate how dis-ability studies can take a position on the ecological crisis. Together, dis-ability theory, animal advocacy, and ecology can be brought together in a philosophy of eco-ability, entailing concepts of interdependency, inclusion, and respecting difference within a community and all life sentient and non-sentient.

CRISIS OF ECOLOGICAL DOMINATION AND NORMALCY

Being "the voice for the voiceless" is a saying that has been used repeatedly by dis-ability rights activists, environmentalists, and animal advocates. These oppressed groups, nonhuman animals, people with disabilities and the ecological world, sharing much in common, have arguably been marginalized more than any other segment of society. In today's colonized and capitalist driven world the worst thing is to be considered an "animal," "wild," or a "freak" (Snyder and Mitchell 2006). If you are not recognized as human by "normal society," you are either an animal or disabled, as was the case for women and people of color less than fifty years ago, who were also identified by law as property. When people of color and women asserted that they were human, white patriarchal science, using the racist, sexist, and ableist theory of eugenics, retorted that they had smaller brains, were mentally disabled and less than human. As Snyder and Mitchell explain,

> American eugenics laid bare the social and national goals newly claimed for medical practices. It promised an empirically sound, cross-disciplinary arena for identifying 'defectives' viewed as a threat to the purity of a modern

S. D. Fassbinder, A. J. Nocella II and R. Kahn (Eds.), Greening the Academy:
Ecopedagogy Through the Liberal Arts, 185–198.

> nation-state. Turn-of-the-century diagnosticians came to rely on the value of bureaucratic surveillance tools, such as census data, medical catalogues, and intelligence testing. (2006, p. 74)

At the early 1870s and onward was the rise of strategic repressive pathological medical categorization of those with mental dis-abilities especially those that were poor; first came immigration laws not allowing any person with mental dis-ability in the U.S.; next came the incarceration of those within the country, and finally came the testing and killing of them in the name of purification (Snyder & Mitchell, 2006). It was a mass genocide in the name of purity and normalcy promoted by the medical field (Snyder & Mitchell 2006).

The only theory to repeatedly argue by environmental ethicists that everyone and everything are interdependent and diverse, and that there exists no norm or normal, is the inherent philosophy within the natural world, when it is in harmony and balance. The ecological world or biosphere is itself an argument for the respect of differing abilities and uniqueness and for humans being species that are part of the "animal kingdom" and nature rather than separate or dominate over it. The ecological world's philosophy was the antithesis of genocide – a love of difference and mutual aid, rather than sameness and individualism.

Eco-ability, a concept that I developed and am first exploring in this article, is a philosophy that respects differences in abilities while promoting values appropriate to the stewardship of ecosystems. Very much in its beginning states, I do not want eco-ability to become dogmatic. Eco-ability studies praises difference, uniqueness and interdependency, while stressing that while every being has differing abilities, all play an important role in the global community and are valuable within the larger ecological global community. Eco-ability respects difference while challenging the concepts of equal, same, and normal as social constructions that fail to respect the uniqueness of individual abilities and differences, which, as the ecological and dis-ability communities realize, are interdependent. Nature, nonhuman animals and people with disabilities have experienced institutionalization, torture, and murder not because they have committed a crime or for profit, but for being recognized as being different. Difference is a threat to the advancement of normalcy, which is the philosophical foundation of social control and discipline.

The label of "different" is important to eco-ability because "different," as labeled through institutions, becomes what I refer to as the 4Ds of Disability Criminology – demonized, deviant, delinquent, and dissenters. If you are not labeled normal by society, you are identified as abnormal, a threat that must be controlled, disciplined, and punished. The history of repressing people with disabilities has always been a complex system of stigmatizing those that are different. Even to this day, some counselors, doctors, and religious leaders state that if an individual has committed a highly controversial act to challenge socio-economic or political conditions, they are determined to be evil and demonized in the news and official reports. If you are a deviant, researchers can determine that you are a delinquent, and if after many tests are conducted and doctors have determined you are not "rational," they will diagnose you as being disabled.

The marginalization of those who were different was first fostered and reinforced by the concept of civilization with its divide between nature and human. (This divide arguably began when human beings first began cultivating the land millennia ago.) Those considered wild, savage, primitive or illiterate were situated on one side, with those considered civilized or normal on the other. In time, civilization took the further step of establishing state borders in what we know today as Europe, amidst the project of global conquest which we today call colonization. Beyond establishing an elitist anti-natural culture at home (i.e., civilization), the goal was to conquer and destroy or assimilate every non-colonial, non-European influenced culture. Where there were other religious establishments, a Christian church was built on top of them. With colonialism spreading across the world, an economic system that held the same values, capitalism, was created, placing a value on everything and everyone; whites were more valuable than people of color, birds, trees, water, and even land. All of nature was viewed as a natural resource, and typically marked as property – something that was owned by someone – to be used any which way by its owners. The concept of property, critiqued by anarchists, created the haves and the have-nots; thus class society developed in the form of owning and working classes. With the establishment of natural resources and ownership of goods, the producer and consumer relationship was forged. This symbiotic relationship was the foundation of the industrial world, and the system was buttressed by institutions ostensibly developed to care for others, keep the public safe and in order, and develop "scientific" treatments to benefit the common good. Institutions such as colleges, prisons, and religions centers worked closely with the political and educational system to justify their violent acts such as experimentation, dissection, and vivisection toward people with disabilities, nonhuman animals, plants, water, and other elements.

DECONSTRUCTING DIS-ABILITY[2]

Behind the colonial concept of "disability" is a normalized level of ability, while dis-ability has at times been the justification to kill, test on, segregate, abort, and abandon. What is "disability" and why does it have a negative connotation? Disability is a negative term because of the notion of being broken, not working properly, or there being something wrong. Disabled, like crippled, lame, and retarded all mean similar things and are all used commonly in U.S. society (Taylor, 1996) to conjure up negative images that are most commonly used to insult and label someone, i.e., "You are being lame," "You are so retarded," "What, are you mad?" "Don't be insane?" and "What are you, crippled or something?" Thus, for example 'feebleminded,' 'retarded,' special educational needs,' special needs,' 'learning difficulties' are all examples of what Corbett (1995) calls 'Bad

Mouthing'" (Armstrong, Armstrong, & Barton 2000, p. 3). Erving Goffman in his article, "Selections from Stigma," writes, "The Greeks, who were apparently strong on visual aids, originated the term *stigma* to refer to bodily signs designed to expose something unusual and bad about the moral status of the signifier" (Davis 1997, p. 203).

And, of course, this is the classic label of "dumb," and this is certainly a term historically applied to both human and nonhuman animals. For example, in St. Thomas Aquanis's thirteenth-century tome *Summa Theologica*, one of the most influential works in Western culture, he stated that "dumb animals and plants are devoid of the life of reason whereby to set themselves in motion; they are moved, as it were by another, by a kind of natural impulse, a sign of which is that they are naturally enslaved and accommodated to the uses of otherss." (1460). Here, dumb is actually not the insult we see it as today. It indicates the nonhuman animal's inability to speak and also his/her lack of intelligence or sense of self. However, although not an insult, it was most certainly a term used to dismiss those creatures labeled as such. Western philosophers after Aquinas would use the same terminology. (Immanuel Kant and René Descartes immediately come to mind.) More than just the import of the word itself, however, is the notion that because a being cannot speak and process the world intellectually as do the white males, that being naturally becomes a slave to be used by others as food, clothing or as science experiments. This stigma against animals is evident, but what is not as immediately apparent is that way the term similarly stigmatizes those with disabilities.

A meaningful example of stigma against the disabled is found in the movie *300* (2006) in which the great fighting 300 Spartans battle the Persians who are depicted as "uncivilized." In the movie *Spartan King*, Leonidas is approached by a Greek who is strong and loyal, but physically disabled, to join the Spartans to fight. However, King Leonidas sees this man as a weak liability, rather than a powerful and strong soldier with wit. The solider with disabilities pleads his case to be part of the Spartans, but the King, after asking the solider to perform a few defensive and offensive moves, said he was not of the level he needed to be. This devastates the solider so much that he becomes a traitor for what the movie portrays as the uncivilized "wild"—the Persians. The meaning of the story is the Spartans, as a perfect society, could never have a person with disabilities among them, but for the uncivilized "wild" Persians, the movie portrays that to be acceptable, and as all marginalized groups are the same, this implies that "non–Spartan" equals non-perfect or not normal. Based on the historical battle, the story had many imperialist lessons, one of them being that "civilized men" are more powerful than all of nature.

"Disability," "people with disabilities" (using first person language) or breaking up "dis" and "ability," (which I and many others do) are terms endorsed and used by dis-ability rights activists, theorists, advocates, and allies. As noted above, there are negative connotations of the term "disability," but the dis-ability rights movement has reclaimed the term out of a universal global understanding of what the definition of disability means and to whom it refers. It is also the only term used to describe the differently abled that holds significant legal and medical value, for it "appears to signify something material and concrete, a physical or psychological condition considered to have predominantly medical significance" (Linton 1998, p. 10). This does not suggest that the term should and must be resisted. Most dis-ability activists would not argue for doing so. However, while many in the movement embrace the term, others (among whom are those who teach dis-ability pedagogy) are now striving to promote new terms that promote positive values of difference. The classic predicament in all names for particular identities is that not everyone will understand the term or even be aware that it exists, thus forcing the focus group to put a great deal of energy into promoting the name and its correct and respected definition.

Much of the theoretical work on dis-ability studies is centered on terminology because of the diverse array of imagery related to people with disabilities. There are currently two major tasks being initiated by the dis-ability rights movement to correct negative perceptions of the differently abled. The first of these is that they are not disabled, meaning they are not deformed, lame, broken, or having something wrong with them. They are perfect the way they are. This point has two sub-concerns. First, that societies' exclusion of difference and the reinforcement of the social construction of normalcy is a problem (Fulcher 1999) which allows capital to exclude people with disabilities from economic life, and second, until all are accepted in society, there is truly an identifiable group that needs assistance and that are challenged in the current exclusionary society we live in.

The second main point is the theoretical understanding of all dis-ability activists, which is that people with disabilities are not disabled, but that all people are different and have unique needs. This point is critical of society and its role in how people are identified: recognizing that "normal," "average," or "able" are all socially constructed terms that can and must be changed. Such activists, moreover, are also critical of the capitalist systeminsofar as it tries to reduce our humanity and citizenship functions to the roles of producer and consumer, both of which support capitalism; consumption supports the engines of production because people have to work to buy and ideologically capitalism captures their desires and support (Gramsci 1989; Marcuse 1969).

Similarly, dis-ability activists should critique the norm of a productive employee, student, daughter/son, and/or parent. There is no measurement for an individual except within the context of that individual. Nothing is objective and able to be measured in a detached state. Let us take a moment to analyze some of the standard definitions of the names given to those identified as disabled. *Illness* is defined as, "Poor health resulting from disease of body or mind; sickness" (Houghton Mifflin Company 2009), while *diseased* is defined as, "A pathological condition of a part, organ, or system of an organism resulting from various causes, such as infection, genetic defect, or environmental stress, and characterized by an identifiable group of signs or symptoms" (Houghton Mifflin Company 2009). Diseased is also defined as, "A condition or tendency, as of society, regarded as abnormal and harmful"

(Houghton Mifflin Company 2009). Disability has traditionally been associated with illness and disease. Yet, this socially constructed meaning cannot be understood without examining the notion of normalcy. The "normal" is defined as "relating to or characterized by average intelligence or development" (Houghton Mifflin Company 2009). A standard dictionary type definition states that normalcy is "free[dom] from mental illness; sane. Conforming to, adhering to, or constituting a norm, standard, pattern, level, or type; typical" (Houghton Mifflin Company 2009). Fulcher writes, "Disability is primarily a political construct rather than a medical phenomenon" (1999, p. 25).

With this backdrop, it comes as no surprise that disability is understood as, "The condition of being disabled; incapacity" (Houghton Mifflin Company 2009).Also, it is stigmatized as "A disadvantage or deficiency, especially a physical or mental impairment that interferes with or prevents normal achievement in a particular area" (Houghton Mifflin Company 2009). It is defined as "Something that hinders or incapacitates" (Houghton Mifflin Company 2009). As the definitions build onto each other, we see the repeated theme of "something wrong with" (Houghton Mifflin Company 2009), be it defined as incapacity, harmful, or sick. In contemporary society, these are the terms that are used interchangeably with disability. But by measuring everyone according to this imaginary notion of a so-called *normal person*, society is inclusive only to certain types of people.

The social constructions of terms such as normalcy, ableism, and civilization have been put in the service of domination for political power, economic gain, and social control. Those in power used them to establish a superior (dominator) vs. inferior (dominated) binary, which has played out over and over again in theories, beliefs, cultures, and identities. People are typically judged against the standard of a "perfect" human; those who choose not to, or simply cannot strive towards the norm because of their identity, politics, social and economic factors are sometimes labeled abnormal. Within this context, ableism is a social construct which suggests that society should manipulate those individuals whose capabilities fall outside the norm in an attempt to reach the same physical and mental abilities as those considered normal, instead of being accepting and inclusive towards all.

While it has been used as a key term to unify and bring attention to the topic, e.g., dis-ability studies, disability is still a term that has been challenged and manipulated from – Dis-Ability, Crip Studies, Mad Studies, and others. Still, dis-ability studies can be regarded as the new special education field, outdated and only reinforcing a particular social constructed binary. Unless we recognize that all are disabled in some way, "disabled" is one of the most demeaning labels and identification a human can be given. A positive and proactive field would truly embrace differing abilities and the theory of ability, hence the notion of developing ability studies and doing away with the concept of disability or dis-ability makes the most amount of sense. To understand one's ability or disability we must also see the similarities and how the two are directly related, but one only has abilities because of one's particular physical and/or mental capabilities, technological assistance, or society's respect for a particular group. When a group is not accepted or an individual is unable to utilize something such as a computer, it is external factors which lead them to become disabled.

CRITICAL EXAMINATION OF ENVIRONMENTAL STUDIES
AND ENVIRONMENTALISM[3]

Environmental studies, which emerged out of the environmental movement, is an interdisciplinary field of study dedicated to examining the relationship between humans and the "natural" environment. Its foundations are attached to a colonialist world view. While many environmental studies programs are committed to protection and preservation of the ecological global community, which these departments see humans as a part of, other programs are dedicated to conservation of natural resources, which humans are not part of but still use. Many of the top environmental studies programs were established in the 1970s within a natural resource and/or forestry college/department. Today, much of environmental studies rooted in a white patriarchal colonial relationship to "nature," i.e., man vs. nature, along with being entrenched in and based on environmental science and natural resources, rather than the liberal arts and humanities. The field of environmental studies has become an increasingly popular marketing tool for the greening of college campuses for students and grants.

While much of the environmental movement in the colonial world is highly problematic because of its patriarchal, racist, ableist, and homophobic philosophical foundation (Best & Nocella 2006), I want to speak to one particular current sub-environmental movement that has received attention not only for its brilliant critiques of colonialism, technology, and civilization, but for its problematic ableist perspectives as well. Among the modern US environmental movement, there is a radical leftist sub-culture/movement known as green anarchism or primitivism.

Based on Do It Yourself (DIY) values, some green anarchists and primitivists are self reliant, independent, and grounded in an anti-technology and anti-civilization "back to nature" philosophy. Concepts such as interdependency, mutual aid and respect of difference are the antithesis of green anarchism because green anarchism promotes an individualistic able bodied competitive belief. The anti-technology society green anarchists argue for would entail us being dominant over nonhuman animals and fail to meet the needs of those in the dis-ability community and transgender community because it excludes technologized medical operations and promotes hunting and gathering. Hunting and gathering takes a great amount of energy and time in the wilderness: picking up, walking, running, and climbing to find food and water are activities that many people with physical disabilities cannot accomplish on their own or without technology. Further, green anarchism promotes not only abled-bodied individuals but the consumption of animals (i.e., wearing them for shoes and clothing, and eating them) which has been critiqued by environmentalists and animal rights activists as highly unsustainable. The process of moving to a primitive lifestyle would utilize more energy than striving to move forward with technology in a sustainable manner: first, because of the destruction of urban areas and the leaking of non-maintained contaminates, and second, because spreading people out rather than condensing human areas of mass impact would damage more areas of the planet with the current population of the planet. While there are those in green anarchism who promote a vegan or animal liberation philosophy as well as an ecological or green technology, they are few and far between. In addressing an audience question about painful deaths and difficult child births in a primitivist society, John Zerzan, one of the leading voices of the green anarchist movement noted:

> ...are we supposed to keep this whole industrialized suicide going for the sake of the people that you don't want to pull the plug on? I don't want to pull the plug either. I'm not comfortable with that answer but to some degree...It's not a full answer, I don't think it's a full answer. If you discover what it is that creates the problem and the problem just keeps on being created, whatever it is, like more people with all kinds of conditions, all kinds of problematic things including [dangerous or risky] child birth, including autism, including health threatening obesity...These are creations of mass society so the healthy... where is the healthy direction? I don't know what to do about disabled people...I don't want to pull the plug on people, but we have a reality too... where do we go with that? You tell me, I don't know.[4]

Dis-ability anarchists and green anarchists are at a crossroads. Rather than aiding and supporting their needs through technology and interdependence, green anarchists and primitivists argue that those who have disabilities, identified by their perspective as the weak in a society, will die off because of the lack of one's ability. While Zerzan might feel uncomfortable about excluding people with dis-abilities at best and accept them being killed or dying off at worst, by being supportive of green anarchism's anti-technology position, this appears to be what he and other green anarchists are advocating when they promote a society that would fail to meet the needs of people with disabilities. Some green anarchists may not understand that disability is a social construct, created by normalcy, and that the goal of taking down civilization and colonialism also includes taking down normalcy, which we are all draped within. Everyone is dis-abled by capitalism, colonialism, civilization, and industrialization throughout their lives. These systems of domination promote standardization, normalcy, equality, and sameness, which are against the respecting of different abilities and identities. Computers, cars, doorways, homes, books, clothes, and pencils are all designed for a particular type of person in mind. While dis-ability anarchists are not for all technology – they agree that some technology is disruptive and are critical of the medical industrial and pharmaceutical complex that the green anarchists also oppose – they support technological innovation that will aid in human freedom.

WHEN ECOLOGY MEETS ABILITY

Like eco-feminism (Gaard 1993), and critical scholarship of eco-racism (Bullard 1993) and eco-colonialism (Best & Nocella 2006), which are social manifestations of oppression and domination such as patriarchy, racism, and colonialization, eco-ability interrogates normalcy, ableism, and civilization. Eco-ability advocates for understanding how nature is diverse and interdependent; not equal, but different. Just like the human who cannot climb Mount Everest or the bird who cannot swim, one is always going to be "disabled" or better stated because of limitations in approaching one's physical landscape. Life is not about the *survival of the fittest* or living life like one is the only resident of an island, or in a social Darwinist notion of competition, where there is a winner and a loser. Rather, we must recognize how the bio-community promotes a win-win situation, and end the win-lose relationship with other species in which humans for the last hundred years wiped out thousands of species from existence. Of greater importance is that the survival of humans and nonhuman animals and the biosphere is intertwined.

When a natural disaster or massive oil spill by a corporation such as BP in the Gulf Coast of the US wipes one species off this planet, that extinction and event affects us all. Therefore, the theory of eco-ability employs the concept of the web of life, which stresses that all are different, unique, with differing abilities (e.g., flying, walking, swimming, slithering, and jumping), inter-relationships and interdependence, therefore, must be respected. Respect means understanding and valuing the needs of another being or element because it liberates, frees, and completes one's self. Respect is greatly different than tolerance or acceptance, which both arise from places of domination. Tolerance is the act of not wanting someone in a place, but managing to act in a way that does not physically force the person out of the place through trying to fire them, beat them, or verbally insult them. Acceptance is an act of approving of one's presences or existance in a place, while having ownership and domination over the place. The action of respect is mutual for all parties involved and not simply for the "other" that is being referred to. We must respect all for their value toward the larger bio-community and strive for a global inclusion of all. Global inclusion is a critical theory that is more of a process and a perspective than a state of being, one that is continuously challenging the notion of community and the barriers, borders, and boundaries we construct. These barriers, borders, and boundaries foster a devaluing and exclusionary relationship to others, found for example, in the many urban parks, apartments, schools, and public transportation vehicles that do not allow dogs and other nonhuman animals. Hence, when we employ universal design to a school, park, or company to challenge speciesism, we must invite the plants and nonhuman animals in.

While dis-ability studies is a powerful emerging field of study which is receiving attention throughout the academy and beyond, it has not made a formal connection with environmental studies. The reason might be rooted in an ableist assumption that people with disabilities should not be in the natural world because ableist claim it is not inclusive and is dangerous for those with disabilities. One of the few arguments made to discuss the complex connections between the two (ecology and people with disabilities) was during a panel I co-organized with Dr. Judy Bentley at the Central New York Peace Studies Consortium's Peace Studies Conference in 2007 at SUNY Cortland.

In one of the papers presented on the panel, "Disability Studies and Social Construction of Environments," Robin M. Smith and Jack P. Manno stressed that disability as well as the environment are social constructions developed through relationships, noting, "These relationships are institutional, cultural, and interpersonal social structures" (Smith and Manno 2007, p. 2). They go on to write in a paper that was presented, "The social construct of the environment is defined through a web of socio-economic relationships that privileges commodities over relationships, where a tree is regarded far more as timber and paper pulp than as oxygen producer, shelter for beings, builder of soil or the many other roles it plays in a complex set of ecosystem relationships (Manno, 2000)" (Smith and Manno 2007, p. 3). Rather than being recognized as members of a large and complex eco-community, domesticated animals such as cows, monkeys, and horses are viewed by human society as mere resources to be exploited for profit. This is promoted in the ideological interests of capital, according to which people are either producers or consumers.

Capitalists and Marxists view people with disabilities as limited consumers, never able to be useful enough to be part of the means of production. On the contrary, people with disabilities are huge consumers of medicine, technology, and therapy, which while important in the relationship of consumer and producer, needs to also be critiqued because much of the medicine produced is tested on nonhuman animals and the production of it causes a great amount of pollution. Further, the medicine that is produced often has negative side-effects and is highly addictive, causing the user to become dependent. Therefore, not only the dis-ability community, but much of the world that uses corporate produced medicine should look for organic natural alternatives, which are sometimes proven to be more effective, and do not support the medical industrial complex. The reason many of these natural medicines, such as herbs, are not promoted is because corporate medical doctors are either (1) not knowledgeable about natural medicines, thus they claim they are not affective, (2) they have economic commitments or interests, and/or (3) there are social and peer pressures of supporting medical traditions, which include vivisection.

Eco-ability argues for the respect of difference and diversity. Diversity and difference challenge social constructions of normal and equal. Eco-ability also challenges labels and categorization which divide and separate rather than unify and collaborate. Eco-ability stresses imperfection and the value of "flaws." Perfection suggests an ideal of not having a flaw or an imaginary ideal, whereas everyone can be defined through the eco-ability lens as unique and different. Perfection is what normalized society has dreamed up and believes can be reached: purity. Perfection and purity, two notions that Nazism strived for, but did not recognize that difference was the essential ingredient for human and global survival. It must be noted that the first to be tortured and killed by the Nazis were those with disabilities, as they were the abnormal and less than (Davis 2002). People with disabilities are the true reality of what nature was based on: difference and uniqueness.

Every living creature has different abilities: some can climb trees or burrow into the ground, some have exceptional hearing, vision or sensing of movement and others can swim, slither or fly. To remove our difference removes the value of diversity. By erecting a standard of normalcy, society devalues diversity. While technology can be a wonderful tool to aid people, some technology destroys at the expense of difference, such as by making a paved path through a forest to accommodate everyone instead of making a wheelchair that is meant for off-roading or admitting that some people simply cannot go down that path. Not everyone with their own abilities can climb Mount Everest, but that does not mean we need to make a road to the top. While some environmentalists believe that society should destroy urban areas and that technology is the cause of ecological destruction, others argue that "going back" to a primitive lifestyle would cause a mass amount of waste and wear on the ecological system. It is not about going back and romanticizing about the past, but building a sustainable future void of exploitation of all life and elements.

Inclusion means access and assistance, which might involve allowing others to have technological assistance like wheelchairs, glasses, or custom computer software to allow one to be successful. It is important to make the difference between technological tools that allow one to be included and technology that is globally destructive to the bio-community such as bombs. This is not to say that computers, cellphones, and other forms of technology do not have destructive impacts; they do and should be challenged, but there is also a great deal of technology that can be phased out first before there is a full boycott on all electronic devices.

Inclusion also means giving up power and challenging all forms of domination, therefore resisting gatekeeper terms such as accept, tolerate, allow, approve, and permit. This initiative for technology is a slippery slope and can cause a destructive rippling effect, but I would argue that tools can be a very beneficial part of the bio-community today. For example, instead of flying to conferences in Europe or across the US, one can Skype on the internet to provide presentations, which eliminates the travel carbon footprint. As we are caught in a life of hypocrisy, we must do our best to minimize the ecological impact we make, while if we do utilize electronic devices we utlize them to make the world a better place and not simply to play video games. The most difficult part of figuring this ethical equation out, is acknowledging that inclusion is terminated by the dominator. The dominator is a socio-political, economic, and ecological gatekeeper, determining who is included and excluded.

This decision comes with great ignorance; for example, it is only recently that social justice movements have called for the inclusion of people of color, people with disabilities, women, children, and nonhuman animals. Social justice activists and the oppressed fight to take down barriers, borders, and boundaries, which exclude those that are dominated, while dominators consciously and ignorantly support and construct those oppressive tools of division. To deconstruct these exclusionary structures, institutions, systems, and tools we must critically examine, resist, dismantle, and transform the global community.

We must move forward rather than backwards, utilizing renewable eco-technology and non-polluting resources. Unfortunately, corporations and governments have promoted destructive technologies through "greenwashing," while their domination is globalized through industrialization, institutionalization, civilization, and capitalism (Tokar 1997). Eco-ability is against GMOs and other science, technologies, and theories that control and manipulate life, a stance that they share with green anarchists (Best and Nocella 2006). Eco-ability favors respect and inclusive change rather than conservationism, which frames the ecosystem as resources and property. Eco-ability is rooted in anarchist principles, which appose competition, domination, and authoritarianism (Ben-Moshe, Hill, Nocella, and Templer 2009). The development of sustainable technology and resources must be implemented from a non-hierarchical community in which everyone recognizes the interests of all – human and nonhuman – as priority over personal profit.

Some technology has the potential if used to advance peace and to give people opportunities to reduce fossil-fuel use and clear-cutting. Technology can also aid a person to read a book, walk across the street, roll to class, and see the birds in the air. These advances toward human simplicity – a decrease in consumption and materialism – and global sustainability cannot be advanced through acts of domination such as testing on fellow humans, species, or ecological communities. Eco-ability argues for social transformation away from acts of domination, towards compassion; there is no need to imprison fellow humans to teach a lesson, drop bombs on other countries for freedom, or put chemicals in the eyes of animals to protect humans from illness. Vivisection, testing, experimentation, and dissection dominate, divide and create a false construction of social and ecological individualism, emphasizing our nonhuman, non-animal, and non-natural identities. Assisting dis-ability through technology allows us to be self reliant and reinforces that dis-ability is a valued quality which should be respected and praised. This assistance stresses the ecological importance of interdependency that the life system is based on, but which, throughout human history, we have been moving as fast as we can away from.

IN CONCLUSION

In order to challenge any system or institution of domination all life must work together in a respectful and harmonious relationship with the hope of global transformation toward a peaceful planet, void of violence toward all elements and life on and off this planet. This will demand the changing of one's diet to being an organic local poly or perma-culture plant based vegan diet, to embrace difference and dismantle normalcy, and end the valuing the natural worlds as mere resources begin a mutual respected l friendship of all life. For the day may come when, as oft envisioned by Hollywood, Earthlings will create a social constructed dominating divide between ourselves and those from another planet,[5] defining them as abnormal, freaks, or a danger, which must be tested on, imprisoned, and destroyed. This occurs in the movie *District 9* in which aliens do not dominate the Earth, as usually takes place in Hollywood iterations of the alien genre. Rather, they become oppressed individuals living in poverty with drugs, gangs and prostitutes their main form of income. Let it be that the day when we meet other non-Earth life forms we come together in a peaceful welcoming manner, rather than a scene from the film *The Day the Earth Stood Still* (Derrickson 2008), where guns were pointed at the aliens that came to the Earth to protect it from humans. In the film, Klaatu (played by Keanu Reeves) expresses what dis-ability advocates and environmentalists have been saying all along, "The universe grows smaller every day, and the threat of aggression by any group, anywhere, can no longer be tolerated. There must be security for all, or no one is secure." Through the colonial mentality, humans have striven to deny themselves as being part of nature and as animals. But those who promote civilization as such deny their interdependence with fellow members of the ecological world. The colonial mindset is a mindset of striving and conquering, but little do its adherents know they are only dominating and conquering themselves. Once the oppression caused by economic, social, and political factors is overcome, the values of intra/inter-dependent life, global inclusion, respect of difference and bio-diversity, and the transformation from domination, marginalization, manipulation, and control can be used to bring about a world of peace, love, and respect of other's beliefs, abilities, and identities. We must acknowledge and transform our relationships with fellow Earthlings and elements into a respectful, inclusive, interdependent, peaceful community or else we will find ourselves traveling down the road of destruction.

NOTES

[1]   This article was adapted and taken from the Introduction co-edit by Anthony J. Nocella II and Judy K.C. Bentley and from Chapter One, The Rise of Eco-Ability: Social Justice and the Intersectionality of Disability, Animals, and Ecology, In, *Earth, Animal, and Disability Liberation: The Rise of Eco-Ability*, (forthcoming) Co-edited by, Anthony J. Nocella II, Judy K.C. Bentley, and Janet Duncan.

[2]   This section of this chapter was adapted from "Emergence of Disability Pedagogy" by Anthony J. Nocella II published in the Journal for Critical Education Policy Studies (December 2008) Volume 6, Number 2.

[3]   Sentences in this section may have come directly from the Introduction of "Igniting a Revolution: Voices in Defense of the Earth" co-edited with Steve Best (2006).

[4]   See http://www.youtube.com/watch?v=F0mlQHwqlpk&feature=related, accessed June 20, 2010.

[5]   As Stephen Hawking suggests in a new documentary, extraterrestrials are almost certain to exist. http://www.timesonline.co.uk/tol/news/science/space/article7107207.ece.

REFERENCES

Aquinas, T. (2007). *Summa theologica, volume 3*. New York, NY: Cosimo, Inc.
Armstrong, F., Armstrong, D., & Barton, L. (2000). *Inclusive education: Policy, contexts and comparative perspectives*. London, UK: David Fulton Publishers.

Ben-Moshe, L., Hill, D., Nocella II, A. J., & Templer, B. (2009). Dis-abling capitalism and an anarchism of "radical equality" in resistance to ideologies of normalcy. In *Contemporary anarchist studies: An introductory anthology of anarchy in the academy*, Eds. Amster, R., DeLeon, A., Nocella II, A. J. & Shannon, D. New York, NY: Routledge.

Best, S., & Nocella II, A J. (2006). *Igniting a revolution: Voices in defense of the Earth*. Oakland, CA: AK Press.

Bullard, R. D. (1993). *Confronting environmental racism: Voices from the grassroots*. Boston, MA: South End Press.

Davis, L. (1997). *The disability studies reader*. New York, NY: Routledge Press.

Davis, L. (2002). *Bending over backwards: Disability, dismodernism & Other difficult positions*. New York, NY: New York University Press.

Derrickson, S. (2008). *The day the Earth stood still*. Los Angeles, CA: Twentieth Century Fox Film Corporation.

Disability. (2009). *The American heritage dictionary of the english language*. Boston, MA: Houghton Mifflin Company. Retrieved from http://www.thefreedictionary.com/disease.

Disease. (2009). *The American heritage dictionary of the english language*. Boston, MA: Houghton Mifflin Company. Retrieved from http://www.thefreedictionary.com/disease.

Fulcher, G. (1999). *Disability policies? A comparative approach to education policy*. Sheffield, UK: Philip Armstrong Publications.

Gaard, G. (1993). *Ecofeminism: Women, animals, nature*. Philadelphia, PA: Temple University Press.

Gramsci, A. (1989). *Selections from the prison notebooks* (10th ed.). New York, NY: International Publishers.

Illness. (2009). *The American heritage dictionary of the english language*. Boston, MA: Houghton Mifflin Company. Retrieved from http://www.thefreedictionary.com/disease.

Linton, S. (1998). *Claiming disability. Knowledge and identity*. New York: New York University Press.

Marcuse, H. (1969). *An essay on liberation*. Boston, MA: Beacon Press.

Nocella II, A. J. (forthcoming). Anarcho-disability criminology. In *Anarchist criminology*. Eds. Ferrell, J, Brisman, A., & Nocella, II, A. J.

Nocella II, A. J. (2008). Emergence of disability pedagogy. In *The Journal for Ccritical Education Ppolicy Studies*. Vo. 6, Issue 2.

Nocella, A. J. II, Bentley, J. K. C., Duncan, J. (forthcoming). *Earth, animal, and disability liberation: The rise of eco-ability*. New York, NY: Peter Lang.

Normal. (2009). *The American heritage dictionary of the english language*. Boston, MA: Houghton Mifflin Company. Retrieved from http://www.thefreedictionary.com/disease.

Normalcy. (2009). *The American heritage dictionary of the english language*. Boston, MA: Houghton Mifflin Company. Retrieved from http://www.thefreedictionary.com/disease.

Snyder, S. L., & Mitchell, D. T. (2006). *Cultural locations of disability*. Chicago: IL: University of Chicago Press.

Snyder, Z. (2006). 300. Hollywood, CA: Warner Bros. Pictures.

Smith, R. M., & Manno, J. P. (2007). *Disability studies and social construction of environments*. http://www.cortland.edu/ids/sasc/vol1_issue1/index.html. In Social Advocacy and Systems Change. Vol. 1, Issue 1.

Taylor, S. (1996). *Disability studies and mental retardation*. Disability studies quarterly. Vol. 16, No. 3.

Tokar, B. (1997). *Earth for sale: Reclaiming ecology in the age of corporate greenwash*. Boston, MA: South End Press.

Van der Pijl, K. (2007). *Nomads, Empires, States*. London and New York: Pluto, 2007.

GREENING FEMINISM

GRETA GAARD

Was Rachel Carson primarily an environmental scientist, a writer of creative nonfiction, or a feminist? Published just two years prior to her death, Carson's *Silent Spring* (1962) combined careful observations, scientific data, and eloquent prose to expose the toxic links between pesticides, environmental degradation, and inter-species health. Carson's work is often credited with sparking the environmental movement of the 1970s and beyond, but rarely is she seen as the foremother of second-wave feminism. Like Carson, the works of Dian Fossey and Jane Goodall are usually classified as primatology, but academic training for these women came well after their field research was already underway. Like Barbara McClintock's work with corn, both Fossey and Goodall had "a feeling for the organism" (Keller, 1983) that powered their work more completely than their belated scientific training. Could their research more aptly be described as communication studies, inter-species anthropology, or environmental feminism?

The interdisciplinary field of feminist and gender studies defies such exclusionary categorizations. With the resurgence of feminism in the 1960s sparked by Betty Friedan's *The Feminine Mystique* (1963)—published just a year after Carson's *Silent Spring* – the women's movement diversified to address all aspects of women's lives. From the recognition of housework and childcare as unwaged labor, to the various mobilizations around domestic violence, pink-collar ghettos, reproductive freedoms and anti-nuclear resistance, feminists worked to improve the material conditions of women's lives and to understand women's viewpoints by moving women's experiences and standpoints "from margin to center" (hooks 1984). At the same time that the women's movement was being built, women's activism in other liberatory movements of the 1960s and beyond—environmentalism, animal rights, gay liberation, the American Indian Movement, Black Power, La Raza—informed and was informed by feminist theory and practice. The feminist slogan, "the personal is political," articulated the critical feminist insight that individual experiences needed to be understood in context: taken alone, a child's mysterious illness at his new residence could be seen as an individual medical problem; placed in context with other sick children and a legacy of landfilled toxic waste, that child's illness provided the impetus for the Love Canal Parents' Movement started in 1978 by his mother, Lois Gibbs, whose work compelled the U.S. Environmental Protection Agency to create the Comprehensive Environmental Response, Compensation and Liability Act—CERCLA, or the Superfund Program–used to clean up toxic

S. D. Fassbinder, A. J. Nocella II and R. Kahn (Eds.), Greening the Academy:
Ecopedagogy Through the Liberal Arts, 199–216.

waste sites throughout the United States today. No wonder that the environmental movement has longstanding connections with the women's movement, and the movements for public health and environmental justice: women's oppression and liberation are inseparable from cultural, socioeconomic, political and ecological environments.

Today, we misperceive environmental studies as largely based in the physical sciences, with Ethnic Studies or Women's, Gender and Sexuality Studies as largely based in the social sciences. Feminist research and activism in a variety of fields corrects these misperceptions. In the field of feminist science studies, for example, scholars such as Evelyn Fox Keller, Sandra Harding, Lynda Birke, and Ruth Hubbard have challenged the androcentric construction of knowledge, the separation between researcher and subject, and the invisibly racialized qualities of scientific research. Their scholarship has provided theoretical groundwork for the women's health movement, and the related movements for public health and environmental justice. Feminist environmental scholar-activists have generated a wealth of knowledge across the curriculum, contributing to and transforming the fields of philosophy, geography, political science, economics, literary studies, as well as in gender, sexuality, and women's studies. Beyond the academy, feminist environmentalists are active internationally, through the climate justice movement, the anti-corporate-globalization movement, and movements to promote fair trade, food security, water sovereignty, gender justice and environmental health.

Some feminist environmentalists identify themselves as ecofeminists, others see themselves as environmental justice activists, and still others self-identify as simply environmentalists or labor activists. Not surprisingly, given the persistence of sexism, racism, and other forms of hierarchical thought and institutionalized power, the intersectional work of feminist environmentalists has faced resistance across the disciplines, in their home communities and in the larger political arena as well. It's well known that prior to winning the Nobel Peace Prize in 2004, Kenya's Green Belt Movement founder Wangari Maathai was persecuted and even beaten for her work, whipped about the head, and jailed, all for speaking out for democracy, organizing women and planting trees: the assaults came from men who felt Maathai was acting out of line from women's assigned role. Anti-nuclear activists still remember Karen Silkwood, who spoke out against unsafe workplace conditions at Kerr-McGee's plutonium processing plant in Oklahoma and was harshly punished for her whistleblowing: Silkwood was mysteriously contaminated with high levels of radioactivity found in her lungs and in her home; on her way to a meeting with an Oil, Chemical and Atomic Workers' union official and a *New York Times* reporter, where Silkwood planned to deliver a stack of documentation for her claims, she allegedly fell asleep at the wheel and drove off the road to her death—her car showing signs of being rammed from behind, and the highway behind her car marked with tire skids.

Despite persistent threats of retribution, women activists for gender and environmental justice have refused to keep silent. Their experiences and standpoints provide vital data on critical issues such as climate change, food production, and the fundamental connections between environmental sustainability and social justice. In short, our knowledge of science, social science, humanities and environmental studies has been transformed and enriched by the critical contributions of women.

FEMINIST PHILOSOPHIES OF SCIENCE, AND THE NATURE/NURTURE DEBATE

A significant contribution of feminist environmentalisms has been the revaluing of women's bodies, experiences, and standpoints as locations of knowledge (Slicer 1998). Traditionally, scientific studies equated biology (sex) with gender, associated women with caregiving, nurturing, spirituality and nature, and then used this association to justify restrictive and conventional gender roles; this approach inspired the feminist rebuttal that "biology is not destiny." But if feminists were to succeed in challenging gender roles and freeing women from lives of compulsory heterosexuality, compulsory motherhood, compulsory housework and the low-waged "pink-collar ghetto," the essentialist perspective on women's "nature" had to be uprooted; the associations and disjuncts between women/nature and men/culture had to be investigated; the alleged "objectivity" of western science had to be unmasked; and the presumed goal of science as providing mastery and dominion over nature had to be challenged.

As more women entered the fields of scientific research, the inherent biases of conventional science became more evident. The standpoint of these new women scientists helped raise questions about scientific methods and objects of study. They discovered not only sexism, but also the more egregious examples of scientific racism that were once considered "good science": consider Samuel Morton's craniometry studies that compared measurements of African and European skulls to justify white intellectual superiority, or the U.S. Public Health Service study of untreated syphilis in black men—the Tuskegee Syphilis Experiment that ran uninterrupted from 1932 to 1972, and provided no treatment to its participants, but sought only to compile data (Harding, 1993). Witty feminist explorations of gender attributions in "bias-free" biological science revealed discourses of egg and sperm as mere projections of cultural stereotypes: while the egg "drifts" or "is swept" along the fallopian tube, the sperm have "velocity", "energy", and "fuel" permitting them to "assault" and then "activate the developmental program of the egg" (Martin, 1991). Feminists realized that conventional scientists studied white male subjects and then made generalizations about all humans, unwittingly projecting cultural stereotypes about race, gender, and sexuality onto the cells beneath their microscopes. Omissions and distortions of data such as these led feminists to propose a strategy for acknowledging standpoint in the construction of knowledge.

In feminist epistemology, the standpoints of those most marginalized are taken as ideal starting points for investigating scientific problems. "Strong objectivity" is knowledge produced through community dialogue, and knowledge that is the most inclusive of diverse standpoints (Harding, 1991). Moreover, motives matter: scientific research should be undertaken not to achieve dominion over nature or to produce knowledge for the sake of knowledge, status, or economic profit, but rather knowledge in the service of social justice; the participants in any scientific study should not only be capable of giving consent for their participation, but they should also be the first to benefit from the research findings (Harding, 1991, 1993; Keller, 1985; Keller and Longino, 1996). In short, feminist epistemology calls into question the science-as-usual practice of animal experimentation, which is at the foundation of modern scientific research (Birke & Hubbard 1995).

From a feminist perspective, knowledge is produced not through greater and greater separation, but through acknowledgement of connection (Keller 1985). Moreover, knowledge is located not solely in the mind but in the body, not solely in the isolated and artificially controlled laboratories of conventional science but in the dynamic living world, encountered as an active entity. Reconceiving research "objects" as subjects, feminist epistemology provides a theory capable of explaining how Barbara McClintock could "listen" to corn, and how primates can reason, empathize, and show willful aggression (Keller, 1983; Haraway, 1989). By reconceiving the relations between nature/culture, male/female, and human/animal as continuities rather than opposed categories, feminist environmentalism *redefines what it means to be human.*

This relational epistemology is both an experientially-based and socially constructed component of women's psychology and self-identity as well as that of many non-dominant, Indigenous cultures. It forms the basis of later ecofeminist theorizing about the "ecofeminist ecological self" (Gaard, 1997b), the "mutual self" (Plumwood, 1993), the "political animal" self-identity of ecological democracy that is articulated through both political and ecological participation (Sandilands 1999), or the sense of ecological "inter-identity" and "interbeing" (Murphy 1995) expressed by ecological feminisms. This self identity stands in stark contrast to the autonomous individualism of dominant western psychology, liberalism, and their dangerous development in deep ecology's "transpersonal self" that incorporates, absorbs, or erases the other (Plumwood, 1993).

Through its explorations of biological science, and its attendant studies of women's bodies and women's health, feminist philosophy of science provides conceptual support for further feminist explorations of nature, race, gender, sexuality, and species. One of the most significant contributions of feminist environmentalisms has involved eschewing the old liberal dualisms of public vs. private, culture vs. nature, and situating human embodiment as a nexus of nature, environment, and culture.

ENVIRONMENTAL JUSTICE, ECOFEMINISM, AND ENVIRONMENTAL HEALTH

The 1990s was a decade of renewed environmental activism growing out of the separate but linked fields of civil rights and feminism, a time during which the environmental justice and ecofeminist movements, respectively, became fully developed. The environmental justice movement traces its roots to a 1982 action in Warren County, NC, where Dollie Burwell helped form Warren County Concerned

Citizens, a group of predominantly black and poor residents who successfully opposed a polychlorinated biphenyl (PCB) disposal landfill in their community. In 1987, the United Church of Christ Commission for Racial Justice produced the study, *Toxic Waste and Race*, showing that race was the most powerful variable predicting the location of toxic waste facilities—more powerful than other variables such as poverty, land values, and home ownership. By 1991, the First National People of Color Environmental Leadership Summit met for four days in Washington D.C. At the conference, Hazel Johnson was named the "mother of the environmental justice movement" for her work organizing on Chicago's south side: in 1982 she had founded People for Community Recovery when she learned that her community, a "toxic doughnut," was surrounded by polluting industries that caused an incidence of cancer higher than any other area in Chicago (EJRC, 2008). In 2002, the Second National People of Color Environmental Leadership Summit was again held in Washington, DC, offering another four-day event that attracted over 1,400 participants. This second summit expanded and extended the environmental and economic justice paradigm to address globalization and international issues (EJRC, 2008). Although the prominent spokespersons for the environmental justice movement are predominantly male, academic, and/or ministerial, the movement itself was formed largely through the work of grassroots women activists who are working class and/or women of color.

Like the environmental justice movement, ecofeminism's roots come from earlier movements—second-wave feminism, the anti-nuclear movement of the 1970s, the women's spirituality movement, the animal rights movement, the environmental movement—and its first manifestations also occurred in the 1980s. WomanEarth Feminist Peace Institute, founded by Ynestra King and Starhawk, grew out of a feminist engagement with the peace movement. During the three years of its existence (1986–89), this educational institution was committed to addressing the conflicts of race among women, and chose the concept of racial parity as its foundation for addressing the connections linking feminist peace politics, ecology, and spirituality. In 1982, Marti Kheel and Tina Frisco formed Feminists for Animal Rights (FAR), a group committed to exploring the connections between the exploitation of women and that of animals. Activists from FAR and from WomanEarth, along with ecofeminists active in the women's spirituality movement, participated as founders of the U.S. Green Movement during the 1980s, and many remained active through the mid-1990s (Gaard, 1998). Feminist interest in environmental issues took on a global focus through the Women's Environment and Development Organization (WEDO), formed in 1991 by former U.S. Congresswoman Bella Abzug (1920–1998) and feminist activist and journalist Mim Kelber (1922–2004). Bringing together women from all around the world to take action in the United Nations and other international policymaking forums, WEDO's primary events in the 1990s included the World Women's Congress for a Healthy Planet (a planning meeting for the 1992 UN Conference on Environment and Development), followed by highly successful Women's Caucuses at key UN conferences throughout the 1990s (WEDO, 2008).

Although ecofeminism is a movement launched primarily by European, Australian, and Euro-American women, significant organizations within the movement have been formed with a commitment to racial and global justice in administration, vision, and action—WomanEarth Feminist Peace Institute and WEDO, respectively—and notable ecofeminists such as Maria Mies and Vandana Shiva (1993) have written and organized in a way that bridges first-world/third-world and racial barriers.

A primary emphasis of feminist environmentalism has been the connection between reproductive cancers and environmental health, and by the mid-1990s a raft of research was published to document this connection. Liane Clorfene-Casten's *Breast Cancer: Poisons, Profits and Prevention* (1996), Theo Colborn's *Our Stolen Future* (1996), Lois Gibbs' *Dying from Dioxin* (1996), and Sandra Steingraber's *Living Downstream: An Ecologist Looks at Cancer and the Environment* (1997) all pointed to the role of pesticides, endocrine-disruptors, phthalates, PCBs, dioxins, and other toxic chemicals in affecting cancers and reproductive health for humans and animals alike. Women's reproductive capacities were the central but not the sole topic of study; these texts also documented reduced sperm counts and feminization among human and animal males. Opening with examples of reduced fertility in bald eagles in Florida (1952), river otters in England (late '50s), mink in Michigan (mid-60's), herring gulls in Michigan (1970), western gulls in California (early '80s), alligators in Florida ('80s), seals in northern Europe (1988), dolphins in the Mediterranean (early '90s), and sperm counts of men worldwide (1992), Colburn's *Our Stolen Future* contains a chapter titled "Fifty Ways to Lose Your Fertility" and a conclusion that hormone-disruptors produced by synthetic chemicals are damaging human and animal reproductive health in females and males alike. Steingraber's *Living Downstream: An Ecologist Looks at Cancer and the Environment* (1997) offers the first study to bring together data on toxic releases with newly released data from U.S. cancer registries, presenting these environmental links to cancer as a human rights issue—though not an animal rights issue.[1]

As Steingraber is careful to emphasize, co-occurrence does not equal causality, and in fact the environmental causes of breast and other reproductive cancers are very difficult to prove: people move, winds change, heredity and lifestyle influence health, chemical production increases or decreases. The inability to prove causality has been a loophole for environmental pollution and workplace discrimination alike: without a direct link between harassment and a woman's protected class status, without a direct link between corporate profit, environmental pollution, and human/animal ill health (such as those links provided by Union Carbide's 1984 explosion in Bhopal, or Chisso's discharges of methylmercury for over thirty years in Japan's Minamata Bay)—perpetrators and polluters go free. To compel accountability and reduce environmental toxins, feminist environmental activists gathered with other environmental health scientists, Indigenous rights activists, physicians, and academics at the Wingspread Center in Racine, Wisconsin, to develop the Wingspread Statement on the Precautionary Principle (1998), a strategy for shifting the burden of proof from citizens to corporations, requiring not the accumulation of cancers and deaths but the prevention of such through independently documented proof of safety prior to a product's release.

At the same time that women's environmental health advocates were accumulating data and performing research, women health advocates were developing a feminist perspective on mothering that can be traced to significant texts of radical feminism, such as Suzanne Arms' *Immaculate Deception: Myth, Magic, and Birth* (1975), Adrienne Rich's *Of Woman Born: Motherhood as Experience and Institution* (1976) and Barbara Ehrenreich and Deidre English's *For Her Own Good: 150 Years of the Experts' Advice to Women* (1979). Already, feminists had uncovered the links between the so-called "Scientific Revolution" and the male-dominanted medical profession's appropriation of midwifery and expulsion of women's knowledge in the witch-burnings (Merchant 1980), and a feminist movement to reclaim the entire process of conception, pregnancy, childbirth and breastfeeding was underway. Sandra Steingraber's *Having Faith: An Ecologist's Journey to Motherhood* (2001) places this feminist reclamation of motherhood in an environmental context by tracing the environmental impacts on reproductive health from conception through the nine months of pregnancy and into the breastfeeding years. Audacious in her advocacy of women and children's health and environmental health alike, Steingraber describes using her standpoint as a scientist and nursing mother to speak against persistent organic pollutants (POPs) at the United Nations by passing around a jar of her own breastmilk as an exhibit. Her action illustrates Deborah Slicer's philosophical explanation of an anti-essentialist ecofeminist standpoint theory that strategically uses "bodies as grounds" (1998).

The field of environmental health has been growing in dialogue with these diverse feminist scientific researchers, using both epidemiological and animal studies to provide its data. In April 2002, a research team of scientists at the University of California-Berkeley, lead by Tyrone Hayes, revealed that the most abundantly used herbicide in the world, atrazine, disrupts the development of frogs at extraordinarily low levels of exposure, producing demasculinization of secondary sexual characteristics and alterations in serum hormone levels. Despite repeated attacks from the chemical industry, Hayes has spoken widely about his research, invoking the Precautionary Principle in advocating for an immediate ban on agricultural chemicals until further research proves their safety. Similar findings are reported in the Vallombrosa Report, *Challenged Conceptions: Environmental Chemicals and Fertility* (Luoma, 2005), a document produced from the national Collaborative on Health and the Environment, Stanford University School of Medicine's Women's Health Program, and 40 experts in infertility and reproductive health, who met together at the Vallombrosa Retreat Center to discuss the relationship between environmental chemicals and fertility. Their findings show that 12% of the reproductive age population in the United States is experiencing infertility, a trend increasing most dramatically in women under the age of 25. Their research produced a list of environmental contaminants affecting human and animal fertility prior to conception, during development, as well as through exposures during adulthood: bisphenol A (BPA), chlorinated hydrocarbons (dioxins, PCBs), organichlorine pesticides, pesticides, phthalates (plasticizers found in plastics, cosmetics, toys, pharmaceuticals, medical devices), solvents (benzene, toluene, xylene, styrene, perchloroethylene), heavy metals (lead, mercury, manganese, cadmium), perfluorinated compounds, polybrominated diphenyl ethers (flame retardants), and cigarette smoke (Luoma, 2005). Many of these chemicals are bioaccumulative, and their effects when encountered in combination are largely unstudied.

A specific aspect of environmental health that has been a focus of environmental feminist activism is the correlation between breast cancer and environmental toxins. In 1994, activists from the Massachusetts Breast Cancer Coalition who had noted elevated breast cancer rates throughout Cape Cod called for an investigation of their causes, and, inspired by Rachel Carson's work, founded the Silent Spring Institute (SSI). Today, this Institute is comprised of not only activists but also scientists, physicians, public health advocates, and elected officials, united around the common goal of identifying and changing the links between the environment and women's health, especially breast cancer. In collaboration with Communities for a Better Environment and Brown University, SSI is assessing household pollutant exposure for endocrine disrupting compounds (EDCs) and developing communications tools to report results to affected individuals and communities. One of this project's specific aims is to link breast cancer advocacy and environmental justice in two communities that differ in racial/ethnic and economic character (Silent Spring Institute 2008).

Breast cancer activists studying the correlation between breast cancer and the environment have uncovered a list of environmental toxins linked with breast cancer, using campaigns such as "think before you pink" (2008) to challenge the privatization of breast cancer as a problem caused primarily by a woman's genetics, reproductive history, and lifestyle, along with the mistaken notion that we can shop our way back to health. Instead, breast cancer researchers and activists like Devra Lee Davis and Ana Soto point to the complexity of breast cancer causation as an intersectional phenomenon of genetic, lifestyle, and environmental factors that include exposure to xenoestrogens and other endocrine disrupting compounds, estrogens and progestins, radiation, and other chemicals of concern (ethylene oxide, organic solvens, aromatic amines, benzene, PVCs, 1,3-Butadiene) (Gray 2008). Numerous epidemiological studies and animal studies (the latter performed on involuntary participants who do not benefit from the research) document these environmental chemicals' impacts on reproductive health and link environmental exposures to breast cancers, yet their findings are interpreted as having relevance primarily for humans.

Another branch of feminist environmentalism, vegan/vegetarian ecofeminism, argues for interspecies justice as integral to a feminist and environmental vision of ecological democracy. Beginning with recognitions of the similarities between sexism and speciesism (Adams, 1990; Donovan, 1990), sexism and racism (Spiegel 1988), or sexism and the oppression of nature (Griffin 1978), this branch of ecofeminism coalesced with a recognition of the similarities among sexism, racism, and speciesism (Collard & Contrucci, 1989; Gaard, 1993) and ultimately shifted analysis from the objects of oppression to the conceptual system that undergirds the logic of domination in western cultures (Warren 1994, 1997, 2000). This system relies on a three-step process of alienation of self from other, and the associated identity formations that emphasize a valued feature possessed only by the self. Alienation is followed by hierarchy, valuing self above other, and concludes by justifying the subordination of an inferior and separate other. This system of alienation, hierarchy, and domination is at work in all major structures of oppression in the west—sexism, racism, classism, heterosexism, ageism, ableism, speciesism, anthropocentrism—and the features of the valued self in each system are associated, just as the features of the devalued self are associated: thus, "real" men are socially constructed as young able-bodied rational productive heterosexual meat-eaters, while women are seen as simultaneously irrational, sexual, animalistic, and reproductive (Gaard, 1997b). The policing of GLBTQ sexual behaviors, and the practice of compulsory gender reassignment for intersexed infants, are additional aspects of domination in the form of reproductive control (Mortimer-Sandilands & Erickson, 2010). A queer, vegetarian ecofeminist analysis suggests that an inclusive vision of reproductive justice will address interspecies, intersexual, and GLBTQ reproductive justice together with environmental justice. Eschewing the human/nonhuman dualism, this perspective explores the ways that the sexual and reproductive capacities of females of all species are affected by social and environmental toxins.

Building on earlier feminist research into the exploitation of female reproduction (Corea, 1985), and the development of reproductive technologies via experimentation on non-human females first, vegetarian ecofeminists emphasize how western systems of industrial animal production ("factory farming") rely specifically on the exploitation of the female (Adams & Donovan, 1995; Donovan & Adams, 2007; Gaard, 2003; Kheel, 2008), harming the health of both nonhuman females and the human females who consume their bodies and their reproductive "products." As Carol Adams (2003) points out, "to control fertility one must have absolute access to the female of the species." (147) The control of female fertility for food production and human reproduction alike uses invasive technologies to manipulate female bodies across the species (Adams, 2003; Corea, 1985; Diamond 1994). Battery chickens are crowded into tiny cages, de-beaked, and inoculated with numerous antibiotics to maximize control of their reproductive output, eggs (Davis 1995). Male chicks are routinely discarded because they are of no use to the battery hen industry, while female chicks are bred to deformity with excessively large breasts and tiny feet, growing up to live a radically shortened lifetime of captivity, unable to perform any of their natural functions (i.e., dustbathing, nesting, flying). Pregnant sows are confined to gestation crates and after they give birth they are allowed to suckle their offspring only through metal bars. Dairy cows are forcibly inseminated, and their male calves are taken from them 24–48 hours after birth and confined in crates, where they will be fed an iron-deprived diet until they are slaughtered for veal. Cows separated from their calves bellow and appear to grieve for days afterwards, sometimes ramming themselves against their stalls in attempt to reunite with their calves; news articles report the "amazing" feats of cows returning across miles of countryside in order to nurse calves from whom they were forcibly separated (Dawn 2008). We understand the frenzy of a human mother separated from her new infant, yet our understanding and empathy seems to halt at the species boundary, since this involuntary weaning and the attendant suffering for cow and calf continues to be the norm for dairy production: the milk that would have fed the cows' offspring is taken for human consumption, and manipulated into overproduction through the use of growth hormones (Dawn, 2008; Gaard, 1994; Gruen, 1993).

In all of these cases, reproductive injustice exploiting nonhuman females is practiced for the economic profit of an elite group—first-world humans. Meanwhile, human females who consume the milk and eggs of other animals face higher risks in their own reproductive organ health: studies published in the *American Journal of Clinical Nutrition* (2004), *Cancer Epidemiology Biomarkers & Prevention* (2004), and the *American Journal of Epidemiology* (1999) all confirm positive associations between ovarian cancer risks for women with a higher consumption of eggs or dairy products (primarily cow's milk) (Gaard, 2010). A vegan ecofeminist perspective on milk- and egg-production makes visible the ill health and suffering of females from all species—from those who are used for their reproductive capacities while their infants are taken from them for slaughter or continued reproductive confinement until slaughter, to those who work in unsafe and illegal conditions in order to slaughter these animals, to those pregnant or lactating mothers who drink the water or breathe the air permeated with the waste of these industrial animal farms as pass on these contaminants to their infants, and finally, to those who consume these products of female reproduction, ingesting their antibiotics and growth hormones along with their suffering, their eggs and their milk. Ecofeminism's contribution to a theory of reproductive justice offers an emphasis on the environmental causes of infertility and compromised reproductive health as well as a vision of reproductive justice for all—women, men, transpersons, and others of all species (Gaard, 2010).

FEMINIST ENVIRONMENTALISMS ACROSS THE DISCIPLINES

Feminist environmentalists have been active across the arts and social sciences, developing artwork and art criticism, literature and literary criticism, queer ecology, psychology and outdoor education. Their critiques of biotechnology, water privatization, population and development, and economic globalization have shaped the dialogues on these issues, both describing and inspiring activism around the world.

Among the first studies of ecofeminist art, Carol Bigwood's *Earth Muse* (1993) explores the culture/nature dualism by alternating interrogations of art criticism and gender with lyrical meditations on specific artworks—from the Minoan snake goddess to Brancusi's *Seal*—and the gendered projections that accompany them. Feminist artist Sue Coe (1995) uses her artwork to draw attention to the violence of industrialized animal "meat" production and animal experimentation; their requisite oppression of female animals, mothers and offspring; and the links to capitalist profit. Minnesota environmental artist Betsy Damon has created Living Water Gardens as artistic sites of water remediation and reclamation around the world, and has founded Keepers of the Water to join art, science, and community in protecting and rehabilitating water. Wisconsin artist Helen Klebesadel depicts nature and women in conjunction, "not ... to express an idea that nature is motherly and feminine," but rather "to acknowledge the meaning and magic that is inherent in our everyday experience as a part of nature and to notice that nature is watching, and wondering how long it will take us to see ourselves as a part of its interconnected web." Klebesadel's work was recently featured in the 2006 Wisconsin-based project, "Paradise Lost? Climate Change in the Northwoods," a multimedia art installation depicting the current and projected effects of global warming on northern Wisconsin and the Great Lakes. "Instead of viewing the arts as adjuncts to political activity or as distractions from political activism," explains Gloria Feman Orenstein, "ecofeminism considers the arts to be essential catalysts of change" (2003). Through site-specific installation, ritual and performance, habitat restoration, and other unconventional media, ecofeminist artists strive to create "a healthy web of interrelationships between humans and others" (Mathews, 2001).

In literature and literary criticism, feminist environmental critics have excavated a large body of work by women writers, illustrators, gardeners, mountaineers and animal advocates, illuminating a history of women's environmental writing (Anderson, 1991, 2003; Anderson & Edwards, 2002; Gates, 1998; Norwood, 1993; Norwood & Monk, 1987). In founding texts of feminist environmental literary criticism such as Annette Kolodny's *The Lay of the Land* (1975) and Louse Westling's *The Green Breast of the New World* (1996), feminist literary critics explored the culture/nature dualism by cataloging masculine literary projections of gender onto nature, and the ways this projection of gender was used strategically to legitimate colonization. With the founding of the Association for the Study of Literature and the Environment (ASLE) in 1992, scholars of environmental literature found a community and a venue for developing environmental literary criticism ("ecocriticism"), and ecofeminist literary criticism was well articulated just a few years later (Carr 2000; Gaard & Murphy 1998; Murphy 1995, 2000; Stein 1997). Under the broad category of ecocriticism, ecocritics who began their scholarly work in ecofeminist politics (Sandilands 1999; Sturgeon 1997) or ecofeminist literary criticism continued to expand their analyses and served as gateway scholars, collecting interviews, essays, and literary criticism to build the new field of environmental justice ecocriticism (Adamson, Evans & Stein 2002; Stein 2004; Sturgeon 2009) and a queer ecocriticism (Mortimer-Sandilands & Erickson 2010).

Feminists have explored the intersections of environmentalisms and lesbian, gay, bisexual, and transgendered (LGBT) studies, or queer studies. Among the first such explorations, Gaard's "Toward a Queer Ecofeminism" (1997b) adds the oppositional pairs "heterosexual/queer" and "reason/the erotic" to Val Plumwood's (1993) list of dualisms underlying the Master Model, "the identity that is at the core of Western culture and that has initiated, perpetuated, and benefited from Western culture's alienation from and domination of nature" (Gaard 1997b:23). A queer ecofeminist perspective uncovers the ways that nature is inextricably linked with not just the female, non-white, non-human animal, but also with the erotic, such that liberation efforts for LGBT equality, feminism, and environmental health will be more effective if they are undertaken with an understanding of these interconnections. Subsequent work has both critiqued the potential for losing lesbian identity and experience in the homogenizing term "queer" for ecofeminism (Lee & Dow 2001), and explored the uses of AIDS as metaphor in addressing environmental degradation and developing a "queer ecological sensibility" (Mortimer-Sandilands, 2002, 2005). Recent work in "queer ecologies" develops these ideas by "queering" eco-cultural criticism, sexual politics, and environmental politics alike, revealing a wealth of same-sex sexual behaviors across species, challenging appeals to nature as covert attempts to bolster dominant social norms and sexualities, and providing extensive documentation for the insight that sexuality and environment are mutually co-constituted (Mortimer-Sandilands & Erickson, 2010).

In psychology and outdoor education, feminist environmentalists initially explored the healing power of environmental engagement for incest and rape survivors, for women in midlife transition, as well as for building women's self-esteem, transforming body image and creating community (Cole, Erdman, Rothblum 1994). A lesser-known component of feminist therapy, women's environmental groups such as Woodswomen and Women in the Wilderness brought women together for personal renewal and empowerment through outdoor education. As these groups developed, they became deeply concerned with empowering local women's communities wherever their groups traveled; now, through feminist ecotourism, these groups regularly plan environmental excursions that simultaneously contribute to improving the livelihoods of women in developing countries while educating first-world outdoorswomen.

The pervasive ecological feminist experience of self-in-connection has also inspired new developments in feminist ecopsychologies. Gay Bradshaw's studies of elephants traumatized through the devastating effects of ivory poaching and slaughter has also included strategies for rehabilitation that use humans as foster-mothers to orphaned elephants; other feminists working on interspecies psychology pair traumatized parrots with traumatized war veterans to build empathy and foster healing for participants of both species (Bradshaw 2009; Bradshaw and Watkins, 2006; Borchers & Bradshaw, 2008). Similarly, pattrice jones' work rehabilitating fighting roosters so that they can be reintegrated with the flock draws on her studies of trauma theory in humans (jones, 2007, 2010b). Jones' decade-long experience founding and operating a bird sanctuary on the Delmarva Peninsula, along with her graduate training in psychology, inspired her explorations of "avian archetypes": people use birds as symbols in ways that erase the actual bird's experience or needs, whereas a more critical consideration of bird psychologies suggests humans and birds participate in a greater collective unconscious, rooted in shared brain architecture

(2010a). Her work lays the foundation for a feminist, embodied ecopsychology that can help heal the harms done to other species, and join with them in devising responses to environmental degradation.

Environmental feminists see the ongoing appropriation and devaluation of women's reproductive labor, Indigenous lives and lands, the bodies and reproductive labor of nonhuman animals, and the earth's regenerative economy as the foundation of global capitalist politics (Mies & Shiva, 1993). By illuminating these intersections, feminist environmentalists and ecofeminists have shaped international dialogues on economic globalization and structures of global political dominance, building an international feminist movement for environmental justice (Agarwal, 1992, 2000, 2007; Eaton & Lorentzen, 2003; Salleh, 2009; Seager, 1993, 2003). Feminist geographer Joni Seager (2008) has produced and regularly updates an *Atlas of Women in the World* that provides global data on many key issues: environmental health, gender equality, motherhood, feminism, women in the global economy, domestic violence, lesbian rights, women in government. Among the most prominent third-world feminists, Indian physicist Vandana Shiva has developed detailed critiques of biotechnology's damage to agriculture, women farmers, consumers, and the economy and political independence of third-world governments (Shiva 1988, 1997; Shiva & Moser 1995). Other third-world women environmentalists have worked to protect women, water, and forests through activisms that foreground their shared well-being, such as Wangari Maathai's Green Belt Movement in Kenya (1985; 2004), and Arundhati Roy's work against water privatization in India (2001). Inspired by New Zealand feminist Marilyn Waring's germinal work, *If Women Counted* (1988), feminist ecological economists have explored the inaccuracies of patriarchal economic systems that exclude the work and the wealth produced by women, children, animals, and the environment, while counting as wealth the pollution created by elite male-controlled production processes (McMahon, 1997; Nelson, 2007; Perkins & Kuiper, 2005). Feminist and ecofeminist critiques of population theory that condemns third-world women as "breeders" whose progeny threaten the planet have pointed to the links between population and consumption, the male ideology of masculinity that includes "fathering" but not raising children, and the persistent uses of rape as a weapon of warfare as some of the many forces that have been used to blame women for systems that are largely under male control, and thereby obsure the real root of the problem and prevent our capacity to craft more effective eco-justice solutions (Hartmann, 1987; Silliman & King, 1999).

First-world feminists such as Ariel Salleh and Susan Hawthorne in Australia, Maria Mies in Germany, Stacy Alaimo and Susan Hekman in the U.S., and Mary Mellor in Great Britain have brought a materialist feminist analysis to explore the ecological, economic, and political legacies of colonialism. Their language in describing this approach varies from "feminist green socialism" (Mellor, 1992, 1997) to an embodied materialist ecofeminism (Salleh, 1997, 2009; Alaimo & Hekman, 2008), an ecological and feminist "body politics" (Mies, 1986), and an ecofeminism that places biodiversity and Indigenous people at the center of policy, analysis, and

G. GAARD

strategy (Hawthorne, 2002). "I want an epistemological multiversity which values the context and real-life experiences of people," writes Susan Hawthorne (2002); "I want a world in which relationship is important, and reciprocity is central to social interaction" (375).

FOR A FEMINIST AND ECOLOGICAL FUTURE

The breakdown of communication between the sciences and the humanities, widely articulated in C. P. Snow's 1959 lecture on "The Two Cultures," relies in fact on the exclusion of women. Today, many environmental studies programs are simply environmental *sciences* as usual, lacking knowledge from the environmental humanities. As an interdisciplinary and transdisciplinary perspective, feminist environmentalisms offer a strategy and an imperative for reconnecting these different ways of knowing, repairing the academic fragmentation of knowledge by placing the experiences of women, queers, and all non-dominant groups at the center of research.

NOTE

[1] Steingraber's feminism omits a critique of her own medical training: she is persistently untroubled by using the results of data derived from animal experimentation, and omits advocacy for these animal species from all of her conclusions regarding human and environmental health.

REFERENCES

Adams, C.J. (1990). *The Sexual Politics of Meat: A Feminist-Vegetarian Critical Theory*. New York: Continuum Publishers.
Adams, C.J. (2003). *The Pornography of Meat*. New York: Continuum, 2003.
Adams, C.J., & Donovan, J. (Eds.) (1995). *Animals and Women: Feminist Theoretical Explorations*. Durham, NC: Duke University Press, 1995.
Adamson, J, Evans, M.M., & Stein, R. (Eds.) (2002). *The Environmental Justice Reader: Politics, Poetics and Pedagogy*. Tucson, AZ: University of Arizona Press.
Agarwal, B. (1992). "The Gender and Environment Debate: Lessons from India." *Feminist Studies 18*, 119–158.
Agarwal, B. (2000). Conceptualizing Environmental Collective Action: Why Gender Matters. *Cambridge Journal of Economics 24*, 283–310.
Agarwal, B. (2007). "Gender Inequality, Cooperation, and Environmental Sustainability." pp. 274–313. In *Inequality, Cooperation, and Environmental Sustainability*. Ed. Jean-Marie Baland, Pranab Bardhahn, and Samuel Bowles. Princeton, NJ: Princeton University Press.
Alaimo, S., & Hekman, S. (Eds.) (2008). *Material Feminisms*. Bloomington: Indiana University Press.
Anderson, L. (Ed.). (1991:2003). *Sisters of the Earth: Women's Prose and Poetry About Nature*. New York: Random House.
Anderson, L., & Edwards, T.S. (2002). *At Home on This Earth: Two Centuries of U.S. Women's Nature Writing*. Hanover, NH: University Press of New England.
Arms, S. (1975: 1994). *Immaculate Deception: Myth, Magic & Birth*. Berkeley: Celestial Arts,
Bigwood, C. (1993) *Earth Muse: Feminism, Nature, and Art*. Philadelphia: Temple University Press, 1993.
Birke, L., & Hubbard,R. (Eds.) (1993) *Reinventing Biology: Respect for Life and the Creation of Knowledge*. Bloomington: Indiana University Press.

Borchers, J G., & Bradshaw, G. A. (2008, December). "How Green Is My Valley—And Mind: Ecotherapy and the Greening of Psychology." *Counseling Today* 38–41.

Bradshaw, G. A. (2009). *Elephants on the Edge: What Animals Teach Us About Humanity.* Yale University Press.

Bradshaw, G.A., & Watkins, M. "Trans-Species Psychology: Theory and Praxis." *Spring: A Journal of Archetype and Culture, 75*(1), (2006): 1–26.

Carr, G, (Ed.) (2000). *New Essays in Ecofeminist Literary Criticism.* Cranbury, NJ: Associated University Presses,

Carson, R. (1962). *Silent Spring.* Boston: Houghton Mifflin Company.

Clorfene-Casten, L. (1996). *Breast Cancer: Poisons, Profits and Prevention.* Monroe, ME: Common Courage Press.

Coe, S. (1985). *Dead Meat.* New York: Four Walls Eight Windows.

Colburn, T, Dumanoski, D., & Myers, J.P. (1996). *Our Stolen Future.* New York: Penguin.

Cole, E, Erdman, E., & Rothblum, E.D. (Eds.) (1994). *Wilderness Therapy for Women: The Power of Adventure.* New York: Harrington Park Press.

Collard, A with Contrucci, J. (1989). *Rape of the Wild: Man's Violence against Animals and the Earth.* Bloomington, IN: Indiana University Press.

Corea, G. (1985). *The Mother Machine: Reproductive Technologies from Artificial Insemination to Artificial Wombs.* New York: Harper & Row.

Damon, B. (2009). *Keepers of the Waters.* http://www.keepersofthewaters.org/default.cfm. Accessed 8/16/09.

Davis, K. (1995). Thinking Like a Chicken: Farm Animals and the Feminine Connection. *Animals and Women: Feminist Theoretical Explorations*, Adams, C., & Donovan, J. (Eds.) (pp. 192–21). Durham, NC: Duke University Press.

Dawn, K. (2008). *Thanking the Monkey: Rethinking the Way We Treat Animals.* New York: HarperCollins Publishers.

Diamond, I. (1994). *Fertile Ground: Women, Earth, and the Limits of Control.* Boston: Beacon Press.

Donovan, J. (1990). Animal Rights and Feminist Theory. *Signs, 15*(2), 350–75.

Donovan, J., & Adams C. J., (Eds.) (2007). *The Feminist Care Tradition in Animal Ethics.* New York: Columbia University Press.

Eaton, H., & Lorentzen, L.A. (Eds.) (2003). *Ecofeminism and Globalization: Exploring Culture, Context, and Religion.* New York: Rowman & Littlefield.

Ehrenreich, B., & English, D. (1978). *For Her Own Good: 150 Years of the Experts' Advice to Women.* New York: Doubleday/Anchor Press.

Environmental Justice Resource Center (2011). Unsung Sheroes and Heroes on the Front Line for Environmental Justice. http://www.ejrc.cau.edu/%28s%29heros.html Accessed June 3, 2011.

Friedan, B. (1963). *The Feminine Mystique.* New York: W. W. Norton.

Gaard, G. (Ed.) (1993). *Ecofeminism: Women, Animals, Nature.* Philadelphia, PA: Temple University Press.

Gaard, G. (1994). Milking Mother Nature: An Ecofeminist Critique of rBGH. *The Ecologist, 24*(6), 1–2.

Gaard, G. (1997, Winter). Toward a Queer Ecofeminism." *Hypatia, 12*(1), 114–37.

Gaard, G. (1998). *Ecological Politics: Ecofeminists and the Greens.* Philadelphia, PA: Temple University Press.

Gaard, G. (2003). Vegetarian Ecofeminism: A Review Essay. *Frontiers, 23*(3), (117–146).

Gaard, G. (2010) Reproductive Technology, or Reproductive Justice? An Ecofeminist, Environmental Justice Perspective on the Rhetoric of Choice." *Ethics and the Environment, 15*(2), 103–130.

Gaard, G., & Murphy, P.D. (Eds.). (1998). *Ecofeminist Literary Criticism: Theory, Interpretation, Pedagogy.* Urbana, IL: University of Illinois Press.

Gates, B. T. (1998). *Kindred Nature: Victorian and Edwardian Women Embrace the Living World.* Chicago, IL: University of Chicago Press.

Gibbs, L.M. (1995). *Dying From Dioxin.* Boston, MA: South End Press.

Gray, J. (Ed.) (2008). *State of the Evidence: The Connection Between Breast Cancer and the Environment* (5th ed.) Breast Cancer Fund. www.breastcancerfund.org/site/pp.asp?c=kwKXLdPaE&b=206137 Accessed June 11, 2008.

Griffin, S. (1978). *Woman and Nature: The Roaring Inside Her.* New York: Harper & Row.

Gruen, L. Dismantling Oppression: An Analysis of the Connection Between Women and Animals. *Ecofeminism: Women, Animals, Nature*, Gaard, G., (Ed.). Philadelphia, PA: Temple University Press. pp. 60–90.

Haraway, D. (1989). *Primate Visions: Gender, Race, and Nature in the World of Modern Science*. New York: Routledge, Chapman & Hall, Inc.

Harding, S. (1991). *Whose Science? Whose Knowledge? Thinking From Women's Lives*. Ithaca, NY: Cornell University Press.

Harding, S. (Ed.) (1993). *The "Racial" Economy of Science: Toward a Democratic Future*. Bloomington, IN: Indiana University Press.

Hartmann, B. (1987). *Reproductive Rights and Wrongs: The Global Politics of Population Control and Contraceptive Choice*. New York: Harper & Row.

Hawthorne, S. (2002). *Wild Politics: Feminism, Globalisation, Bio/Diversity*. North Melbourne, Australia: Spinifex Press.

hooks, b. (1984). *Feminist Theory: From Margin to Center*. Boston, MA: South End Press.

jones, p. (2007). *Aftershock: Confronting Trauma in a Violent World*. New York: Lantern Books.

jones, p. (2010a). Harbingers of (Silent) Spring: Archetypal Avians, Avian Archetypes, and the Truly Collective Unconscious." *Spring, 83*, 185–212.

jones, p. (2010b). Roosters, Hawks and Dawgs: Toward an Inclusive, Embodied Eco/Feminist Psychology." *Feminism and Psychology, 20*(3), 365–80.

Keller, E.F. (1983). *A Feeling for the Organism: The Life and Work of Barbara McClintock*. New York: W. H. Freeman and Company.

Keller, E.F. (1985). *Reflections on Gender and Science*. New Haven: Yale University Press.

Keller, E.F., & Lontging, H.E. (Eds.) (1996). *Feminism and Science*. New York: Oxford University Press.

Kheel, M. (2008). *Nature Ethics: An Ecofeminist Perspective*. New York: Rowman & Littlefield.

Klebesadel, H. K. (2011). Transparent Watercolors: Helen R. Kebesadel. http://65.254.48.21/ Accessed June 3, 2011.

Kolodny, A. (1975). *The Lay of the Land: Metaphor as Experience and History in American Life and Letters*. Chapel Hill: University of North Carolina Press.

Lee, W.L., & Dow, L.M. (2001). Queering Ecological Feminism: Erotophobia, Commodification, Art, and Lesbian Identity. *Ethics & the Environment, 6*(2), pp. 1–21.

Luoma, J. (2005, October). *Challenged Conceptions: Environmental Chemicals and Fertility*. www.rhtp. org/fertility/vallombrosa/documents/Challenged_Conceptions.pdf Accessed March 22, 2008.

Maathai, W. (2004: 1985). *The Green Belt Movement*. New York: Lantern Books.

Martin, E. (1991). "The Egg and the Sperm: How Science has Constructed a Romance Based on Stereotypical Male-Female Roles." *Signs, 16*(3), pp. 485–501.

Mathews, D. (2001, Fall.) "What is Ecofeminist Art?" Women and Environments: pp. 10–11.

McMahon, M. (1997). "From the Ground Up: Ecofeminism and Ecological Economics." *Ecological Economics, 20*, pp.163–173.

Mellor, M. (1992). *Breaking the Boundaries: Towards a Feminist Green Socialism*. London: Virago Press.

Mellor, M. (1997). *Feminism and Ecology*. Washington Square, NY: New York University Press.

Merchant, C. (1980). *The Death of Nature: Women, Ecology, and the Scientific Revolution*. New York: Harper & Row.

Mies, M. (1986). *Patriarchy and Accumulation on a World Scale: Women in the International Division of Labour*. London: Zed Books.

Mies, M., & Shiva, V. (1993). *Ecofeminism*. London: Zed Books.

Mortimer-Sandilands, C. (2002, Fall). Landdykes and Landscape: Reflections on Sex and Nature in Southern Oregon. *Women & Environments*, pp. 13–16.

Mortimer-Sandilands, C. (2005). Unnatural Passions: Notes Toward a Queer Ecology." *Invisible Culture, Issue 9: Nature Loving*. http://www.roc, hester.edu/in_visible_culture/Issue_9/title9.html Accessed June 32010.

Mortimer-Sandilands, C., & Erickson, B. (Eds.) (2010). *Queer Ecologies: Sex, Nature, Politics and Desire*. Bloomington: Indiana University Press.

Murphy, P. D. (1995). *Literature, Nature, and Other: Ecofeminist Critiques*. Albany, NY: State University of New York Press.

Murphy, P. D. (2000). *Farther Afield in the Study of Nature-Oriented Literature.* Charlottesville, VA: University Press of Virginia.

Nelson, J. A. (2007). Feminism, Ecology, and the Philosophy of Economics. *Ecological Economics, 20,* pp. 155–162.

Norwood, V. (1993). *Made From This Earth: American Women and Nature.* Chapel Hill: University of North Carolina Press.

Norwood, V., & Monk, J. (Eds.) (1987). *The Desert is No Lady.* New Haven: Yale University Press.

Orenstein, G. F. (2003, Spring). The Greening of Gaia: Ecofeminist Artists Revisit the Garden. *Ethics & the Environment, 8,* pp. 103–111.

Perkins, E., & Kuiper, E. (Eds.) (2005, November). Explorations in Feminist Ecological Economics. Special Issue. *Feminist Economics, 11*(3), pp. 107–150.

Plumwood, V. (1993). *Feminism and the Mastery of Nature.* New York: Routledge.

Rich, A. (1976). *Of Woman Born: Motherhood as Experience and Institution.* New York: Bantam.

Roy, A. (2001). *Power Politics.* Boston: South End Press.

Salleh, A. (1997). *Ecofeminism as Politics: Nature, Marx, and the Postmodern.* London: Zed Books.

Salleh, A. (Ed.) (2009). *Eco-Sufficiency & Global Justice: Women Write Political Ecology.* London and Australia: Pluto Press and Spinifex.

Sandilands, C. (1999). *The Good-Natured Feminist: Ecofeminism and the Quest for Democracy.* Minneapolis: University of Minnesota Press.

Seager, J. (1993). *Earth Follies: Coming to Feminist Terms with the Global Environmental Crisis.* New York: Routledge.

Seager, J. (2003). Rachel Carson died of breast cancer: The Coming of Age of Feminist Environmentalis." *SIGNS, 28*(3), pp. 945–972.

Seager, J. (2008). *The Penguin Atlas of Women in the World.* 4th ed. New York: Penguin Books, 2008.

Shiva, V. (1997). *Biopiracy: The Plunder of Nature and Knowledge.* Boston: South End Press.

Shiva, V. (1988). *Staying Alive: Women, Ecology and Development.* London: Zed Books.

Shiva, V., & Moser, I. (Eds.). (1995). *Biopolitics: A Feminist and Ecological Reader on Biotechnology.* London: Zed Books.

Silent Spring Institute. (2008). Environment and Breast Cancer: Science Review. http://sciencereview. silentspring.org/ Accessed June 20, 2009.

Silliman, J., & King, Y. (Eds.) (1999). *Dangerous Intersections: Feminist Perspectives on Population, Environment and Development.* Cambridge, MA: South End Press.

Slicer, D. (1998). Toward an Ecofeminist Standpoint Theory: Bodies as Grounds. 49–73 Gaard, G. & Murphy, P.D. (Eds.), *Ecofeminist Literary Criticism: Theory, Interpretation, Pedagogy.* Urbana, IL: University of Illinois Press.

Spiegel, M. (1988). *The Dreaded Comparison: Human and Animal Slavery.* New York: Mirror Books.

Srinivas, H. Wingspread Statement on the Precautionary Principle. http://www.gdrc.org/u-gov/ precaution-3.html Accessed 08/20/09.

Stein, R. (1997). *Shifting the Ground: American Women Writers' Revisions of Nature, Gender, and Race.* Charlottesville, VA: University Press of Virginia.

Stein, R. (Ed.) (2004). *New Perspectives on Environmental Justice: Gender, Sexuality, and Activism.* New Brunswick, NJ: Rutgers University Press.

Steingraber, S. (2001). *Having Faith: An Ecologist's Journey to Motherhood.* New York: Berkley Books.

Steingraber, S. (1997). *Living Downstream: An Ecologist Looks at Cancer and the Environment.* New York: Addison Wesley.

Sturgeon, N. (1997). *Ecofeminist Natures: Race, Gender, Feminist Theory and Political Action.* New York: Routledge.

Sturgeon, N. (2009). *Environmentalism in Popular Culture: Gender, Race, Sexuality, and the Politics of the Natural.* Tucson: University of Arizona Press.

University of Wisconsin-Madison Center for Biology Education. Paradise Lost? Climate Change in the Northwoods. 2006. http://cbe.wisc.edu/assets/docs/pdf/paradiselost/paradise_lost.pdf Accessed June 3, 2011.

Waring, M. (1988). *If Women Counted: A New Feminist Economics.* San Francisco, CA: HarperCollins.

Warren, K. J. (Ed.) (1994). *Ecological Feminism.* New York: Routledge, 1994.

Warren, K. J. (Ed.) (1997). *Ecofeminism: Women, Culture, Nature*. Bloomington: Indiana University Press.

Warren, K. J. (2000). *Ecofeminist Philosophy: A Western Perspective on What It Is and Why It Matters*. New York: Rowman & Littlefield.

Westling, L. H. (1996). *The Green Breast of the New World: Landscape, Gender, and American Fiction*. Athens, GA: University of Georgia Press, 1996.

Women's Environment and Development Organization (WEDO). http://www.wedo.org/ Accessed on June 3, 2011.

CAN HIGHER EDUCATION TAKE CLIMATE CHANGE AS SERIOUSLY AS THE CIA AND THE STRATIGRAPHY COMMISSION OF THE GEOLOGICAL SOCIETY OF LONDON?

DAVID A. GREENWOOD

In the year 2000, the Nobel Prize-winning atmospheric chemist Paul Crutzen coined a new geological term for the current human epoch: the Anthropocene. Crutzen and other scientists recently described the Anthropocene as "a new phase in the history of both humankind and of the Earth, when natural forces and human forces became intertwined, so that the fate of one determines the fate of the other. Geologically, this is a remarkable episode in the history of this planet" (Zalasiewicz, Williams, Steffen & Crutzen, 2010). That human beings live in and have literally formed through their technologies a *new geological epoch* now needs to be taken seriously by a much broader public, and we need to develop the language capable of communicating what now needs to be learned, understood, questioned, and acted on.

Educators and learners worldwide need to pay attention: since the post-WWII acceleration and globalization of the industrial economy, and the rapid growth in human population (expected to reach 9 billion by mid-century), we now live on a biophysically different planet than the one in which modern civilization developed and in which our common assumptions about culture, environment and education were formed. At the time of this writing, a very conservative group of geologists— the Stratigraphy Commission of the Geological Society of London—is considering formalizing the new epoch. That is, the Anthropocene may soon join the Cambrian, the Jurassic, the Pleistocene and other such units on the Geological Time Scale (Zalasiewicz, Williams, Steffen & Crutzen, 2010). Are college and university educators taking sufficient notice of the times we are living in? If serious geologists are talking about changing the geological time scale to reflect the new realities, what is the corresponding response within higher education?

One could point to such movements as the American College and University Presidents' Climate Commitment and the growth of sustainability-related programs across academe as a progressive response to mitigate and adapt to fast changing social and ecological conditions worldwide. But only rarely does green university discourse convey the seriousness and urgency of the situation that has for nearly a decade been expressed in mainstream military and foreign policy analyses that describe and forecast the already catastrophic cultural impacts of climate change. While geologists, atmospheric scientists and other scientist that comprise the Intergovernmental Panel on Climate Change (IPCC) are proposing dramatic actions including renaming our geological epoch, military strategists are predicting in earnest a new dark age for humanity. In the 2007 report, *The Age of Consequences: The Foreign Policy National Security Implications of Global Climate Change*, ex-CIA director James Woolsey describes a plausible near future:

In a world that sees two meter sea level rise, with continued flooding ahead, it will take extraordinary effort for the United States, or indeed any country, to look beyond its own salvation. All of the ways in which human beings have dealt with natural disasters in the past... could come together in one conflagration: rage at government's inability to deal with the abrupt and unpredictable crises; religious fervor, perhaps even a dramatic rise in millennial end-of-days cults; hostility and violence toward migrants and minority groups, at a time of demographic change and increased global migration; and intra- and interstate conflict over resources, particularly food and fresh water. Altruism and generosity would likely be blunted. (Campbell et al., 85–86)

Woolsey's concern for future altruism and generosity is of course noble and ironic, considering the past and present horrors exported globally by the US military and the massive social and ecological debts accrued by Western industrial "progress." But neither foreign policy experts predicting global climate crises nor scientists describing anthropogenic biophysical cataclysm have given much thought to the idea that climate change is only one symptom of modern civilization's ungenerous and non-altruistic record of socio-ecological colonization, development, and energy intensive economic globalization, a mission the modern university uncritically serves.

With *Greening the Academy*, Samuel Day Fassbinder, Anthony Nocella, Richard Kahn and their contributors have asked the right questions to the right audience: What is the role of higher education—and the role traditional liberal arts disciplines—in responding to diverse communities, species, and nations living on a planet in the throes of converging socio-political-ecological crises rooted in centuries of colonization, genocide, and ecocide? I have a fantasy that all of my university colleagues start taking such a question seriously, and that my workplace becomes a space of spirited deliberation about its fundamental purposes in our changing times—with interdisciplinary study groups reading *Greening the Academy* and planning and enacting meaningful transformative actions. But as the authors of this volume suggest through their critiques of higher education and its relation to cultural production and reproduction, my fantasy will likely remain wishful thinking. What appears a more likely scenario for university workplaces is that the discourse of "sustainability" and "the green campus" will function as a cover that will make deeper green-brown critiques of educational convention appear unnecessary or overblown.

As partners with the corporate sector, universities will very likely continue to spin prosperity while avoiding and even suppressing the reflective work of examining the corrupt foundations of much prosperity. Indeed, at my own university, sustainability has recently been promoted and marketed as a major new campus initiative—but its meaning is purely *economic sustainability* in rough economic times with scant acknowledgement of the broader socio-political-ecological meanings of the term.

Simply put, while many university faculty and leaders may be prepared to discuss changes in the name of the sustainability revolution in higher education, they remain seemingly unable to acknowledge the many ways that these state- and corporate-sponsored institutions of learning continue to promote *unsustainability* in structures, processes, and the epistemological assumptions underlying the meaning of a university education. It is my hope that the sustainability revolution, well documented in the many activities and reports from the Association for the Advancement of Sustainability in Higher Education (AASHE), will continue to build momentum toward a truly transformative movement. But if we are to see a real change in direction, people within the university system need to confront the contradictions and the gaps between sustainability rhetoric and serious attempts to retrofit and reimagine the institution for the coming decades. *Greening the Academy* is the first book to critically accept this challenge.

REFERENCES

Campbell, K. M. et al. (2007). *The age of consequences: The foreign policy national security implications of global climate change*. Washington DC: Center for Strategicand International Studies and the Center for New American Security.

Zalasiewicz, J., Williams, M., Steffen, W., & Crutzen, P. (2010). The New World of the Anthropocene. *Environmental Science and Technology, 44*(7), 2228–2231.

CONTRIBUTORS' BIOGRAPHIES

Piers Beirne *is Professor of Sociology and Legal Studies in the Department of Criminology at the University of Southern Maine. The founding co-editor of the journal* Theoretical Criminology, *his forthcoming books include* Law, Criminology and Animal Abuse *(2009, Rowman and Littlefield) and* Criminology: A Critical Approach *(2010, with James W. Messerschmidt, Oxford University Press). His current research interests include the development of concepts of cruelty, green criminology, and agrarian outrage in nineteenth-century Ireland.*

Steven Best is Associate Professor of Humanities and Philosophy at University of Texas, El Paso. Author and editor of 8 books and over 100 articles and reviews, Best works in the areas of philosophy, cultural criticism, mass media, social theory, postmodern theory, animal rights, bioethics, and environmental theory. Two of his books, *The Postmodern Turn* and *The Postmodern Adventure* (both co-authored with Douglas Kellner) won awards for philosophy books of the year. With Tony Nocella, he is co-editor of the acclaimed volumes *Terrorists or Freedom Fighters? Reflections on the Liberation of Animals* (Lantern Books, 2004) and *Igniting a Revolution: Voice in Defense of the Earth* (AK Press, 2006). His newest book is *Animal Rights and Moral Progress: The Struggle for Human Evolution* (Rowman and Littlefield, Forthcoming). Many of his writings can be found at: www.drstevebest.com.

Michelle Gale De Oliveira is CEO of the Gender Progress Consortium and a director of the Green Economics Institute, UK. She is a member of the Law School of the University of London School of Oriental and African Studies (SOAS), holding an MA in Human Rights Law with a focus on Islamic Law, Peace-Building, and Developing Countries. She holds degrees in Political Science and International Relations from Richmond, the American International University in London (RAIUL), and is currently deputy editor of the *International Journal of Green Economics*. Her writing has been featured in Europe's World, one of the foremost European policy magazines. She lectures and speaks on Human Rights, Environmental and Social Justice, Gender Equity, International Development and Green Economics internationally. Recently she ran a conference on women's unequal pay and poverty in Reading, UK, lectured at the Oxford University Club on the human rights of land reform, was invited to lecture on human rights and gender progress at a Cambridge University conference, lectured on green economics in Berlin, at retreats in Glastonbury, UK, and is a regular speaker at international conferences. She has appeared in the media in Africa, Europe, and Latin America.

Kishi Animashaun Ducre is an Assistant Professor in the Department of African American Studies at Syracuse University. She received her Ph.D. in the Environmental

Justice Program of the University of Michigan's School of Natural Resources and Environment in 2005. Kishi has been a committed advocate for environmental justice for over a decade. Her first foray in environmental activism was as a Toxics Campaigner for Greenpeace from 1994–1997. Under her coordination, her team at Greenpeace assisted in the victories of the nation's key environmental justice battles: defeating an AES power plant in San Francisco, halting the licenses of a uranium enrichment facility in rural Louisiana and the nation's largest proposed plastic manufacturing complex by Shintech in Convent, Louisiana. She combines her experiences on the frontlines of the environmental justice movement and academic training in geographic information systems and demography for a unique perspective on economic and environmental inequality in the Southern region of the United States. In 2006, Kishi along with her colleague, Linda Carty in the Department of African American Studies were awarded a grant from the Ford Foundation to expand the curriculum around the themes of Gender and Environmental Justice. Her next project includes a manuscript on Black Women and the Environment based on the research from the Ford project. She can be reached at kanimash@syr.edu.

Samuel Day Fassbinder is currently a "visiting professor" of English with DeVry University Online. He has published work in *Green Theory and Praxis*, the *Journal of Critical Education Policy Studies*, *Capitalism Nature Socialism*, and a number of other journals. He works with Food Not Bombs and posts regularly in a political weblog that can be found at http://www.dailykos.com/blog/cassiodorus.

Greta Gaard an ecofeminist writer, scholar, activist and educator, is editor and contributor to both Ecofeminism: *Women, Animals, Nature* (1993) and *Ecofeminist Literary Criticism: Theory, Interpretation, Pedagogy* (1998). Her other books include *Ecological Politics: Ecofeminists and the Greens* (1998), and a volume of ecofeminist creative nonfiction, *The Nature of Home* (2007). She currently teaches English at the University of Wisconsin-River Falls, and Women's Studies at Metropolitan State University in St. Paul, Minnesota.

David Greenwood (formerly Gruenewald) is Associate Professor and Canada Research Chair in Environmental Education at Lakehead University, where he co-directs the Centre for Place and Sustainability Studies. His many research articles exploring place, environment, culture, education and sustainability are frequently cited in literature across several fields. In 2008 he co-edited with Greg Smith, *Place-based Education in the Global Age* (Routledge). He has also co-edited three previous special issues on environment and education in *Educational Studies*, the *Canadian Journal for Environmental Education*, and *Cultural Studies in Science Education*.

Donna Houston is a Lecturer in the Griffith School of the Environment at Griffith University, Australia. She obtained her Ph.D. in Geography from the University of Southern California. Her research expertise is in: cultural geography, urban and environmental history, indigenous geographies, human rights and land justice, as well as critical pedagogies of the environment. She is the recent co-editor of *The Havoc of Capitalism: Educating for Social and Environmental Justice* (Sense Publishers, 2007).

Richard Kahn is a Core Faculty member in Education at Antioch University Los Angeles. He is the noted author of *Critical Pedagogy, Ecoliteracy, and Planetary Crisis: The Ecopedagogy Movement* (Peter Lang, 2010), which has just appeared in a Chinese edition (Higher Education Press, 2012). He is also the co-author of *Education Out of Bounds: Cultural Studies for a Posthuman Age* (Palgrave Macmillan, 2010) and co-editor of *The Global Industrial Complex: Systems of Domination* (Lexington Books, 2011). He is currently finalizing the forthcoming title, *Ecopedagogy: Educating for Sustainability in Schools and Society* (Routledge). An author of over 50 articles, his work has been collected in a wide variety of books and journals, including *The Critical Pedagogy Reader* (2nd edition); *The Blackwell Companion to Globalization*; *New Media & Society*, and *Cultural Studies: Keyworks*. Additional information about him, including many of his publications, can be obtained at: http:// richardkahn.org.

Miriam Kennet is a member of Mansfield College, Oxford University and is currently doing postgraduate research at Keele University into supply chain and stakeholder theory from a Green Economics perspective. She is co-editor of one of the few books on green economic theory – *Green Economics, Beyond Supply and Demand to Meeting People's Needs* (Green Audit Books, 1999) and the author of many articles on the subject. She is Director and Co-Founder of the Green Economics Institute, is founder and Editor of the *International Journal of Green Economics*, and is on the Editorial Board of the *International Journal of Ecological Economics and Statistics* and of the *International Journal of Industrial Ecology*.

Corey Lee Lewis is a professor of English at Humboldt State University where he teaches both campus and field-based courses in environmental literature and writing. He is author of *Reading the Trail: Exploring the Literature and Natural History of the California Crest,* which explores the literary and activist efforts of Mary Austin, John Muir and Gary Snyder, while recounting stories of teaching their work to students in the field. Dr. Lewis regularly writes on issues such as environmental literature, education, and activism, and is an environmental author himself. Raised on a small farm in Kansas, Dr. Lewis witnessed massive losses of family farms and wild habitat to corporate agribusiness, which launched him into eco-defense at the early age of fourteen; he founded his high school's first environmental club, a direct action EarthFirst! organization, and went on to study creative writing and environmental literature at Kansas State University, and the University of Nevada, Reno. Since that time he has helped establish two wilderness education programs at the university level as well as the Nevada Conservation Corps, and worked to triple the acreage of designated Wilderness in Nevada in seven short years. Dr. Lewis's involvement in the environmental movement has ranged from civilly disobedient direct actions and protests to trail building and habitat restoration efforts, as well as legislative, legal and literary campaigns. His current book project, *Conversations with Cassandra,* explores the coming collapse of civilization and the environmental and political forces pushing us toward that brink.

Timothy W. Luke is University Distinguished Professor of Political Science at Virginia Polytechnic Institute and State University in Blacksburg, Virginia. He also is the Program Chair for Government and International Affairs in the School of Public and International Affairs, and he serves as Director of the Center for Digital Discourse and Culture in the College of Liberal Arts and Human Sciences at Virginia Tech. In addition to his new co-edited book with Ben Agger, *There is a Gunman on Campus: Tragedy and Terror at Virginia Tech* (Rowman & Littlefield, 2008), his recent books include *Museum Politics: Powerplays at the Departing at the Exhibition* (University of Minnesota Press, 2002), *Capitalism, Democracy, and Ecology: Departing From Marx* (University of Illinois Press, 1999), *The Politics of Cyberspace*, ed. With Chris Toulouse (Routledge, 1998), and *Ecocritique: Contesting the Politics of Nature, Economy, and Culture* (University of Minnesota Press, 1997). All of these works investigate questions rooted in civic engagement with the issues of sustainability and culture in the fine arts, civil society, natural environments, and global economy. Much of his recent research focuses on the ethical, political, and social problems associated with global warming, the scientific-technological processes of climate change monitoring, and the political responses needed to avert and/or adapt to the multiple policy challenges posed by these threatening developments.

Brian McKenna, Ph.D. (University of Michigan-Dearborn) is an anthropologist who researches topics in health, medicine, environment, sustainability, political ecology, critical pedagogy and Indians of North America. He is an applied anthropologist and journalist with more than two decades of experience as an applied anthropologist. Brian received his Masters Degree from Temple University and his Ph.D. from Michigan State University. In the 1980s he worked in Philadelphia as a health policy analyst for a number of non-profits including Temple University's Institute for Public Policy Studies and the United Way's Community Services Planning Council. He also worked for National Public Radio's Fresh Air. Dr. McKenna worked for six years in medical education (1992–98) as an evaluator for the W. K. Kellogg Foundation to create community-oriented primary care practitioners, the topic of his dissertation. Brian coordinated a study on Lansing, Michigan's environmental health for the Ingham County Health Department between 1998 and 2001 for which he received an environmental achievement award from Ann Arbor's Ecology Center. He worked as Executive Director of Localmotion, an environmental health non-profit in Ann Arbor. Dr. McKenna writes a regular column in the Society for

Applied Anthropology Newsletter and is a regular contributor to CounterPunch. He is faculty advisor for UMD's American Student Medical Association. Brian is on the Editorial Board of the Journal of Medical Humanities and serves on the Board of Directors for American Indian Health and Family Services in Detroit.

Bill McKibben, Environmentalist, is a scholar in environmental studies at Middlebury College. He is the author of a dozen books including *The End of Nature* (1989), the first book for a general audience about global warming; *Enough* (2004), which critiques human genetic engineering and other rapidly advancing technologies; *Deep Economy* (2007), that explores the possibility of a local gastronomic economy and the effects of the globalization of food; and *The Bill McKibben Reader* (2008), that collects his most trenchant work from the past 25 years. He is co-founder of the new grassroots climate movement 350.org.

Tema Milstein is an assistant professor at the University of New Mexico in the Communication and Journalism Department where she teaches courses in critical and cultural studies and eco-culture. Her research explores how communication as a cultural force closes and opens doors to the re-examination of the human relationship with the environment. One of her long-term projects examines the ways people communicate about the environment and endangered species in the setting of wildlife tourism. This long-term ethnographic study is focused on the cultural and communicative dimensions of human-nature relations within the highest concentration of whale watching in the world, located in transboundaried Pacific waters off the coast of U.S. and Canada. Other projects include critical empirical analyses of discourse in zoos and investigations of environmental meaning systems in the rural Southwest. For links to her research, visit her web site at www.unm. edu/~tema/.

Anthony J. Nocella II, author, community organizer, and educator, teaches at Hamline University as a Visiting Professor of Urban Education in the School of Education. He received his Ph.D. in Social Science at the Maxwell School at Syracuse University. Nocella focuses his attention on critical urban education, peace and conflict studies, inclusive social justice education, environmental education, disability pedagogy, queer pedagogy, feminist pedagogy, critical pedagogy, anarchist studies, critical animal studies, and hip-hop pedagogy. He is a co-founder of more than fifteen active political organizations including Institute for Critical Animal Studies (ICAS), Outdoor Empowerment (OE), Save the Kids (STK), and Sacco and Vanzetti Foundation, and four scholarly journals, which include *Green Theory and Praxis*, *Peace Studies Journal*, *Journal on Critical Animal Studies*, and *Journal on Terrorism and Security*. He is a board member of the American Friends Service Committee (AFSC) and has published more than twenty-five scholarly articles and is working on his eleventh book. His books include such edited collections as: *Contemporary Anarchist Studies: An Introductory Anthology of Anarchy in the*

Academy (Routledge, 2009), *Academic Repression: Reflections from the Academic Industrial Complex* (AK Press, 2010), *Terrorists or Freedom Fighters? Reflections on the Liberation of Animals* (Lantern Books, 2004); and *Igniting a Revolution Voices in Defense of the Earth* (AK Press, 2006). He is also the primary author of the volume, *A Peacemaker's Guide for Building Peace with a Revolutionary Group* (PARC, 2004) His site is http://www.anthonynocella.org.

Nigel South Ph.D. is a Professor of Sociology at the University of Essex, Colchester, UK. He has taught at universities in London and New York and worked as a Research Sociologist at the Institute for the Study of Drug Dependence (now Drugscope), London. Research interests and publications include the development of a green perspective in criminology; drug use, related health and crime issues; crime, inequalities and citizenship; and theoretical and comparative criminology. He has served on various editorial boards and continues to serve on the international editorial board of *Critical Criminology* and as an Associate Editor of the journal *Deviant Behavior*.

Eva-Maria Swidler is Faculty in History at Villanova University. She received her Ph.D. in History from Temple University in 2004 with her dissertation on *The Politics of Economics: Sustainability and Paradigms in World Environmental History and Agriculture*. Her most recent publication is Defending Western Civ: Or How I Learned to Stop Worrying and Love the Course (World History Connected, 2007). She is the H-Net Editor for the H-W-Civ listserv. Her general areas of research include Environmental, Rural and Agricultural History, with a special emphasis on placing these in the context of World History.

Lightning Source UK Ltd.
Milton Keynes UK
UKOW04f2052251014

240628UK00003B/126/P